POSUKA DEMIZU

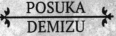

KAIU SHIRAI

If you were one of the children...

- Would you want to know the secret of Grace Field House?

- Or would you want to live your life without knowing?

- Or can you not decide until you read a little bit further?

The plot thickens even more in volume 4.

Writer Shirai's interesting tidbits for *The Promised Neverland* fanatics:

To everyone who reads the chapters in *Weekly Shonen Jump*! Did any of you notice that Demizu Sensei secretly put HAPPY NEW YEAR in the chapter featured in issue 6?

If you only buy the graphic novels, it might be a little small, but see if you can spot it in this version.

Search for it in chapter 21.

Okay, please enjoy this volume!

Posuka Demizu debuted as a manga artist with the 2013 *CoroCoro* series *Oreca Monster Bouken Retsuden*. A collection of illustrations, *The Art of Posuka Demizu*, was released in 2016 by PIE International.

Kaiu Shirai debuted in 2015 with *Ashley Gate no Yukue* on the *Shonen Jump+* website. Shirai first worked with Posuka Demizu on the two-shot *Poppy no Negai*, which was released in February 2016.

THE PROMISED NEVERLAND

VOLUME 3
SHONEN JUMP Manga Edition

STORY BY KAIU SHIRAI
ART BY POSUKA DEMIZU

Translation/Satsuki Yamashita
Touch-Up Art & Lettering/Mark McMurray
Design/Julian [JR] Robinson
Editor/Alexis Kirsch

YAKUSOKU NO NEVERLAND © 2016 by Kaiu Shirai, Posuka Demizu
All rights reserved.
First published in Japan in 2016 by SHUEISHA Inc., Tokyo.
English translation rights arranged by SHUEISHA Inc.

The stories, characters and incidents mentioned in this publication are
entirely fictional.

Printed in the U.S.A.

Published by VIZ Media, LLC
P.O. Box 77010
San Francisco, CA 94107

10 9 8 7 6 5 4 3
First printing, April 2018
Third printing, April 2019

PARENTAL ADVISORY
THE PROMISED NEVERLAND is rated T+
and is recommended for ages 16 and up.
This volume contains fantasy violence and
adult themes.

THE PROMISED NEVERLAND

3
Destroy!

STORY	KAIU SHIRAI
ART	POSUKA DEMIZU

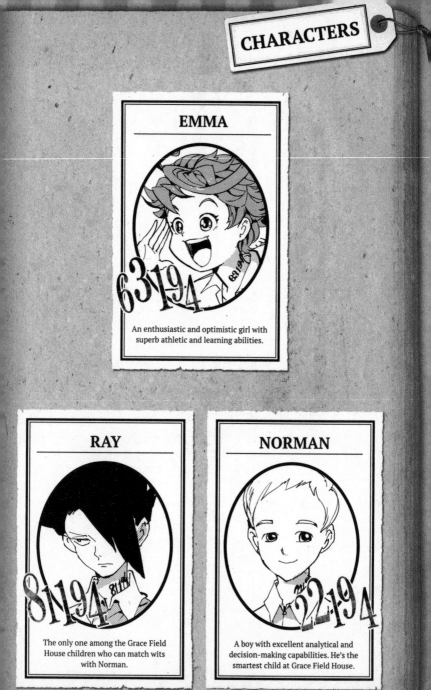

CHARACTERS

EMMA

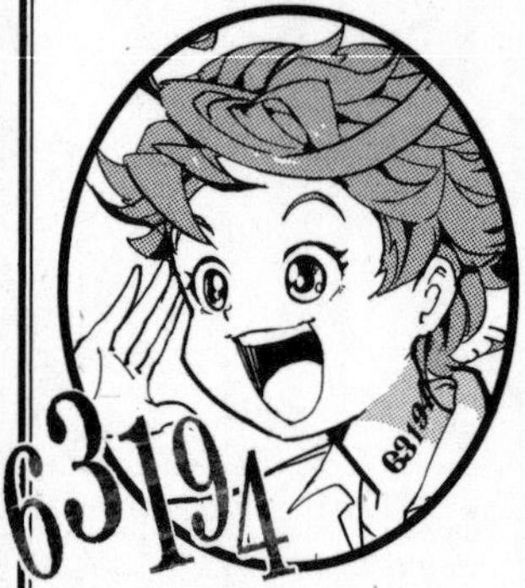
63194

An enthusiastic and optimistic girl with superb athletic and learning abilities.

RAY

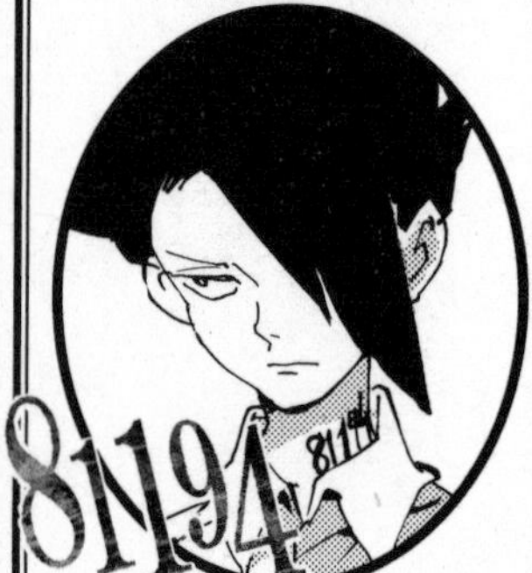
81194

The only one among the Grace Field House children who can match wits with Norman.

NORMAN

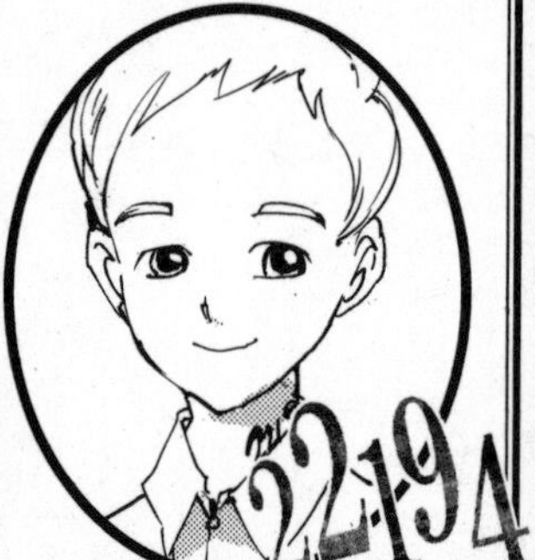
22194

A boy with excellent analytical and decision-making capabilities. He's the smartest child at Grace Field House.

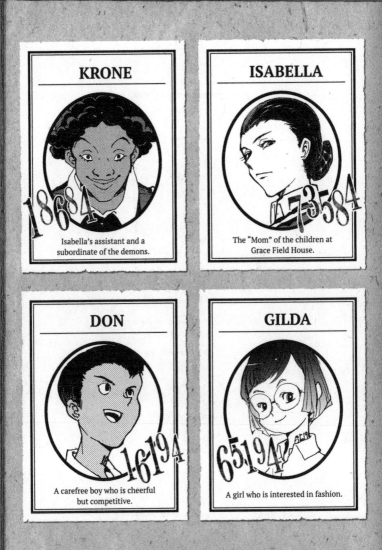

KRONE

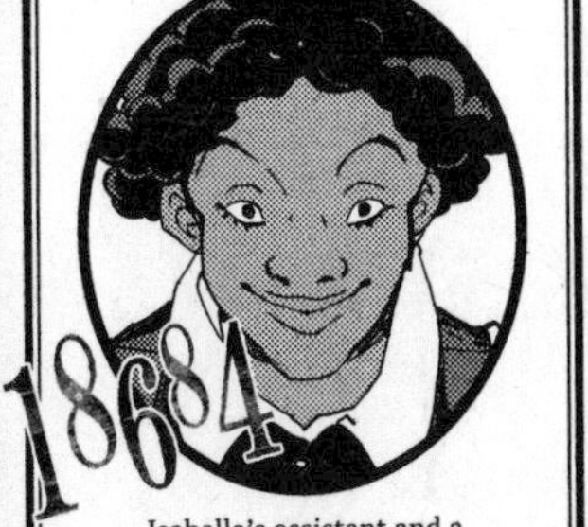
18684

Isabella's assistant and a subordinate of the demons.

ISABELLA

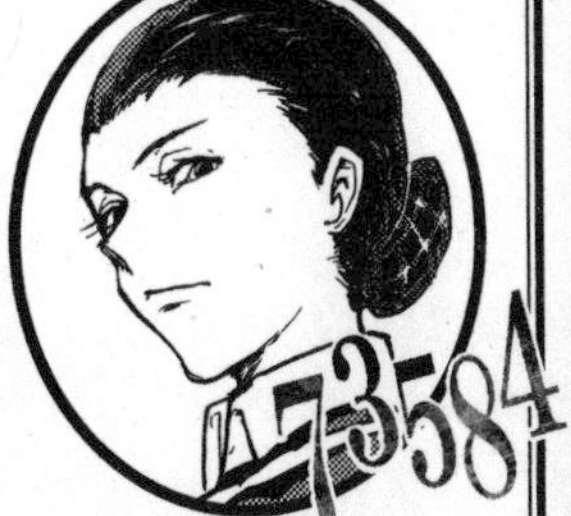
73584

The "Mom" of the children at Grace Field House.

DON

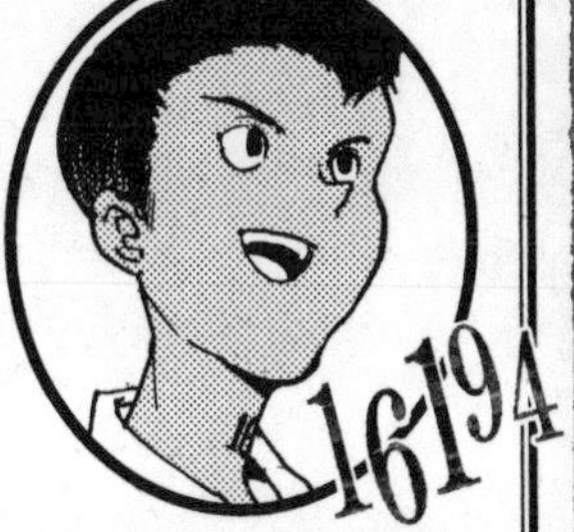
16194

A carefree boy who is cheerful but competitive.

GILDA

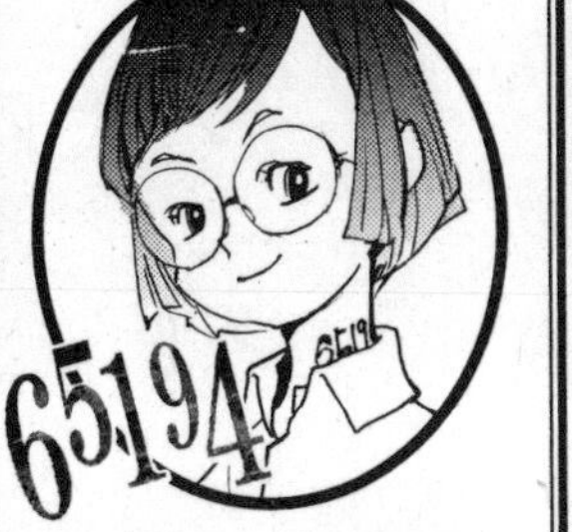
65194

A girl who is interested in fashion.

The Story So Far

The 38 children of Grace Field House orphanage are all living happily with their "Mom," Isabella, treating her as if she were their real mother. One day, one of the children leaves the orphanage to live with her new foster family. But when Emma and Norman go to the gate to deliver something she's left behind, they witness her lifeless body and some terrible demons. In addition, they discover that Mom is raising them as food for the demons. Emma swears that she'll never lose another family member and starts gathering information in order to survive. She and Norman figure out that the daily tests they take are to develop their brains, the demons' favorite part to eat. They eventually get Ray to join their side, and the three start planning a way to escape.

THE PROMISED NEVERLAND 3

Destroy!

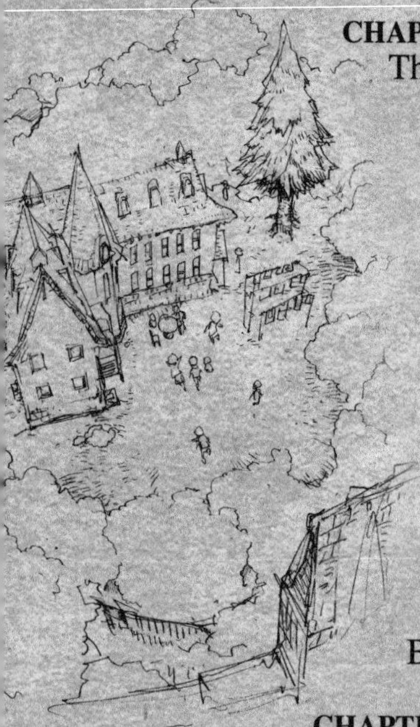

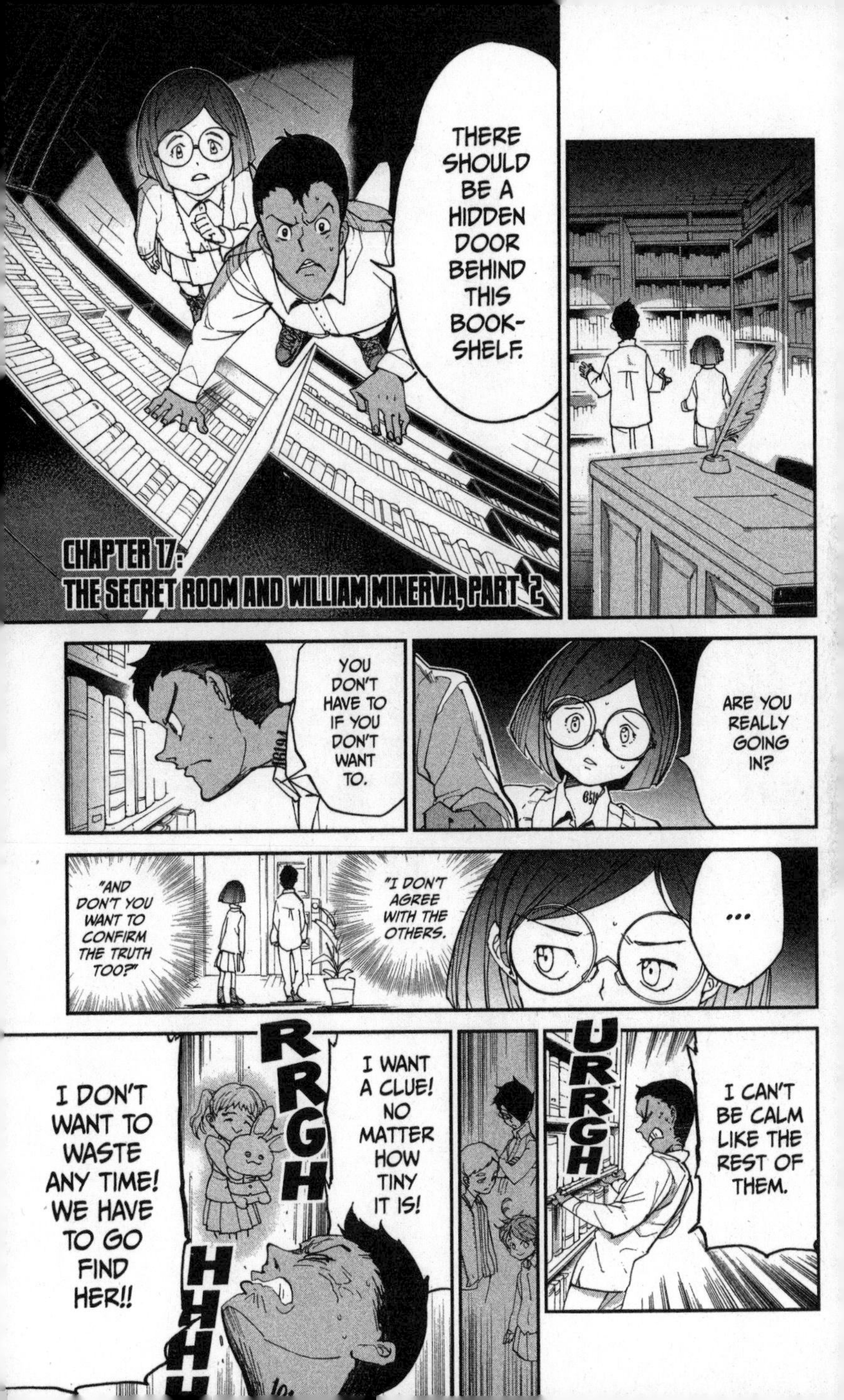
THERE SHOULD BE A HIDDEN DOOR BEHIND THIS BOOK-SHELF.
CHAPTER 17:
THE SECRET ROOM AND WILLIAM MINERVA, PART 2
ARE YOU REALLY GOING IN?
YOU DON'T HAVE TO IF YOU DON'T WANT TO.
...
"I DON'T AGREE WITH THE OTHERS.
"AND DON'T YOU WANT TO CONFIRM THE TRUTH TOO?"
URRGH
I CAN'T BE CALM LIKE THE REST OF THEM.
I WANT A CLUE! NO MATTER HOW TINY IT IS!
RRGH
I DON'T WANT TO WASTE ANY TIME! WE HAVE TO GO FIND HER!!
HHHH

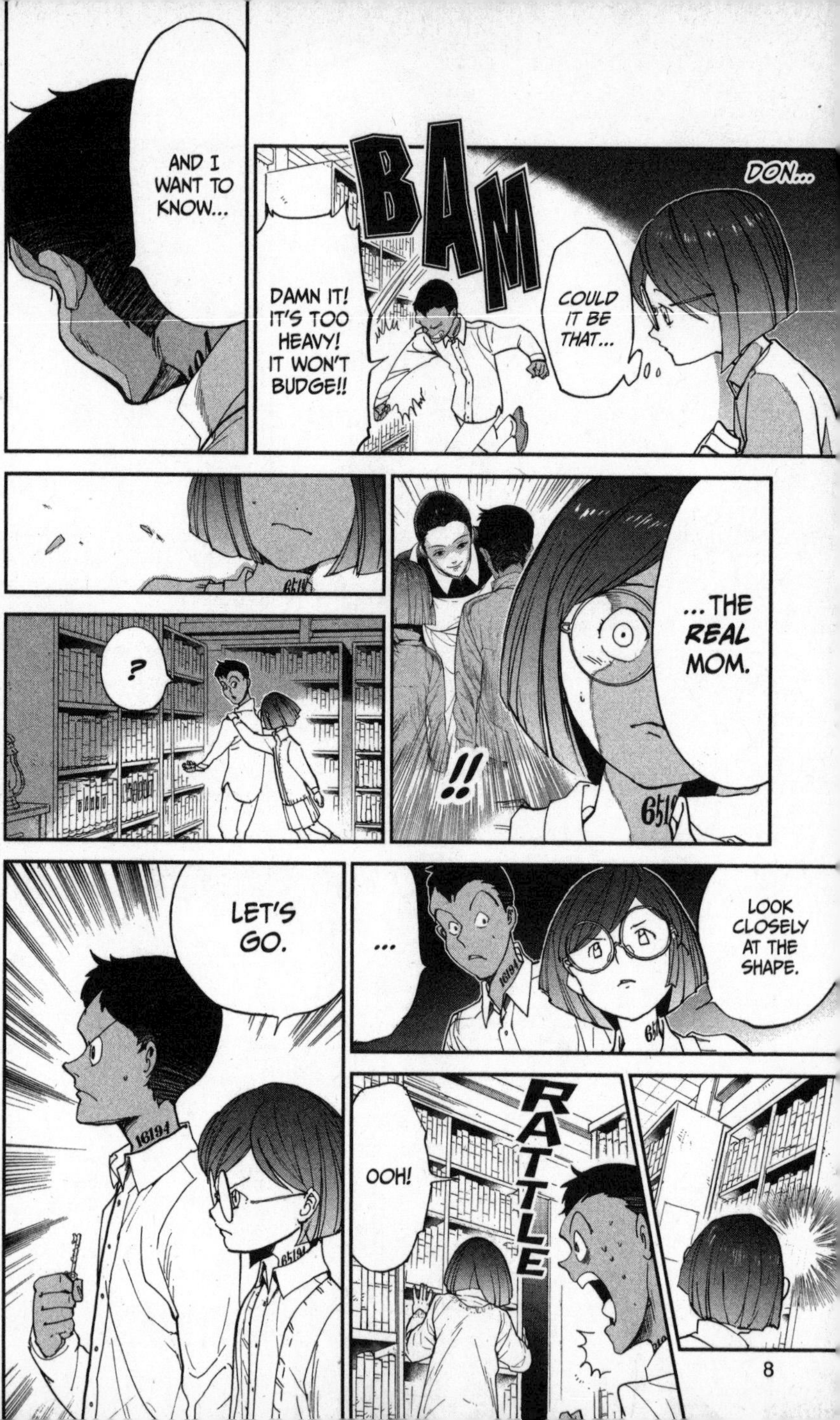
DON...
COULD IT BE THAT...
BAM
DAMN IT! IT'S TOO HEAVY! IT WON'T BUDGE!!
AND I WANT TO KNOW...
...THE REAL MOM.
!!
?
LOOK CLOSELY AT THE SHAPE.
...
RATTLE
OOH!
LET'S GO.

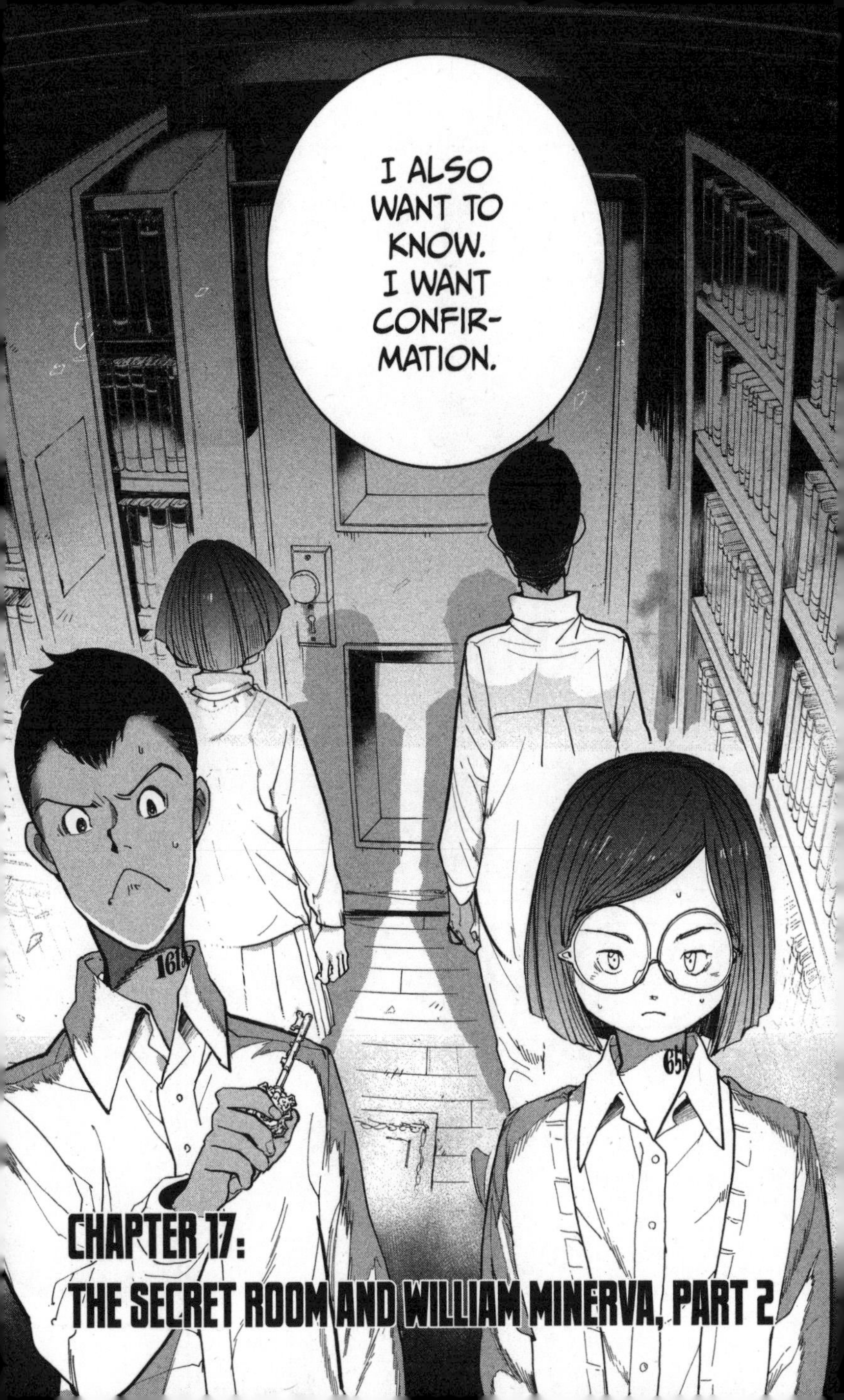
I ALSO WANT TO KNOW. I WANT CONFIRMATION.
CHAPTER 17:
THE SECRET ROOM AND WILLIAM MINERVA, PART 2

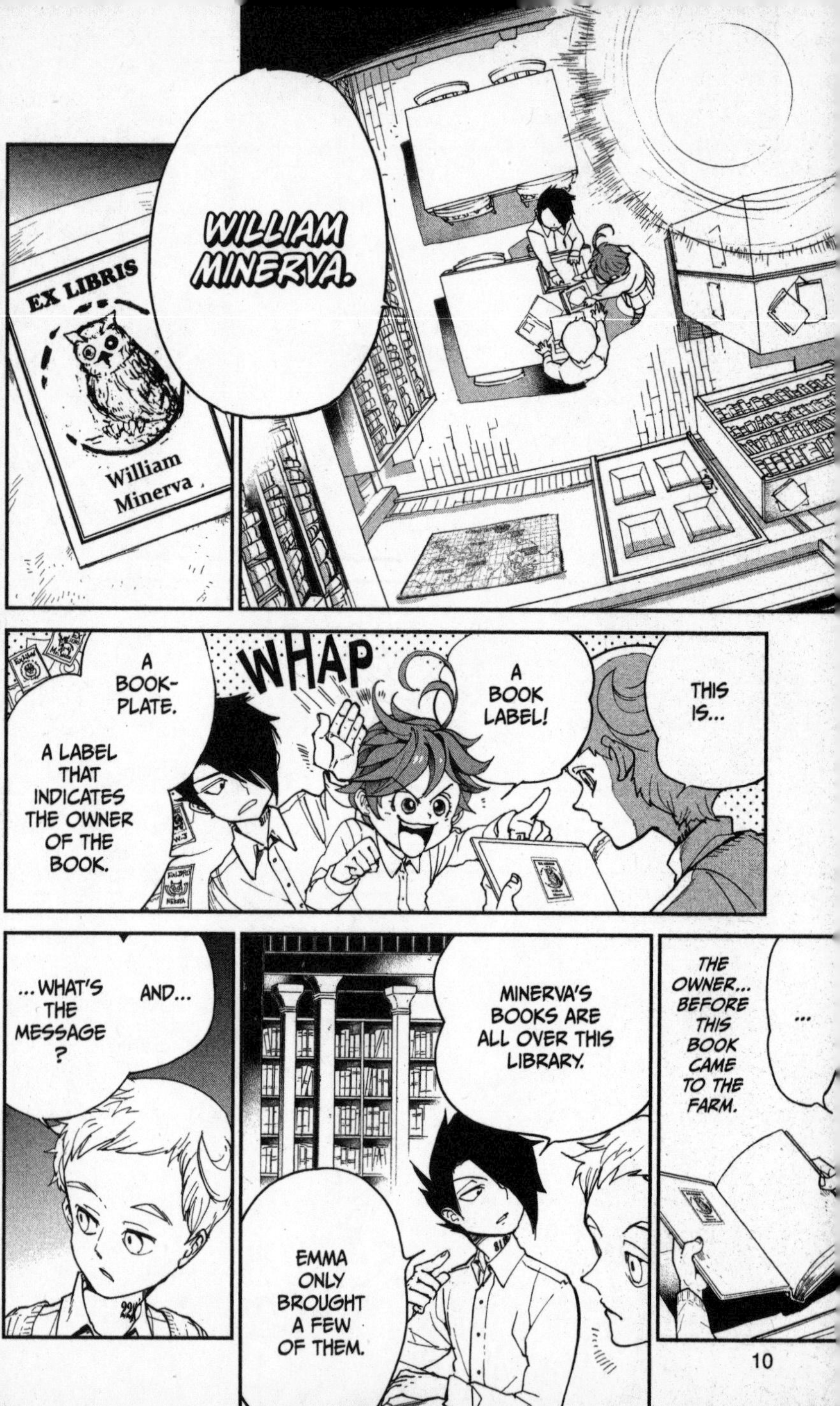
WILLIAM MINERVA.
EX LIBRIS
William Minerva
THIS IS...
A BOOK LABEL!
WHAP
A BOOK-PLATE.
A LABEL THAT INDICATES THE OWNER OF THE BOOK.
...
THE OWNER... BEFORE THIS BOOK CAME TO THE FARM.
MINERVA'S BOOKS ARE ALL OVER THIS LIBRARY.
EMMA ONLY BROUGHT A FEW OF THEM.
AND...
...WHAT'S THE MESSAGE?

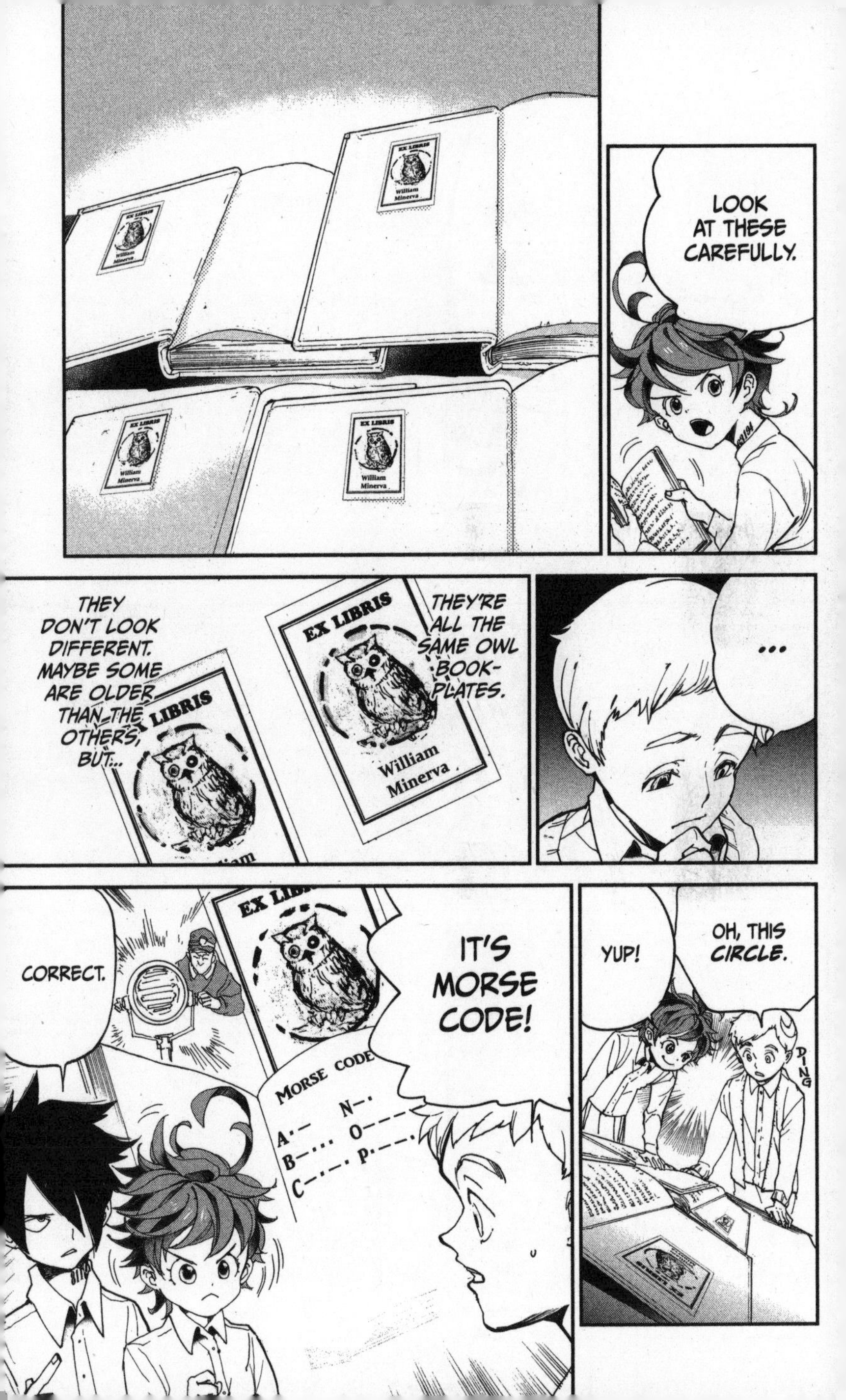
LOOK AT THESE CAREFULLY.
EX LIBRIS
William Minerva
...
THEY'RE ALL THE SAME OWL BOOK-PLATES.
THEY DON'T LOOK DIFFERENT. MAYBE SOME ARE OLDER THAN THE OTHERS, BUT...
EX LIBRIS
William Minerva
OH, THIS CIRCLE.
YUP!
DING
IT'S MORSE CODE!
MORSE CODE
CORRECT.

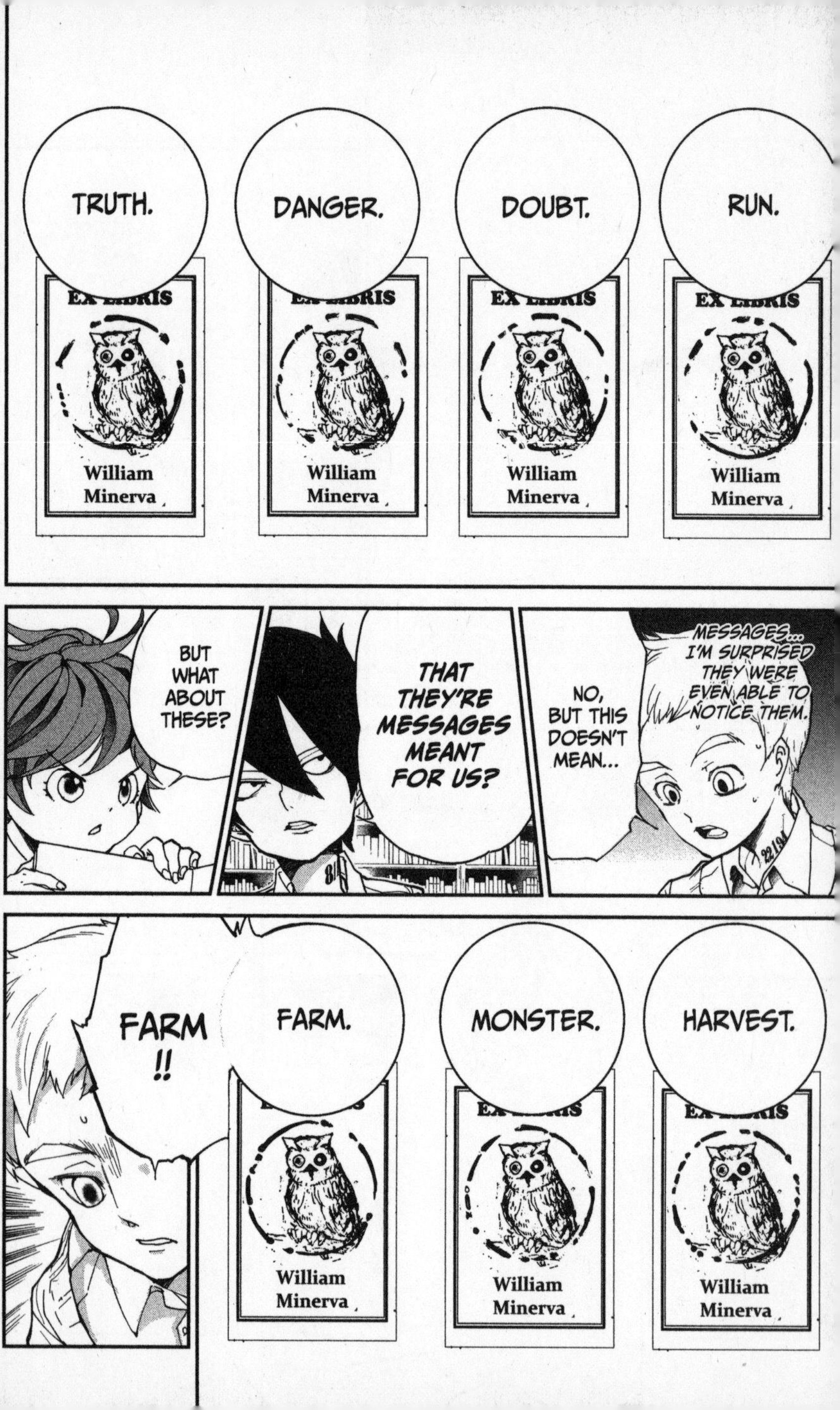
RUN.
EX LIBRIS William Minerva
DOUBT.
William Minerva
DANGER.
William Minerva
TRUTH.
EX LIBRIS William Minerva
MESSAGES... I'M SURPRISED THEY WERE EVEN ABLE TO NOTICE THEM.
NO, BUT THIS DOESN'T MEAN...
THAT THEY'RE MESSAGES MEANT FOR US?
BUT WHAT ABOUT THESE?
HARVEST.
William Minerva
MONSTER.
William Minerva
FARM.
William Minerva
FARM !!

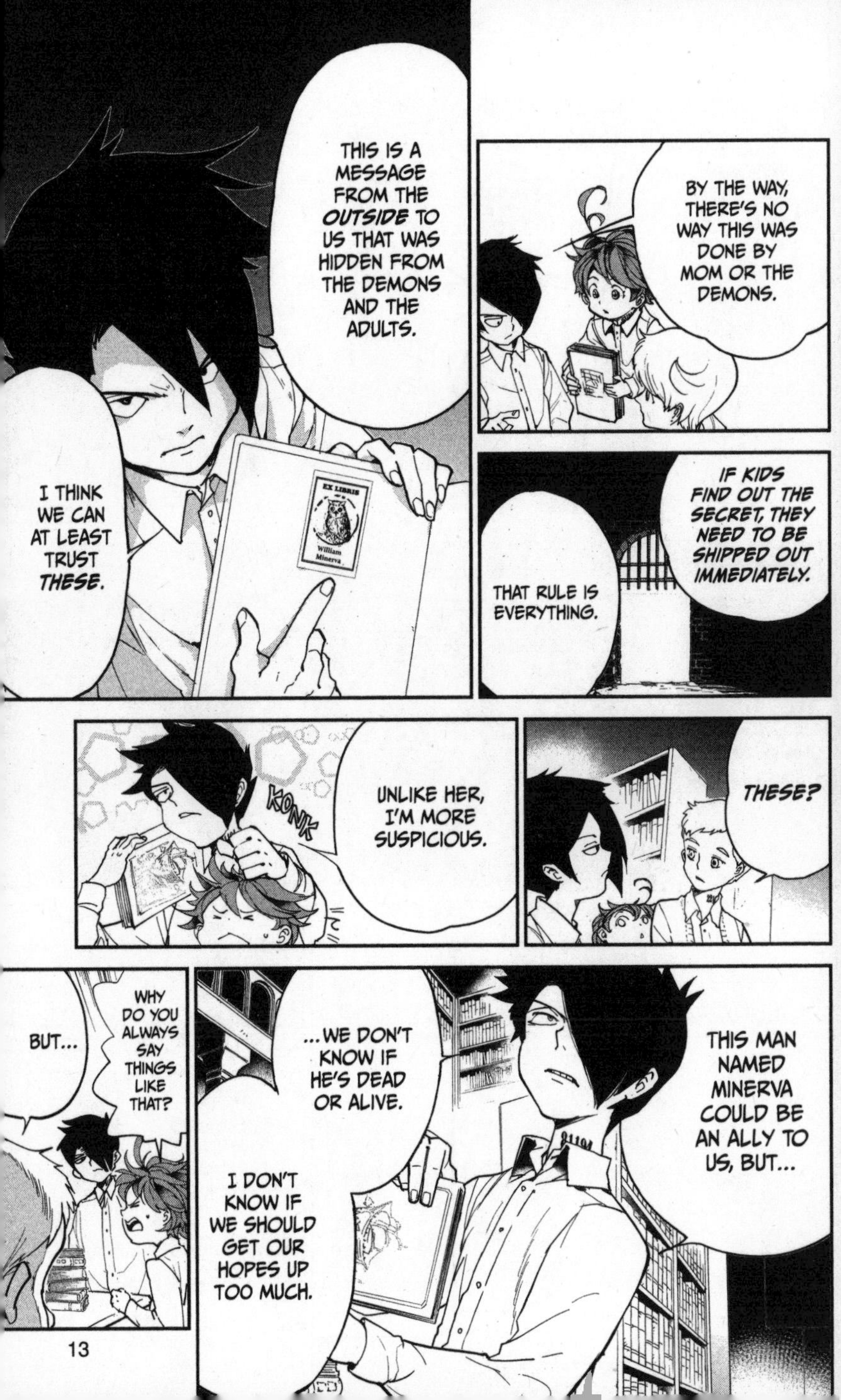
BY THE WAY, THERE'S NO WAY THIS WAS DONE BY MOM OR THE DEMONS.
IF KIDS FIND OUT THE SECRET, THEY NEED TO BE SHIPPED OUT IMMEDIATELY.
THAT RULE IS EVERYTHING.
THIS IS A MESSAGE FROM THE OUTSIDE TO US THAT WAS HIDDEN FROM THE DEMONS AND THE ADULTS.
EX LIBRIS
William Minerva
I THINK WE CAN AT LEAST TRUST THESE.
THESE?
UNLIKE HER, I'M MORE SUSPICIOUS.
KONK
THIS MAN NAMED MINERVA COULD BE AN ALLY TO US, BUT...
...WE DON'T KNOW IF HE'S DEAD OR ALIVE.
I DON'T KNOW IF WE SHOULD GET OUR HOPES UP TOO MUCH.
WHY DO YOU ALWAYS SAY THINGS LIKE THAT?
BUT...

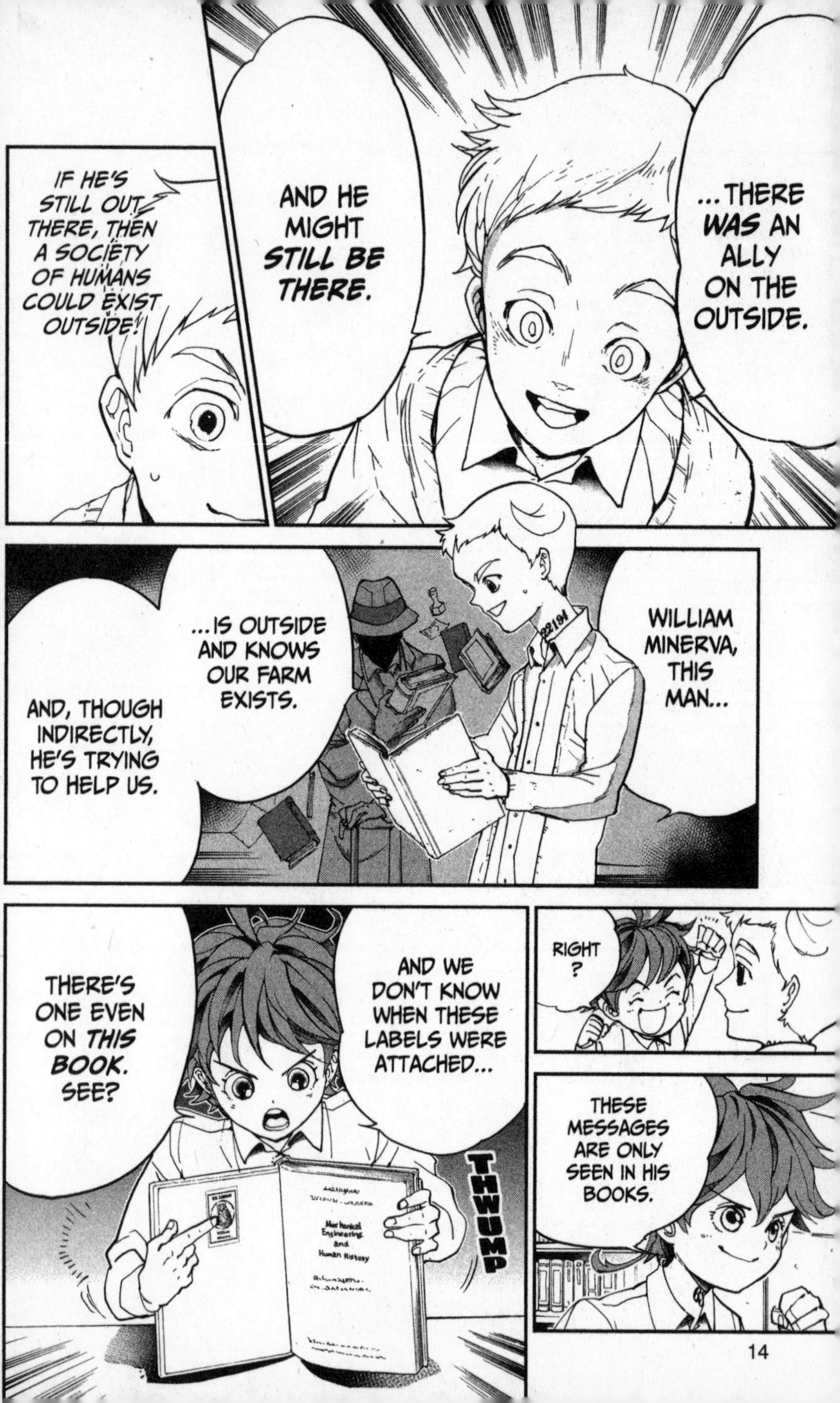
...THERE WAS AN ALLY ON THE OUTSIDE.
AND HE MIGHT STILL BE THERE.
IF HE'S STILL OUT THERE, THEN A SOCIETY OF HUMANS COULD EXIST OUTSIDE!
WILLIAM MINERVA, THIS MAN...
...IS OUTSIDE AND KNOWS OUR FARM EXISTS.
AND, THOUGH INDIRECTLY, HE'S TRYING TO HELP US.
RIGHT?
THESE MESSAGES ARE ONLY SEEN IN HIS BOOKS.
AND WE DON'T KNOW WHEN THESE LABELS WERE ATTACHED...
THERE'S ONE EVEN ON THIS BOOK. SEE?
THWUMP
Mechanical Engineering and Human History

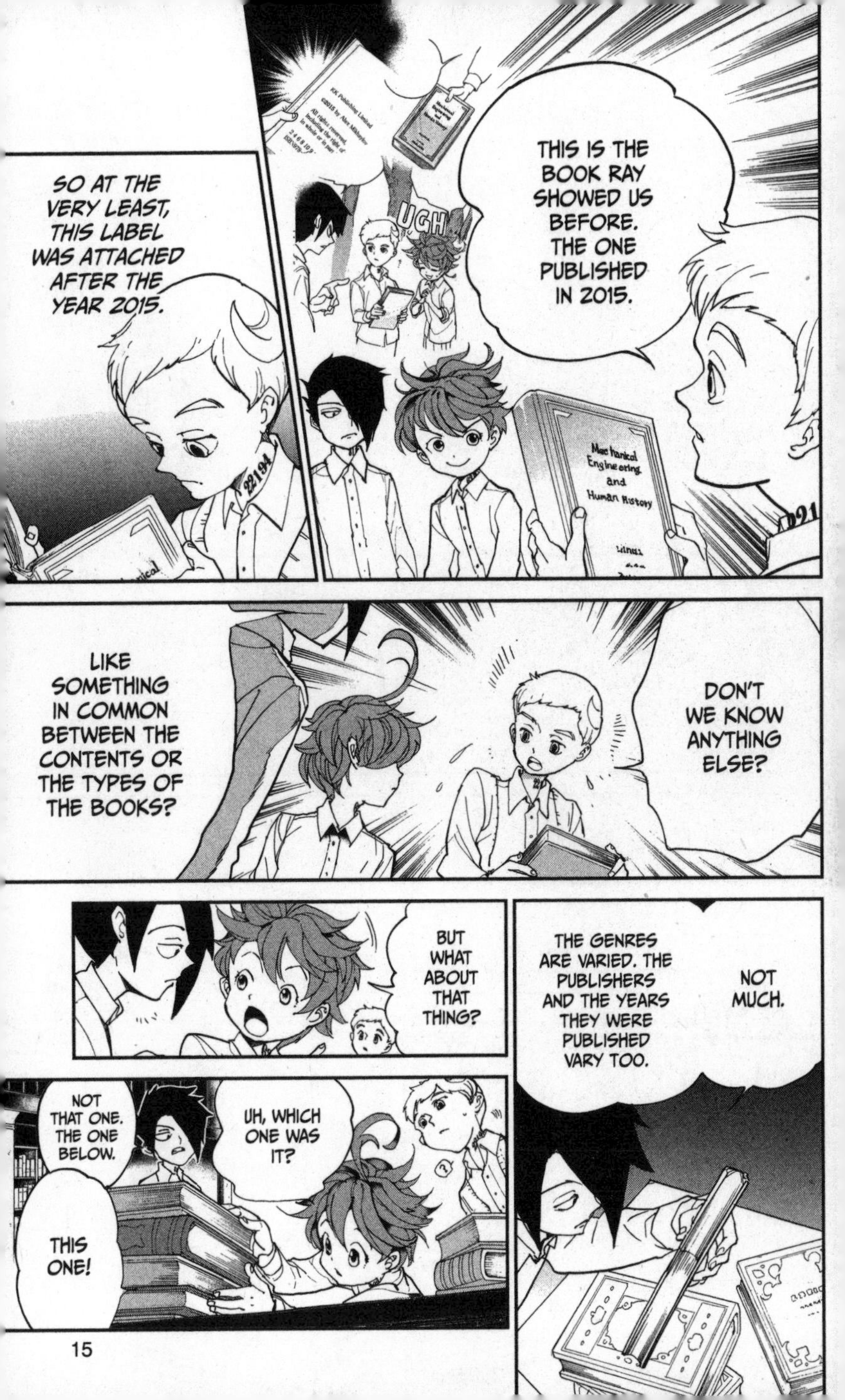
THIS IS THE BOOK RAY SHOWED US BEFORE. THE ONE PUBLISHED IN 2015.
UGH
Mechanical Engineering and Human History
SO AT THE VERY LEAST, THIS LABEL WAS ATTACHED AFTER THE YEAR 2015.
DON'T WE KNOW ANYTHING ELSE?
LIKE SOMETHING IN COMMON BETWEEN THE CONTENTS OR THE TYPES OF THE BOOKS?
NOT MUCH.
THE GENRES ARE VARIED. THE PUBLISHERS AND THE YEARS THEY WERE PUBLISHED VARY TOO.
BUT WHAT ABOUT THAT THING?
UH, WHICH ONE WAS IT?
NOT THAT ONE. THE ONE BELOW.
THIS ONE!

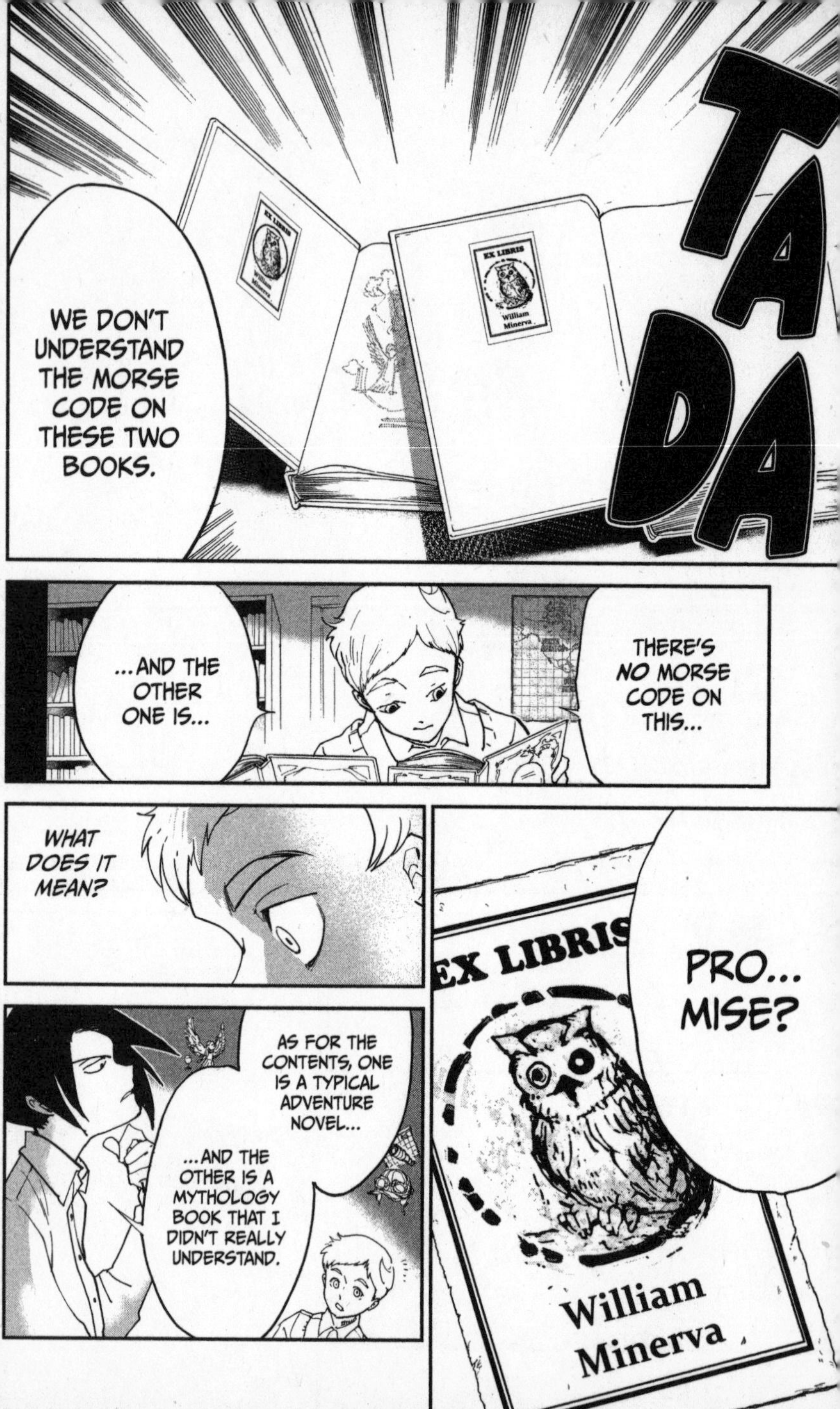
TA DA
WE DON'T UNDERSTAND THE MORSE CODE ON THESE TWO BOOKS.
THERE'S NO MORSE CODE ON THIS...
...AND THE OTHER ONE IS...
PRO... MISE?
EX LIBRIS
William Minerva
WHAT DOES IT MEAN?
AS FOR THE CONTENTS, ONE IS A TYPICAL ADVENTURE NOVEL...
...AND THE OTHER IS A MYTHOLOGY BOOK THAT I DIDN'T REALLY UNDERSTAND.

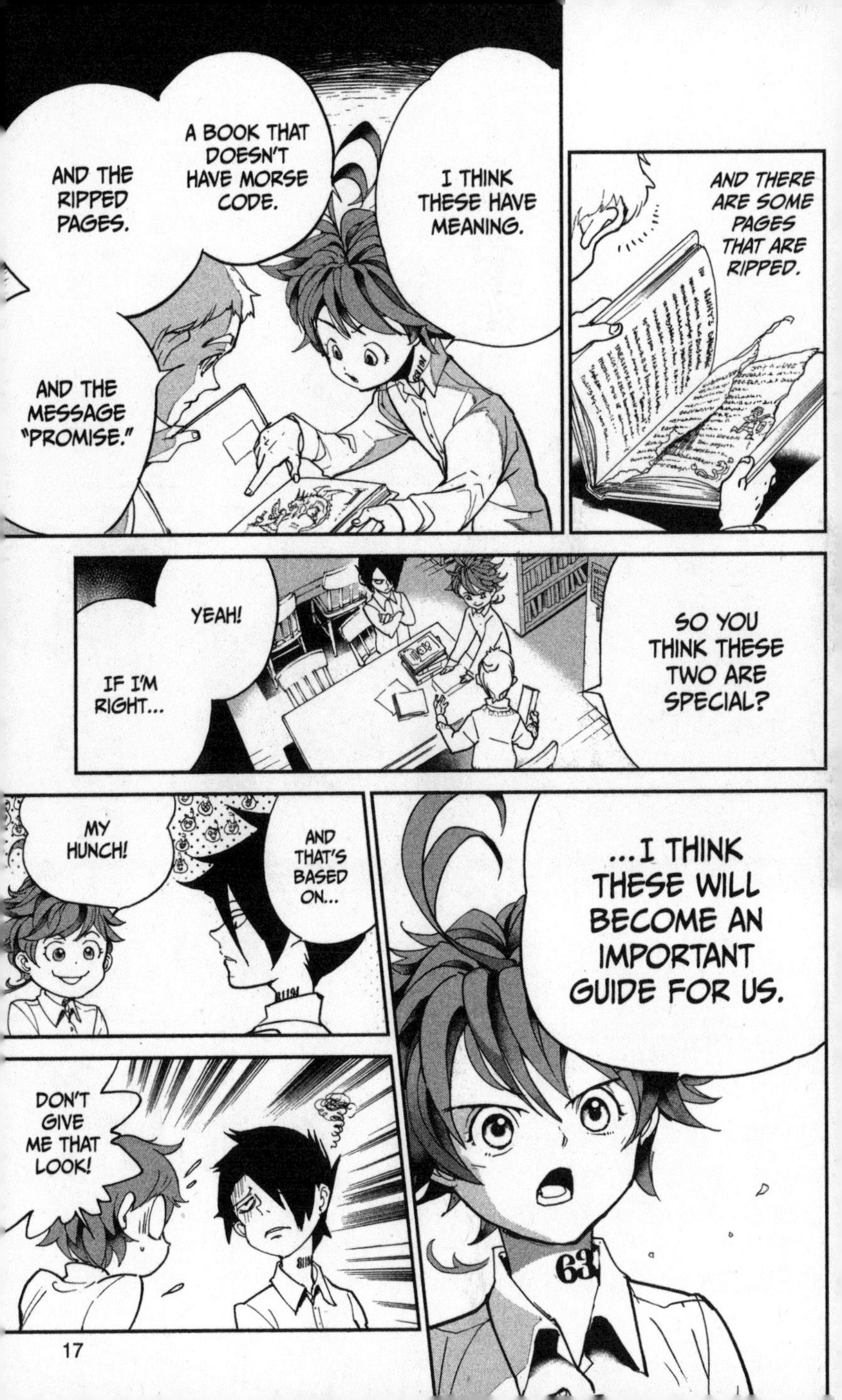
AND THERE ARE SOME PAGES THAT ARE RIPPED.
I THINK THESE HAVE MEANING.
A BOOK THAT DOESN'T HAVE MORSE CODE.
AND THE RIPPED PAGES.
AND THE MESSAGE "PROMISE."
SO YOU THINK THESE TWO ARE SPECIAL?
YEAH!
IF I'M RIGHT...
...I THINK THESE WILL BECOME AN IMPORTANT GUIDE FOR US.
AND THAT'S BASED ON...
MY HUNCH!
DON'T GIVE ME THAT LOOK!

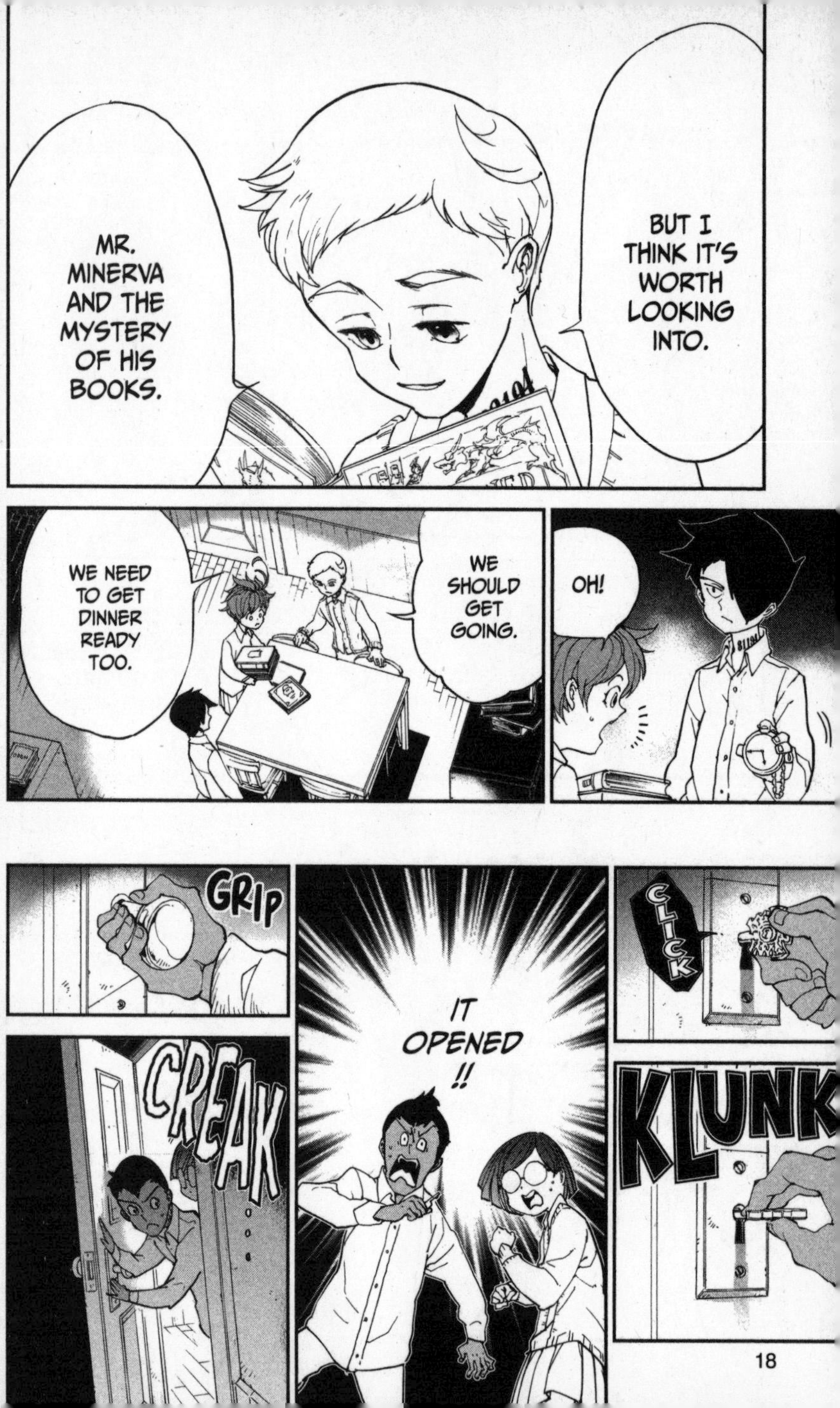
BUT I THINK IT'S WORTH LOOKING INTO.
MR. MINERVA AND THE MYSTERY OF HIS BOOKS.
OH!
WE SHOULD GET GOING.
WE NEED TO GET DINNER READY TOO.
CLICK
KLUNK
IT OPENED !!
GRIP
CREAK

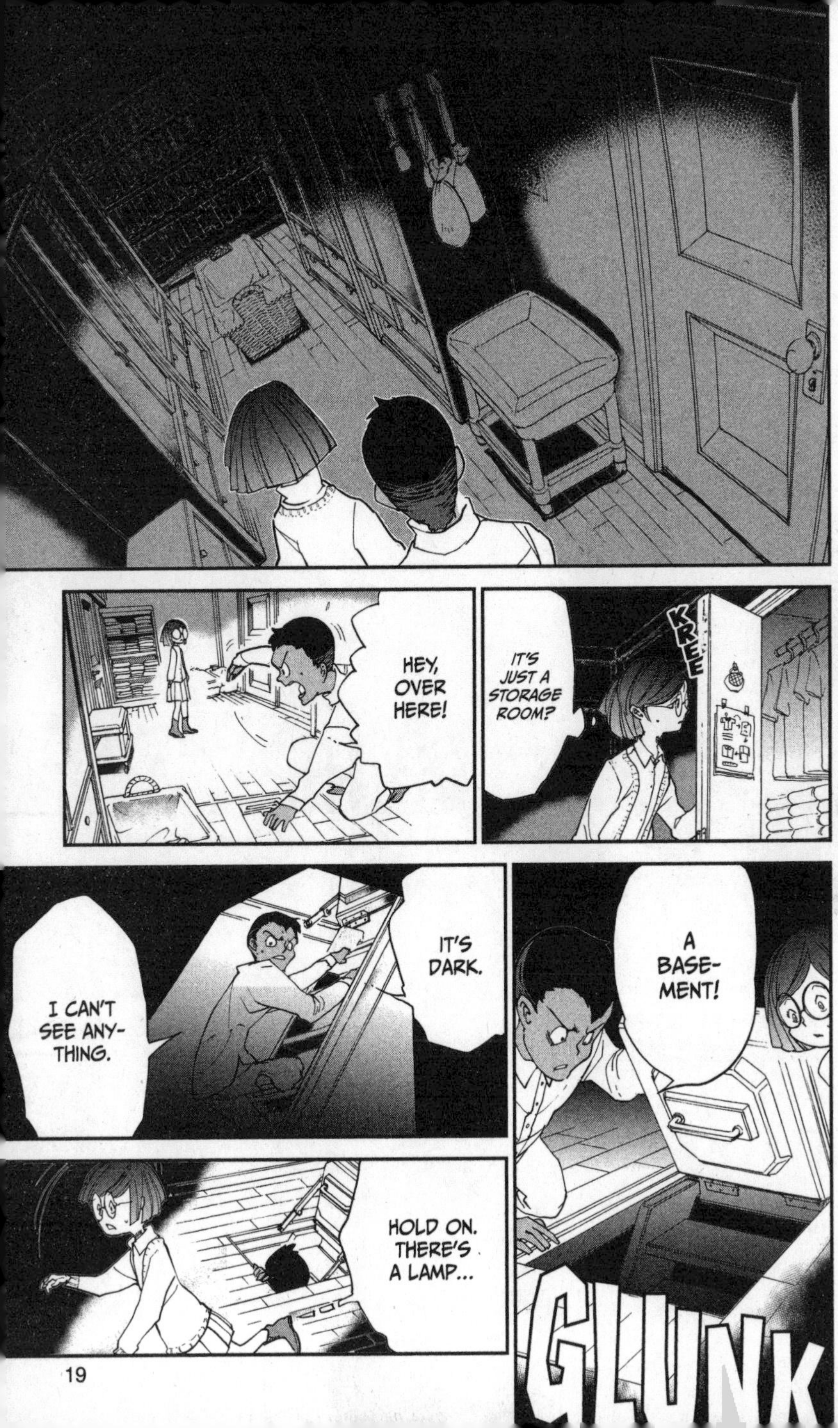
KREE
IT'S JUST A STORAGE ROOM?
HEY, OVER HERE!
A BASEMENT!
GLUNK
IT'S DARK.
I CAN'T SEE ANYTHING.
HOLD ON. THERE'S A LAMP...

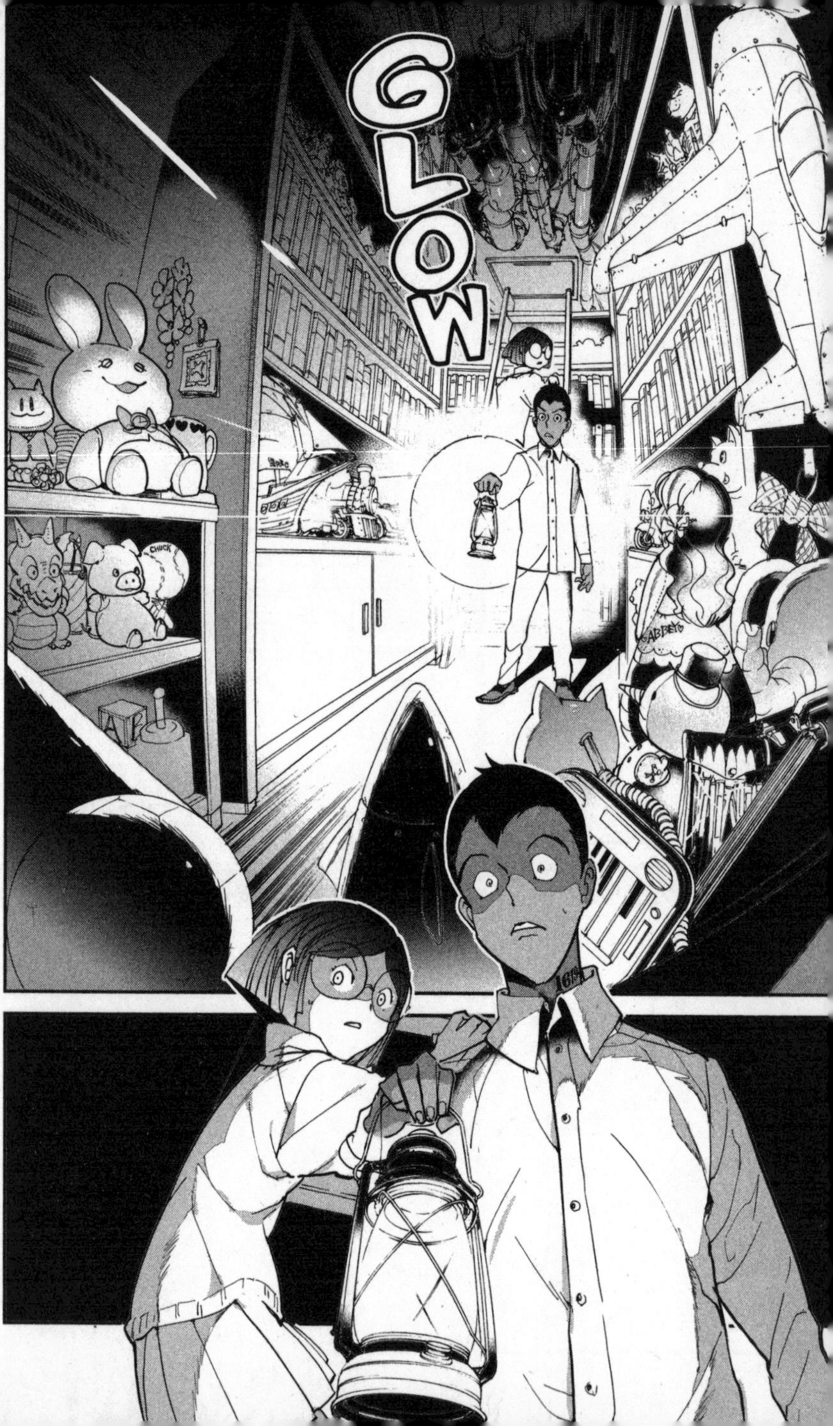
GLOW
CHUCK
ABBEY

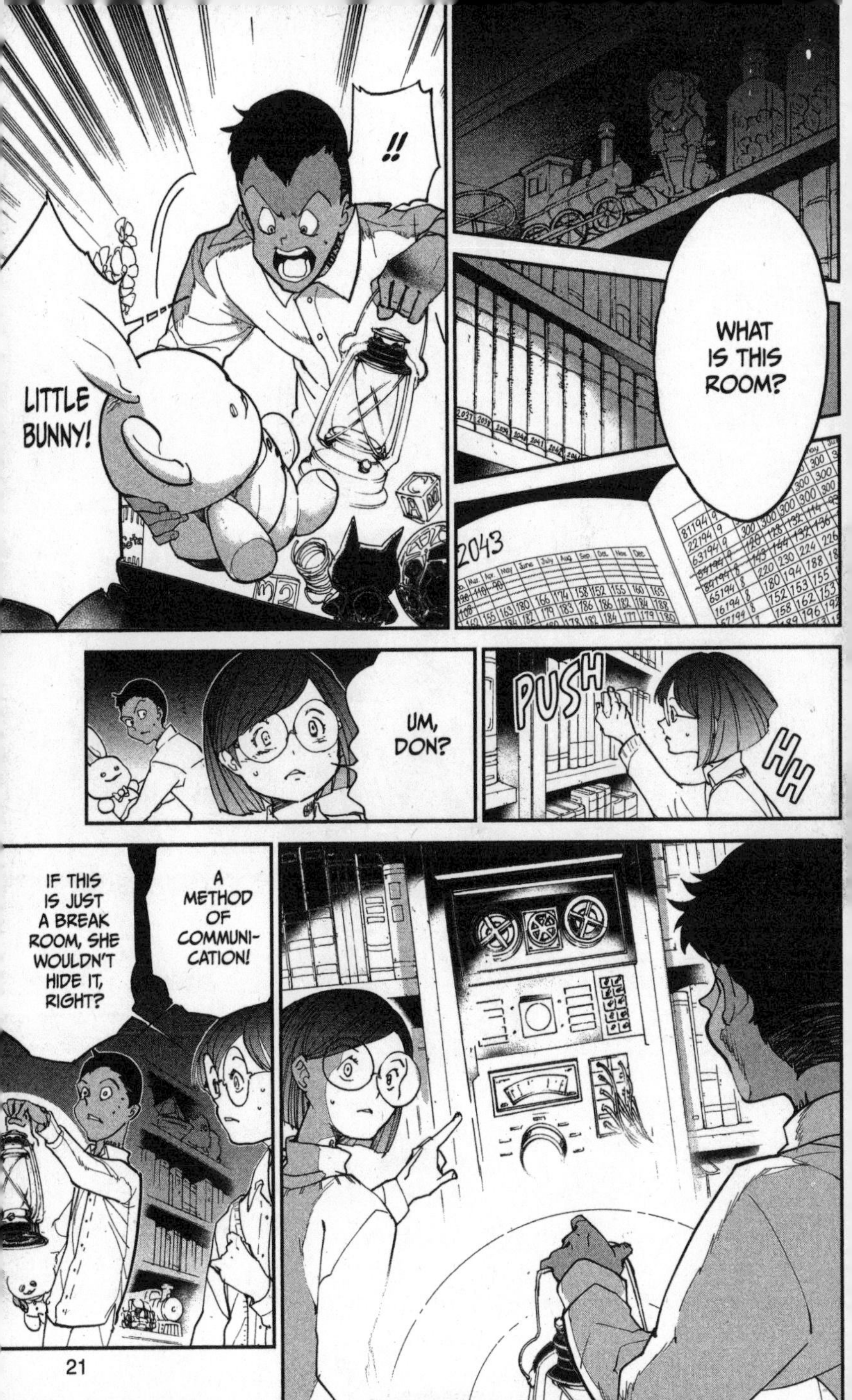

WHAT IS THIS ROOM?
2043
!!
LITTLE BUNNY!
PUSHHH
UM, DON?
A METHOD OF COMMUNICATION!
IF THIS IS JUST A BREAK ROOM, SHE WOULDN'T HIDE IT, RIGHT?

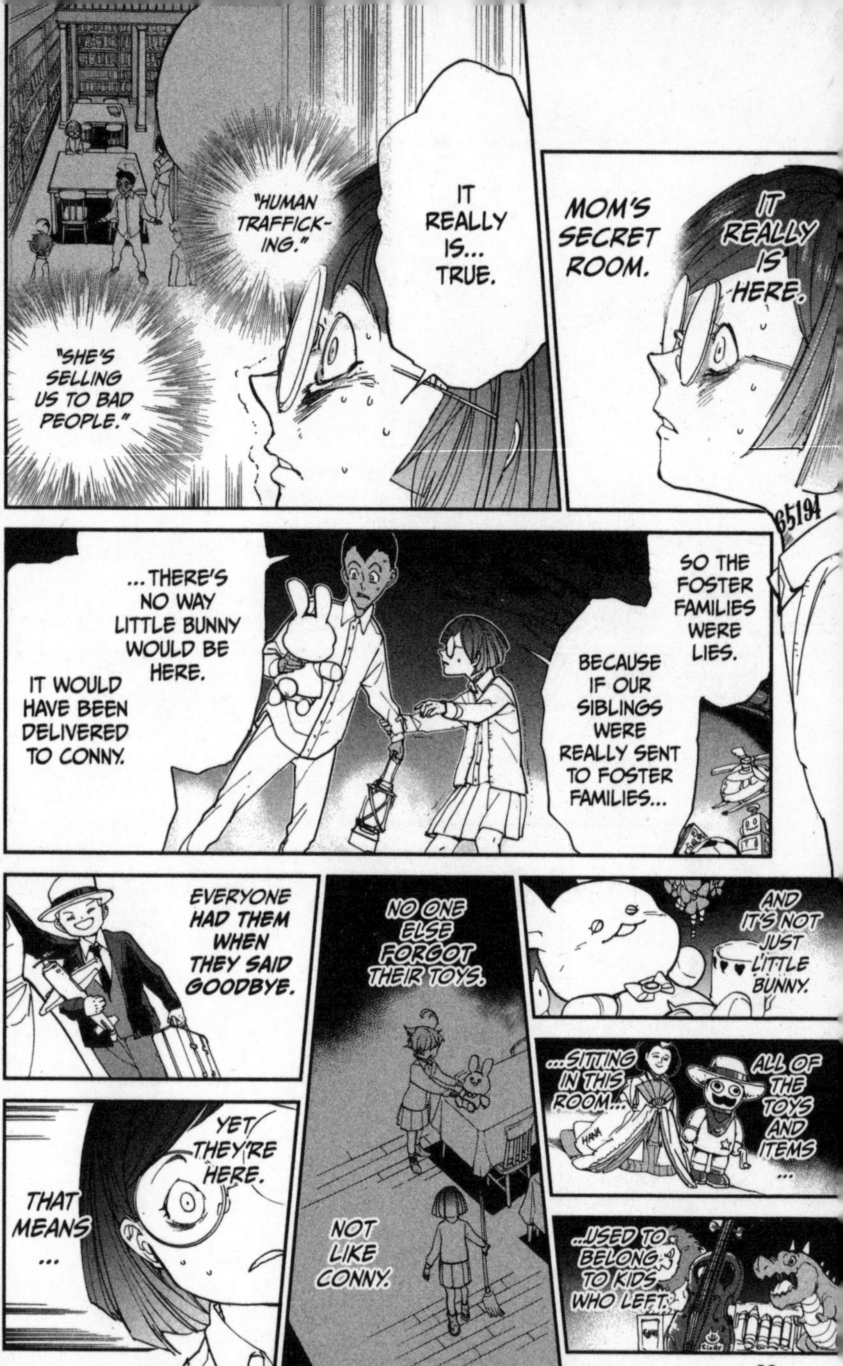
IT REALLY IS HERE.
MOM'S SECRET ROOM.
IT REALLY IS... TRUE.
"HUMAN TRAFFICKING."
"SHE'S SELLING US TO BAD PEOPLE."
65194
SO THE FOSTER FAMILIES WERE LIES.
BECAUSE IF OUR SIBLINGS WERE REALLY SENT TO FOSTER FAMILIES...
...THERE'S NO WAY LITTLE BUNNY WOULD BE HERE.
IT WOULD HAVE BEEN DELIVERED TO CONNY.
AND IT'S NOT JUST LITTLE BUNNY.
ALL OF THE TOYS AND ITEMS...
...SITTING IN THIS ROOM...
...USED TO BELONG TO KIDS WHO LEFT.
NO ONE ELSE FORGOT THEIR TOYS.
NOT LIKE CONNY.
EVERYONE HAD THEM WHEN THEY SAID GOODBYE.
YET THEY'RE HERE.
THAT MEANS...

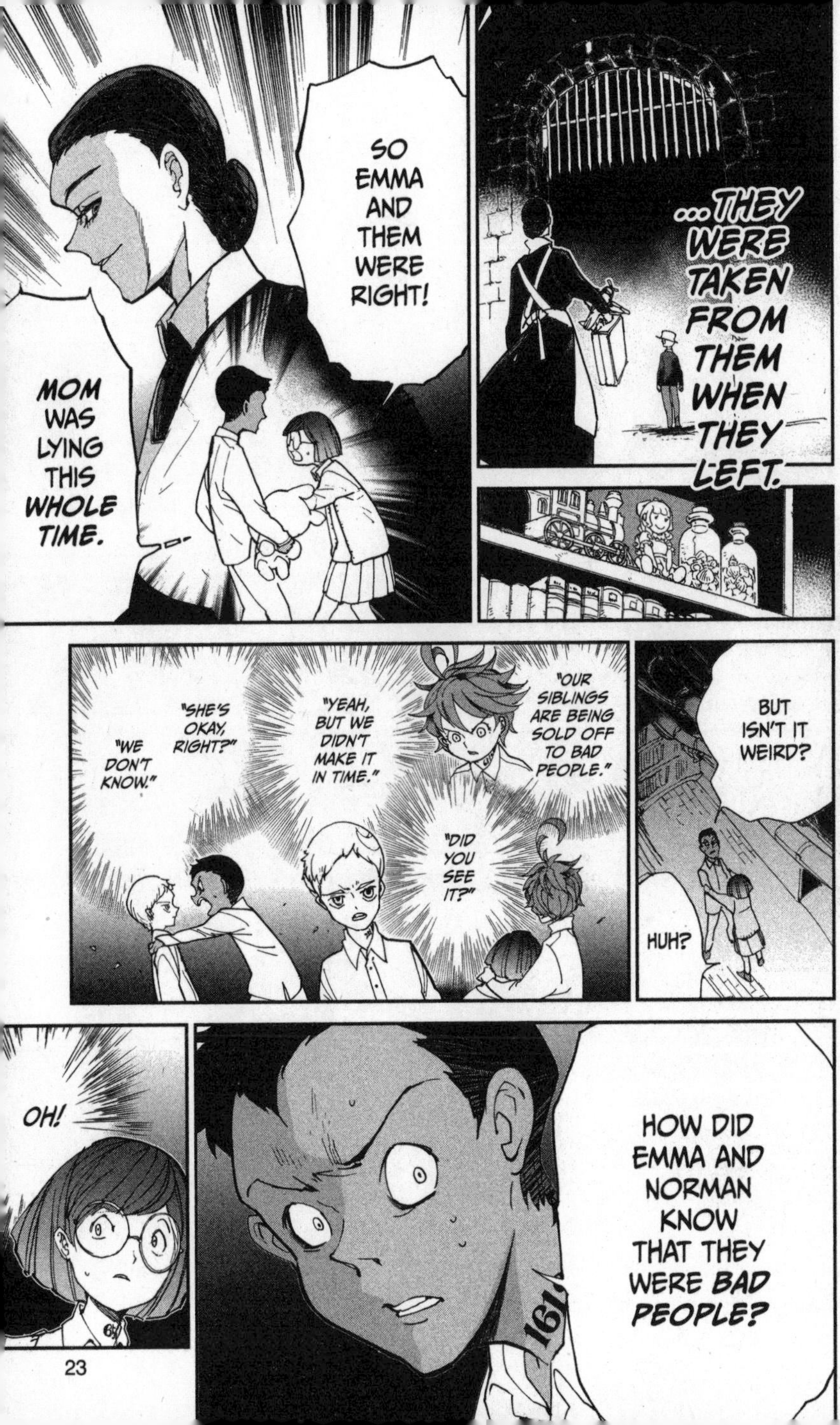
...THEY WERE TAKEN FROM THEM WHEN THEY LEFT.
SO EMMA AND THEM WERE RIGHT!
MOM WAS LYING THIS WHOLE TIME.
BUT ISN'T IT WEIRD?
HUH?
"OUR SIBLINGS ARE BEING SOLD OFF TO BAD PEOPLE."
"YEAH, BUT WE DIDN'T MAKE IT IN TIME."
"SHE'S OKAY, RIGHT?"
"WE DON'T KNOW."
"DID YOU SEE IT?"
HOW DID EMMA AND NORMAN KNOW THAT THEY WERE BAD PEOPLE?
OH!

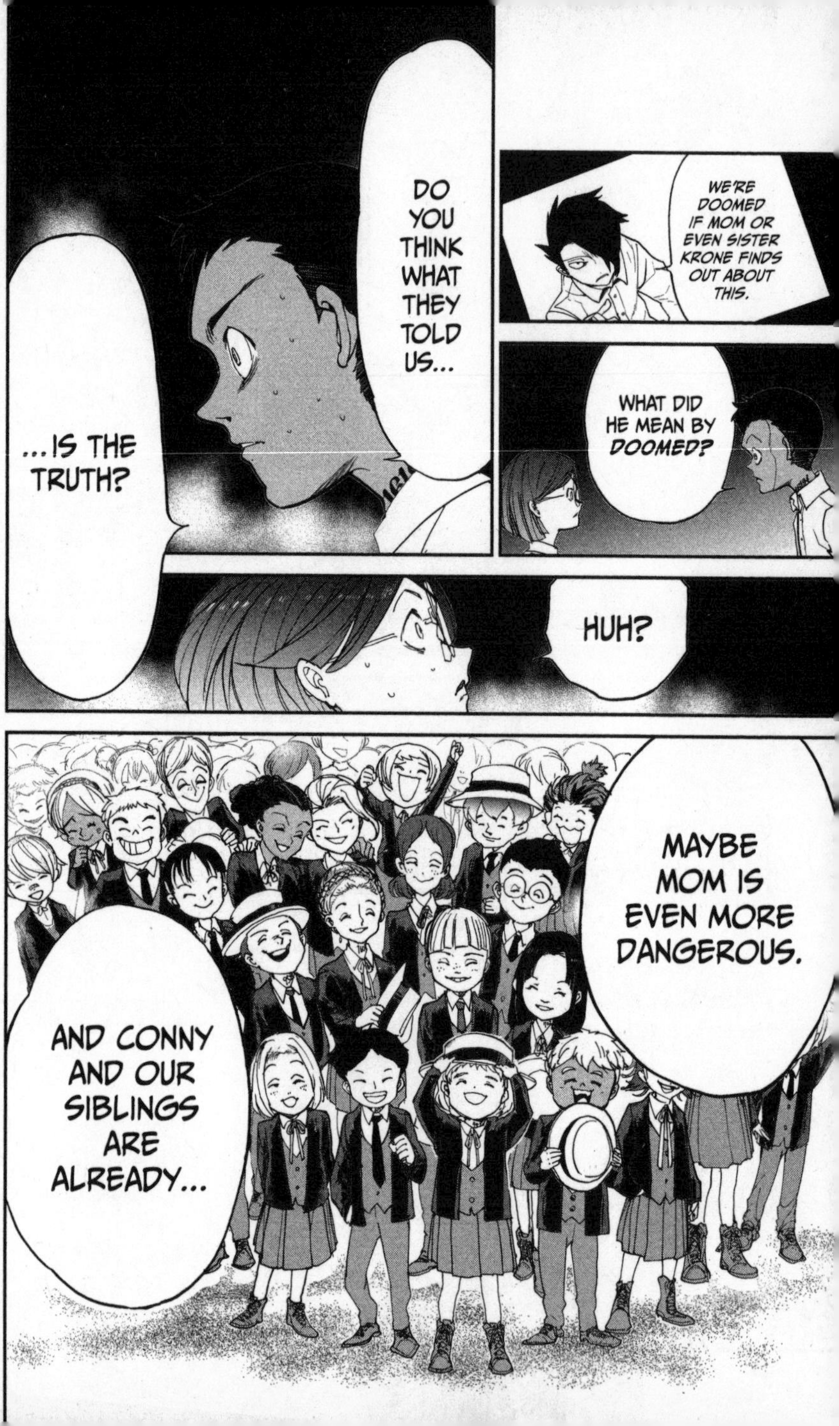
WE'RE DOOMED IF MOM OR EVEN SISTER KRONE FINDS OUT ABOUT THIS.
WHAT DID HE MEAN BY DOOMED?
HUH?
DO YOU THINK WHAT THEY TOLD US...
...IS THE TRUTH?
MAYBE MOM IS EVEN MORE DANGEROUS.
AND CONNY AND OUR SIBLINGS ARE ALREADY...

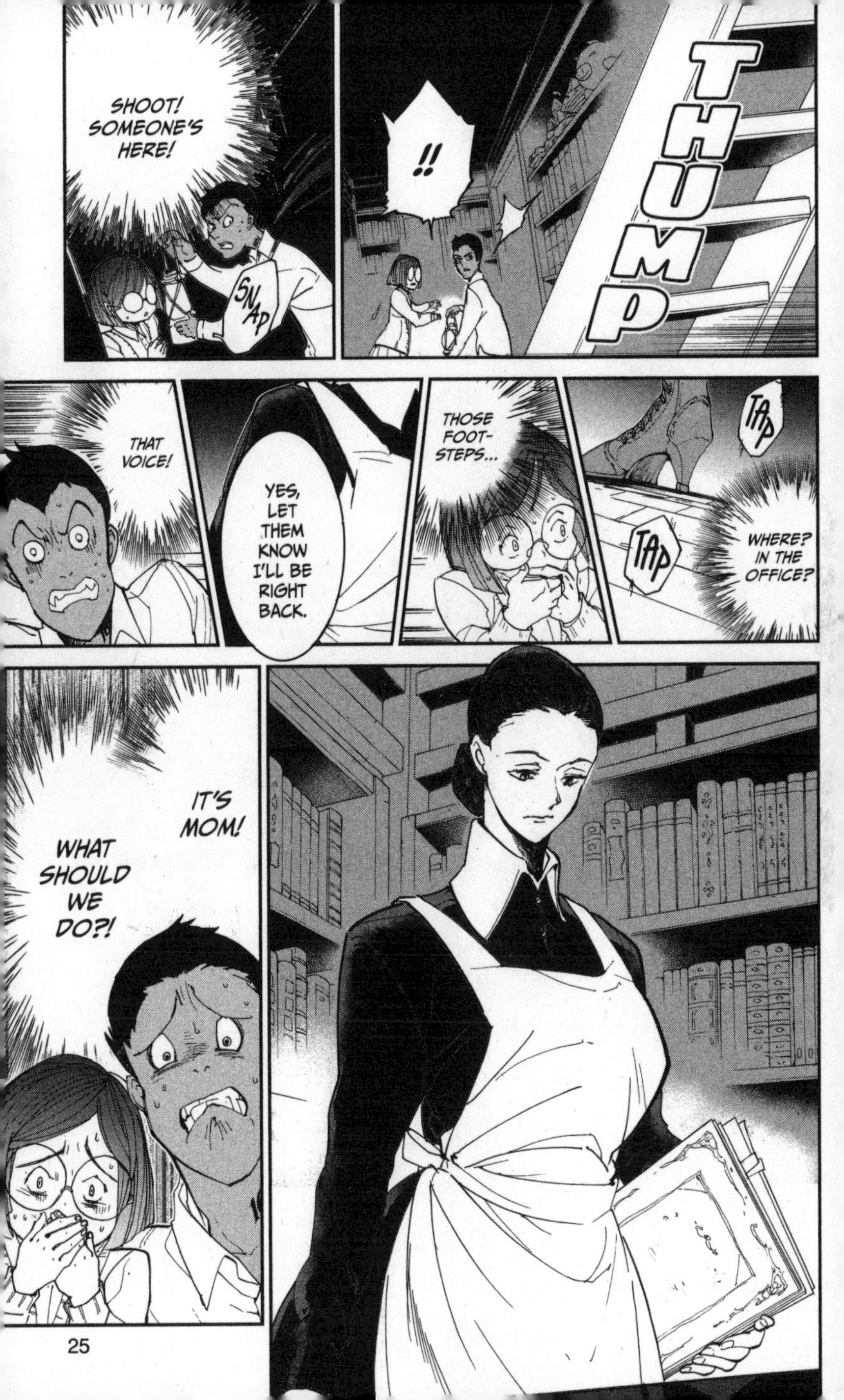
THUMP
!!
SHOOT! SOMEONE'S HERE!
SNAP
TAP
TAP
WHERE? IN THE OFFICE?
THOSE FOOT-STEPS...
YES, LET THEM KNOW I'LL BE RIGHT BACK.
THAT VOICE!
IT'S MOM!
WHAT SHOULD WE DO?!

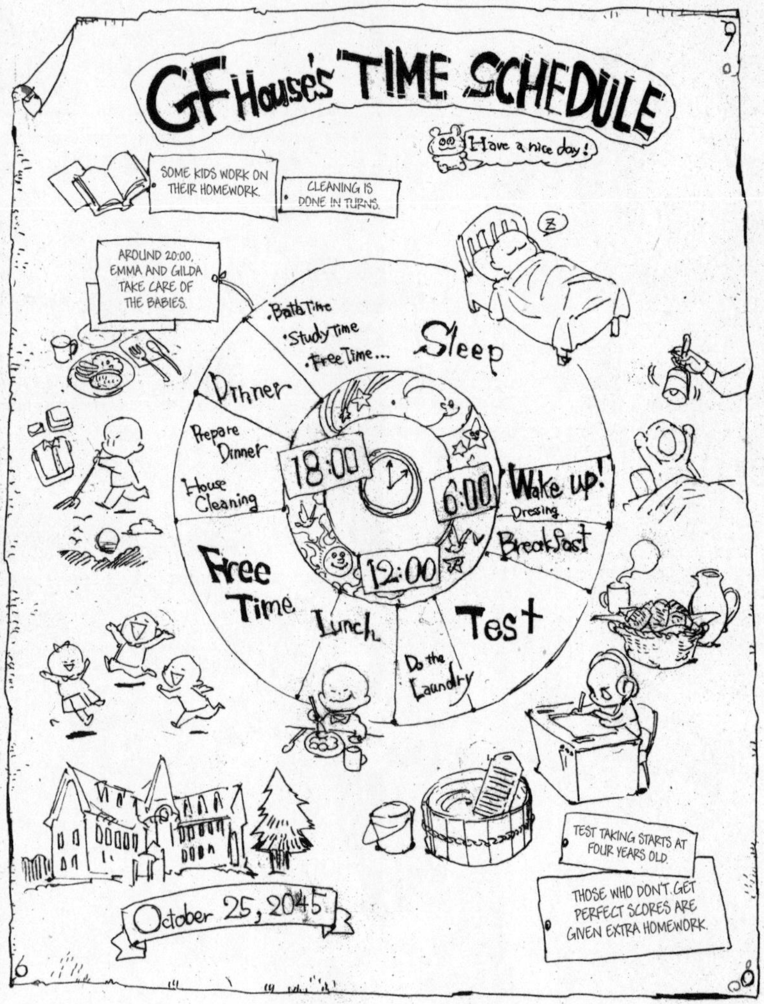
GF House's TIME SCHEDULE
Have a nice day!
SOME KIDS WORK ON THEIR HOMEWORK.
CLEANING IS DONE IN TURNS.
AROUND 20:00, EMMA AND GILDA TAKE CARE OF THE BABIES.
Z
•Bath Time
•Study Time
•Free Time...
Sleep
Dinner
Prepare Dinner
House Cleaning
18:00
6:00
Wake up!
Dressing
Breakfast
12:00
Free Time
Lunch
Test
Do the Laundry
TEST TAKING STARTS AT FOUR YEARS OLD.
THOSE WHO DON'T GET PERFECT SCORES ARE GIVEN EXTRA HOMEWORK.
October 25, 2045

CHAPTER 18: PREPARED

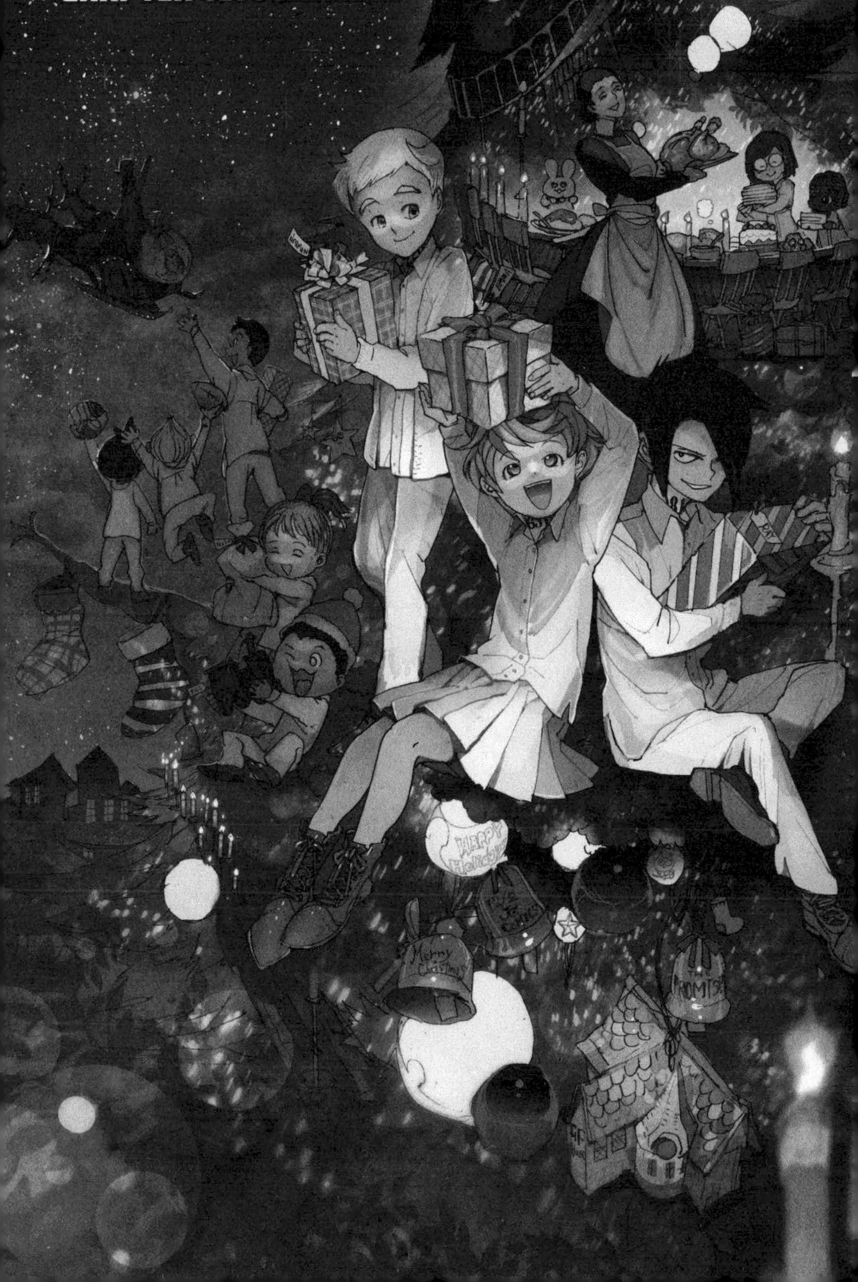

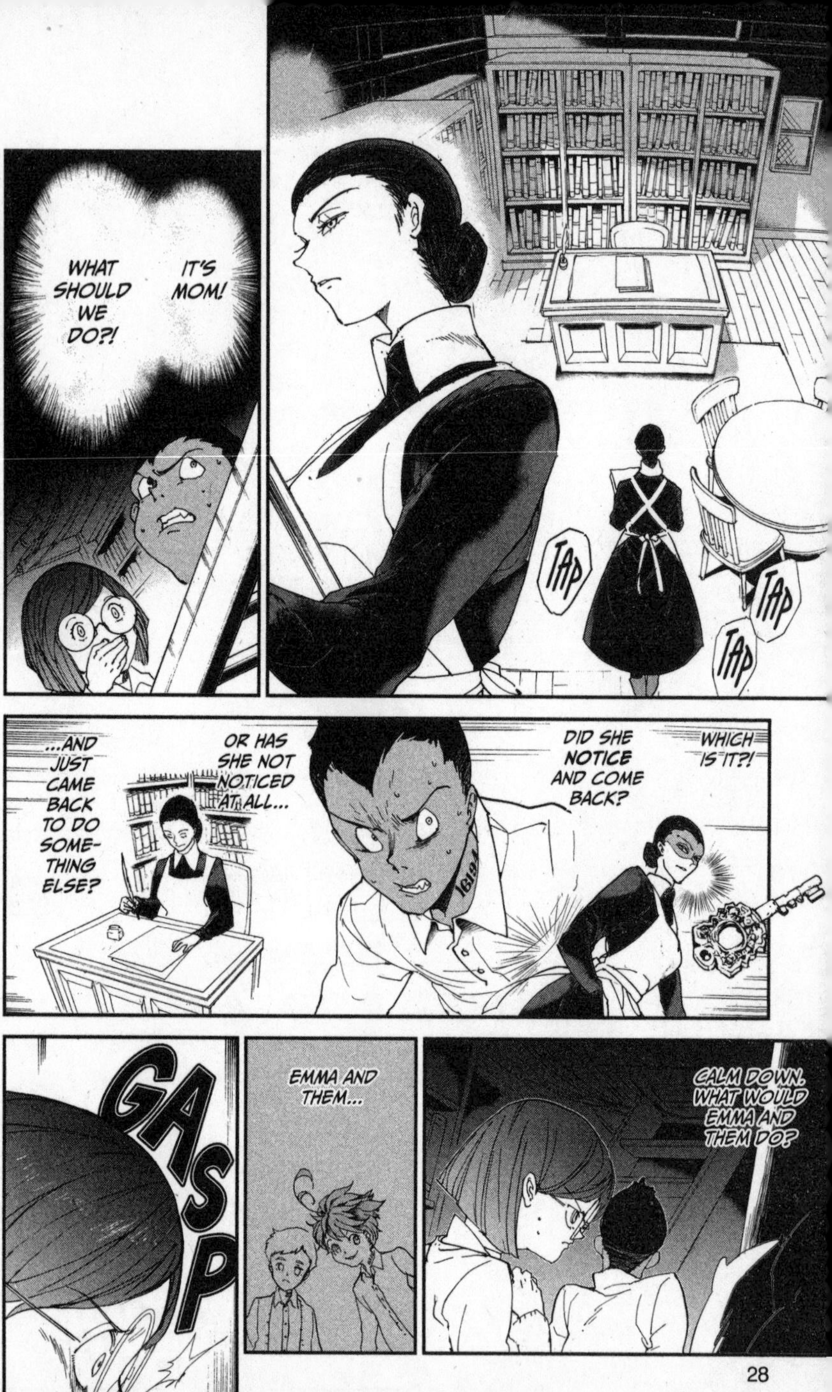
TAP
TAP
TAP
IT'S MOM!
WHAT SHOULD WE DO?!
WHICH IS IT?!
DID SHE NOTICE AND COME BACK?
OR HAS SHE NOT NOTICED AT ALL...
...AND JUST CAME BACK TO DO SOMETHING ELSE?
CALM DOWN. WHAT WOULD EMMA AND THEM DO?
EMMA AND THEM...
GASP

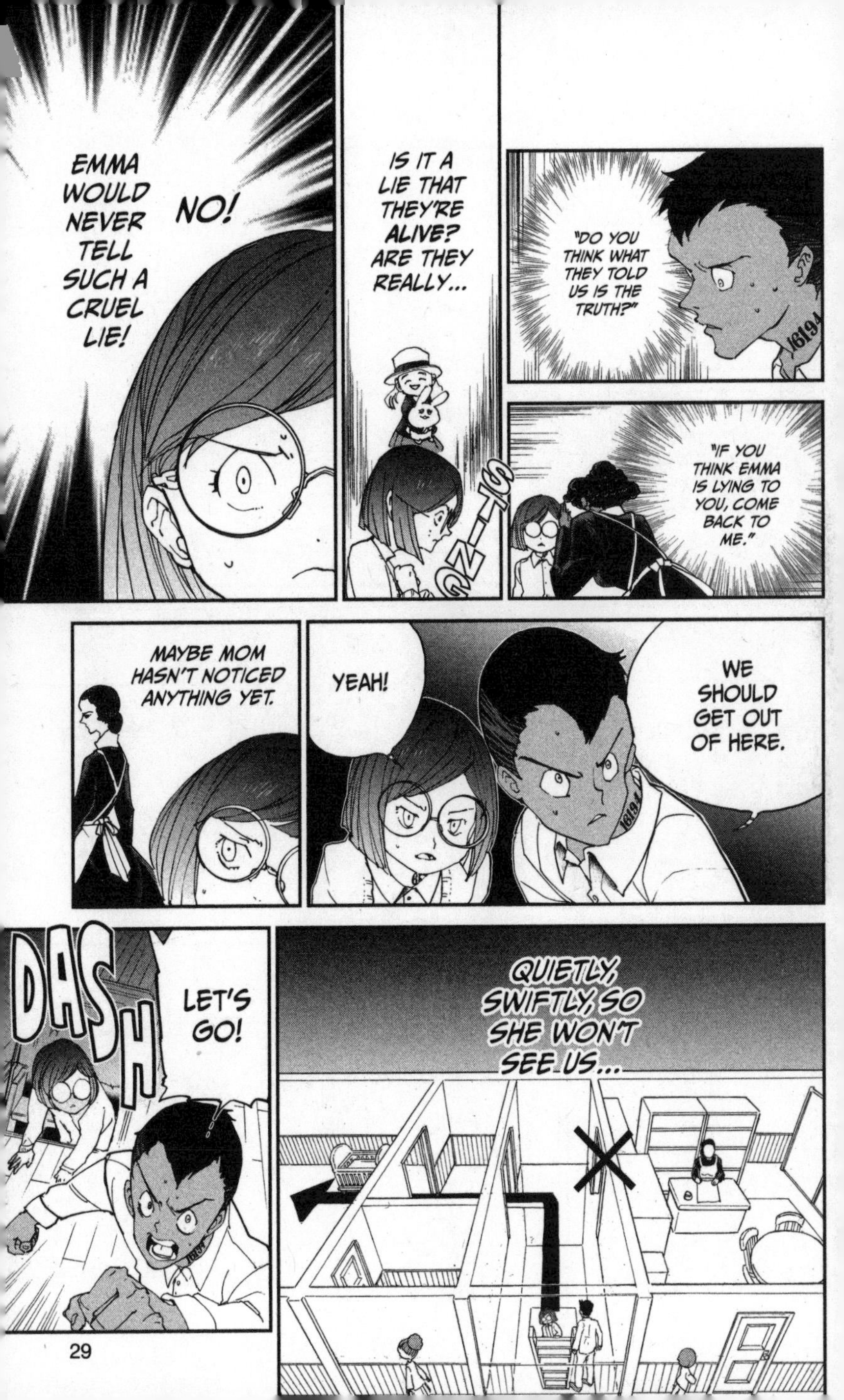
"DO YOU THINK WHAT THEY TOLD US IS THE TRUTH?"
"IF YOU THINK EMMA IS LYING TO YOU, COME BACK TO ME."
IS IT A LIE THAT THEY'RE ALIVE? ARE THEY REALLY...
STING
NO!
EMMA WOULD NEVER TELL SUCH A CRUEL LIE!
WE SHOULD GET OUT OF HERE.
YEAH!
MAYBE MOM HASN'T NOTICED ANYTHING YET.
QUIETLY, SWIFTLY, SO SHE WON'T SEE US...
LET'S GO!
DASH

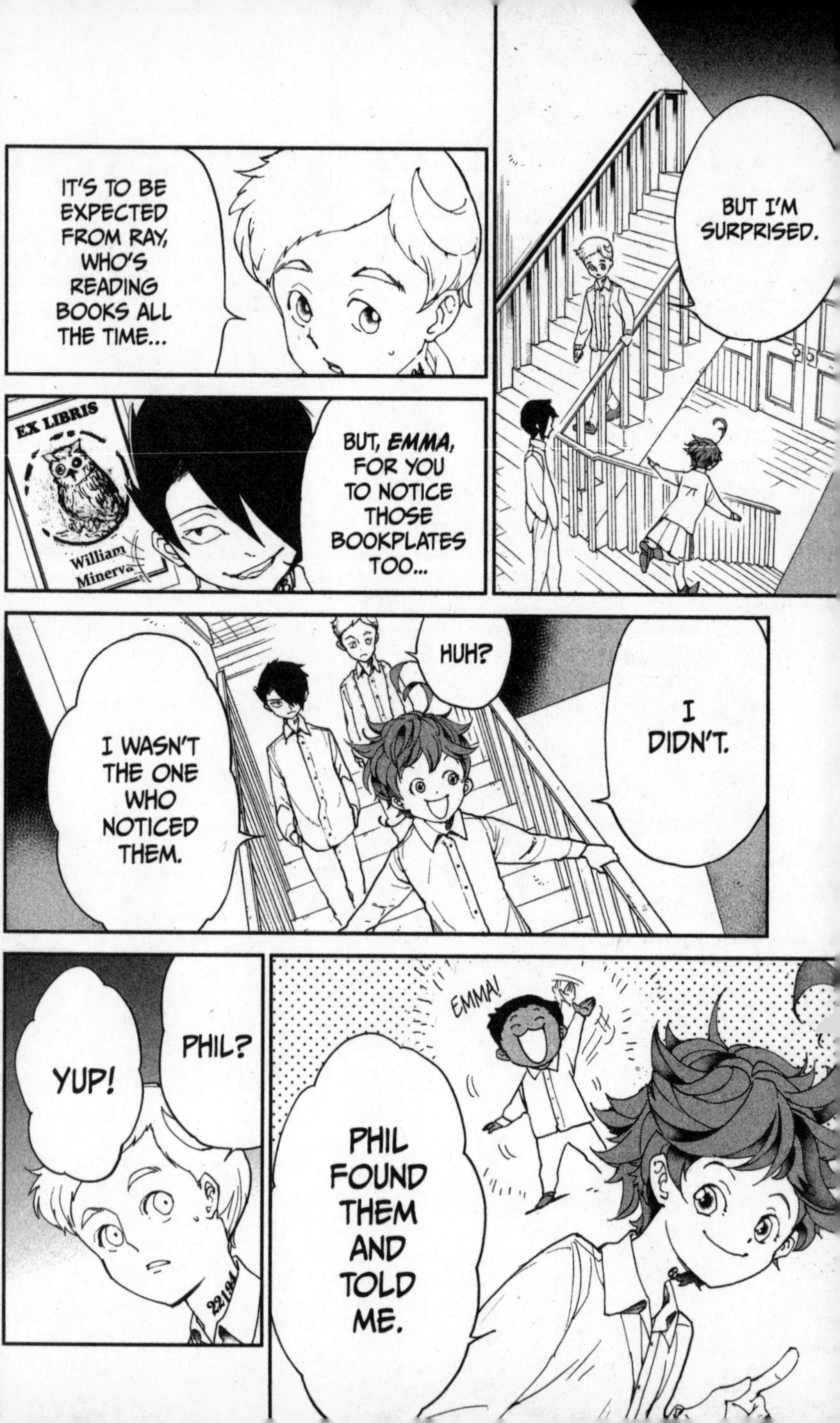
BUT I'M SURPRISED.
IT'S TO BE EXPECTED FROM RAY, WHO'S READING BOOKS ALL THE TIME...
EX LIBRIS
William Minerva
BUT, *EMMA*, FOR YOU TO NOTICE THOSE BOOKPLATES TOO...
I DIDN'T.
HUH?
I WASN'T THE ONE WHO NOTICED THEM.
EMMA!
PHIL FOUND THEM AND TOLD ME.
PHIL?
YUP!
22194

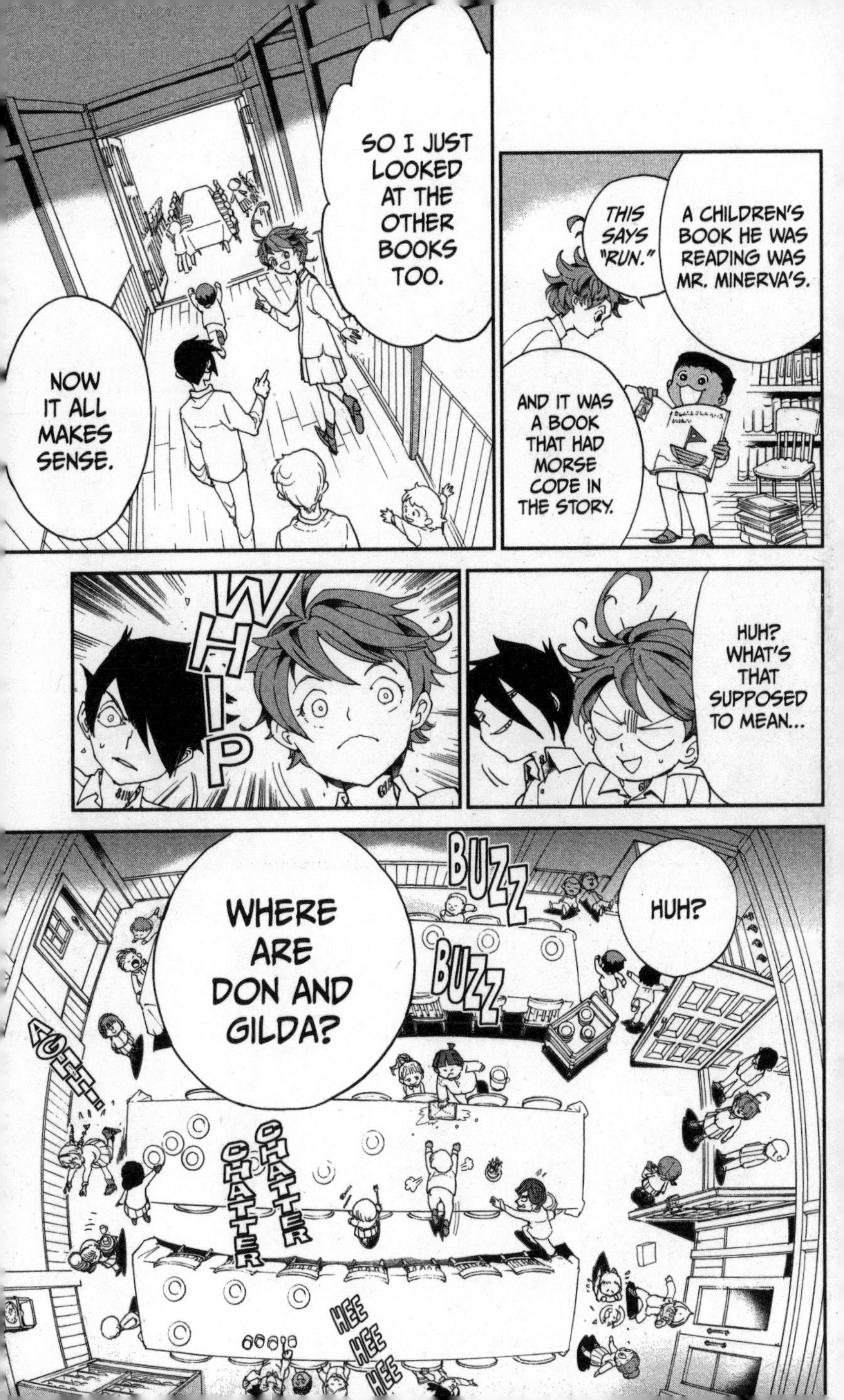
A CHILDREN'S BOOK HE WAS READING WAS MR. MINERVA'S.
THIS SAYS "RUN."
AND IT WAS A BOOK THAT HAD MORSE CODE IN THE STORY.
SO I JUST LOOKED AT THE OTHER BOOKS TOO.
NOW IT ALL MAKES SENSE.
HUH? WHAT'S THAT SUPPOSED TO MEAN...
WHIP
HUH?
BUZZ
BUZZ
WHERE ARE DON AND GILDA?
CHATTER
CHATTER
HEE
HEE
HEE

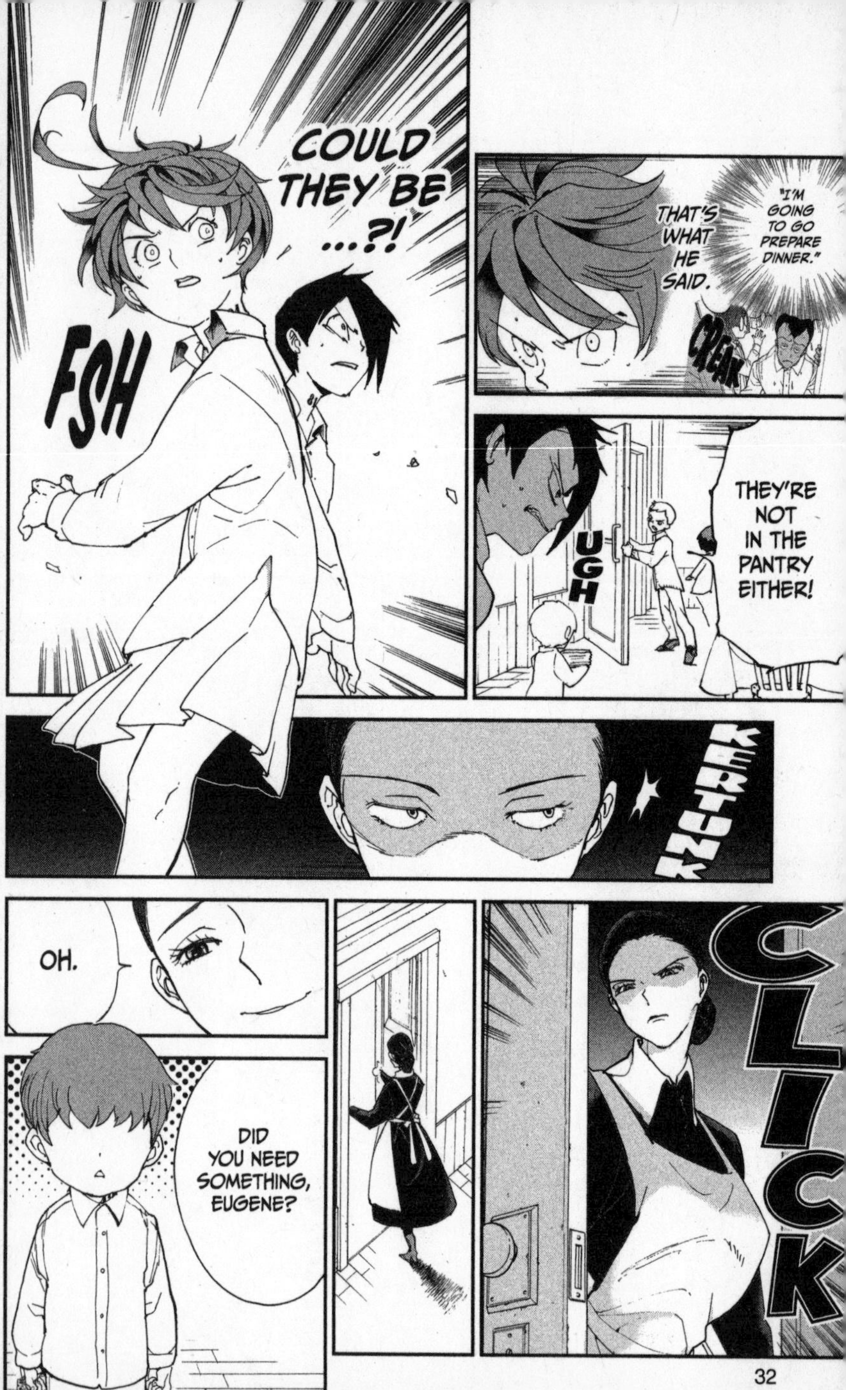
"I'M GOING TO GO PREPARE DINNER."
THAT'S WHAT HE SAID.
CREAK
THEY'RE NOT IN THE PANTRY EITHER!
UGH
COULD THEY BE ...?!
FSH
KERTUNK
CLICK
OH.
DID YOU NEED SOMETHING, EUGENE?

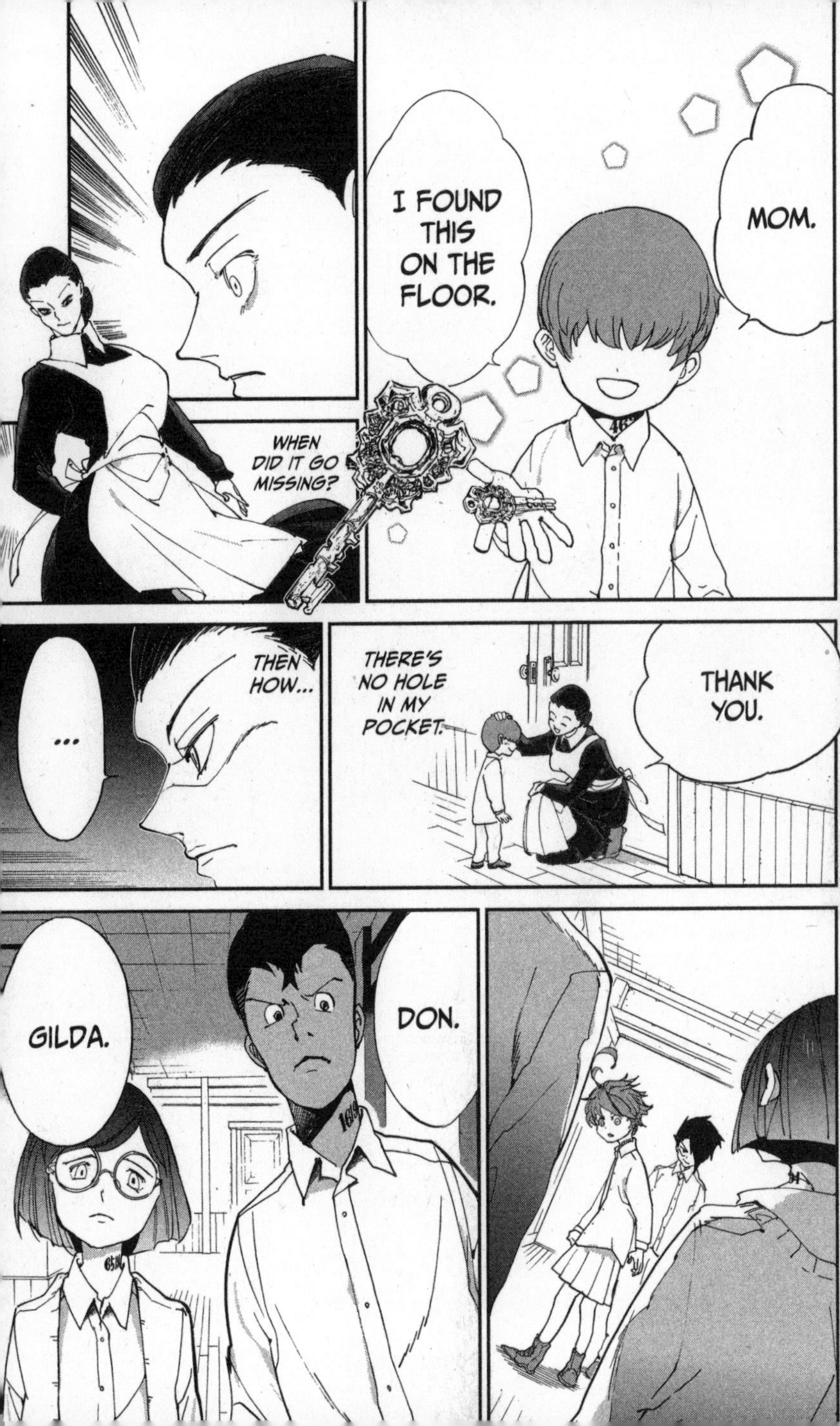
MOM.
I FOUND THIS ON THE FLOOR.
WHEN DID IT GO MISSING?
THANK YOU.
THERE'S NO HOLE IN MY POCKET.
THEN HOW...
...
DON.
GILDA.

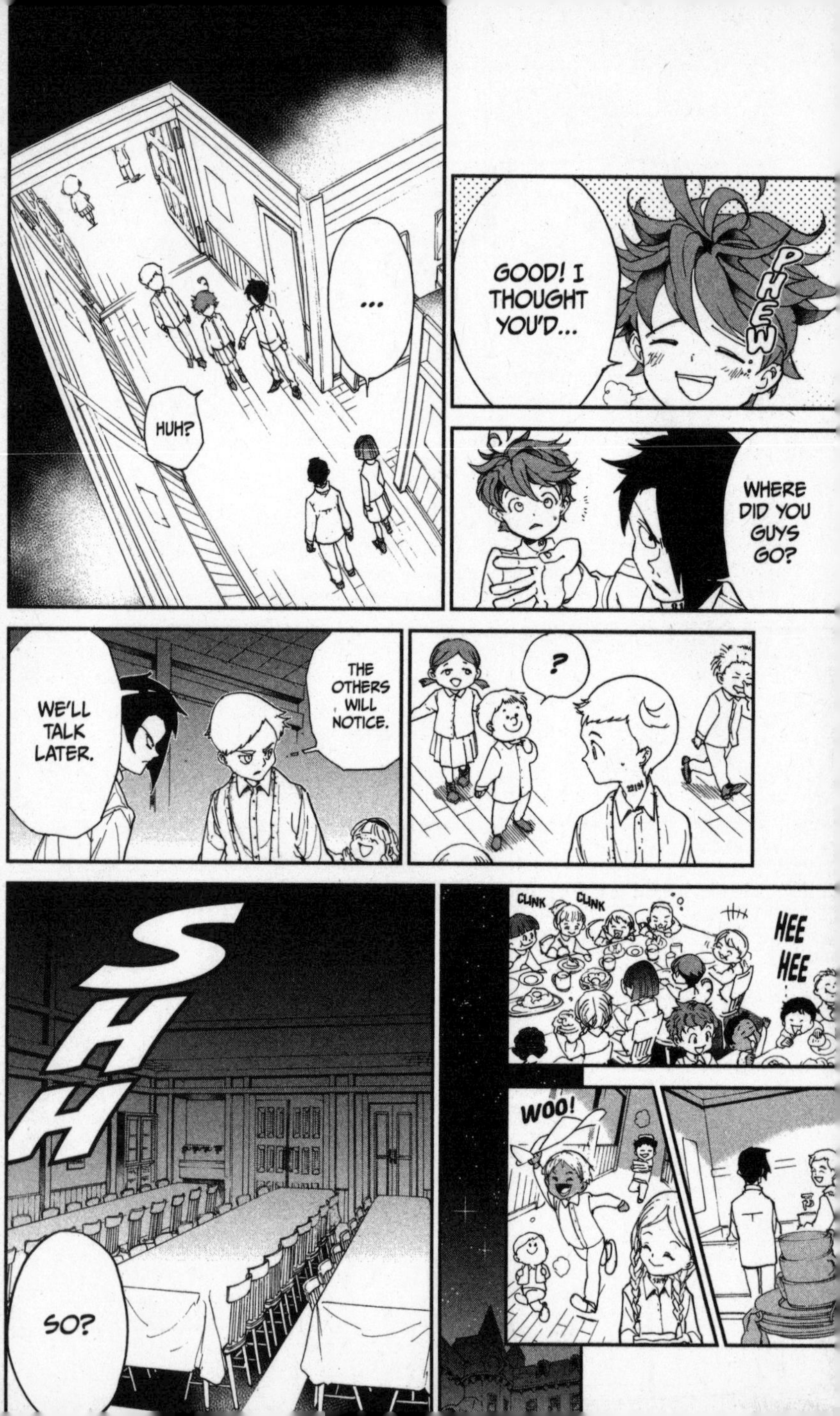
PHEW
GOOD! I THOUGHT YOU'D...
WHERE DID YOU GUYS GO?
...
HUH?
?
THE OTHERS WILL NOTICE.
WE'LL TALK LATER.
HEE HEE
CLINK
CLINK
WOO!
SHHH
SO?

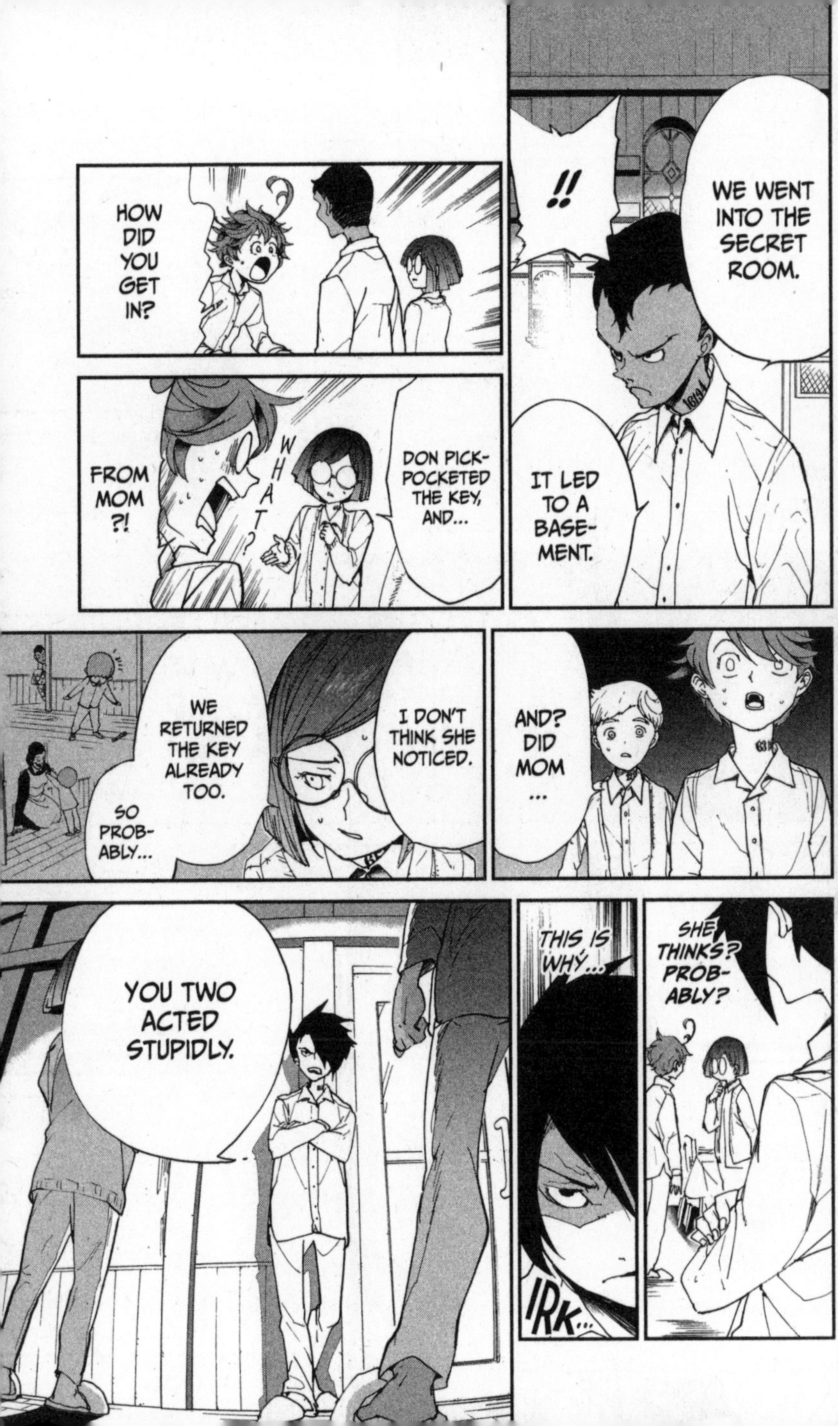
WE WENT INTO THE SECRET ROOM.
!!
IT LED TO A BASEMENT.
HOW DID YOU GET IN?
DON PICK-POCKETED THE KEY, AND...
WHAT?
FROM MOM ?!
AND? DID MOM ...
I DON'T THINK SHE NOTICED.
WE RETURNED THE KEY ALREADY TOO.
SO PROBABLY...
SHE THINKS? PROBABLY?
THIS IS WHY...
IRK...
YOU TWO ACTED STUPIDLY.

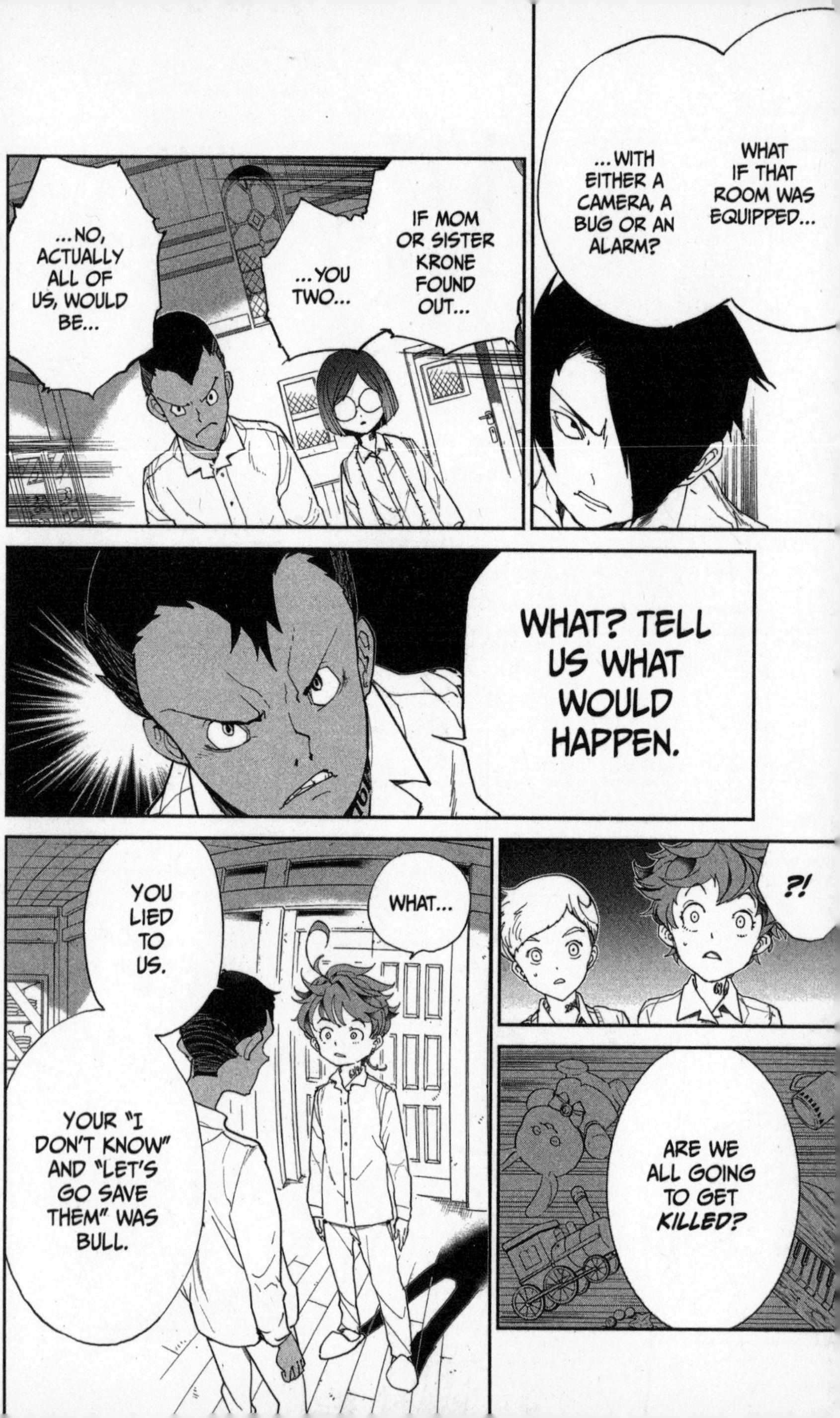
WHAT IF THAT ROOM WAS EQUIPPED...
...WITH EITHER A CAMERA, A BUG OR AN ALARM?
IF MOM OR SISTER KRONE FOUND OUT...
...YOU TWO...
...NO, ACTUALLY ALL OF US, WOULD BE...
WHAT? TELL US WHAT WOULD HAPPEN.
?!
ARE WE ALL GOING TO GET *KILLED?*
WHAT...
YOU LIED TO US.
YOUR "I DON'T KNOW" AND "LET'S GO SAVE THEM" WAS BULL.

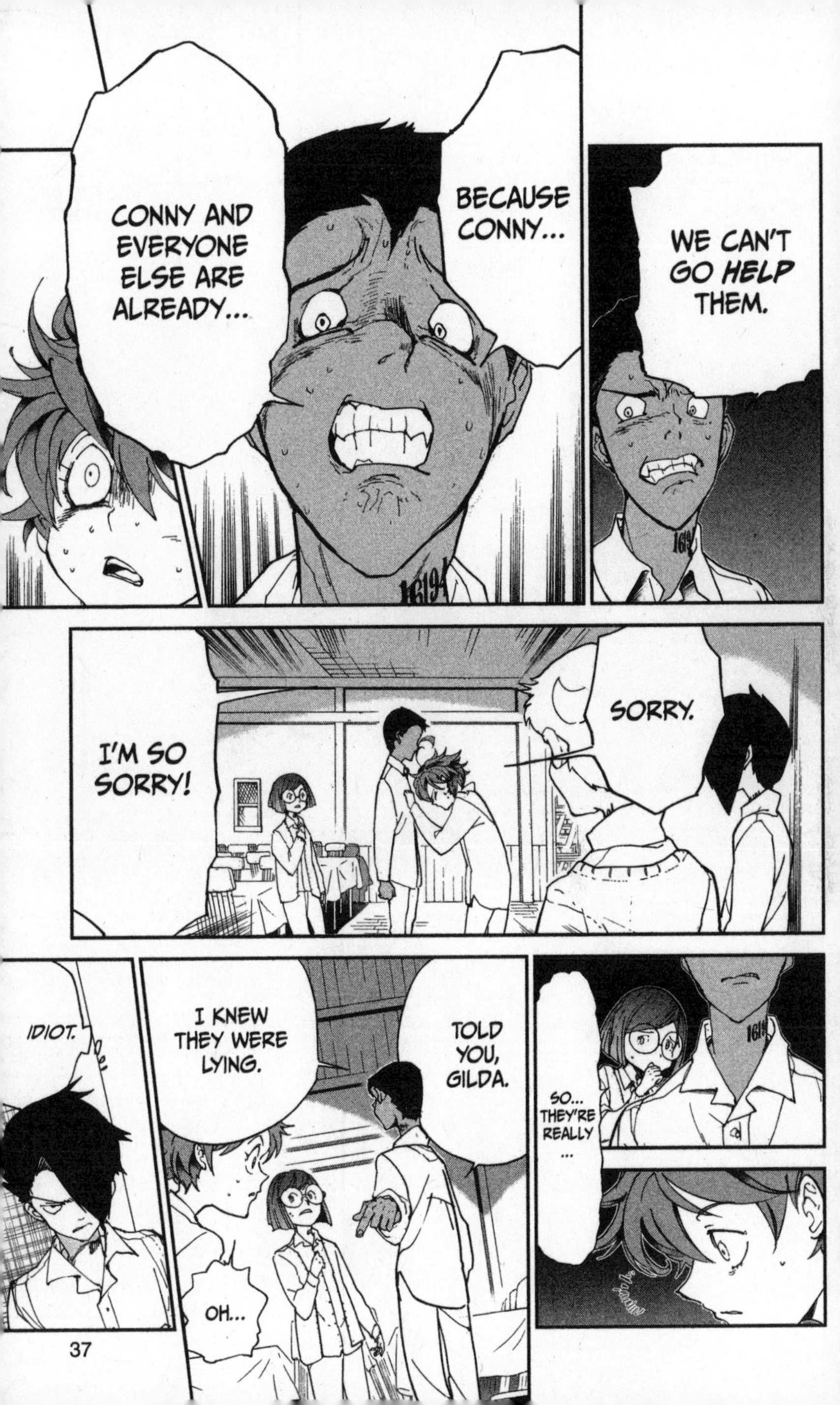
WE CAN'T GO *HELP* THEM.
BECAUSE CONNY...
CONNY AND EVERYONE ELSE ARE ALREADY...
SORRY.
I'M SO SORRY!
SO... THEY'RE REALLY ...
TOLD YOU, GILDA.
I KNEW THEY WERE LYING.
OH...
IDIOT.

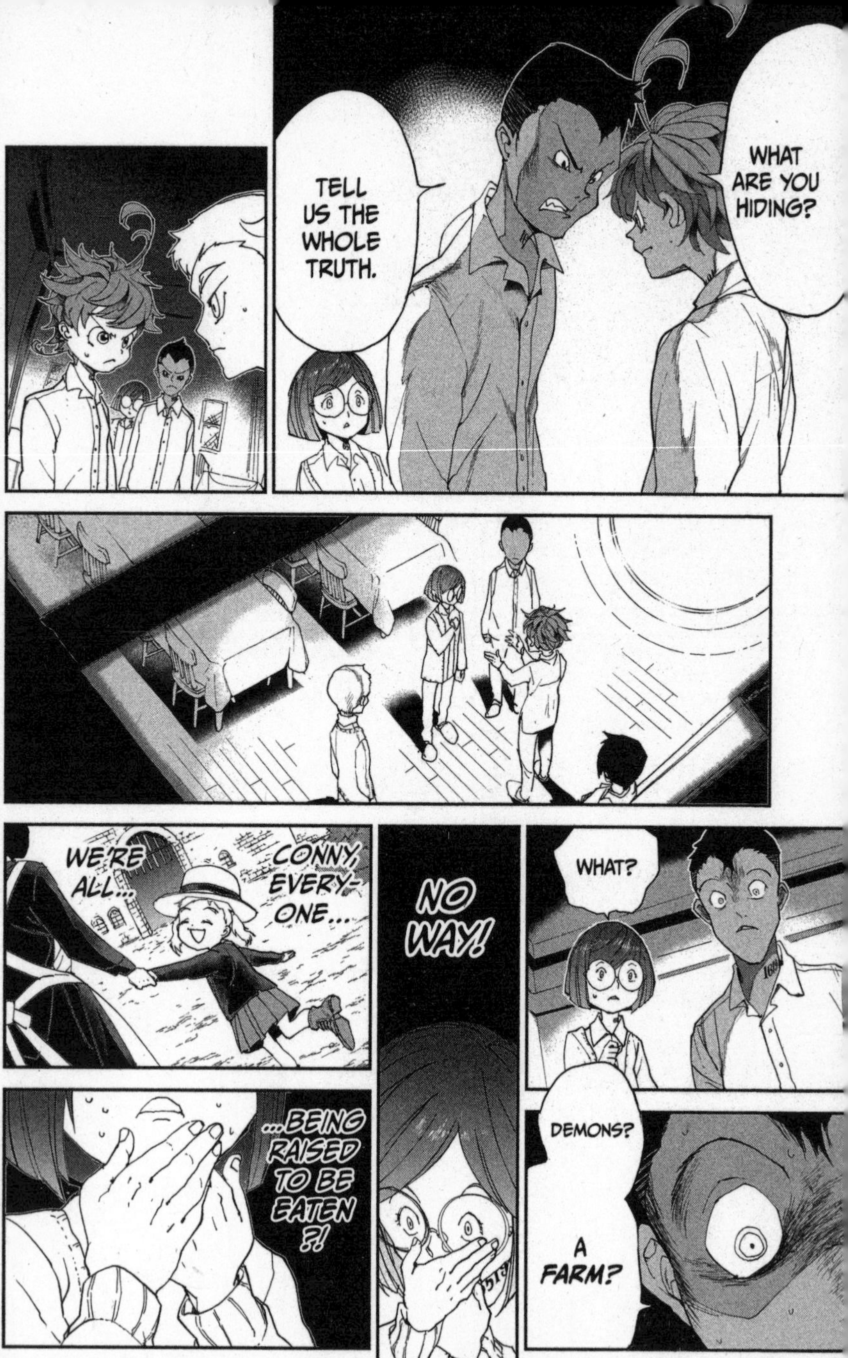
WHAT ARE YOU HIDING?
TELL US THE WHOLE TRUTH.
WHAT?
DEMONS?
A FARM?
NO WAY!
CONNY, EVERY-ONE...
WE'RE ALL...
...BEING RAISED TO BE EATEN ?!

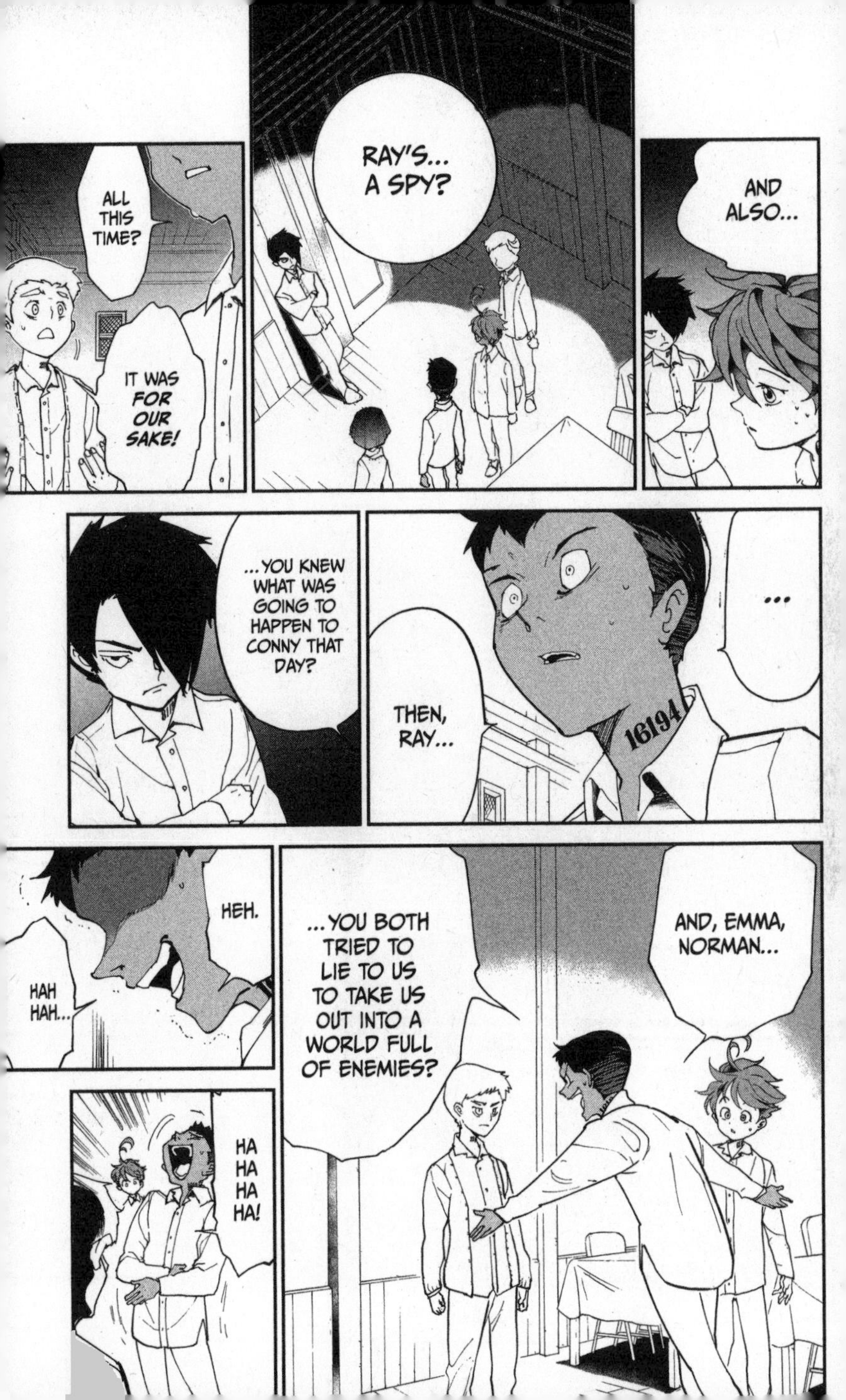
AND ALSO...
RAY'S... A SPY?
ALL THIS TIME?
IT WAS FOR OUR SAKE!
...
THEN, RAY...
...YOU KNEW WHAT WAS GOING TO HAPPEN TO CONNY THAT DAY?
16194
AND, EMMA, NORMAN...
...YOU BOTH TRIED TO LIE TO US TO TAKE US OUT INTO A WORLD FULL OF ENEMIES?
HEH.
HAH HAH...
HA HA HA HA!

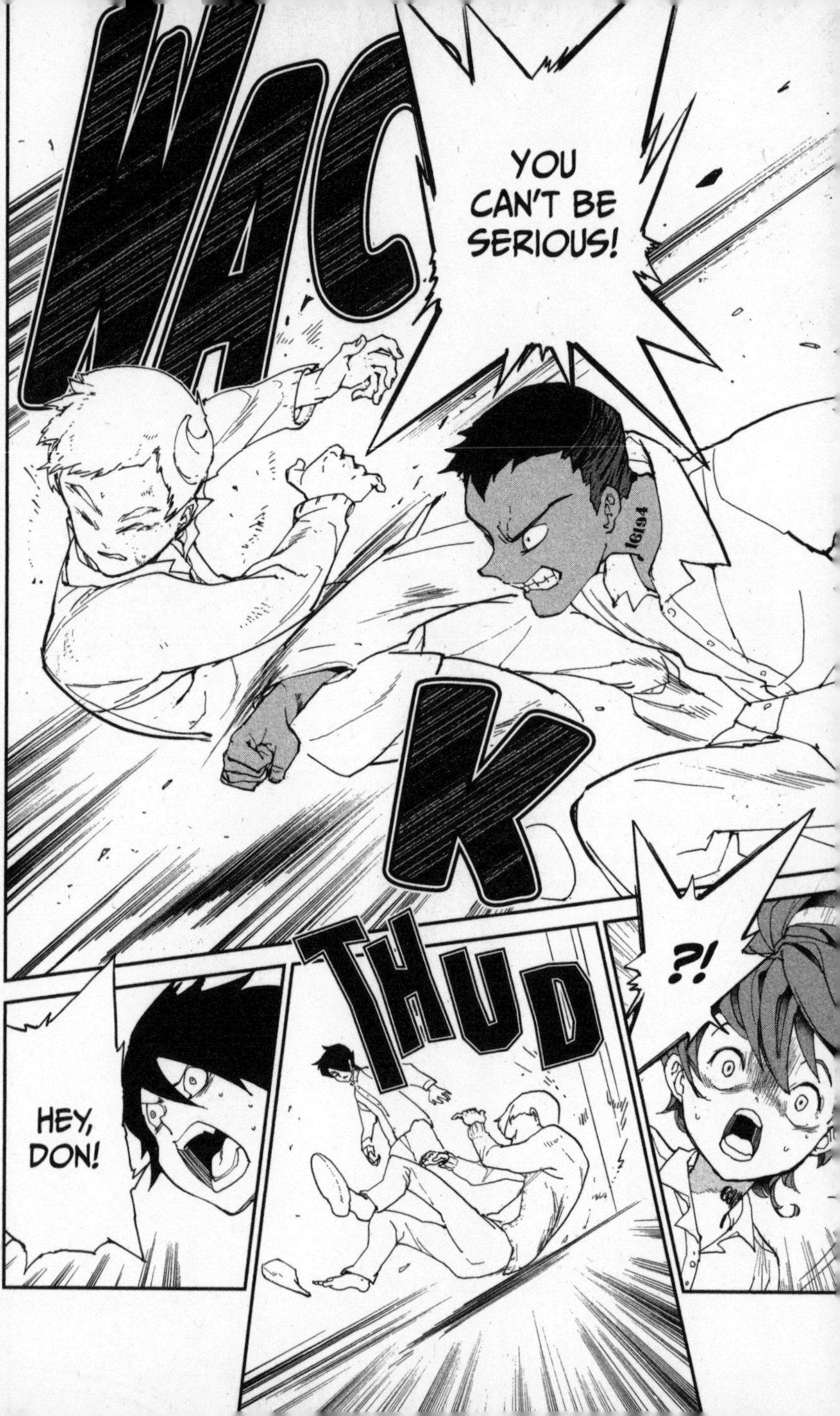
YOU CAN'T BE SERIOUS!
WAC
K
?!
THUD
HEY, DON!

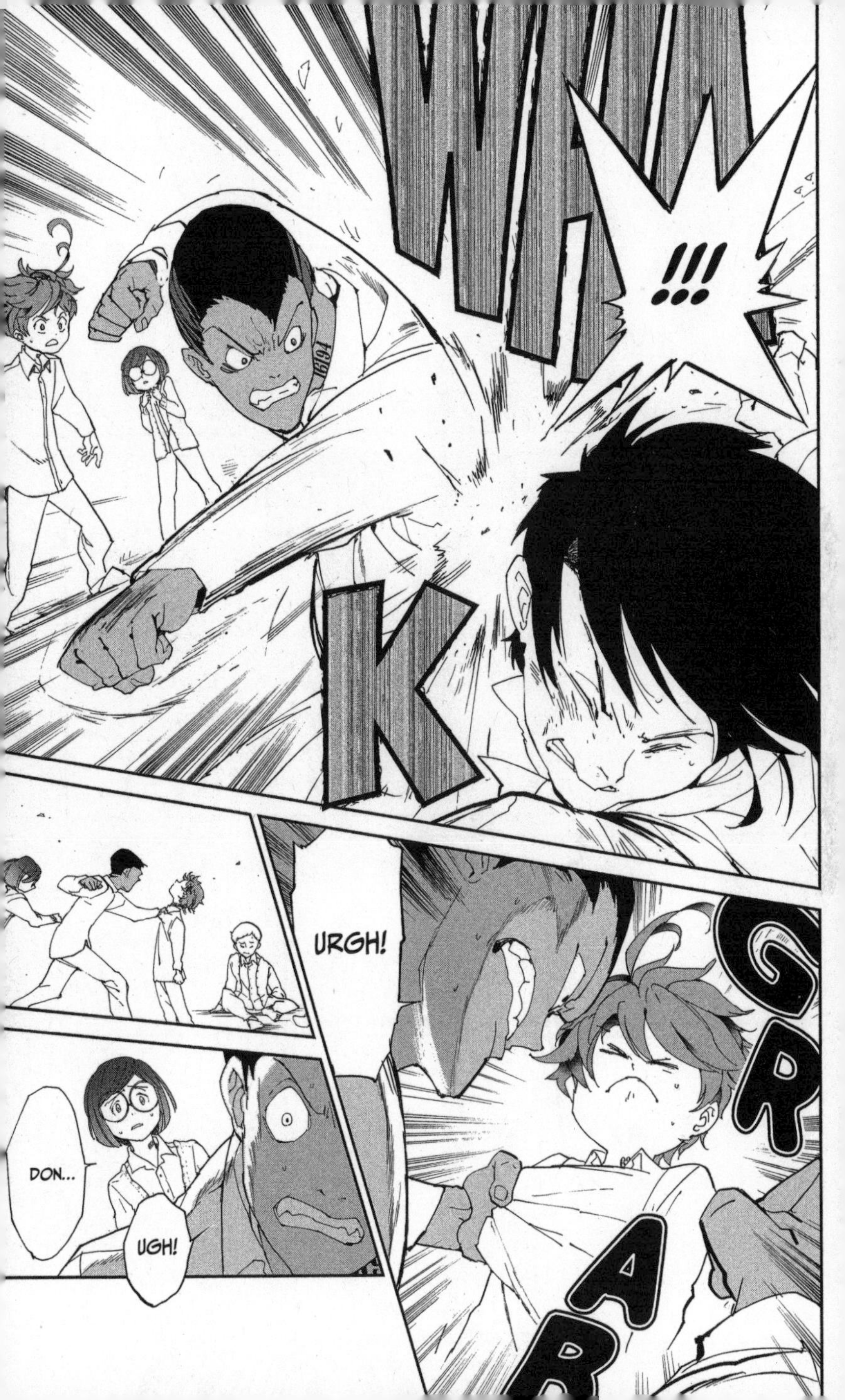

WHA
!!!
K
GR
AR
URGH!
DON...
UGH!

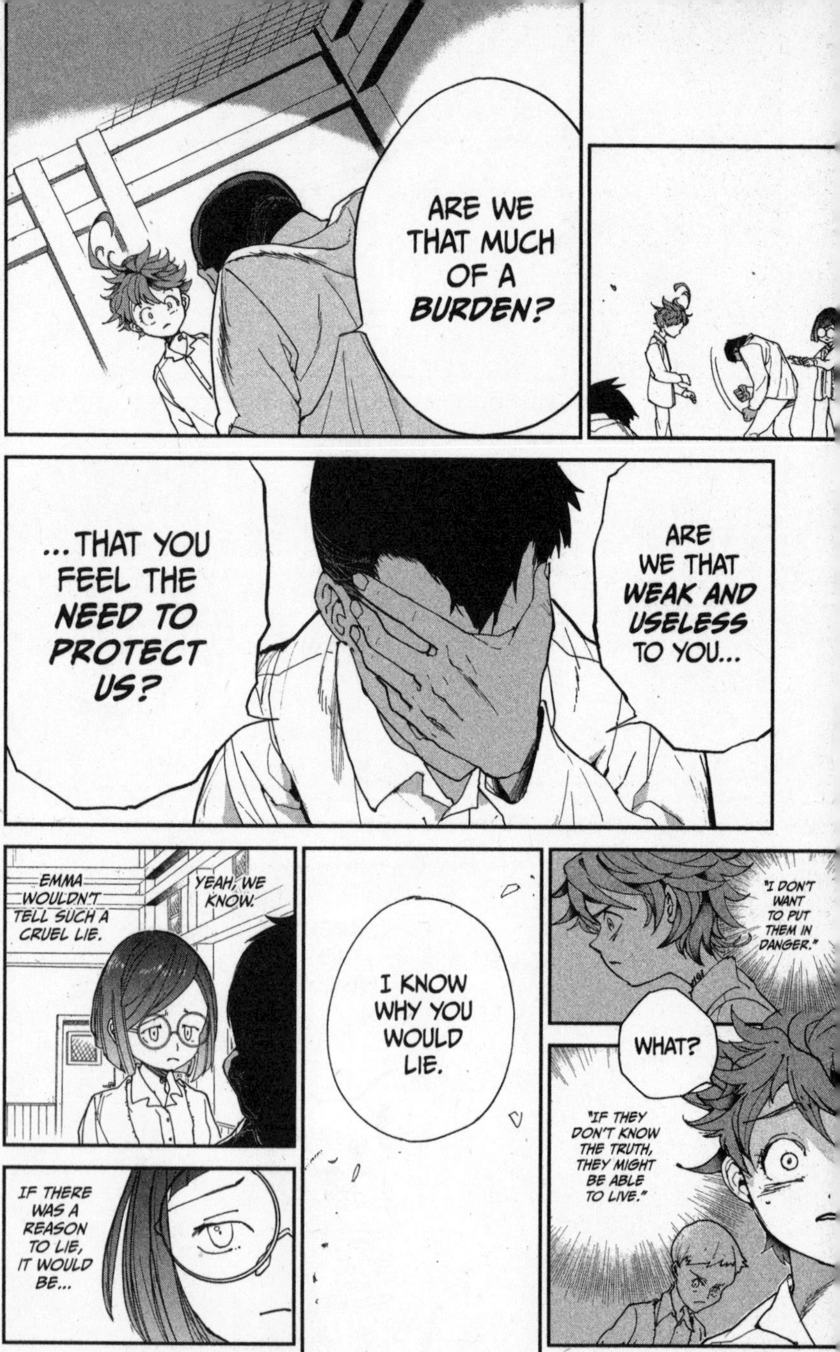
ARE WE THAT MUCH OF A BURDEN?
ARE WE THAT WEAK AND USELESS TO YOU...
...THAT YOU FEEL THE NEED TO PROTECT US?
"I DON'T WANT TO PUT THEM IN DANGER."
WHAT?
"IF THEY DON'T KNOW THE TRUTH, THEY MIGHT BE ABLE TO LIVE."
I KNOW WHY YOU WOULD LIE.
YEAH, WE KNOW.
EMMA WOULDN'T TELL SUCH A CRUEL LIE.
IF THERE WAS A REASON TO LIE, IT WOULD BE...

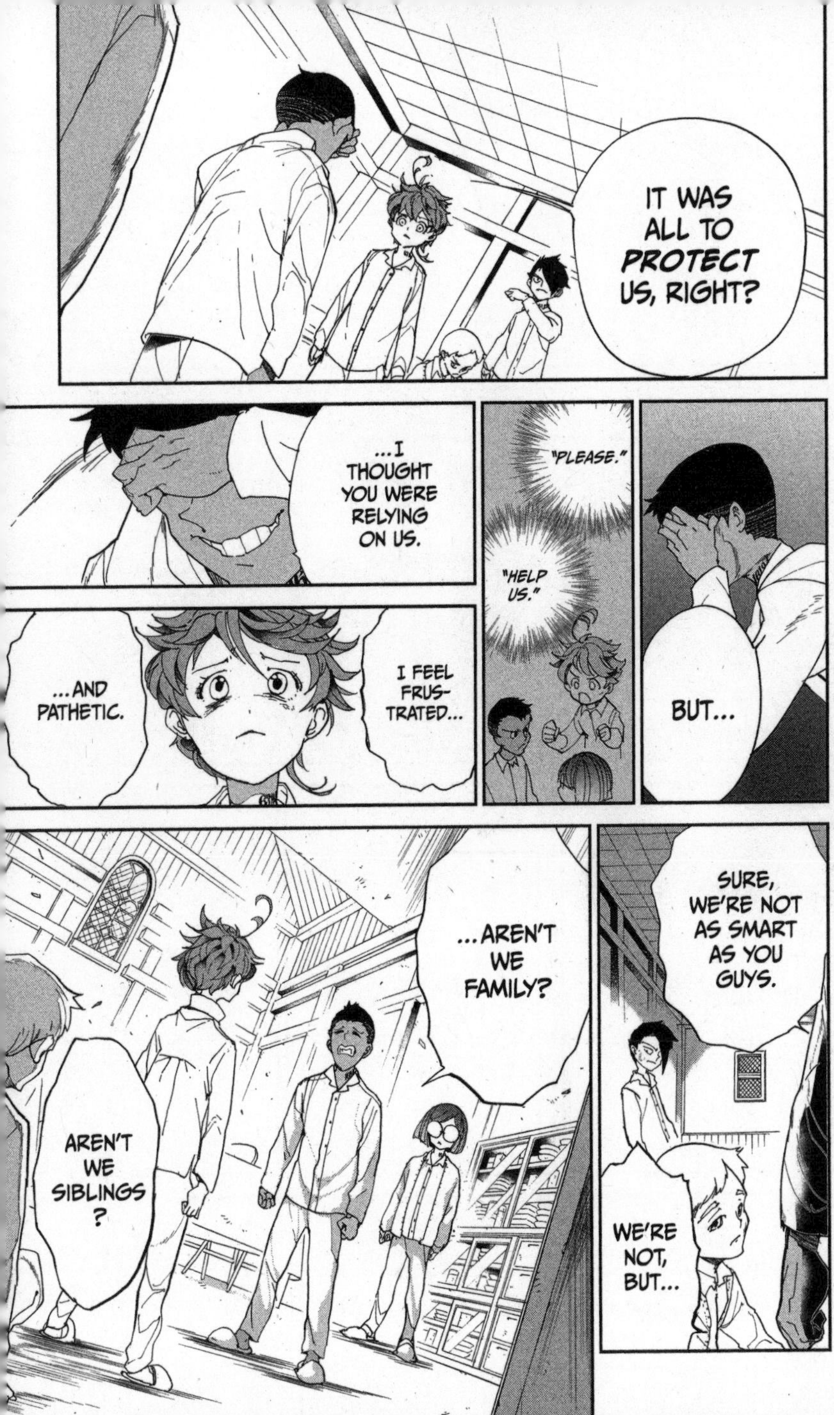
IT WAS ALL TO *PROTECT* US, RIGHT?
BUT...
"PLEASE."
"HELP US."
...I THOUGHT YOU WERE RELYING ON US.
I FEEL FRUS-TRATED...
...AND PATHETIC.
SURE, WE'RE NOT AS SMART AS YOU GUYS.
WE'RE NOT, BUT...
...AREN'T WE FAMILY?
AREN'T WE SIBLINGS?

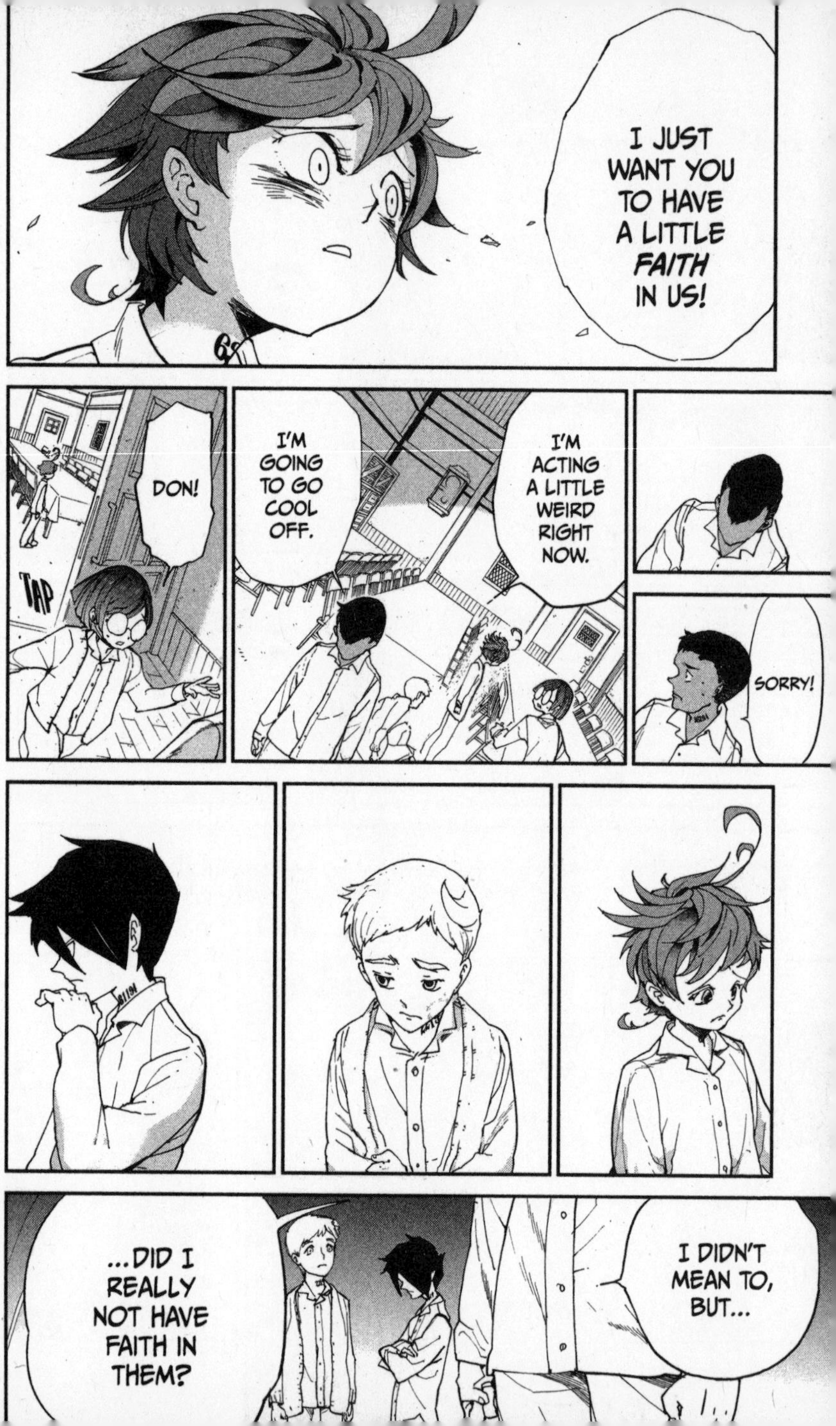
I JUST WANT YOU TO HAVE A LITTLE *FAITH* IN US!
SORRY!
I'M ACTING A LITTLE WEIRD RIGHT NOW.
I'M GOING TO GO COOL OFF.
DON!
TAP
I DIDN'T MEAN TO, BUT...
...DID I REALLY NOT HAVE FAITH IN THEM?

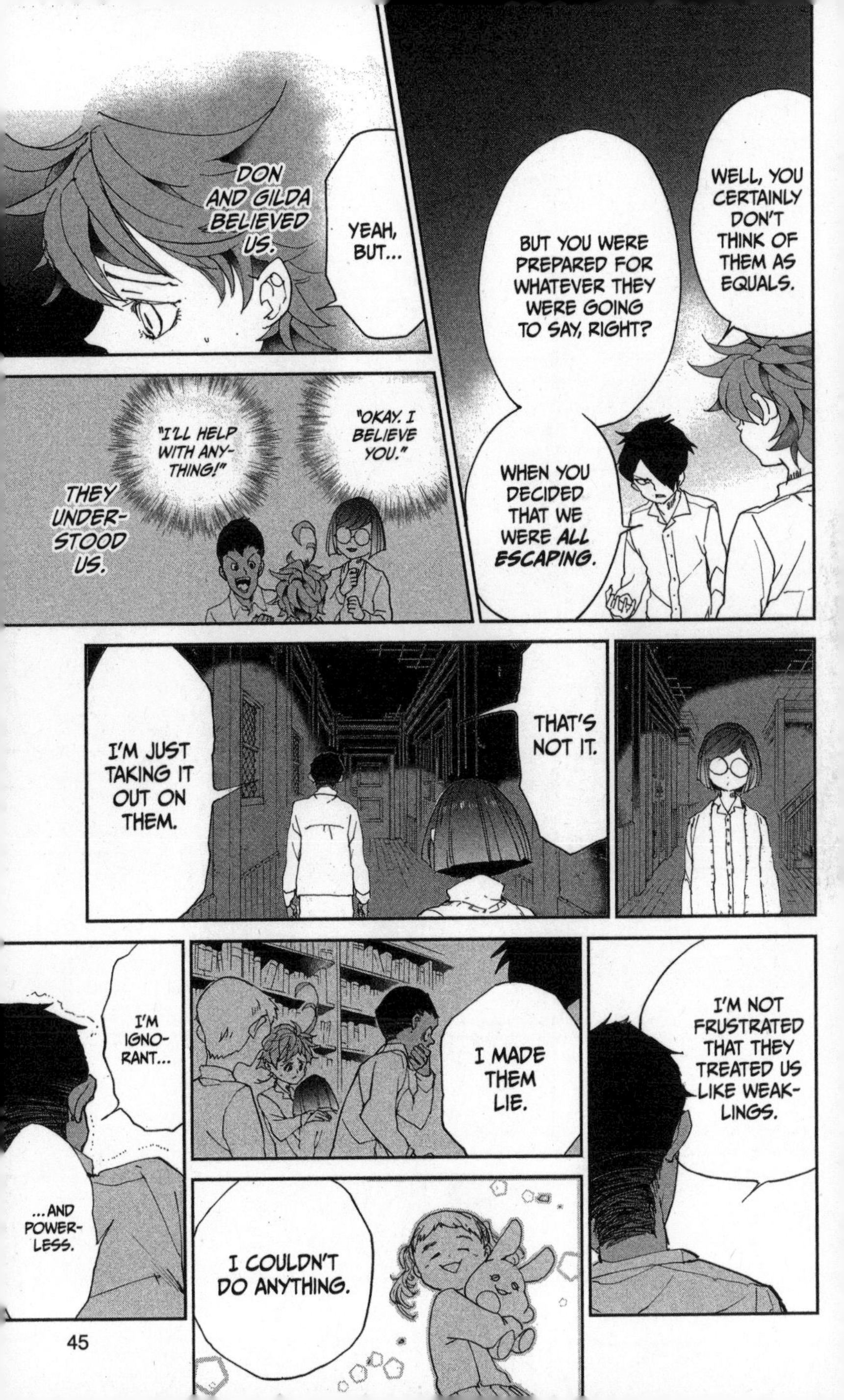
WELL, YOU CERTAINLY DON'T THINK OF THEM AS EQUALS.
BUT YOU WERE PREPARED FOR WHATEVER THEY WERE GOING TO SAY, RIGHT?
WHEN YOU DECIDED THAT WE WERE ALL ESCAPING.
YEAH, BUT...
DON AND GILDA BELIEVED US.
"OKAY. I BELIEVE YOU."
"I'LL HELP WITH ANYTHING!"
THEY UNDERSTOOD US.
THAT'S NOT IT.
I'M JUST TAKING IT OUT ON THEM.
I'M NOT FRUSTRATED THAT THEY TREATED US LIKE WEAKLINGS.
I MADE THEM LIE.
I COULDN'T DO ANYTHING.
I'M IGNORANT...
...AND POWERLESS.

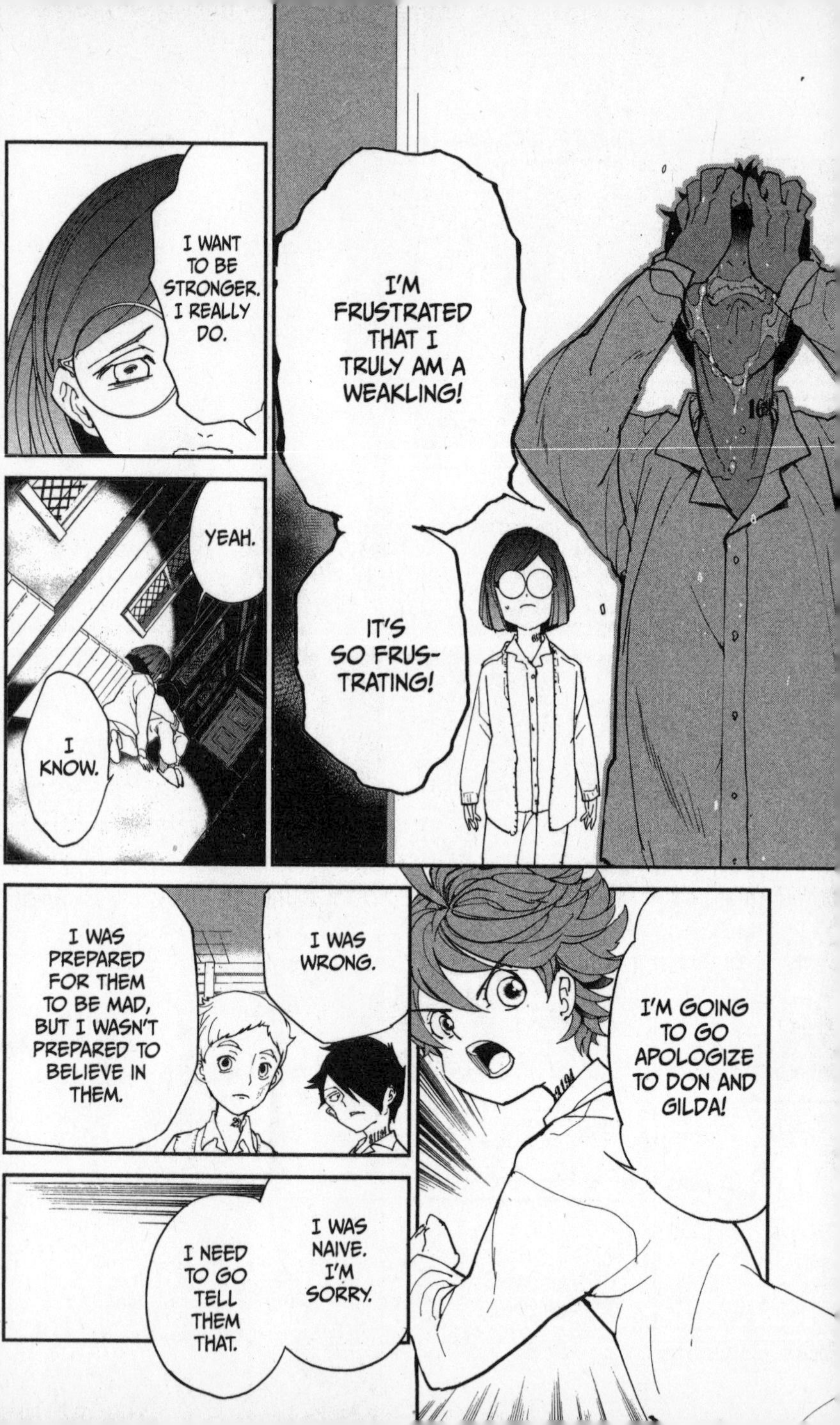
I'M FRUSTRATED THAT I TRULY AM A WEAKLING!
IT'S SO FRUSTRATING!
I WANT TO BE STRONGER. I REALLY DO.
YEAH.
I KNOW.
I'M GOING TO GO APOLOGIZE TO DON AND GILDA!
I WAS WRONG.
I WAS PREPARED FOR THEM TO BE MAD, BUT I WASN'T PREPARED TO BELIEVE IN THEM.
I WAS NAIVE. I'M SORRY.
I NEED TO GO TELL THEM THAT.

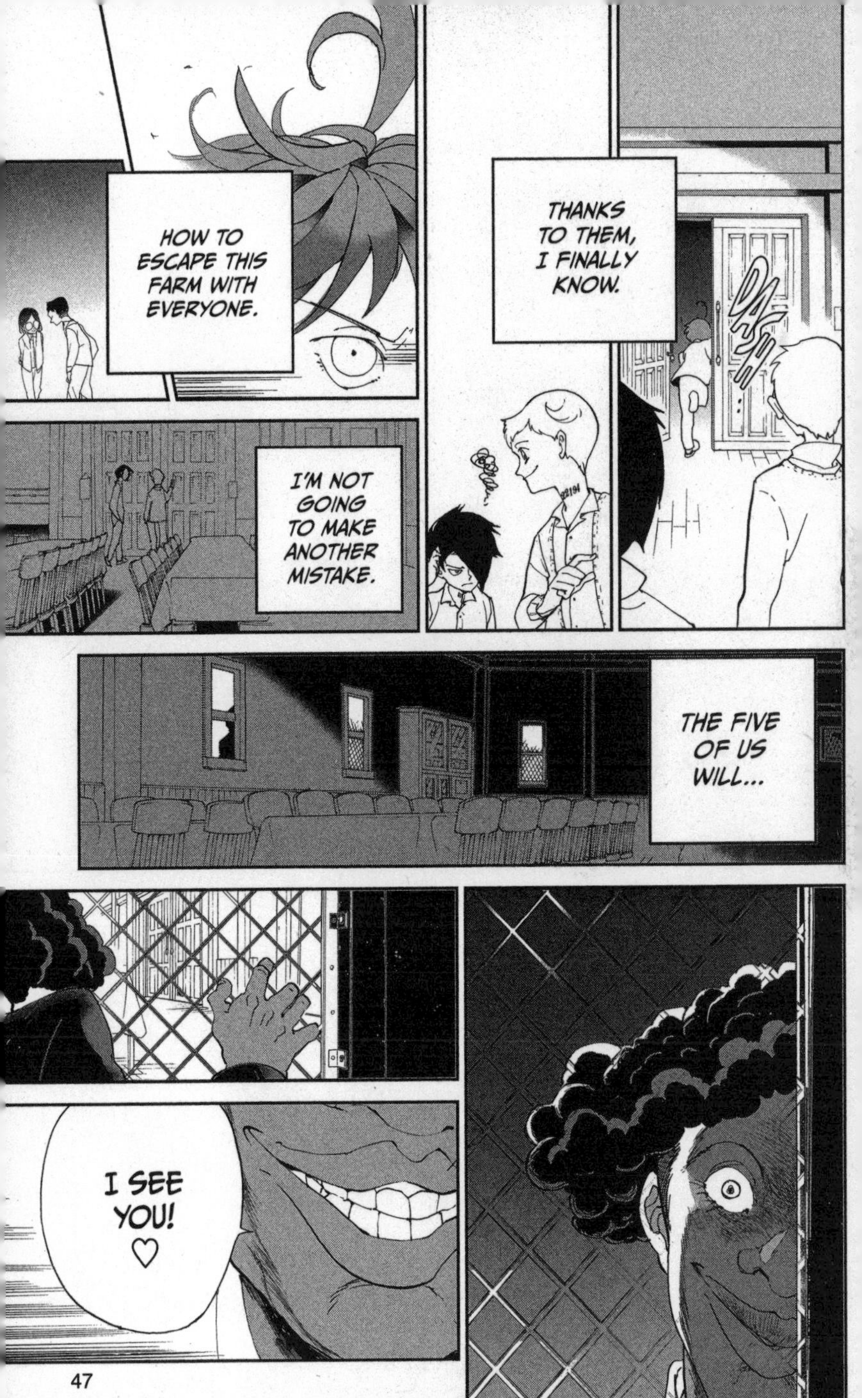
THANKS TO THEM, I FINALLY KNOW.
DASH
HOW TO ESCAPE THIS FARM WITH EVERYONE.
I'M NOT GOING TO MAKE ANOTHER MISTAKE.
THE FIVE OF US WILL...
I SEE YOU! ♡

Cleaning Time

THE DAILY CLEANING IS DONE IN TURNS.

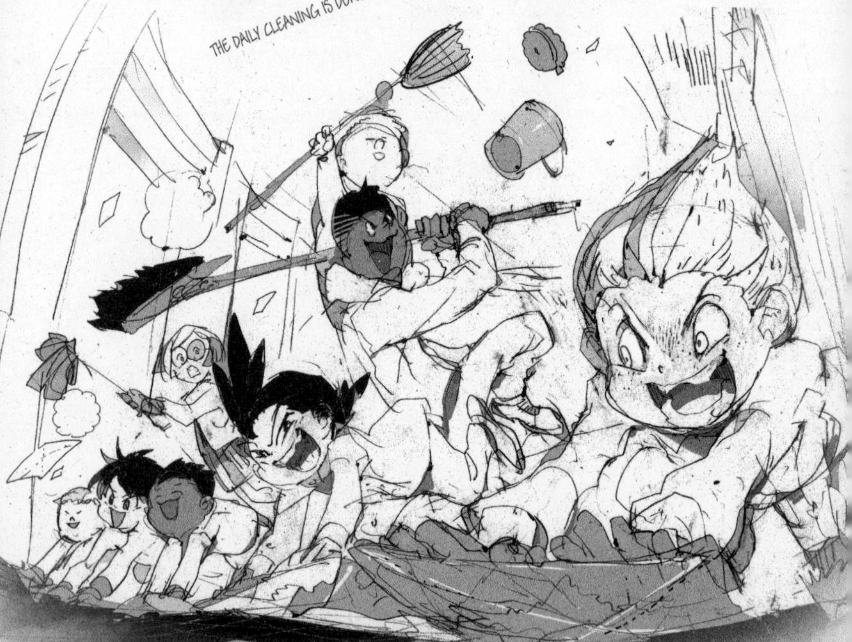

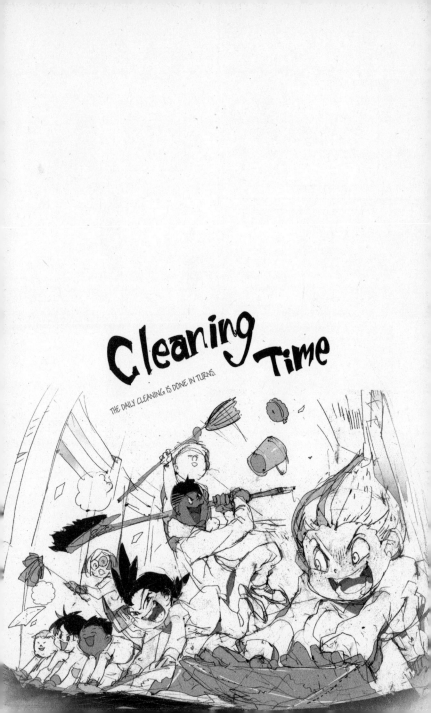

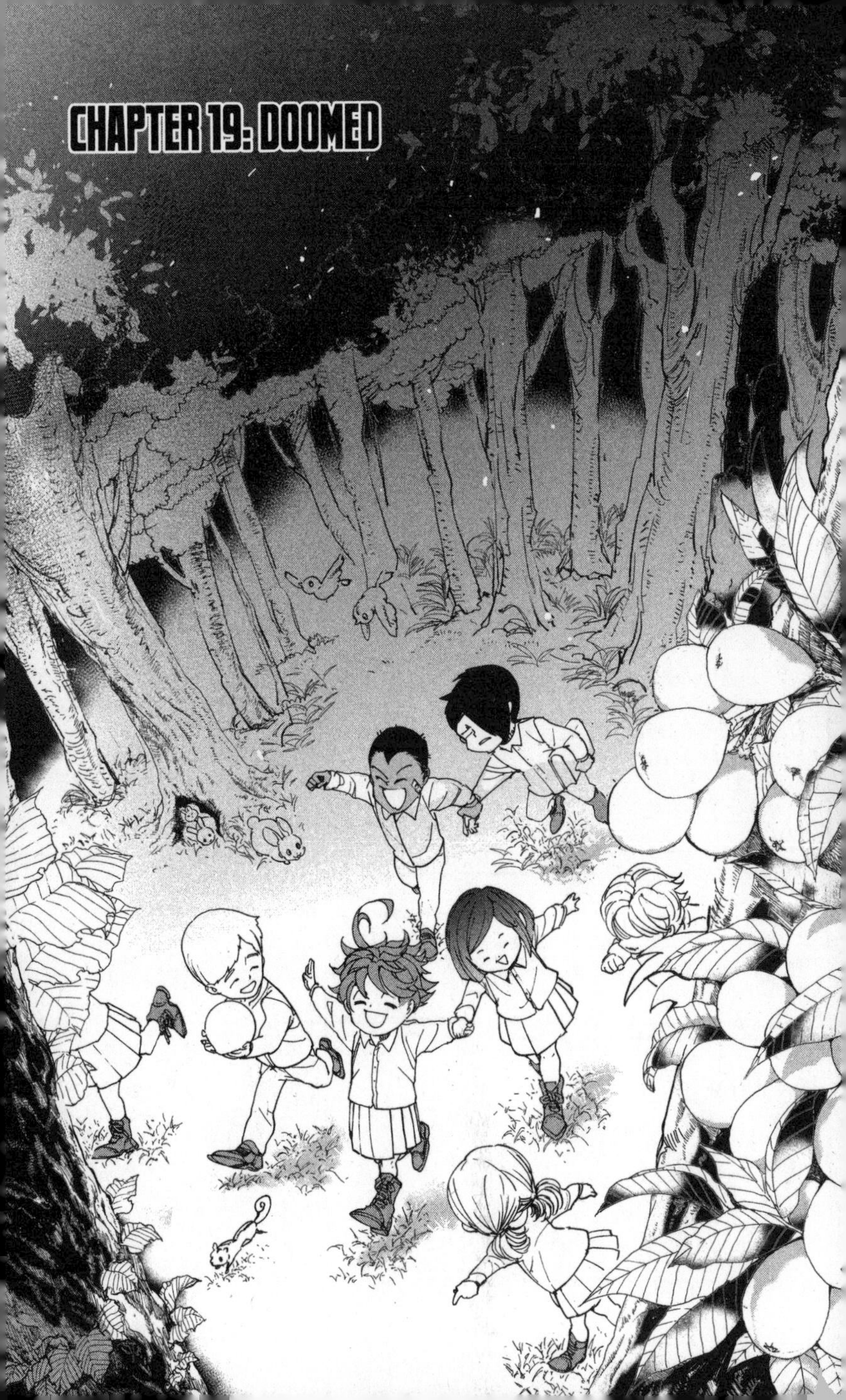
CHAPTER 19: DOOMED

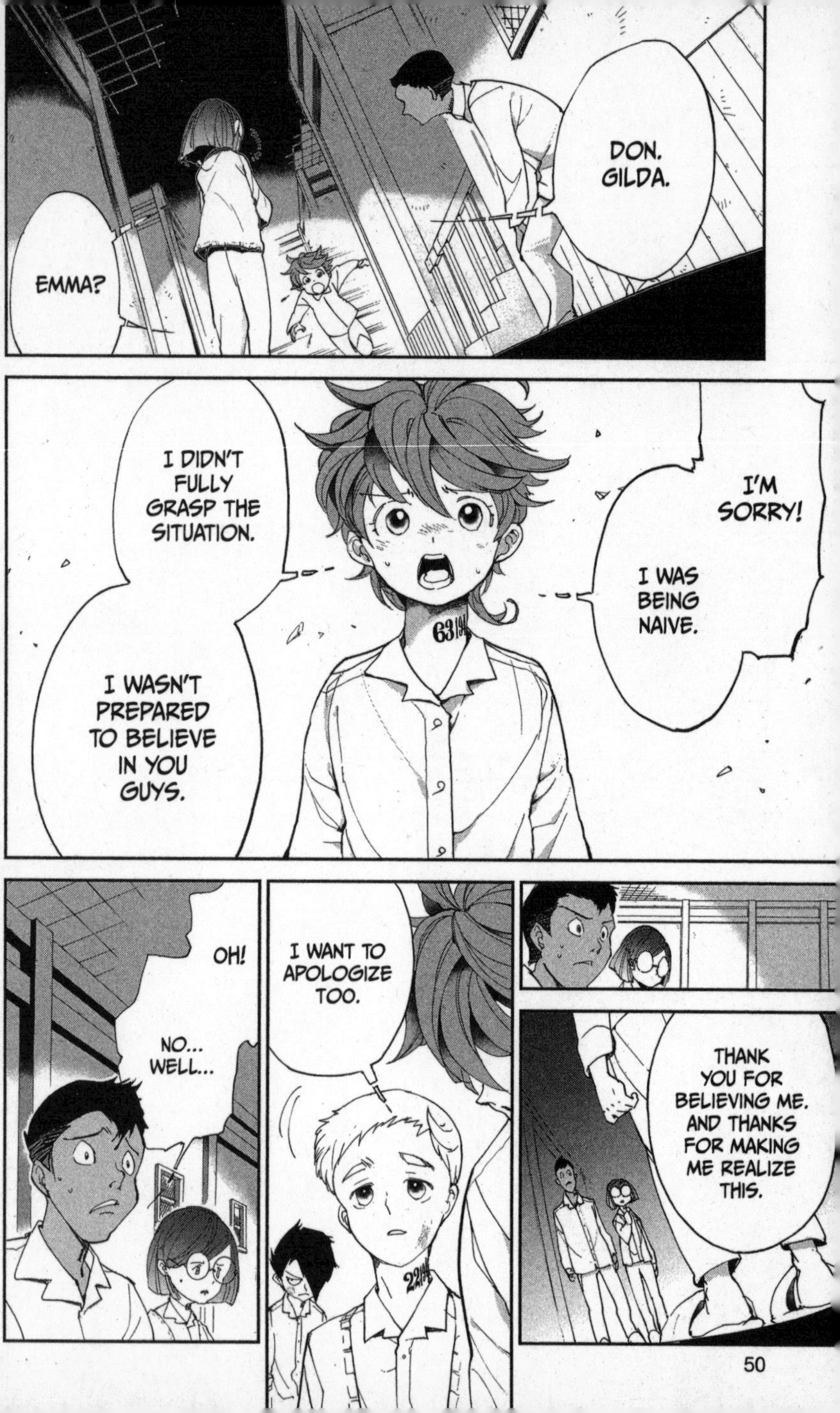
DON. GILDA.
EMMA?
I'M SORRY!
I WAS BEING NAIVE.
I DIDN'T FULLY GRASP THE SITUATION.
I WASN'T PREPARED TO BELIEVE IN YOU GUYS.
THANK YOU FOR BELIEVING ME. AND THANKS FOR MAKING ME REALIZE THIS.
I WANT TO APOLOGIZE TOO.
OH!
NO... WELL...

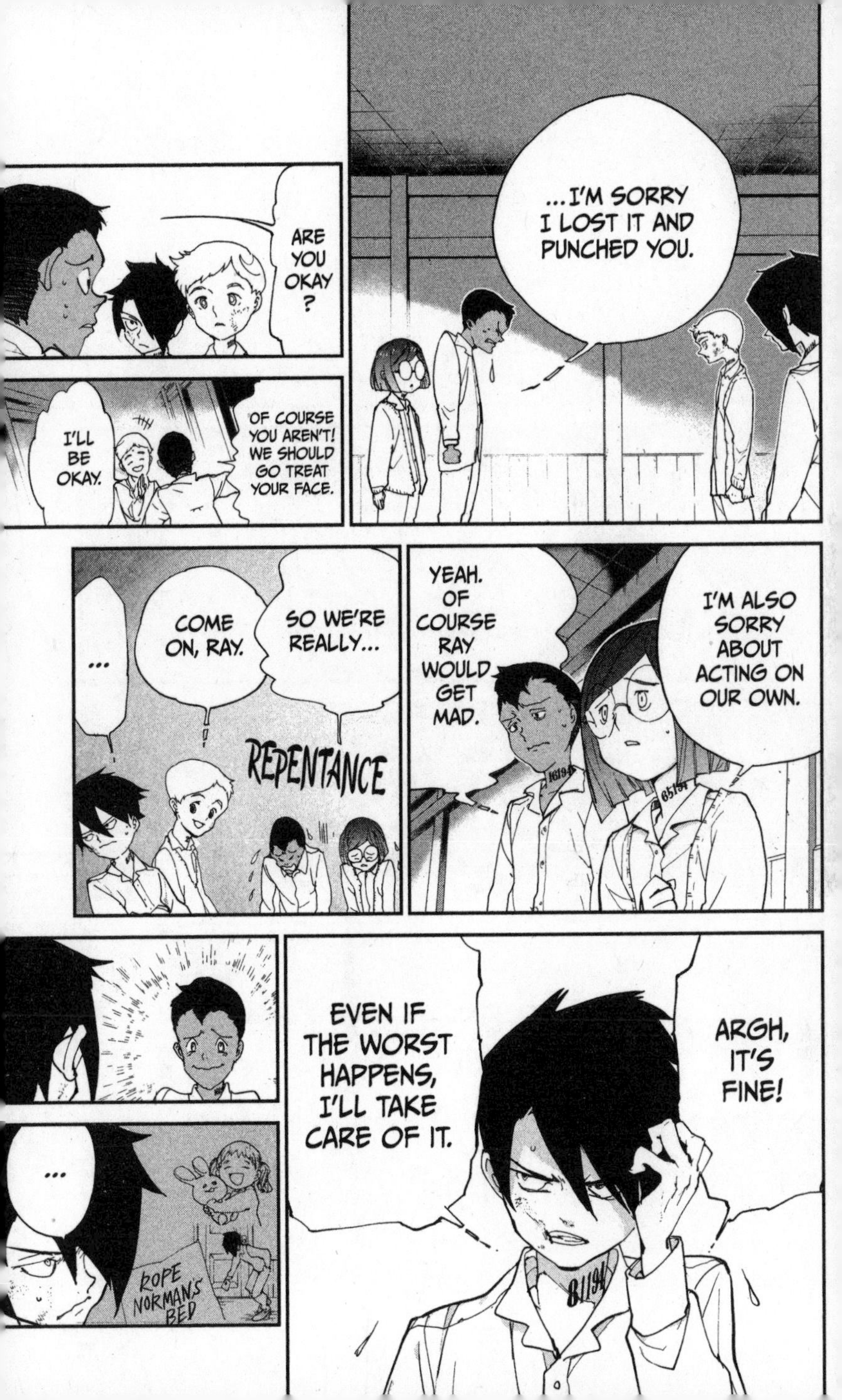
...I'M SORRY I LOST IT AND PUNCHED YOU.
ARE YOU OKAY?
OF COURSE YOU AREN'T! WE SHOULD GO TREAT YOUR FACE.
I'LL BE OKAY.
I'M ALSO SORRY ABOUT ACTING ON OUR OWN.
YEAH. OF COURSE RAY WOULD GET MAD.
SO WE'RE REALLY...
COME ON, RAY.
...
REPENTANCE
ARGH, IT'S FINE!
EVEN IF THE WORST HAPPENS, I'LL TAKE CARE OF IT.
...
ROPE
NORMAN'S BED

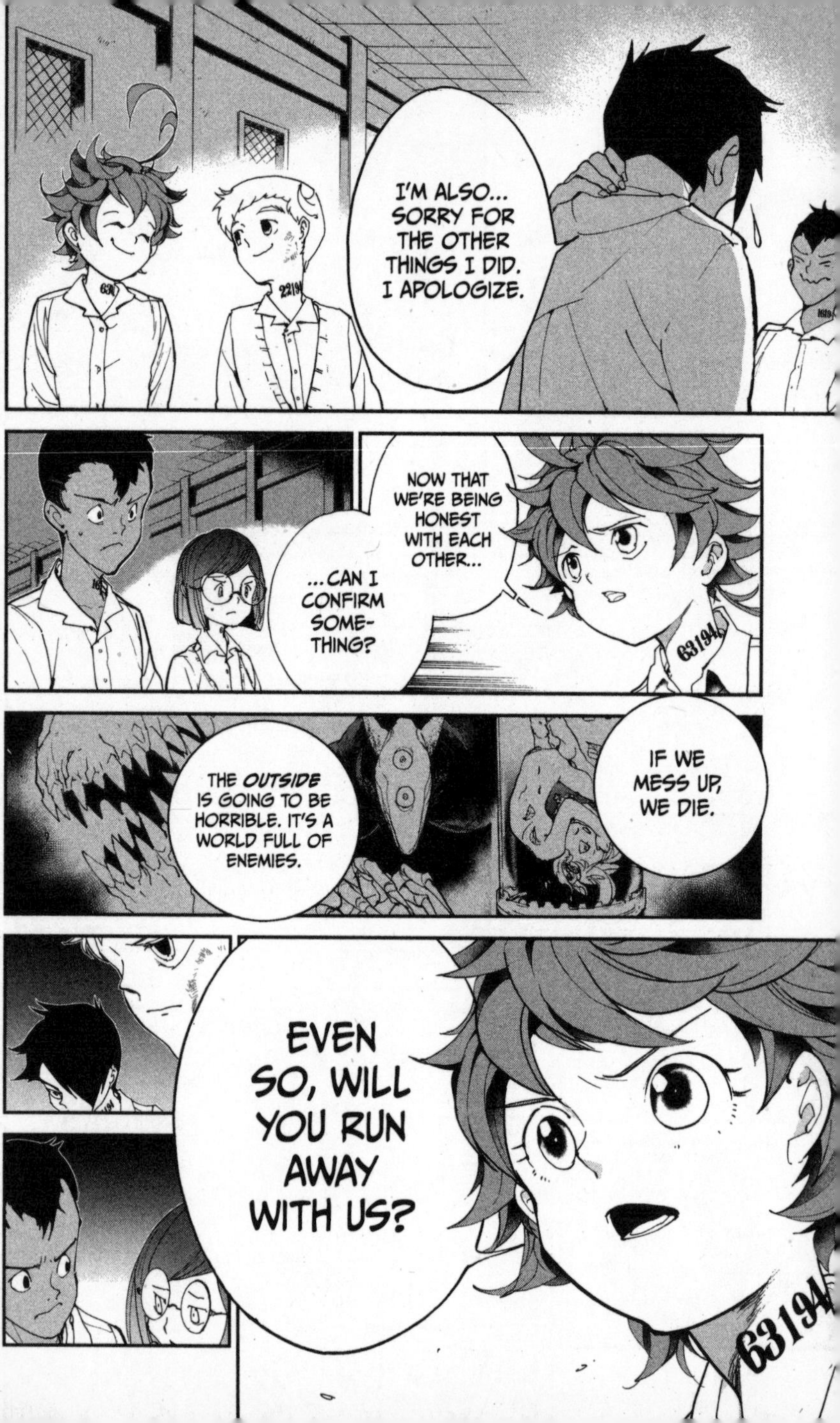
I'M ALSO... SORRY FOR THE OTHER THINGS I DID. I APOLOGIZE.
NOW THAT WE'RE BEING HONEST WITH EACH OTHER...
...CAN I CONFIRM SOME-THING?
IF WE MESS UP, WE DIE.
THE OUTSIDE IS GOING TO BE HORRIBLE. IT'S A WORLD FULL OF ENEMIES.
EVEN SO, WILL YOU RUN AWAY WITH US?

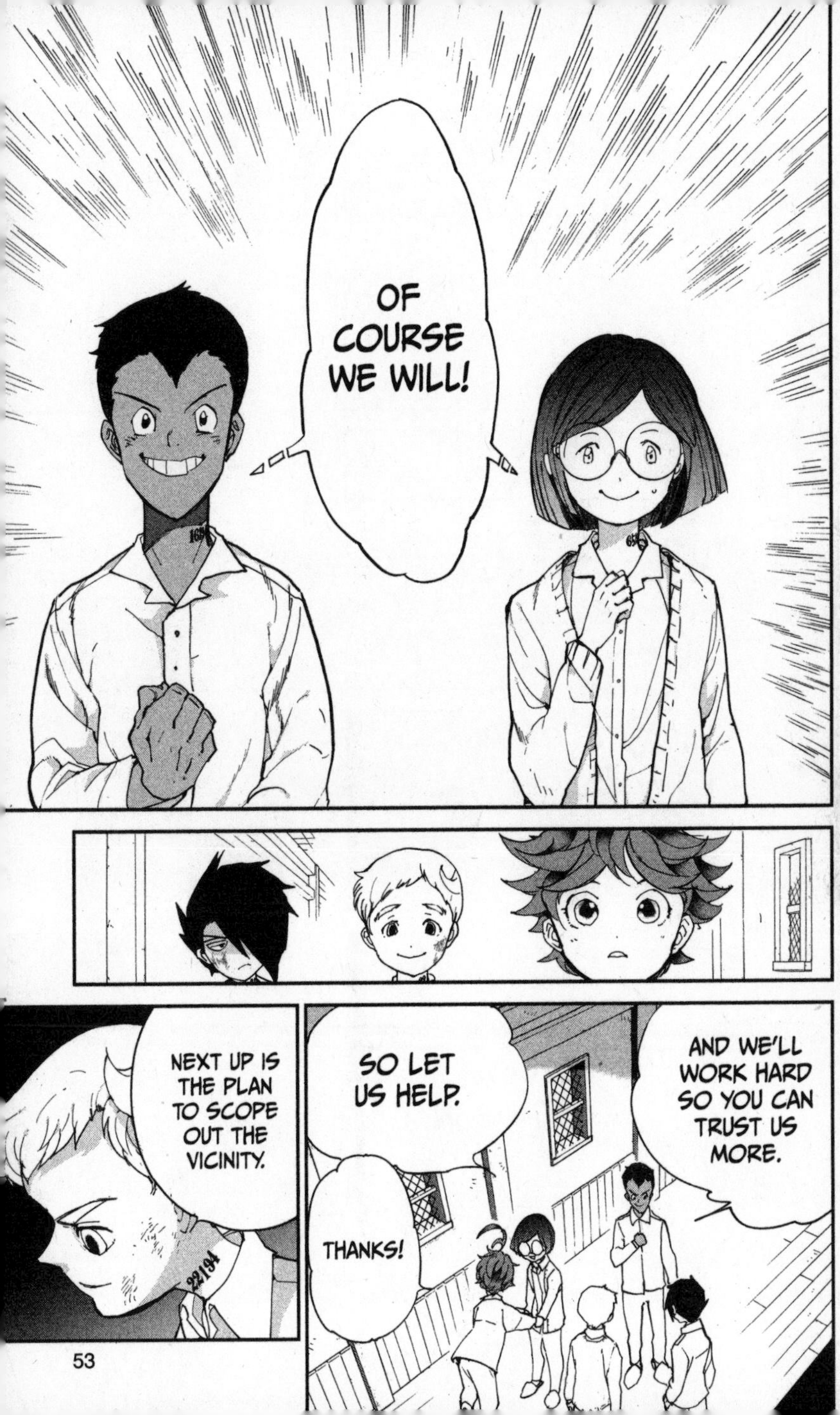
OF COURSE WE WILL!
AND WE'LL WORK HARD SO YOU CAN TRUST US MORE.
SO LET US HELP.
THANKS!
NEXT UP IS THE PLAN TO SCOPE OUT THE VICINITY.

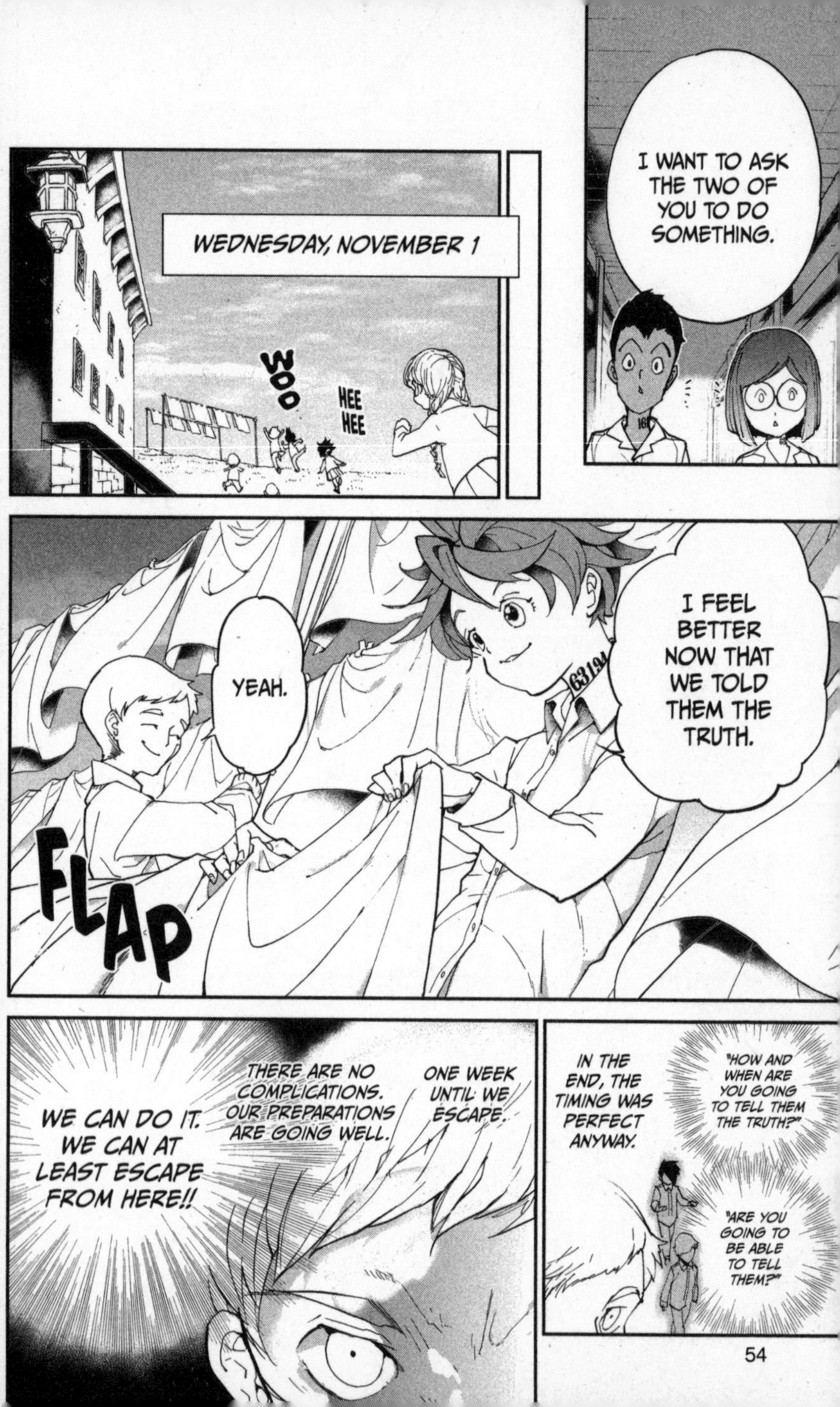
I WANT TO ASK THE TWO OF YOU TO DO SOMETHING.
WEDNESDAY, NOVEMBER 1
WOO
HEE HEE
I FEEL BETTER NOW THAT WE TOLD THEM THE TRUTH.
YEAH.
FLAP
IN THE END, THE TIMING WAS PERFECT ANYWAY.
"HOW AND WHEN ARE YOU GOING TO TELL THEM THE TRUTH?"
"ARE YOU GOING TO BE ABLE TO TELL THEM?"
ONE WEEK UNTIL WE ESCAPE.
THERE ARE NO COMPLICATIONS. OUR PREPARATIONS ARE GOING WELL.
WE CAN DO IT. WE CAN AT LEAST ESCAPE FROM HERE!!

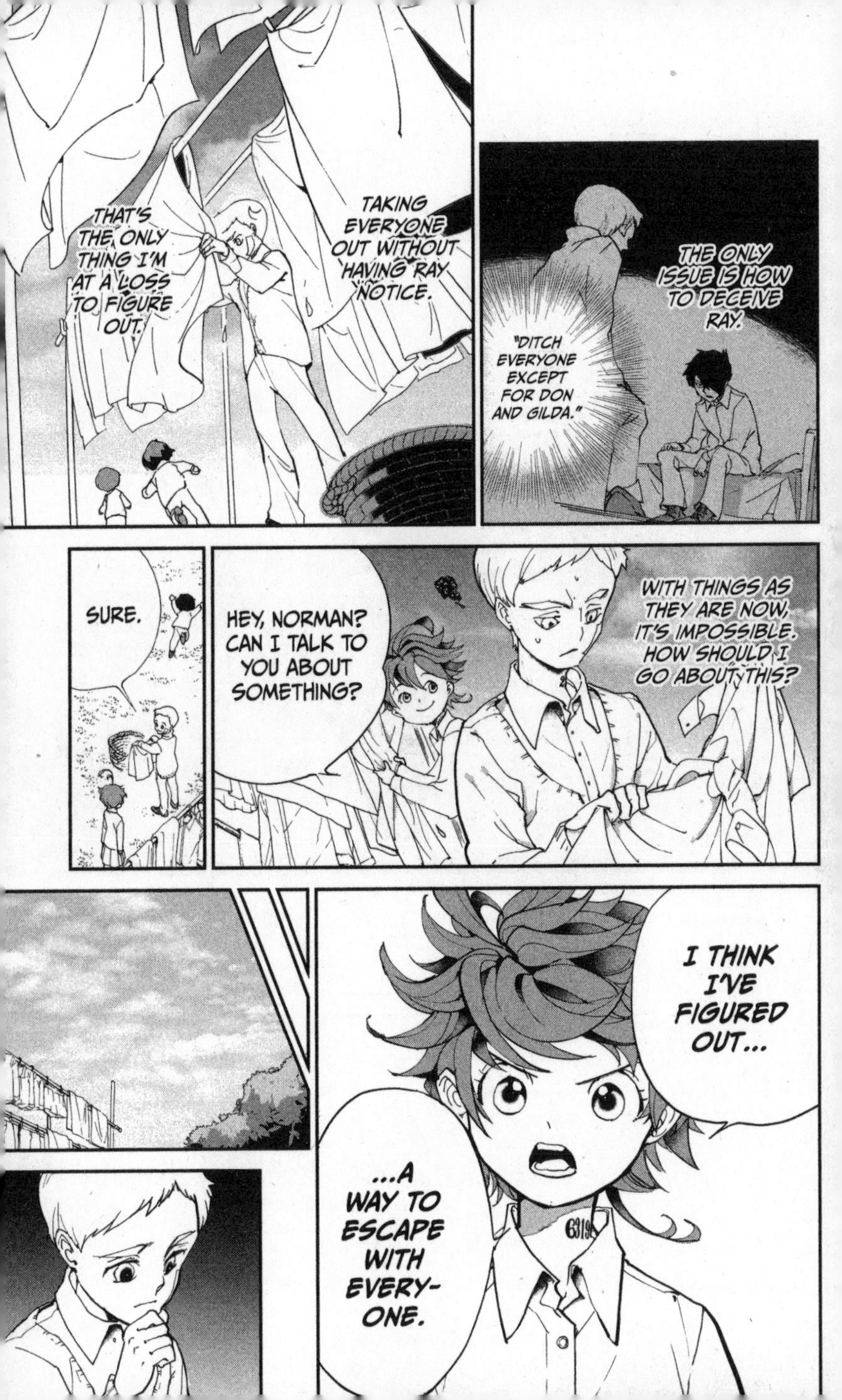
THE ONLY ISSUE IS HOW TO DECEIVE RAY.
"DITCH EVERYONE EXCEPT FOR DON AND GILDA."
TAKING EVERYONE OUT WITHOUT HAVING RAY NOTICE.
THAT'S THE ONLY THING I'M AT A LOSS TO FIGURE OUT.
WITH THINGS AS THEY ARE NOW, IT'S IMPOSSIBLE. HOW SHOULD I GO ABOUT THIS?
HEY, NORMAN? CAN I TALK TO YOU ABOUT SOMETHING?
SURE.
I THINK I'VE FIGURED OUT...
...A WAY TO ESCAPE WITH EVERY-ONE.

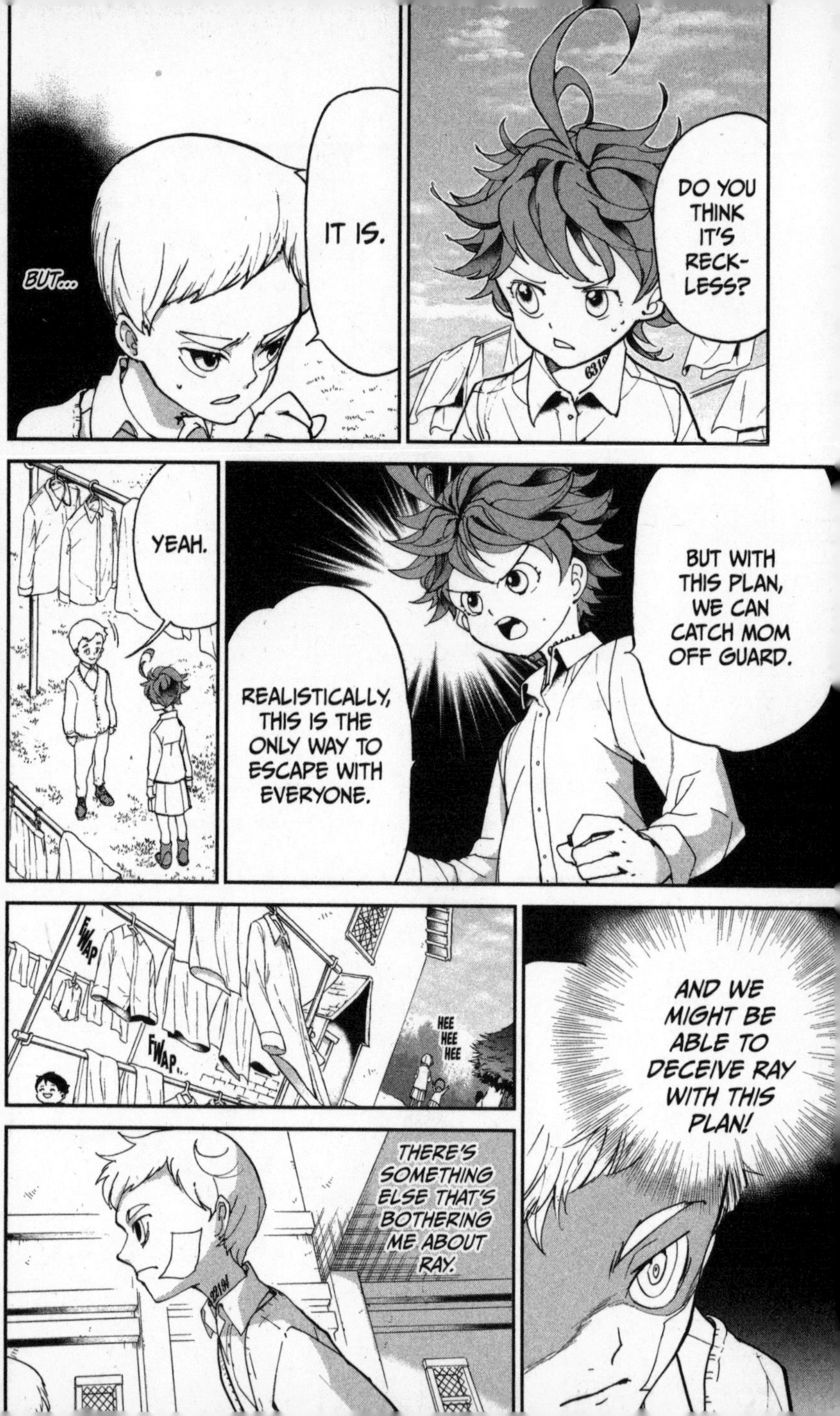
DO YOU THINK IT'S RECK-LESS?
IT IS.
BUT...
BUT WITH THIS PLAN, WE CAN CATCH MOM OFF GUARD.
REALISTICALLY, THIS IS THE ONLY WAY TO ESCAPE WITH EVERYONE.
YEAH.
AND WE MIGHT BE ABLE TO DECEIVE RAY WITH THIS PLAN!
FWAP
FWAP...
HEE HEE HEE
THERE'S SOMETHING ELSE THAT'S BOTHERING ME ABOUT RAY.

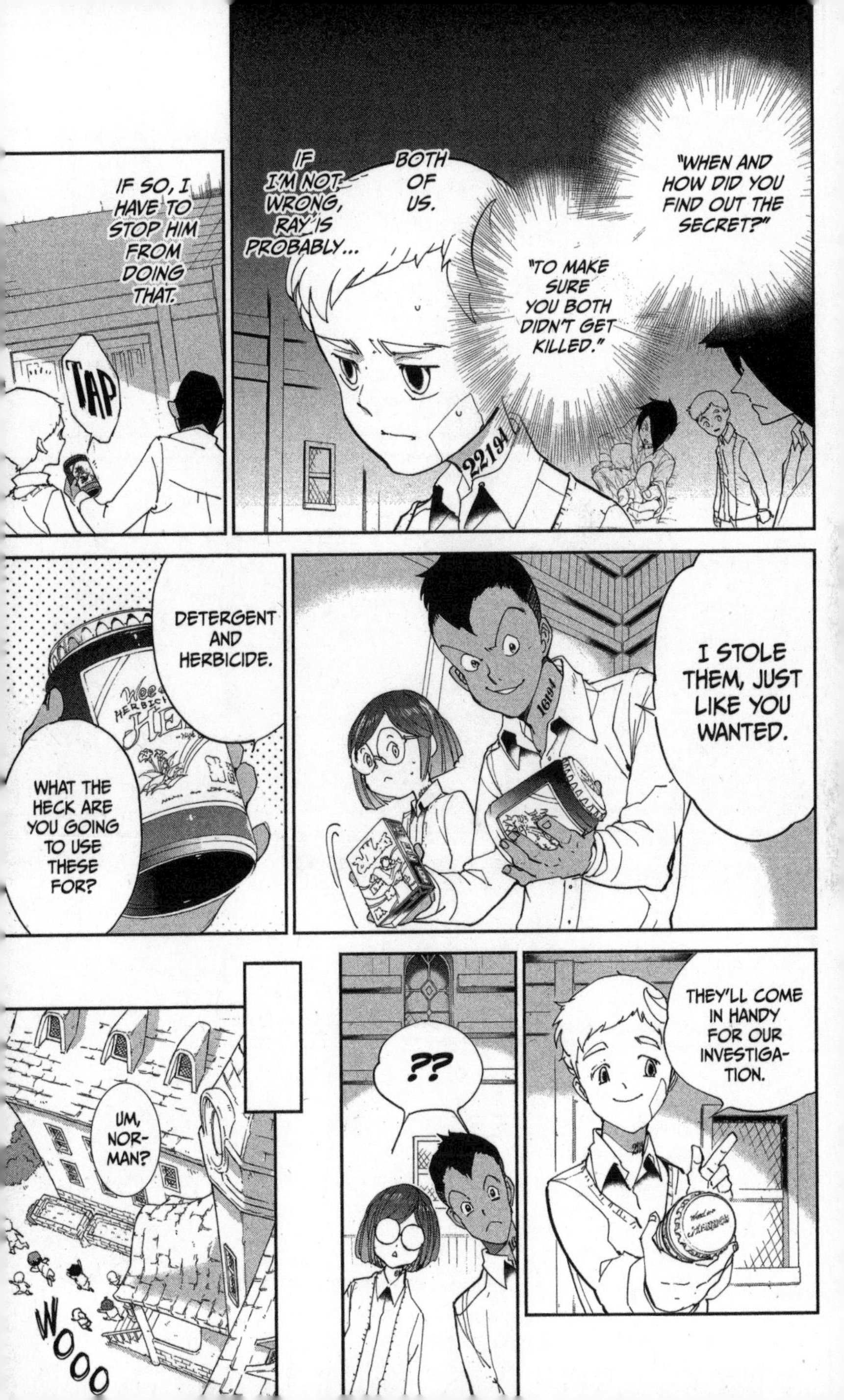
"WHEN AND HOW DID YOU FIND OUT THE SECRET?"
"TO MAKE SURE YOU BOTH DIDN'T GET KILLED."
BOTH OF US.
IF I'M NOT WRONG, RAY IS PROBABLY...
IF SO, I HAVE TO STOP HIM FROM DOING THAT.
TAP
I STOLE THEM, JUST LIKE YOU WANTED.
DETERGENT AND HERBICIDE.
WHAT THE HECK ARE YOU GOING TO USE THESE FOR?
THEY'LL COME IN HANDY FOR OUR INVESTIGA-TION.
??
UM, NOR-MAN?
WOOO

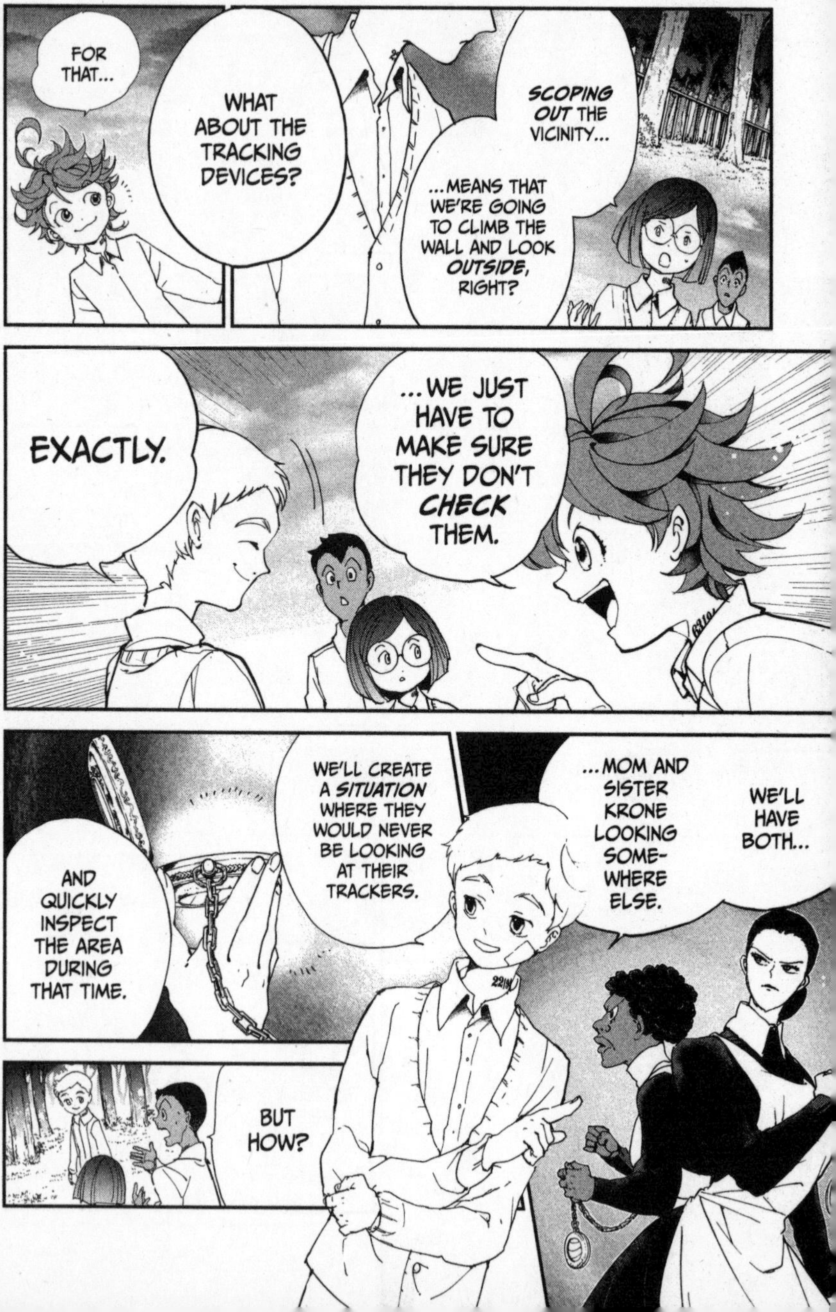

SCOPING OUT THE VICINITY...
...MEANS THAT WE'RE GOING TO CLIMB THE WALL AND LOOK OUTSIDE, RIGHT?
WHAT ABOUT THE TRACKING DEVICES?
FOR THAT...
...WE JUST HAVE TO MAKE SURE THEY DON'T CHECK THEM.
EXACTLY.
WE'LL HAVE BOTH...
...MOM AND SISTER KRONE LOOKING SOME-WHERE ELSE.
WE'LL CREATE A SITUATION WHERE THEY WOULD NEVER BE LOOKING AT THEIR TRACKERS.
AND QUICKLY INSPECT THE AREA DURING THAT TIME.
BUT HOW?

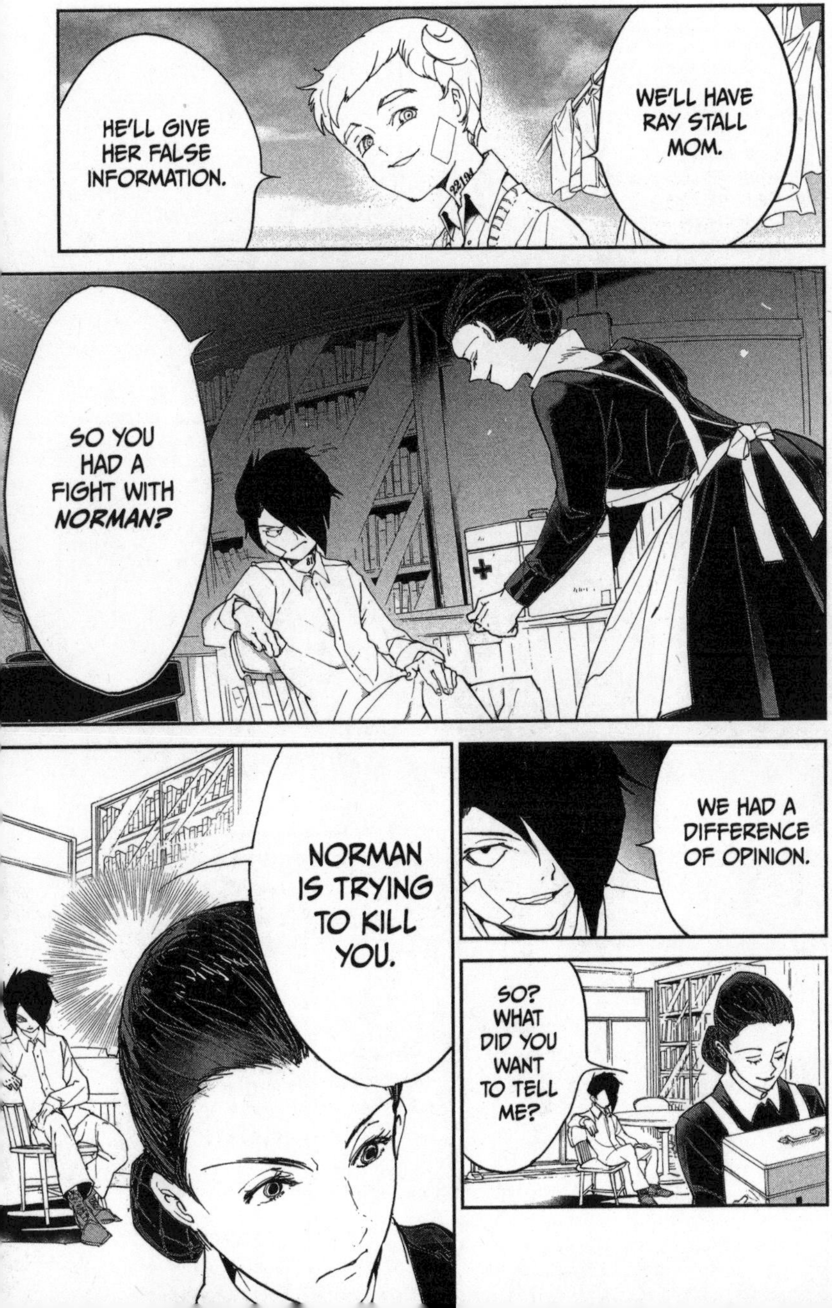
WE'LL HAVE RAY STALL MOM.
HE'LL GIVE HER FALSE INFORMATION.
SO YOU HAD A FIGHT WITH *NORMAN?*
WE HAD A DIFFERENCE OF OPINION.
SO? WHAT DID YOU WANT TO TELL ME?
NORMAN IS TRYING TO KILL YOU.

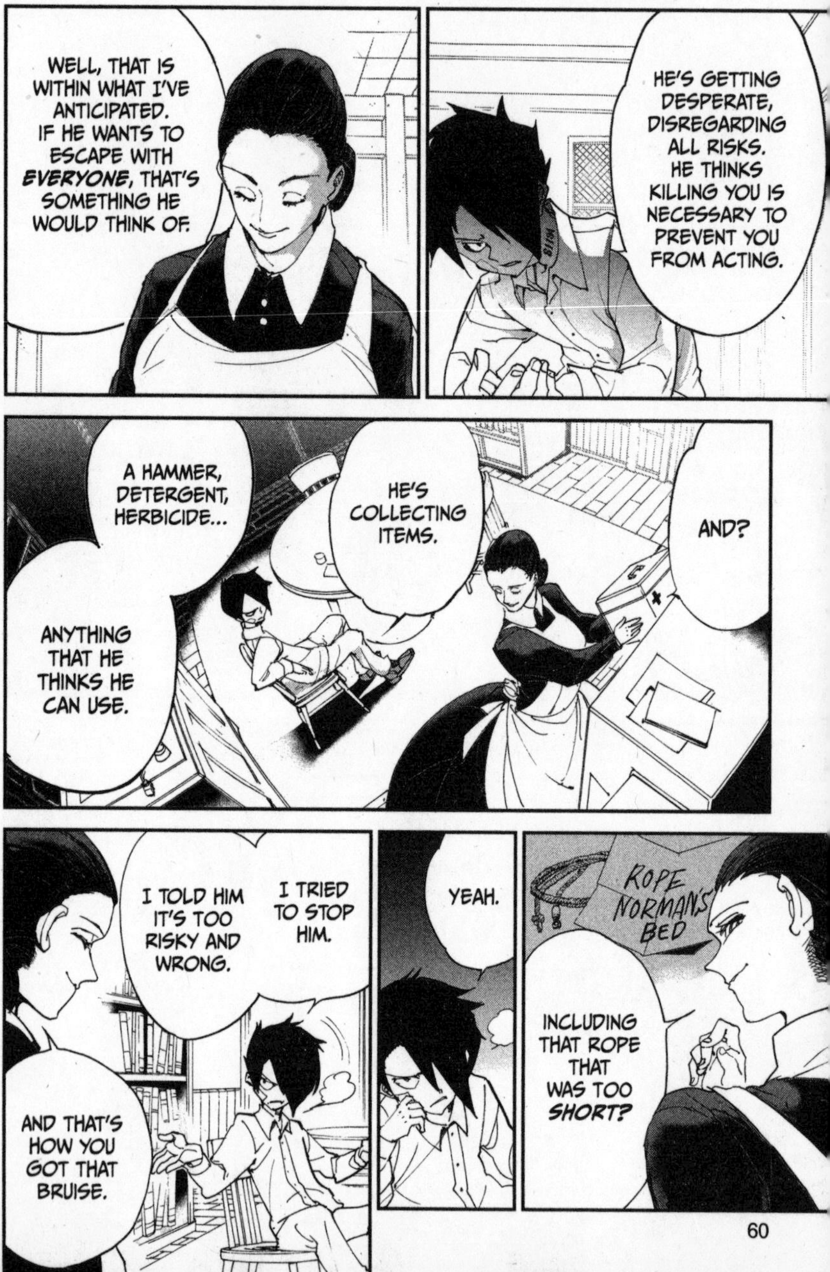
HE'S GETTING DESPERATE, DISREGARDING ALL RISKS. HE THINKS KILLING YOU IS NECESSARY TO PREVENT YOU FROM ACTING.
WELL, THAT IS WITHIN WHAT I'VE ANTICIPATED. IF HE WANTS TO ESCAPE WITH *EVERYONE*, THAT'S SOMETHING HE WOULD THINK OF.
AND?
HE'S COLLECTING ITEMS.
A HAMMER, DETERGENT, HERBICIDE...
ANYTHING THAT HE THINKS HE CAN USE.
ROPE
NORMAN'S BED
INCLUDING THAT ROPE THAT WAS TOO *SHORT?*
YEAH.
I TRIED TO STOP HIM.
I TOLD HIM IT'S TOO RISKY AND WRONG.
AND THAT'S HOW YOU GOT THAT BRUISE.

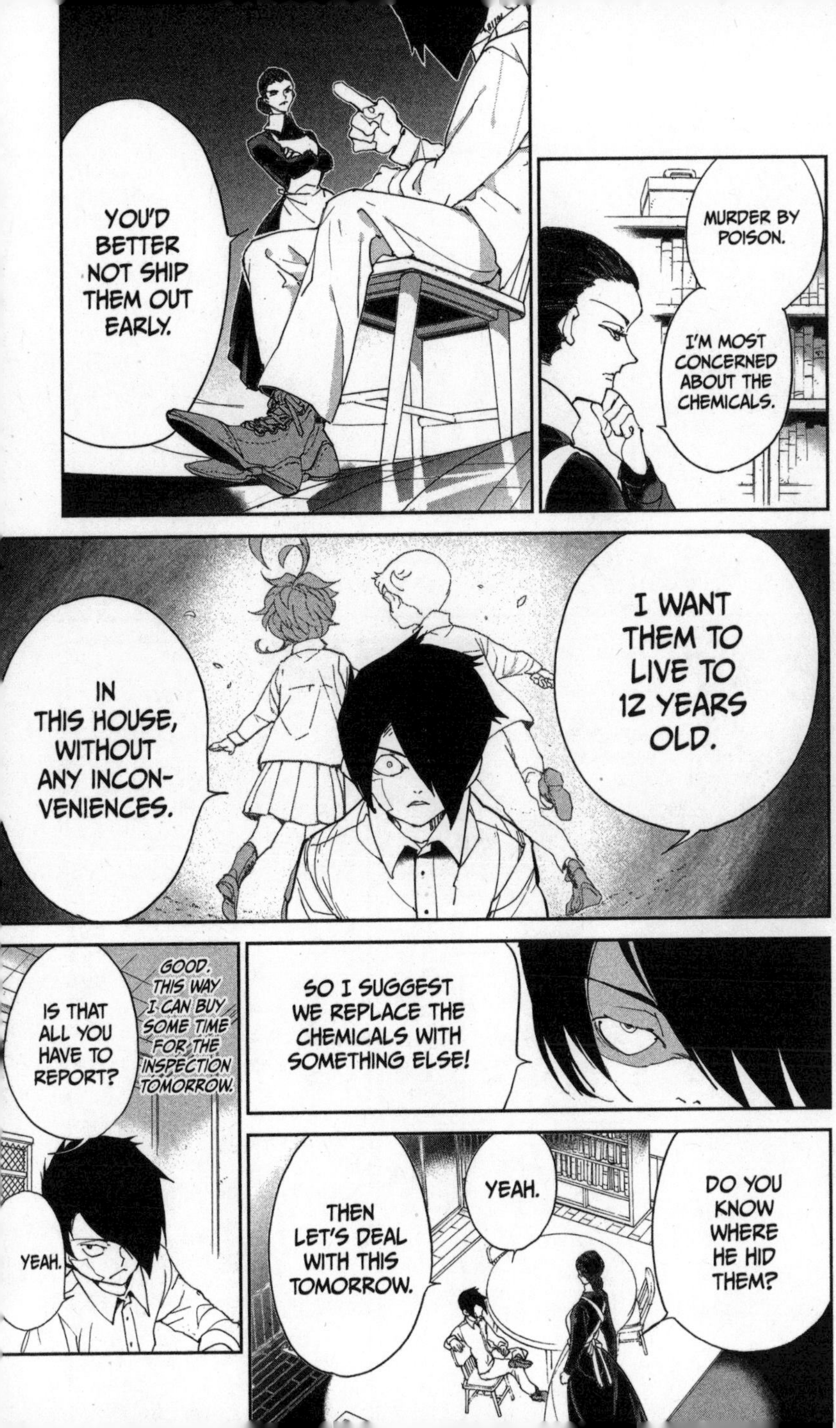
MURDER BY POISON.
I'M MOST CONCERNED ABOUT THE CHEMICALS.
YOU'D BETTER NOT SHIP THEM OUT EARLY.
I WANT THEM TO LIVE TO 12 YEARS OLD.
IN THIS HOUSE, WITHOUT ANY INCONVENIENCES.
SO I SUGGEST WE REPLACE THE CHEMICALS WITH SOMETHING ELSE!
DO YOU KNOW WHERE HE HID THEM?
YEAH.
THEN LET'S DEAL WITH THIS TOMORROW.
GOOD. THIS WAY I CAN BUY SOME TIME FOR THE INSPECTION TOMORROW.
IS THAT ALL YOU HAVE TO REPORT?
YEAH.

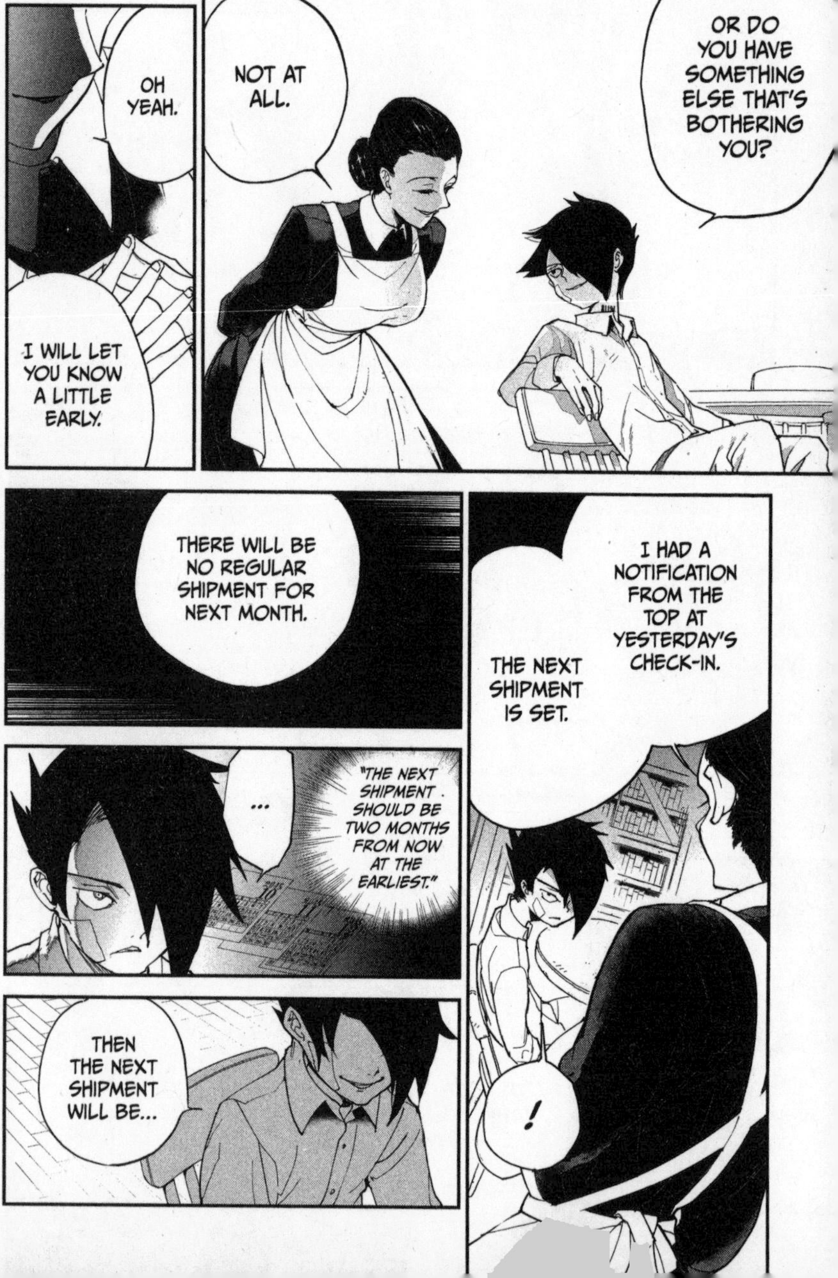
OR DO YOU HAVE SOMETHING ELSE THAT'S BOTHERING YOU?
NOT AT ALL.
OH YEAH.
I WILL LET YOU KNOW A LITTLE EARLY.
I HAD A NOTIFICATION FROM THE TOP AT YESTERDAY'S CHECK-IN.
THE NEXT SHIPMENT IS SET.
!
THERE WILL BE NO REGULAR SHIPMENT FOR NEXT MONTH.
...
"THE NEXT SHIPMENT SHOULD BE TWO MONTHS FROM NOW AT THE EARLIEST."
THEN THE NEXT SHIPMENT WILL BE...

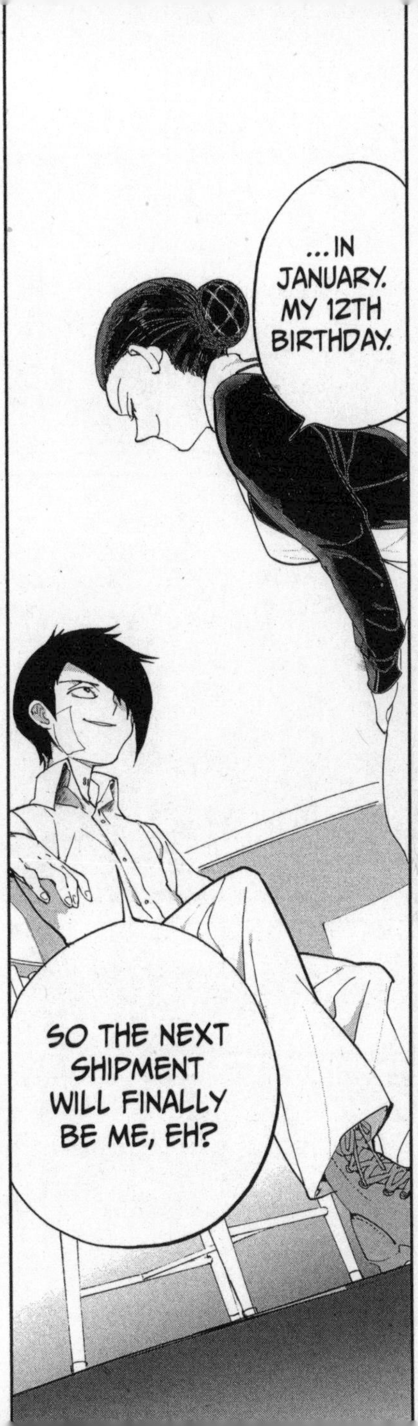
...IN JANUARY. MY 12TH BIRTHDAY.
SO THE NEXT SHIPMENT WILL FINALLY BE ME, EH?
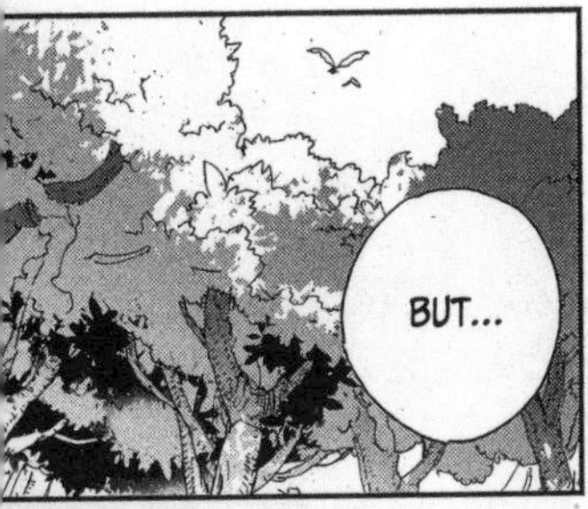
BUT...
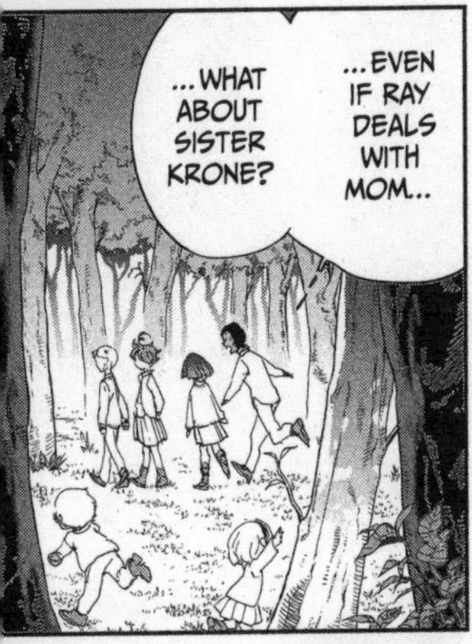
...EVEN IF RAY DEALS WITH MOM...
...WHAT ABOUT SISTER KRONE?
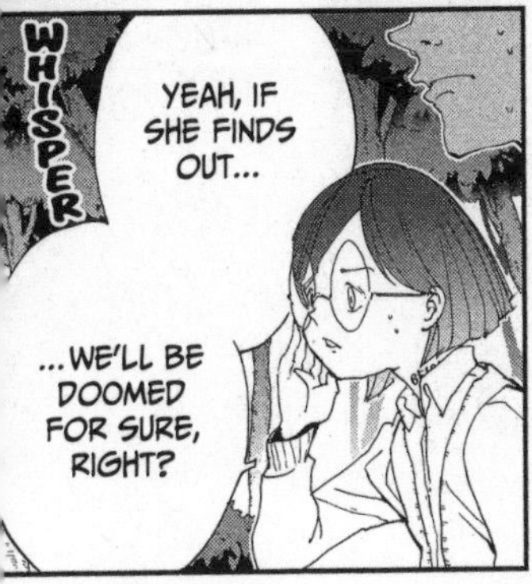
YEAH, IF SHE FINDS OUT...
WHISPER
...WE'LL BE DOOMED FOR SURE, RIGHT?

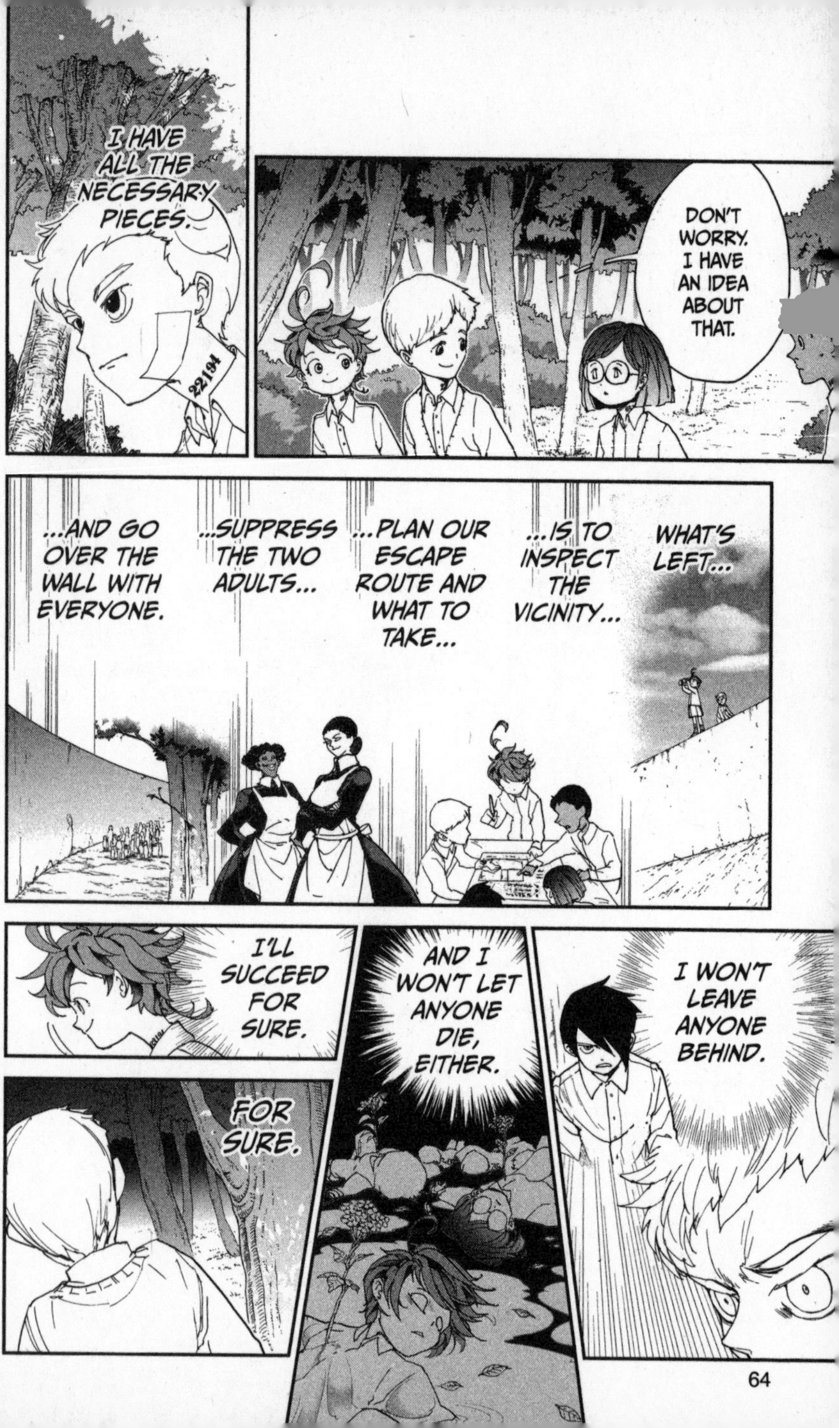
DON'T WORRY. I HAVE AN IDEA ABOUT THAT.
I HAVE ALL THE NECESSARY PIECES.
22194
WHAT'S LEFT...
...IS TO INSPECT THE VICINITY...
...PLAN OUR ESCAPE ROUTE AND WHAT TO TAKE...
...SUPPRESS THE TWO ADULTS...
...AND GO OVER THE WALL WITH EVERYONE.
I WON'T LEAVE ANYONE BEHIND.
AND I WON'T LET ANYONE DIE, EITHER.
I'LL SUCCEED FOR SURE.
FOR SURE.

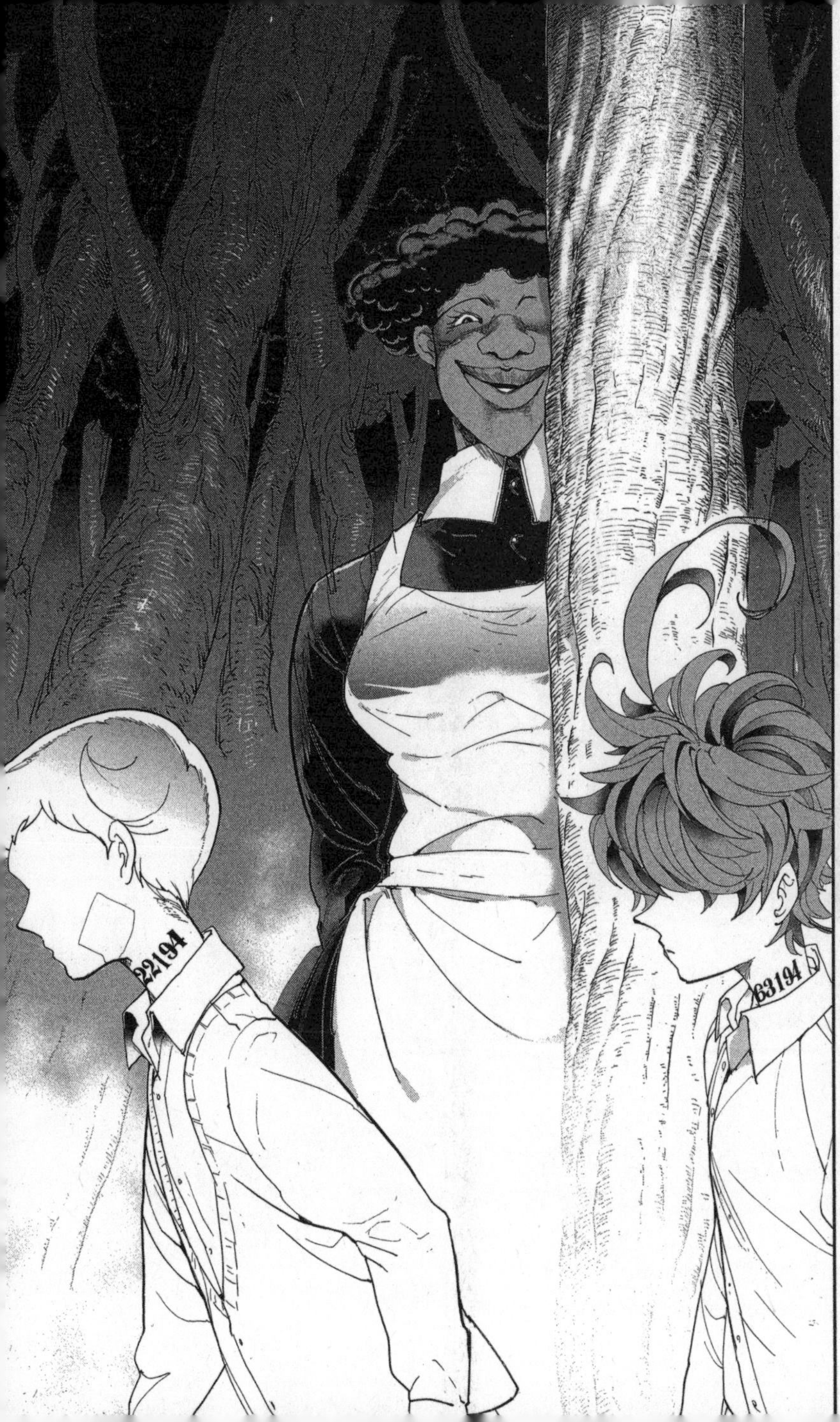
63194
22194

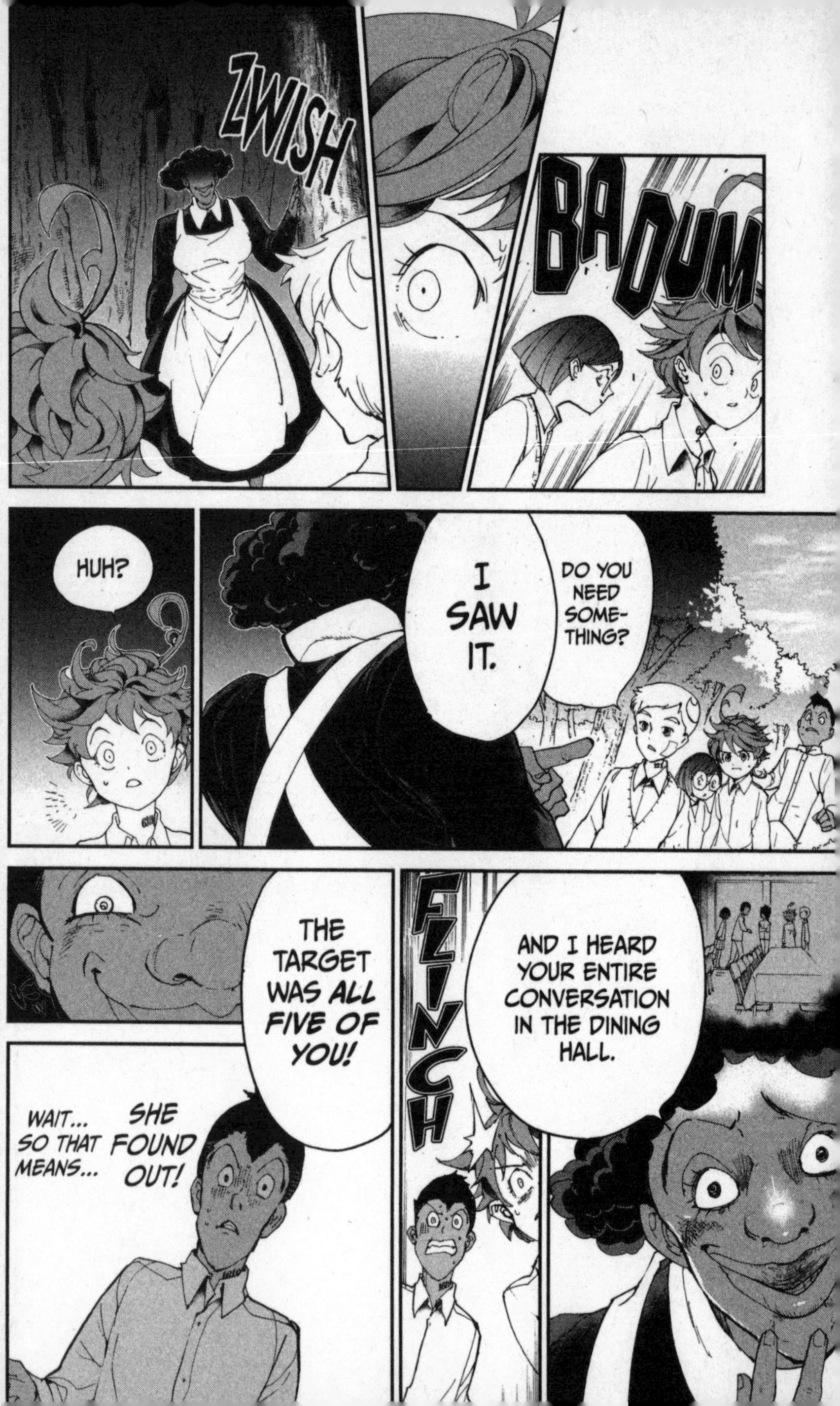
BADUM
ZWISH
DO YOU NEED SOMETHING?
I SAW IT.
HUH?
AND I HEARD YOUR ENTIRE CONVERSATION IN THE DINING HALL.
FLINCH
THE TARGET WAS ALL FIVE OF YOU!
SHE FOUND OUT!
WAIT... SO THAT MEANS...

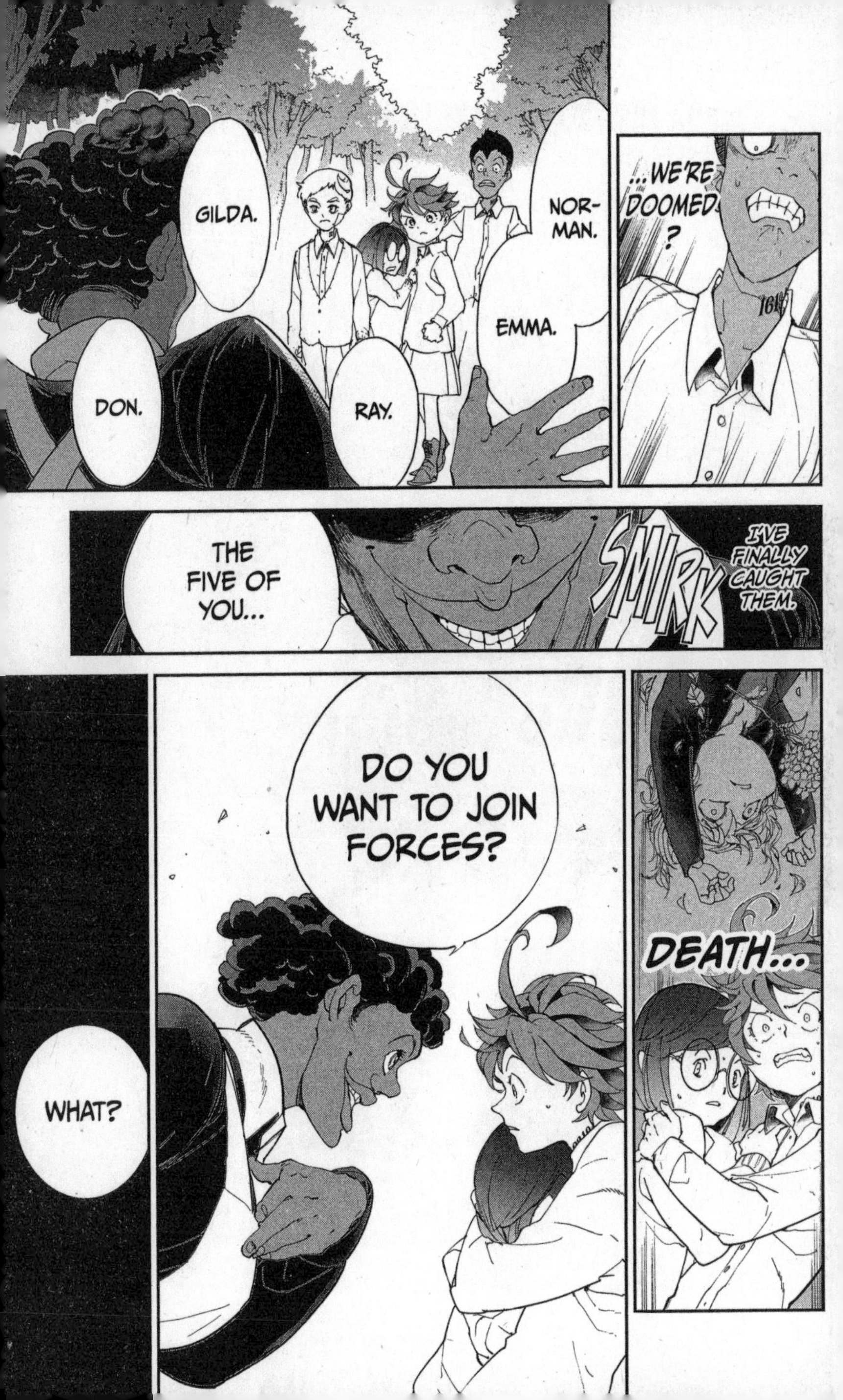
...WE'RE DOOMED?
NOR-MAN.
GILDA.
EMMA.
RAY.
DON.
I'VE FINALLY CAUGHT THEM.
SMIRK
THE FIVE OF YOU...
DEATH...
DO YOU WANT TO JOIN FORCES?
WHAT?

THE PROMISED NEVERLAND SIDE SCENE 002, TAKE 0

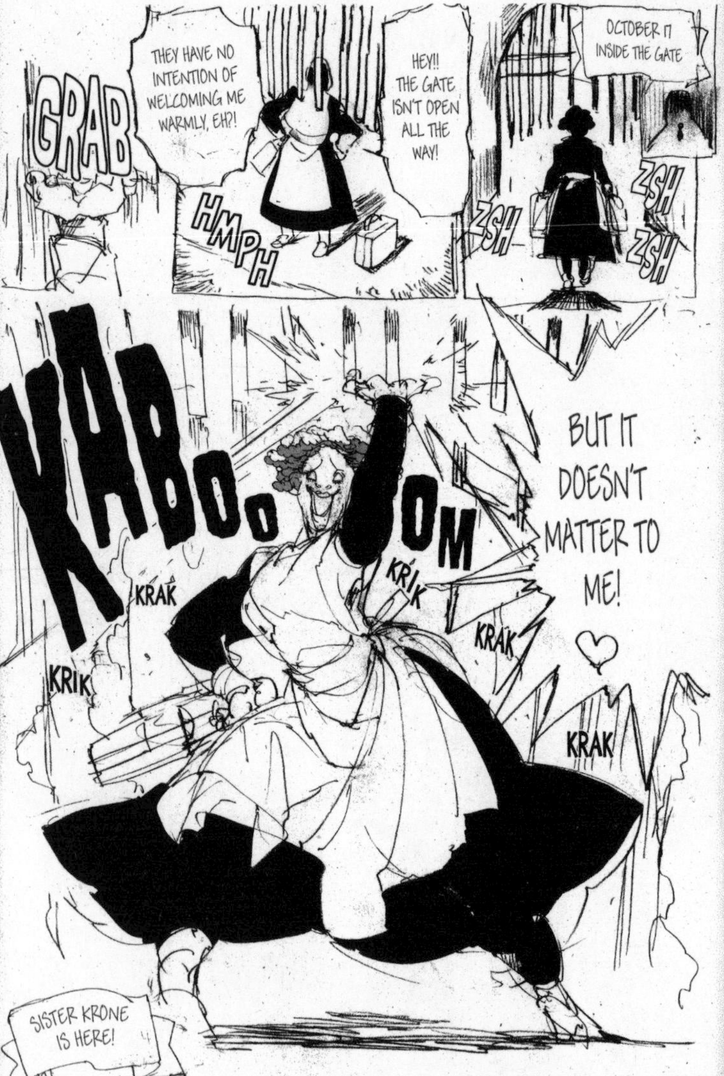
OCTOBER 17
INSIDE THE GATE
ZSH
ZSH
ZSH
HEY!! THE GATE ISN'T OPEN ALL THE WAY!
THEY HAVE NO INTENTION OF WELCOMING ME WARMLY, EH?!
HMPH
GRAB
BUT IT DOESN'T MATTER TO ME!
KABOOOM
KRIK
KRAK
KRAK
KRAK
KRIK
SISTER KRONE IS HERE!

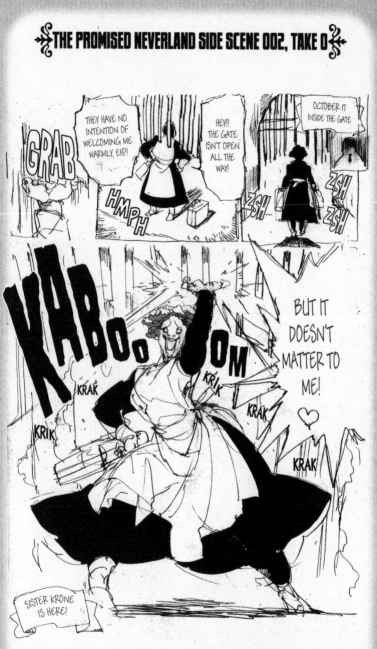

*THIS IS AN ALTERNATE VERSION OF SIDE SCENE 002
THAT WAS INCLUDED IN VOLUME 1.

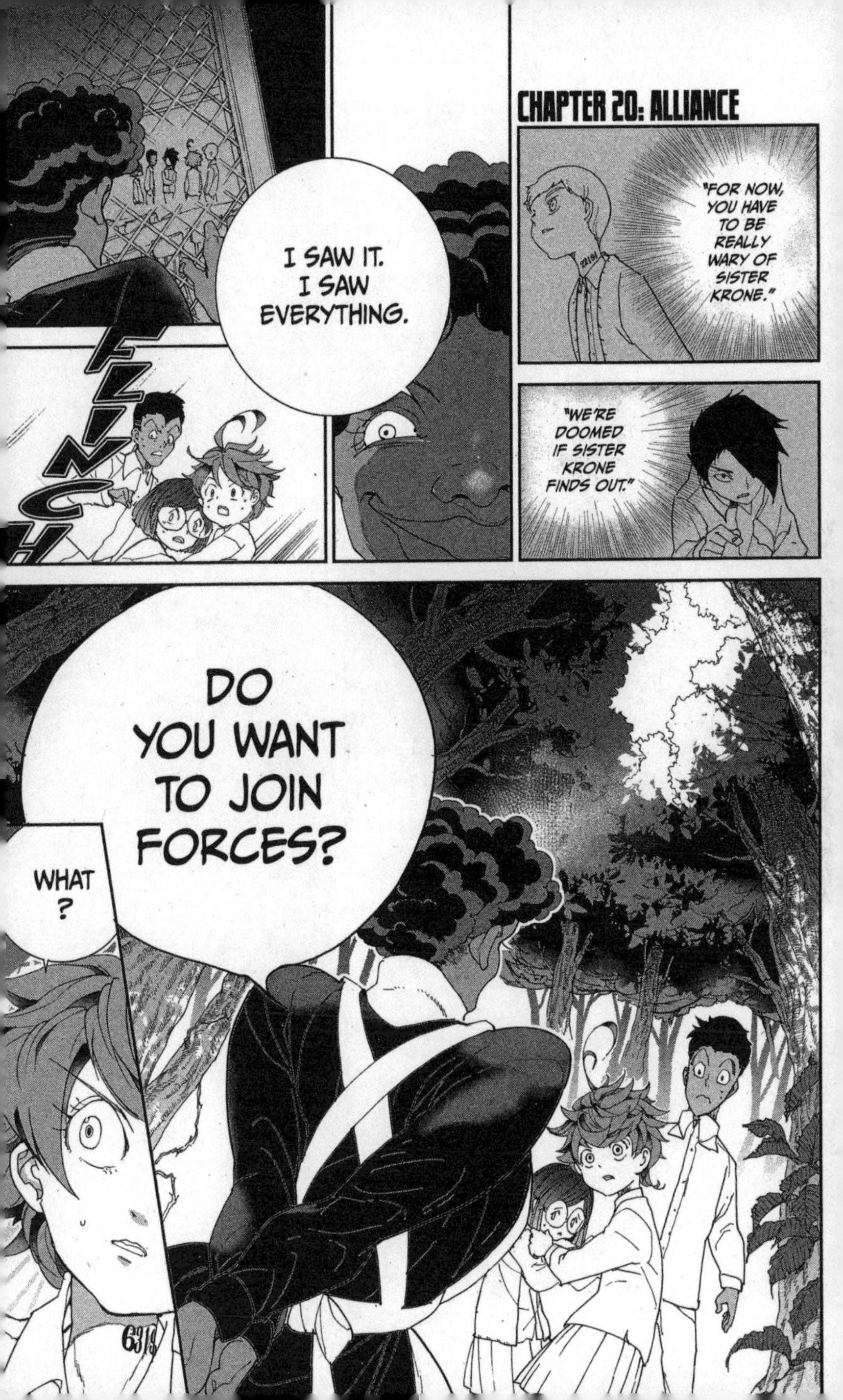
CHAPTER 20: ALLIANCE
"FOR NOW, YOU HAVE TO BE REALLY WARY OF SISTER KRONE."
"WE'RE DOOMED IF SISTER KRONE FINDS OUT."
I SAW IT. I SAW EVERYTHING.
FLINCH!
DO YOU WANT TO JOIN FORCES?
WHAT?

CHAPTER 20: ALLIANCE

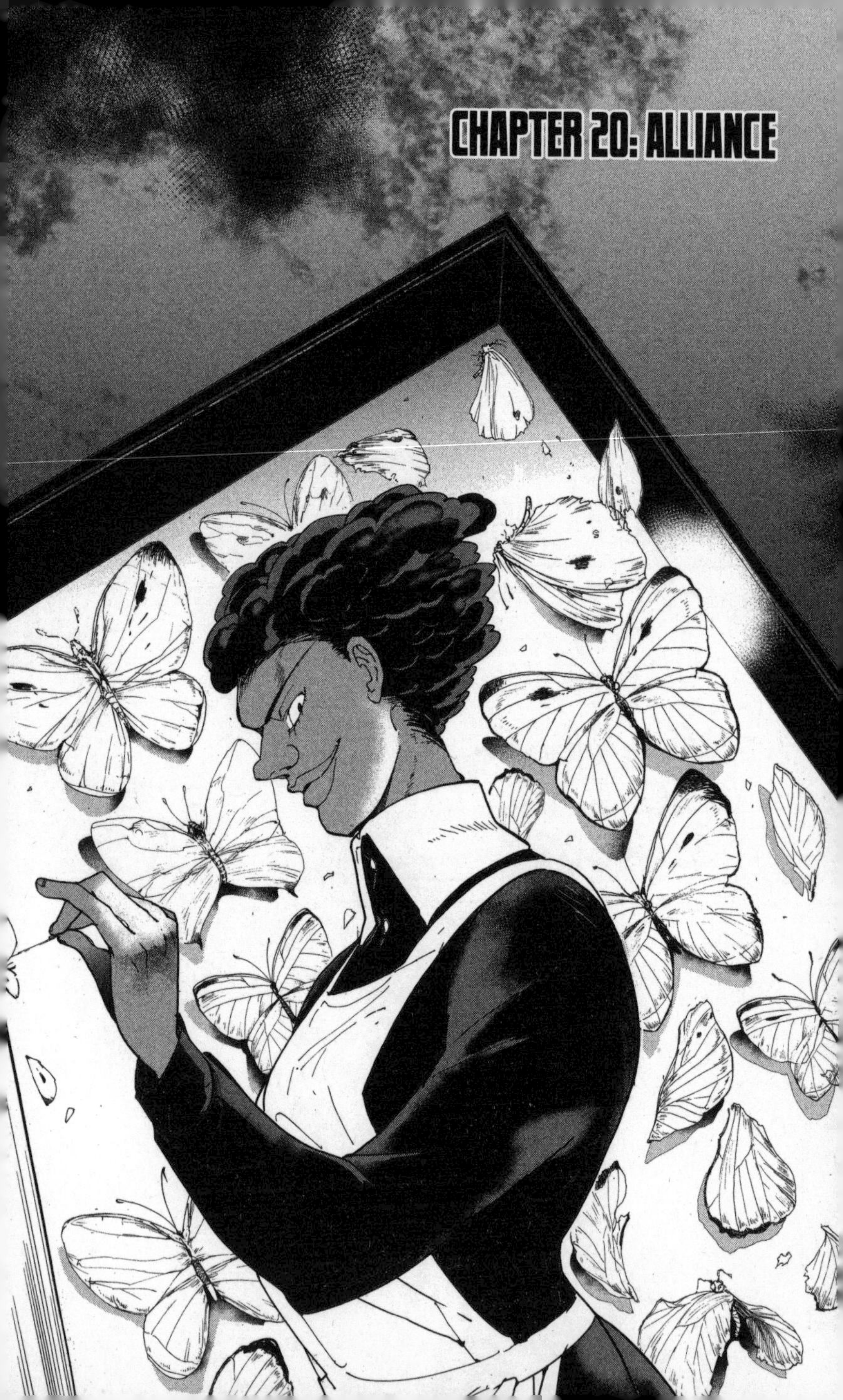

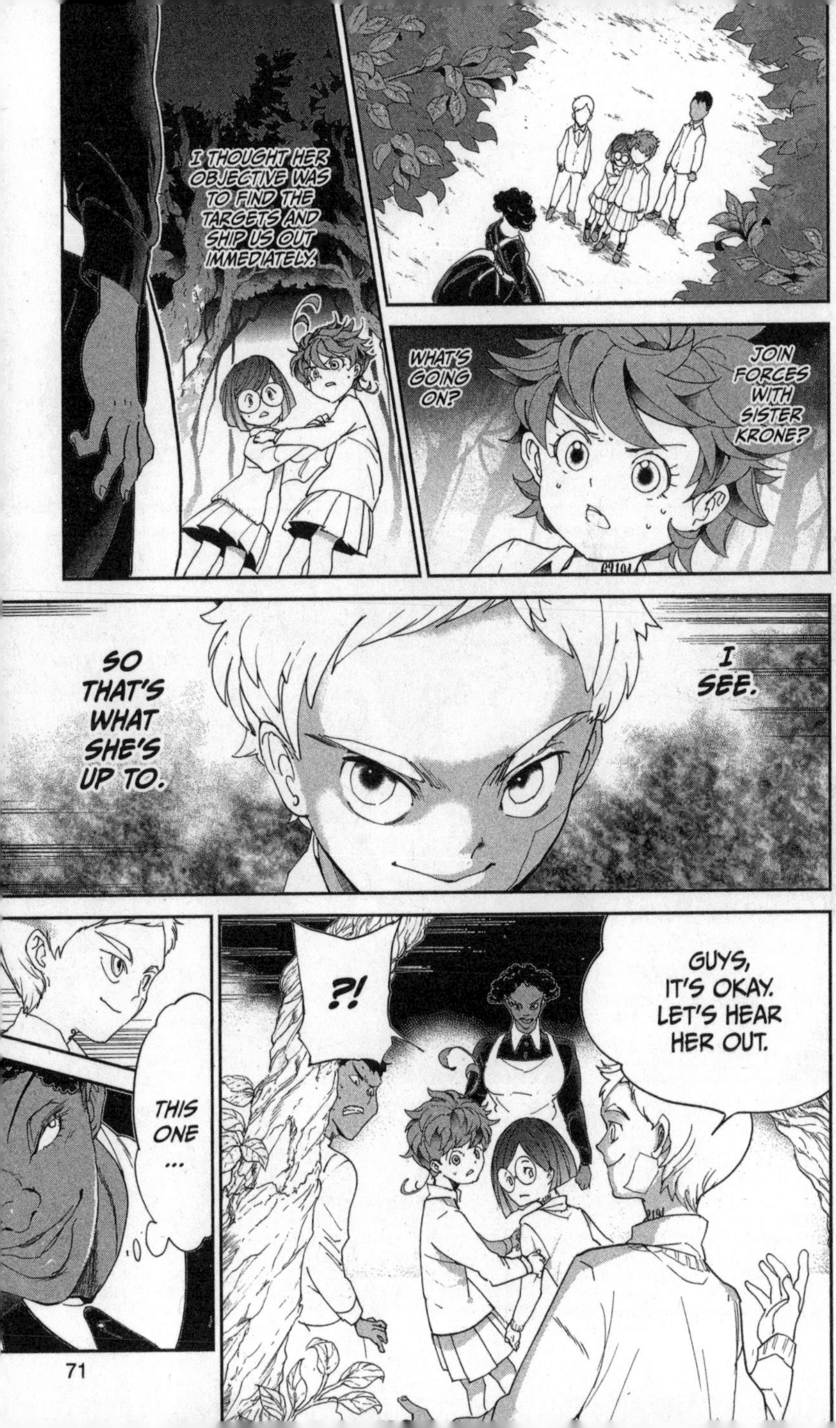
JOIN FORCES WITH SISTER KRONE?
WHAT'S GOING ON?
I THOUGHT HER OBJECTIVE WAS TO FIND THE TARGETS AND SHIP US OUT IMMEDIATELY.
I SEE.
SO THAT'S WHAT SHE'S UP TO.
GUYS, IT'S OKAY. LET'S HEAR HER OUT.
?!
THIS ONE ...

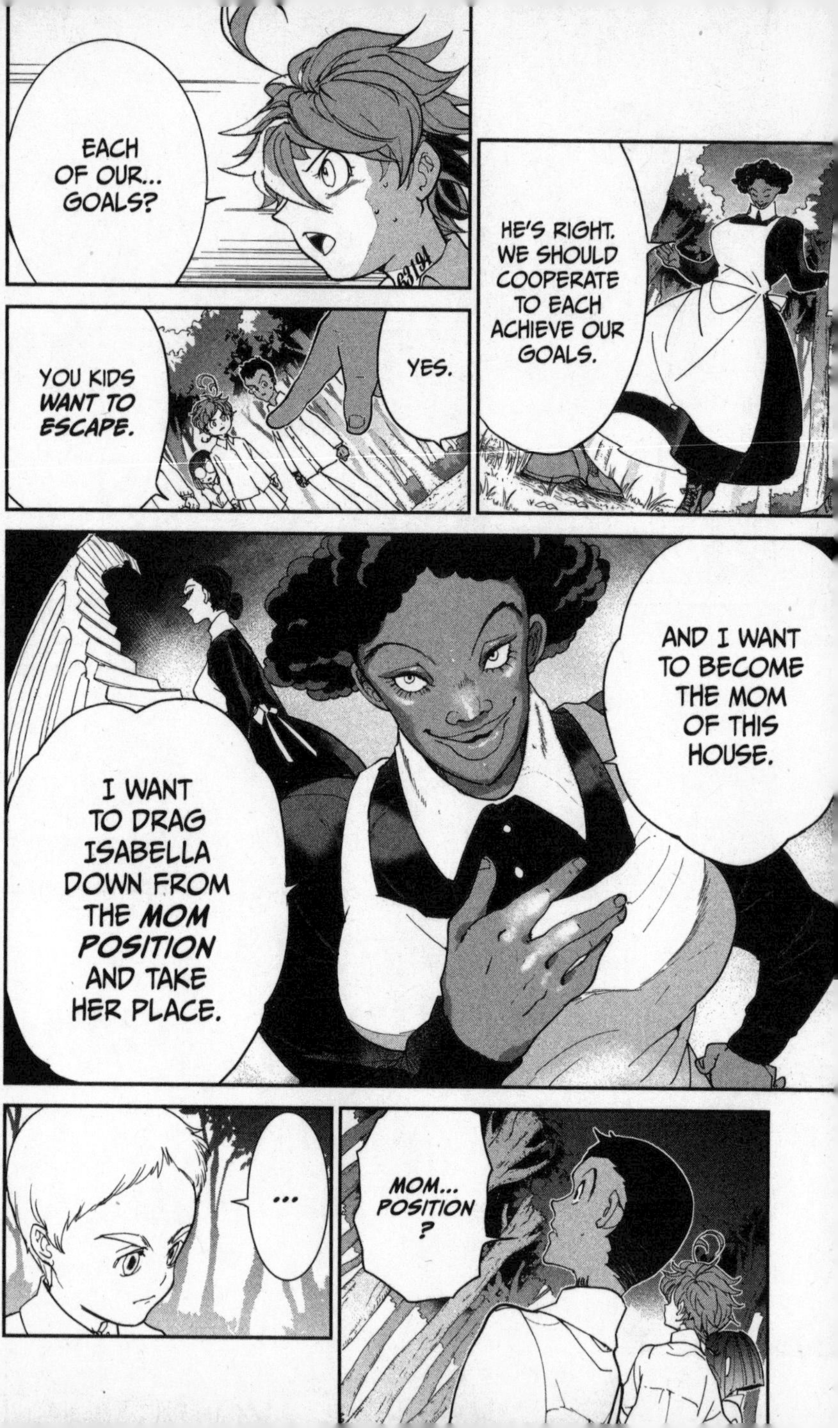
HE'S RIGHT. WE SHOULD COOPERATE TO EACH ACHIEVE OUR GOALS.
EACH OF OUR... GOALS?
YES.
YOU KIDS *WANT TO ESCAPE.*
AND I WANT TO BECOME THE MOM OF THIS HOUSE.
I WANT TO DRAG ISABELLA DOWN FROM THE *MOM POSITION* AND TAKE HER PLACE.
MOM... POSITION ?
...

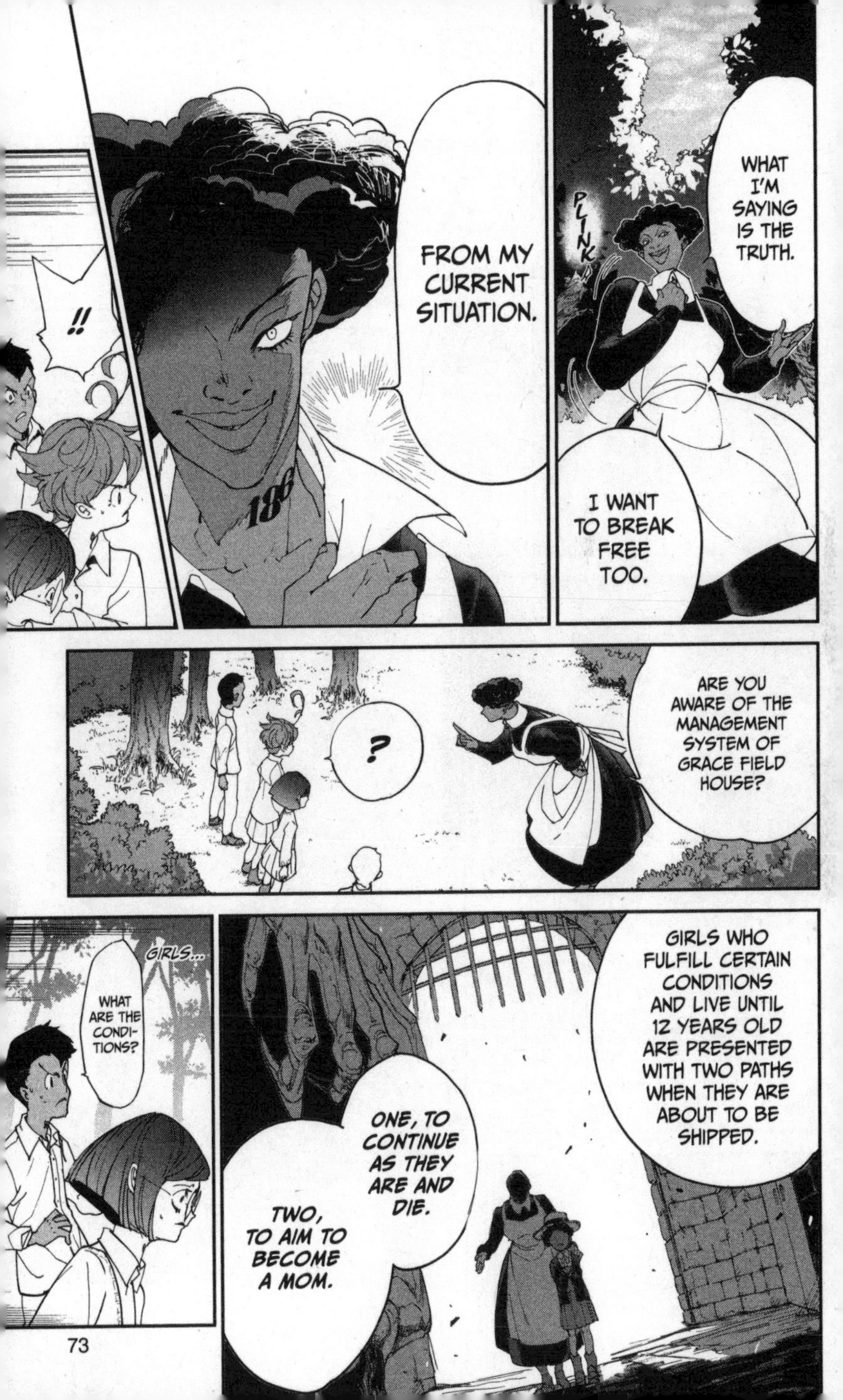
WHAT I'M SAYING IS THE TRUTH.
PLINK
I WANT TO BREAK FREE TOO.
FROM MY CURRENT SITUATION.
!!
ARE YOU AWARE OF THE MANAGEMENT SYSTEM OF GRACE FIELD HOUSE?
?
GIRLS WHO FULFILL CERTAIN CONDITIONS AND LIVE UNTIL 12 YEARS OLD ARE PRESENTED WITH TWO PATHS WHEN THEY ARE ABOUT TO BE SHIPPED.
ONE, TO CONTINUE AS THEY ARE AND DIE.
TWO, TO AIM TO BECOME A MOM.
GIRLS...
WHAT ARE THE CONDITIONS?

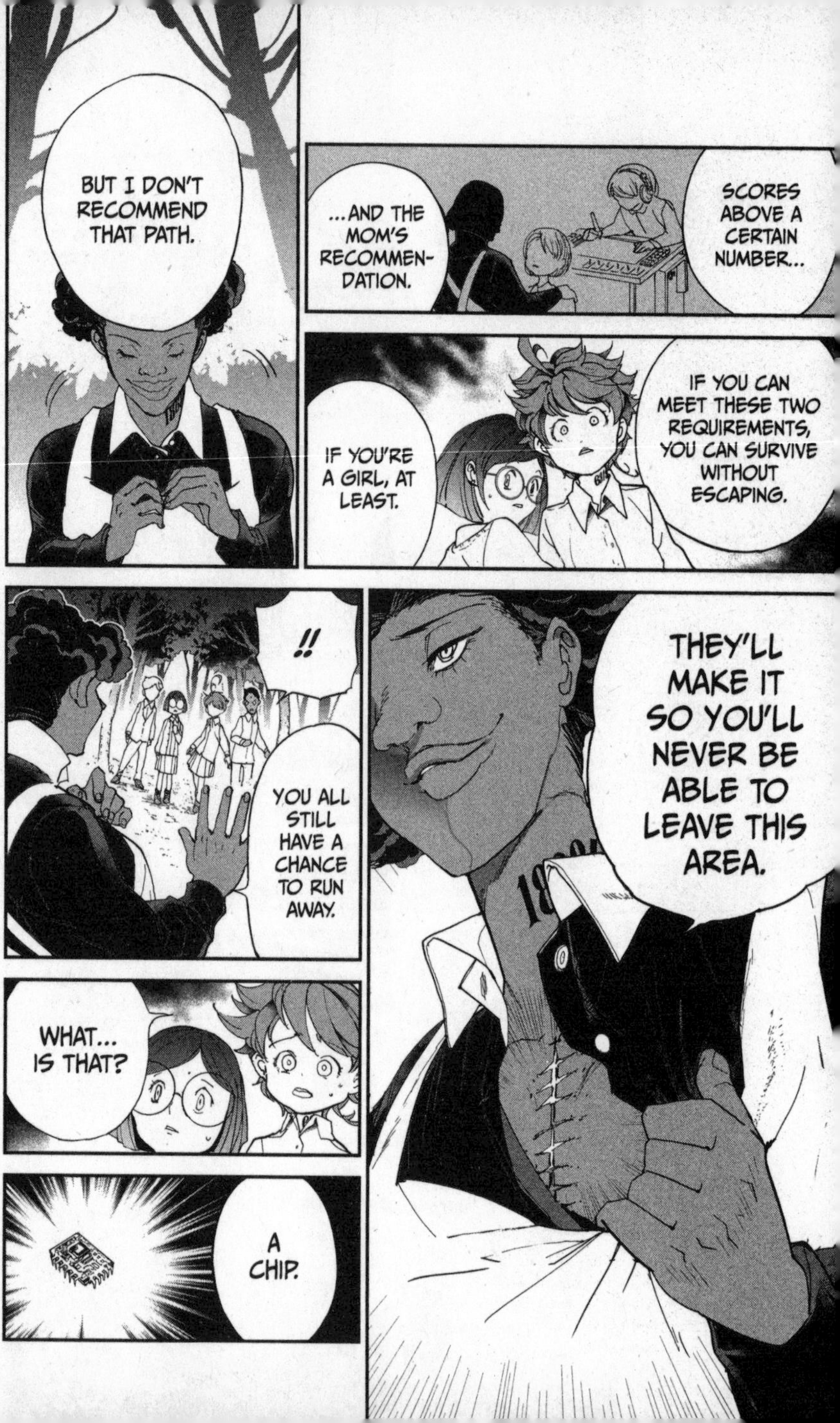
SCORES ABOVE A CERTAIN NUMBER...
...AND THE MOM'S RECOMMEN-DATION.
IF YOU CAN MEET THESE TWO REQUIREMENTS, YOU CAN SURVIVE WITHOUT ESCAPING.
IF YOU'RE A GIRL, AT LEAST.
BUT I DON'T RECOMMEND THAT PATH.
THEY'LL MAKE IT SO YOU'LL NEVER BE ABLE TO LEAVE THIS AREA.
!!
YOU ALL STILL HAVE A CHANCE TO RUN AWAY.
WHAT... IS THAT?
A CHIP.

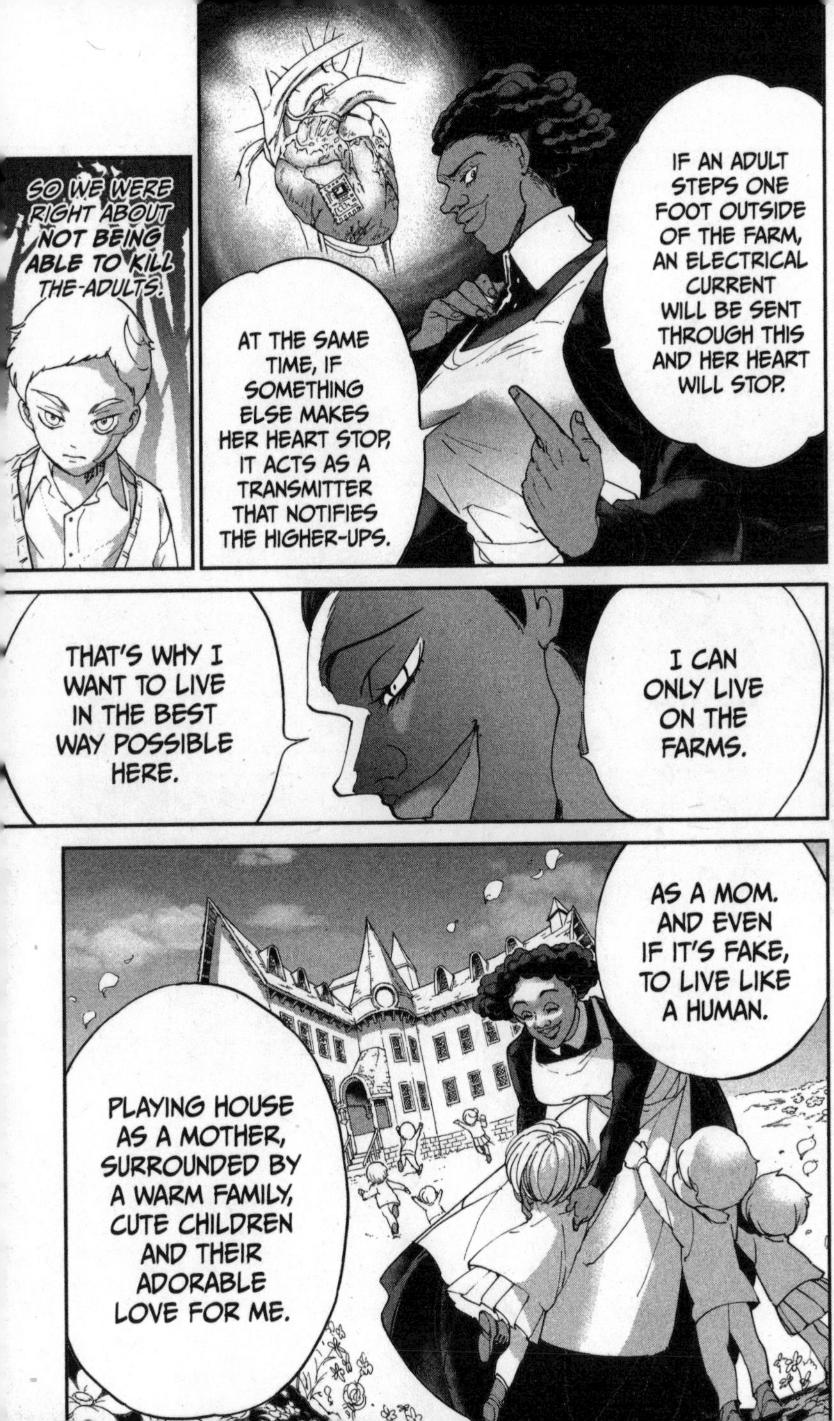
IF AN ADULT STEPS ONE FOOT OUTSIDE OF THE FARM, AN ELECTRICAL CURRENT WILL BE SENT THROUGH THIS AND HER HEART WILL STOP.
AT THE SAME TIME, IF SOMETHING ELSE MAKES HER HEART STOP, IT ACTS AS A TRANSMITTER THAT NOTIFIES THE HIGHER-UPS.
SO WE WERE RIGHT ABOUT NOT BEING ABLE TO KILL THE ADULTS.
I CAN ONLY LIVE ON THE FARMS.
THAT'S WHY I WANT TO LIVE IN THE BEST WAY POSSIBLE HERE.
AS A MOM. AND EVEN IF IT'S FAKE, TO LIVE LIKE A HUMAN.
PLAYING HOUSE AS A MOTHER, SURROUNDED BY A WARM FAMILY, CUTE CHILDREN AND THEIR ADORABLE LOVE FOR ME.

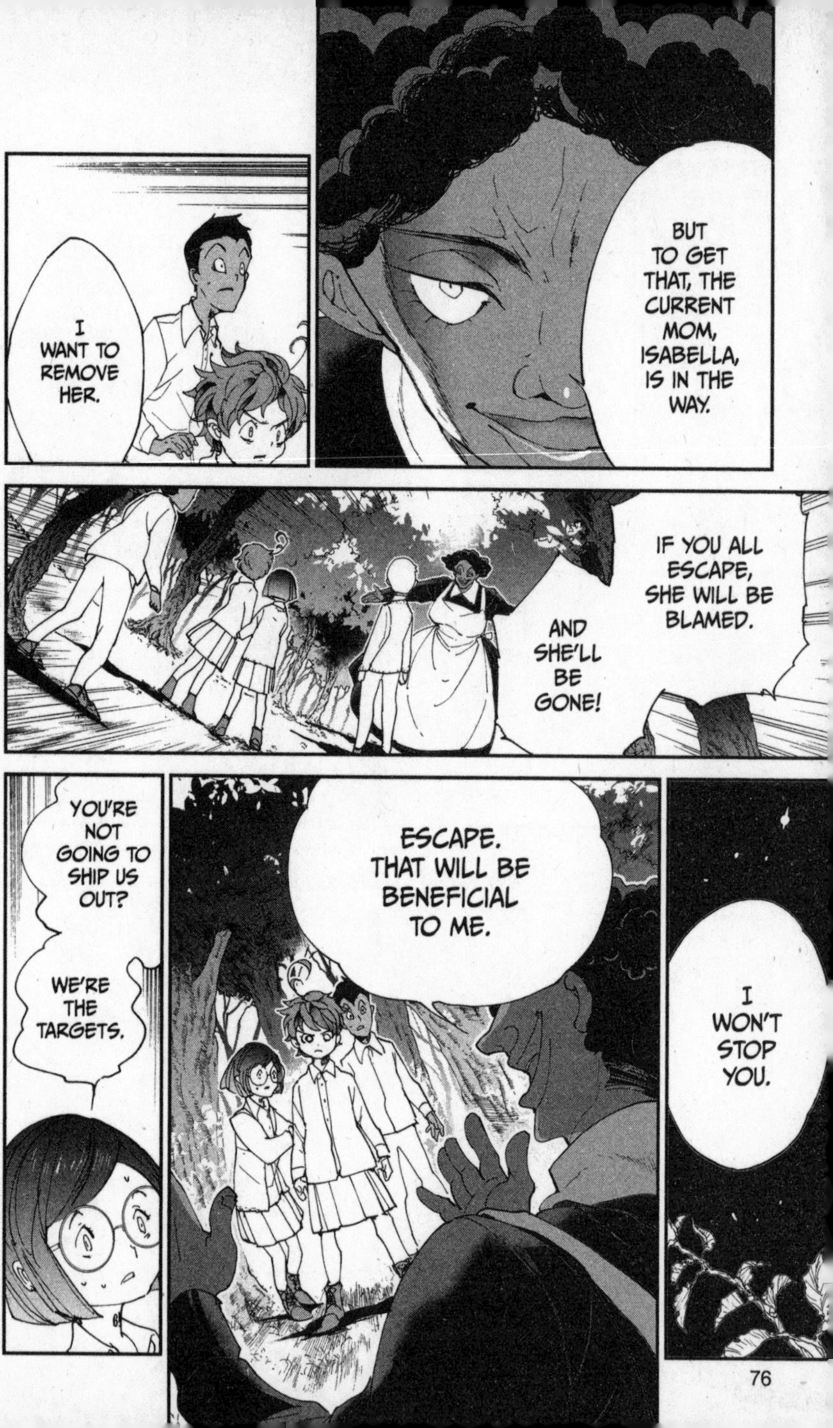
BUT TO GET THAT, THE CURRENT MOM, ISABELLA, IS IN THE WAY.
I WANT TO REMOVE HER.
IF YOU ALL ESCAPE, SHE WILL BE BLAMED.
AND SHE'LL BE GONE!
I WON'T STOP YOU.
ESCAPE. THAT WILL BE BENEFICIAL TO ME.
YOU'RE NOT GOING TO SHIP US OUT?
WE'RE THE TARGETS.

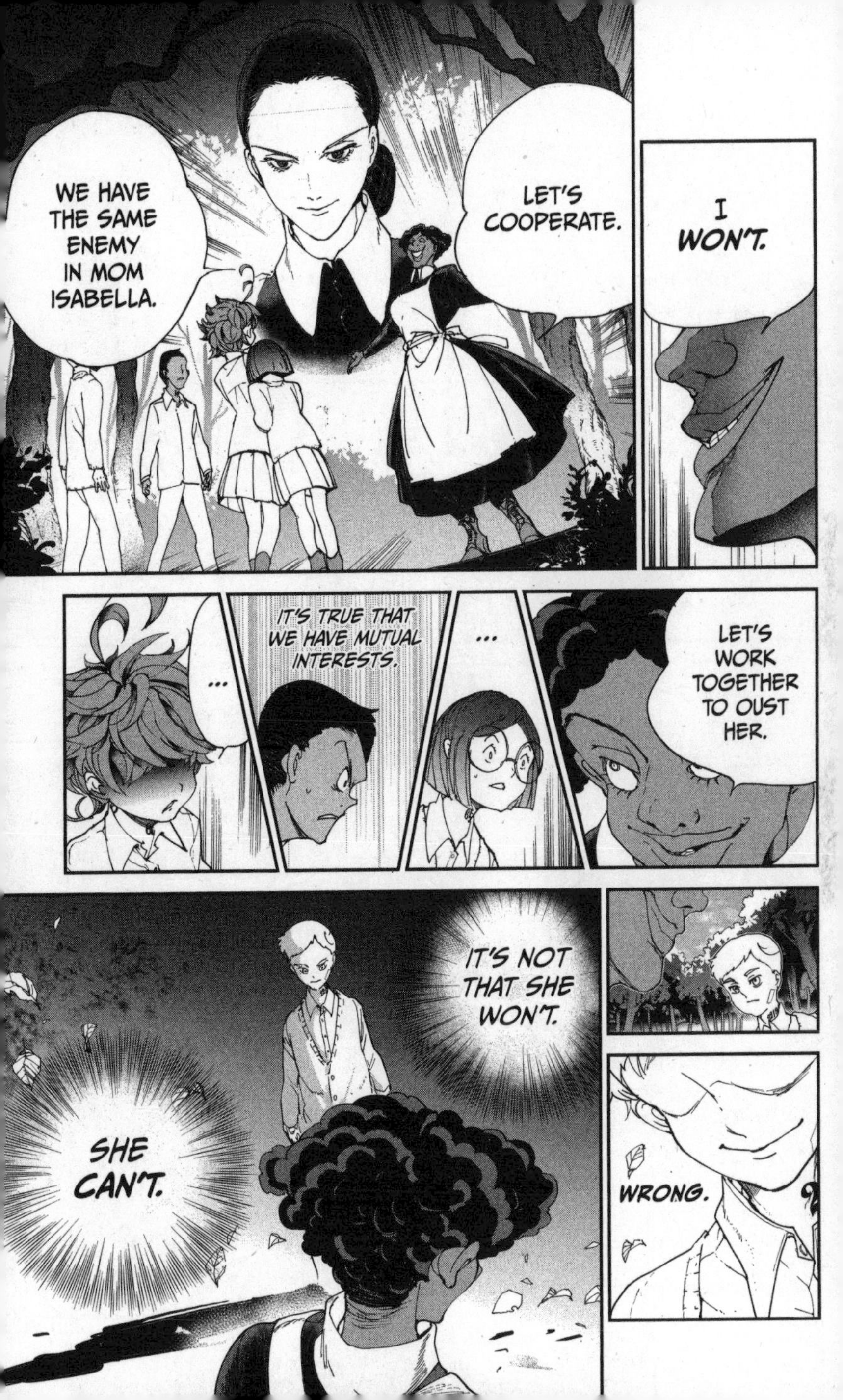
LET'S COOPERATE.
WE HAVE THE SAME ENEMY IN MOM ISABELLA.
I WON'T.
LET'S WORK TOGETHER TO OUST HER.
...
IT'S TRUE THAT WE HAVE MUTUAL INTERESTS.
...
WRONG.
IT'S NOT THAT SHE WON'T.
SHE CAN'T.

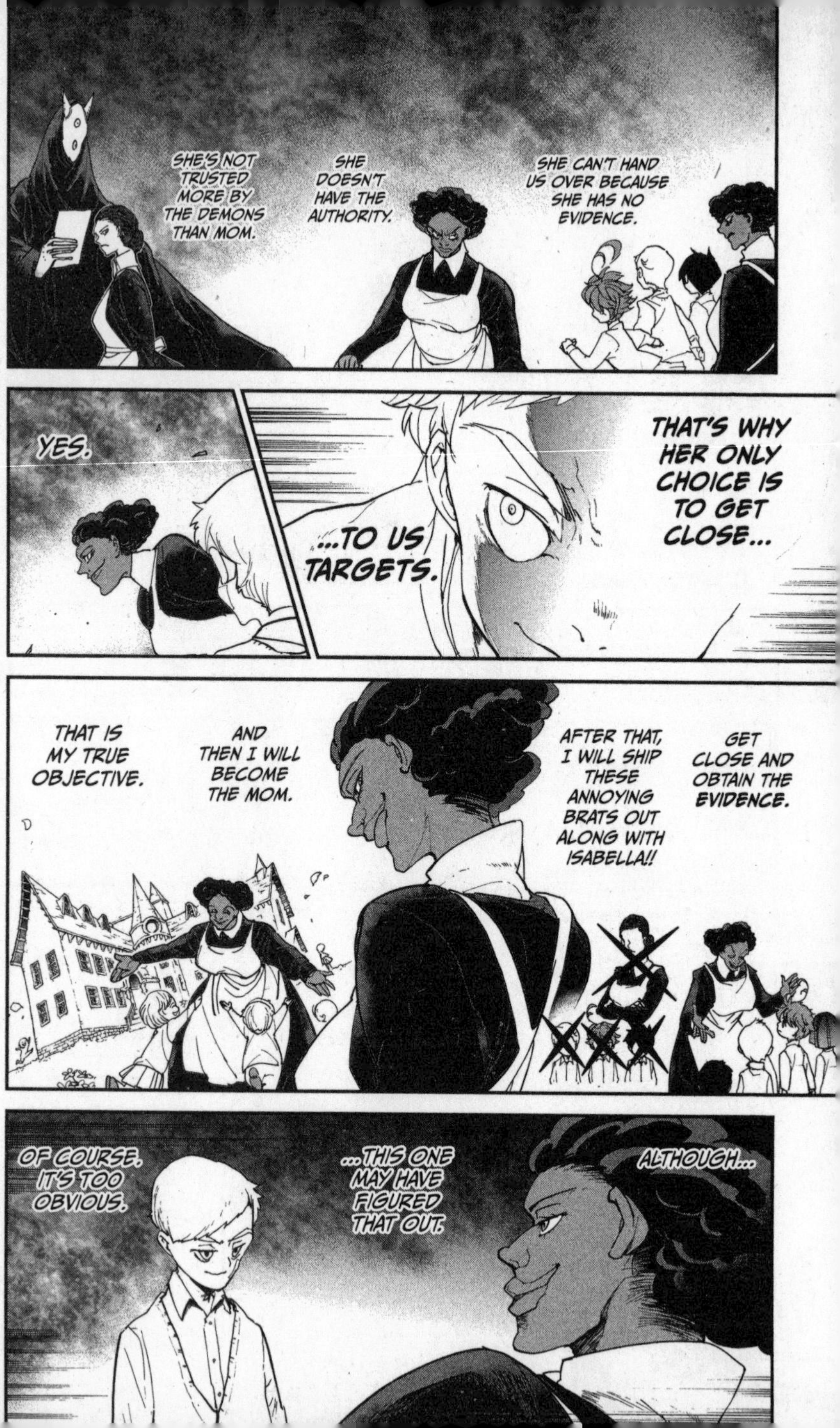
SHE CAN'T HAND US OVER BECAUSE SHE HAS NO EVIDENCE.
SHE DOESN'T HAVE THE AUTHORITY.
SHE'S NOT TRUSTED MORE BY THE DEMONS THAN MOM.
THAT'S WHY HER ONLY CHOICE IS TO GET CLOSE...
...TO US TARGETS.
YES.
GET CLOSE AND OBTAIN THE EVIDENCE.
AFTER THAT, I WILL SHIP THESE ANNOYING BRATS OUT ALONG WITH ISABELLA!!
AND THEN I WILL BECOME THE MOM.
THAT IS MY TRUE OBJECTIVE.
ALTHOUGH...
...THIS ONE MAY HAVE FIGURED THAT OUT.
OF COURSE. IT'S TOO OBVIOUS.

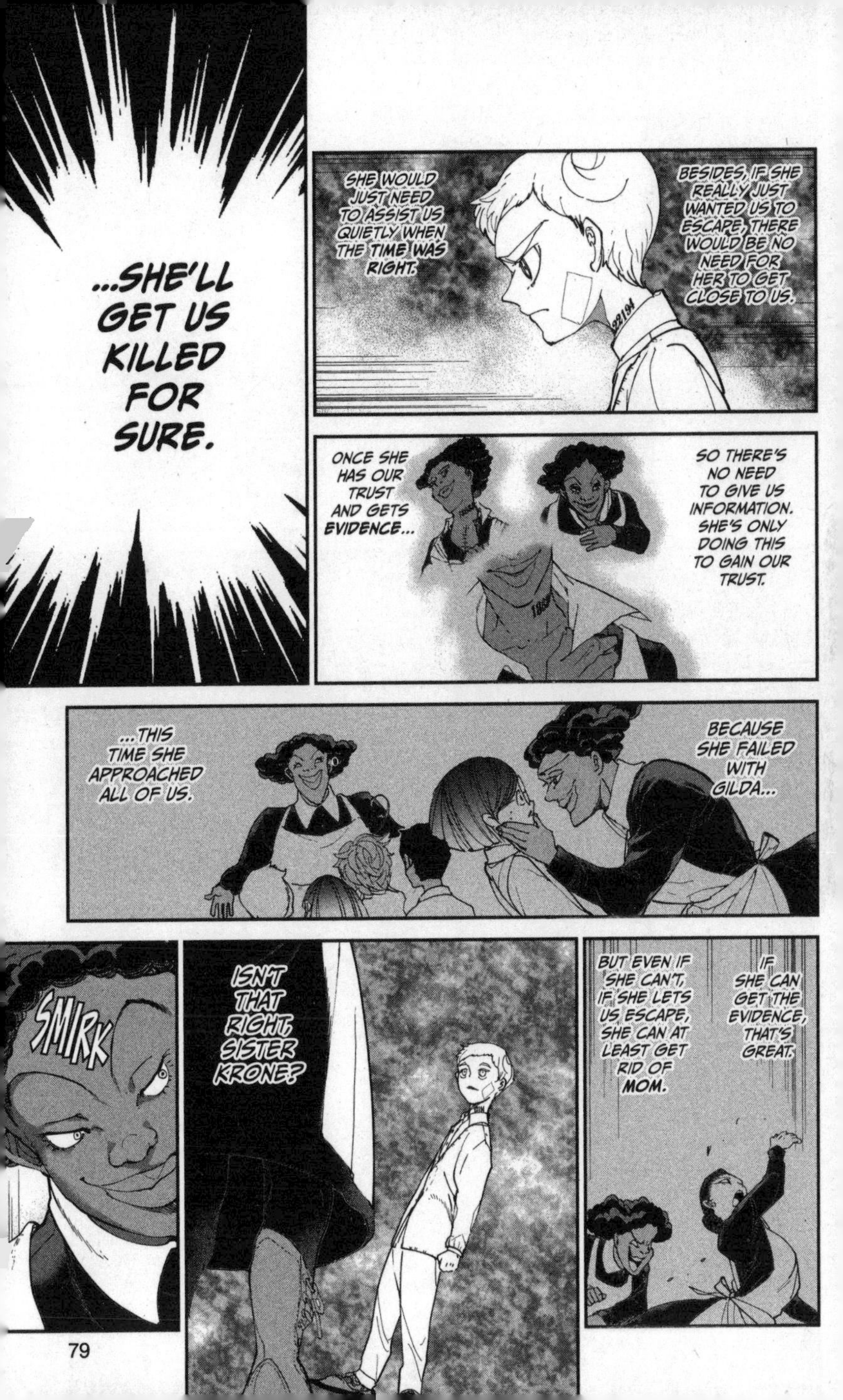
BESIDES, IF SHE REALLY JUST WANTED US TO ESCAPE, THERE WOULD BE NO NEED FOR HER TO GET CLOSE TO US.
SHE WOULD JUST NEED TO ASSIST US QUIETLY WHEN THE TIME WAS RIGHT.
SO THERE'S NO NEED TO GIVE US INFORMATION. SHE'S ONLY DOING THIS TO GAIN OUR TRUST.
ONCE SHE HAS OUR TRUST AND GETS EVIDENCE...
...SHE'LL GET US KILLED FOR SURE.
BECAUSE SHE FAILED WITH GILDA...
...THIS TIME SHE APPROACHED ALL OF US.
IF SHE CAN GET THE EVIDENCE, THAT'S GREAT.
BUT EVEN IF SHE CAN'T, IF SHE LETS US ESCAPE, SHE CAN AT LEAST GET RID OF MOM.
ISN'T THAT RIGHT, SISTER KRONE?
SMIRK

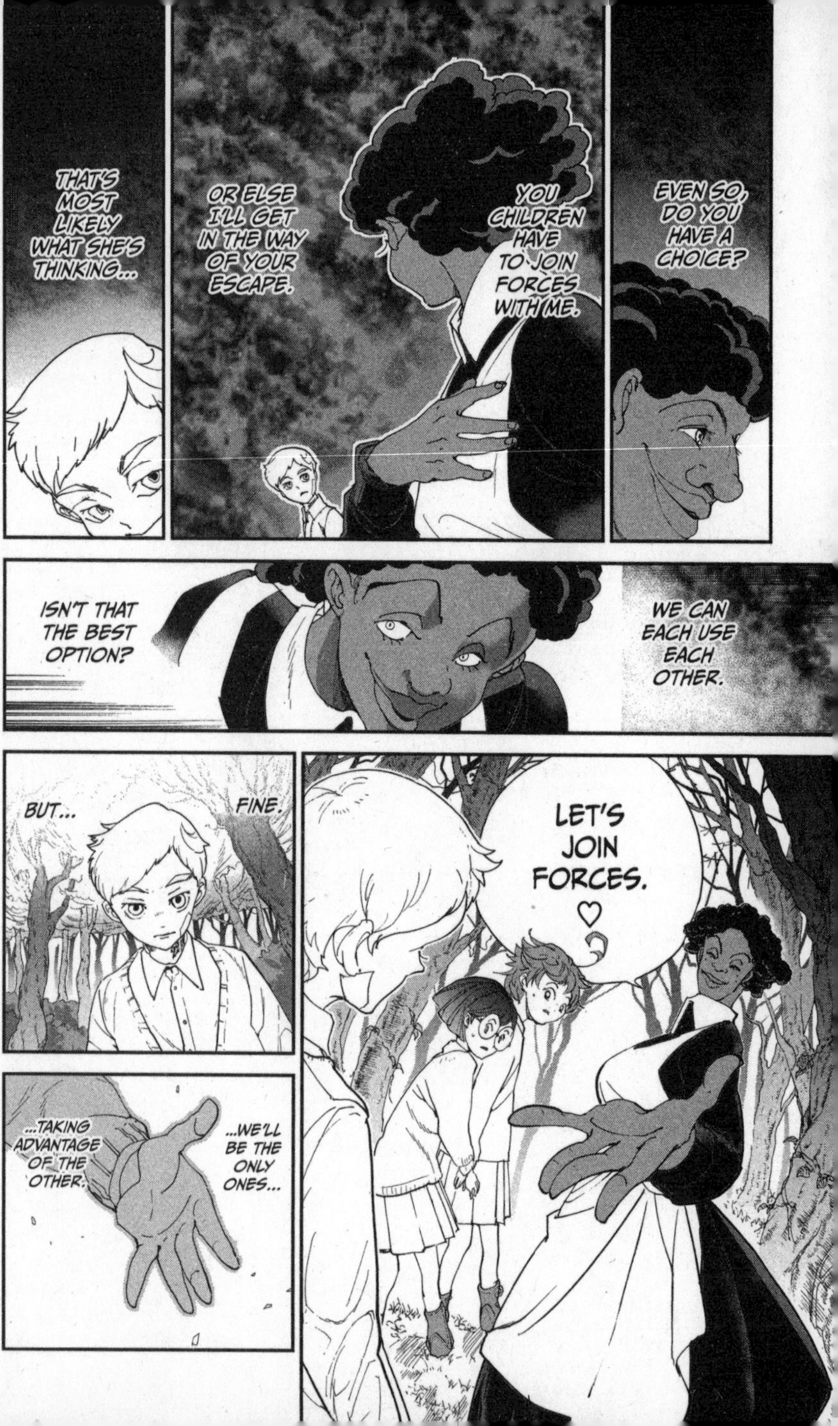
EVEN SO, DO YOU HAVE A CHOICE?
YOU CHILDREN HAVE TO JOIN FORCES WITH ME.
OR ELSE I'LL GET IN THE WAY OF YOUR ESCAPE.
THAT'S MOST LIKELY WHAT SHE'S THINKING...
WE CAN EACH USE EACH OTHER.
ISN'T THAT THE BEST OPTION?
LET'S JOIN FORCES. ♡
FINE.
BUT...
...WE'LL BE THE ONLY ONES...
...TAKING ADVANTAGE OF THE OTHER.

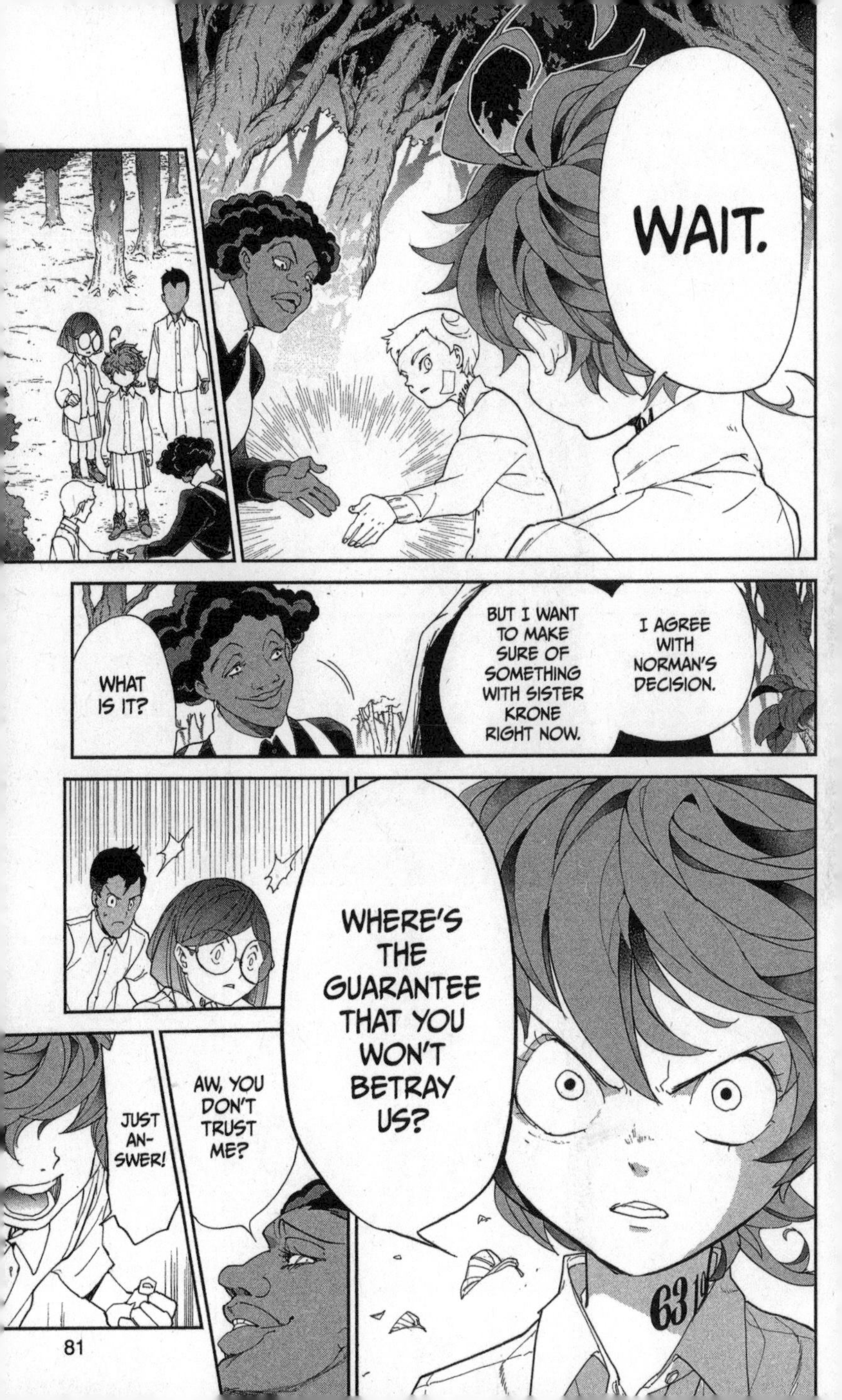
WAIT.
I AGREE WITH NORMAN'S DECISION.
BUT I WANT TO MAKE SURE OF SOMETHING WITH SISTER KRONE RIGHT NOW.
WHAT IS IT?
WHERE'S THE GUARANTEE THAT YOU WON'T BETRAY US?
AW, YOU DON'T TRUST ME?
JUST AN-SWER!

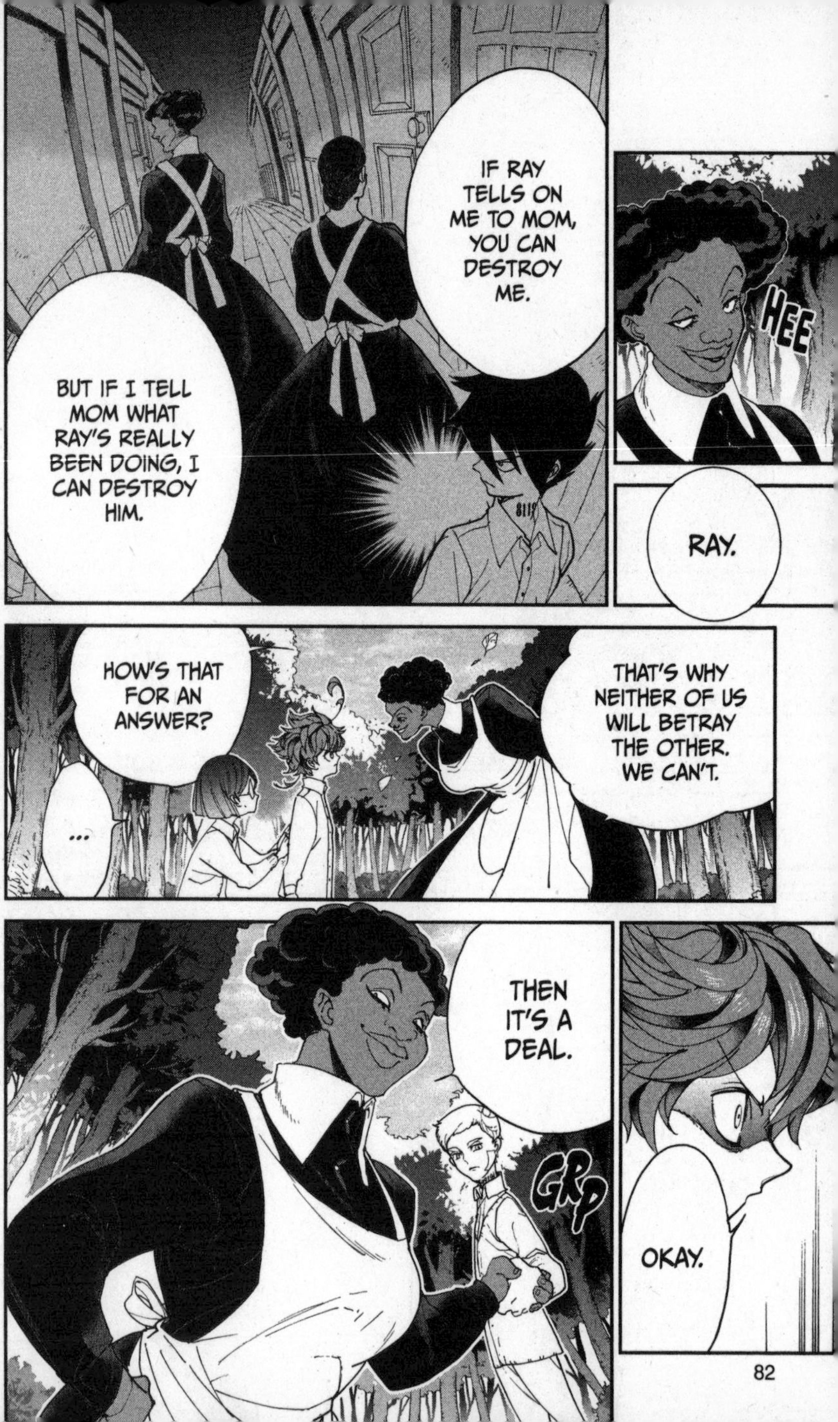
HEE
RAY.
IF RAY TELLS ON ME TO MOM, YOU CAN DESTROY ME.
BUT IF I TELL MOM WHAT RAY'S REALLY BEEN DOING, I CAN DESTROY HIM.
THAT'S WHY NEITHER OF US WILL BETRAY THE OTHER. WE CAN'T.
HOW'S THAT FOR AN ANSWER?
...
OKAY.
THEN IT'S A DEAL.
GRP

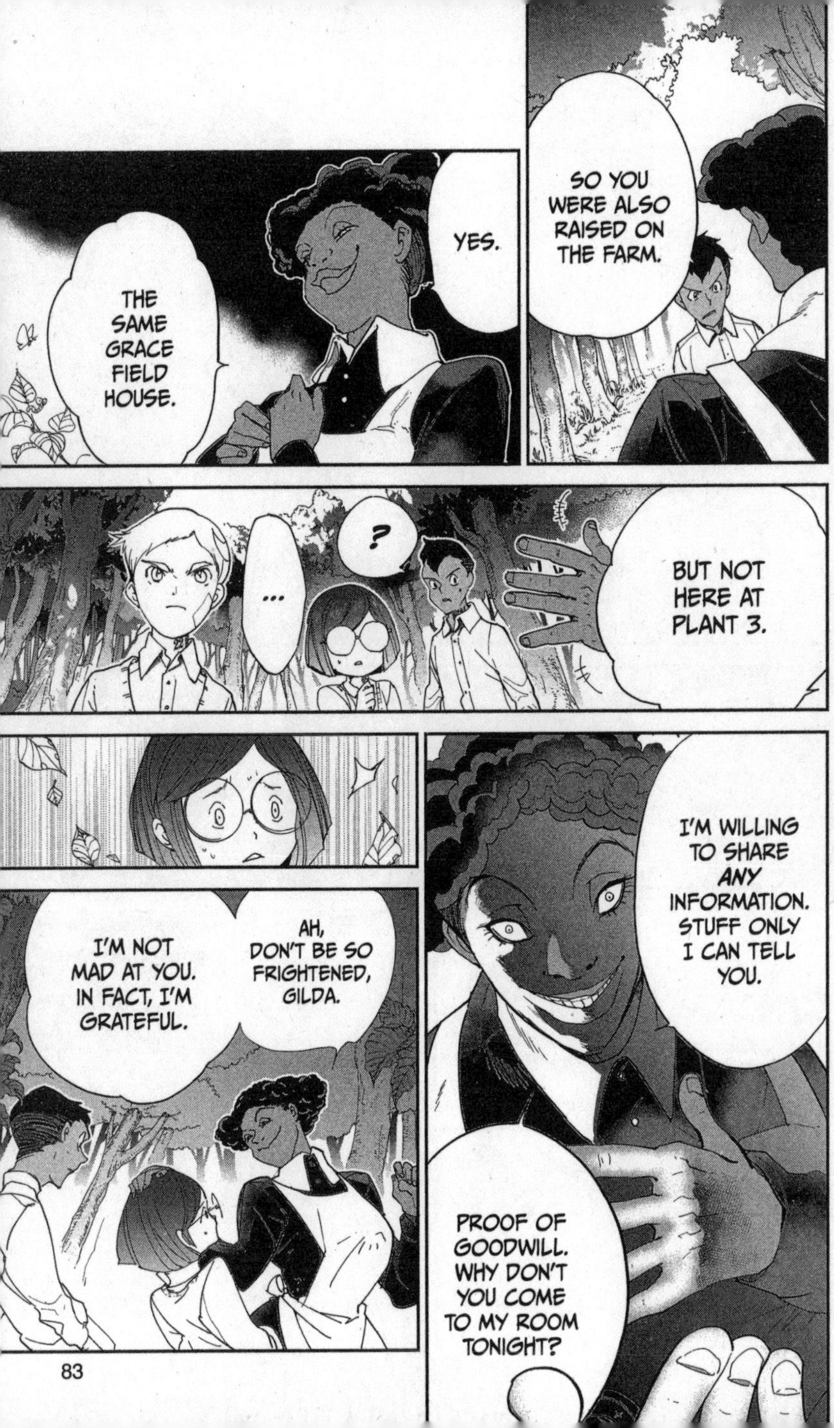
SO YOU WERE ALSO RAISED ON THE FARM.
YES.
THE SAME GRACE FIELD HOUSE.
BUT NOT HERE AT PLANT 3.
?
...
I'M WILLING TO SHARE *ANY* INFORMATION. STUFF ONLY I CAN TELL YOU.
PROOF OF GOODWILL. WHY DON'T YOU COME TO MY ROOM TONIGHT?
AH, DON'T BE SO FRIGHTENED, GILDA.
I'M NOT MAD AT YOU. IN FACT, I'M GRATEFUL.

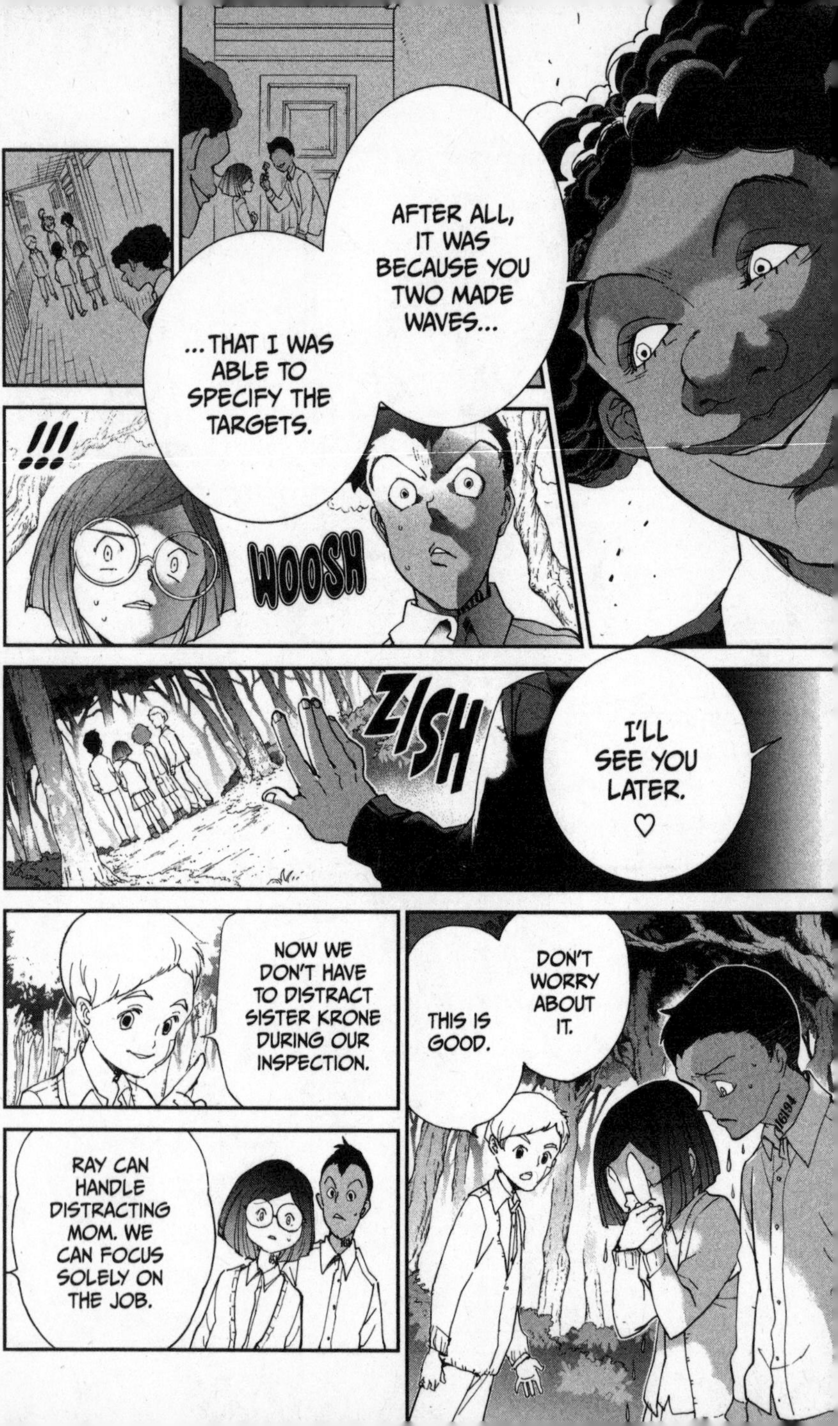
AFTER ALL, IT WAS BECAUSE YOU TWO MADE WAVES...
...THAT I WAS ABLE TO SPECIFY THE TARGETS.
!!!
WOOSH
I'LL SEE YOU LATER. ♡
ZISH
DON'T WORRY ABOUT IT.
THIS IS GOOD.
NOW WE DON'T HAVE TO DISTRACT SISTER KRONE DURING OUR INSPECTION.
RAY CAN HANDLE DISTRACTING MOM. WE CAN FOCUS SOLELY ON THE JOB.

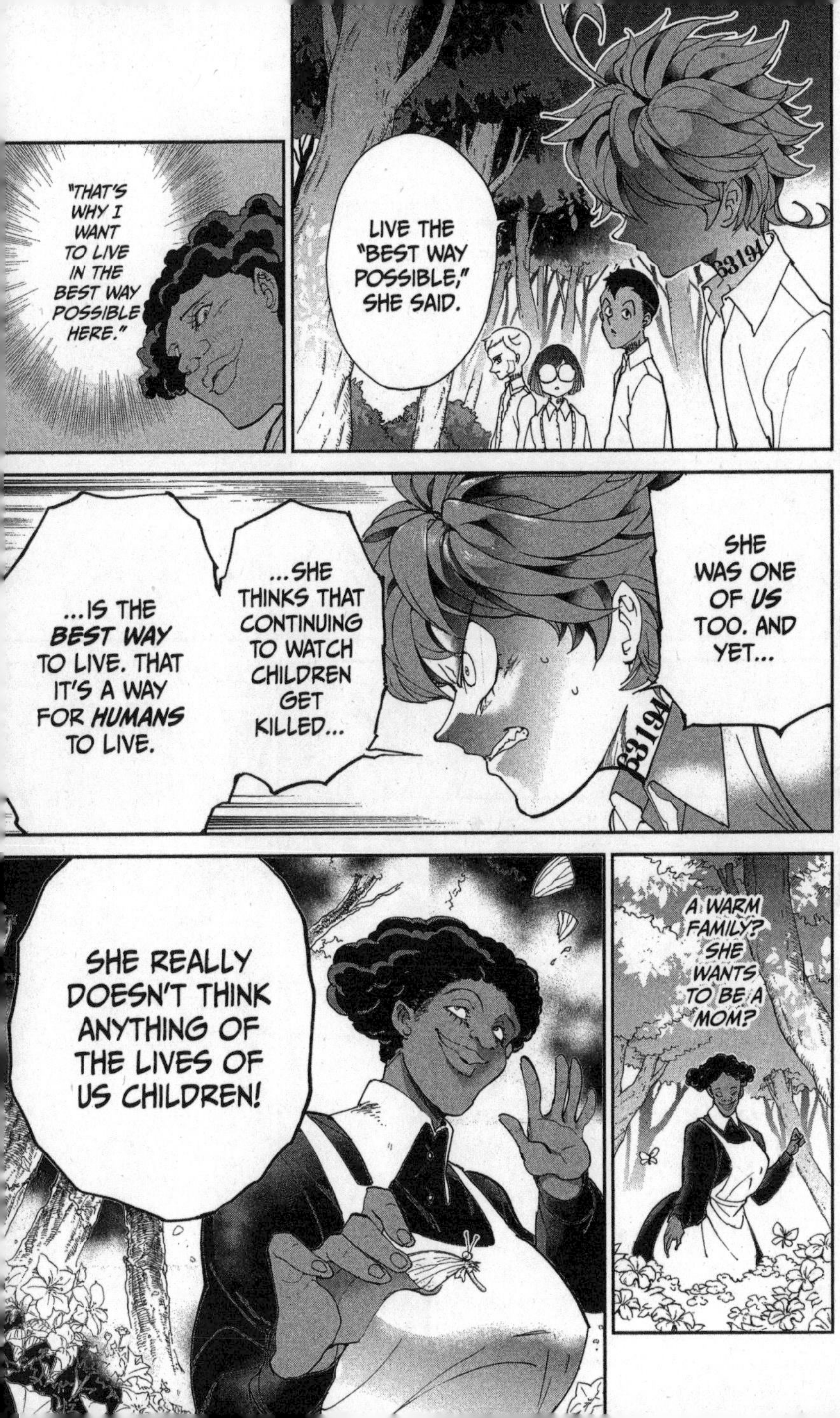
LIVE THE "BEST WAY POSSIBLE," SHE SAID.
"THAT'S WHY I WANT TO LIVE IN THE BEST WAY POSSIBLE HERE."
SHE WAS ONE OF US TOO. AND YET...
...SHE THINKS THAT CONTINUING TO WATCH CHILDREN GET KILLED...
...IS THE BEST WAY TO LIVE. THAT IT'S A WAY FOR HUMANS TO LIVE.
A WARM FAMILY? SHE WANTS TO BE A MOM?
SHE REALLY DOESN'T THINK ANYTHING OF THE LIVES OF US CHILDREN!

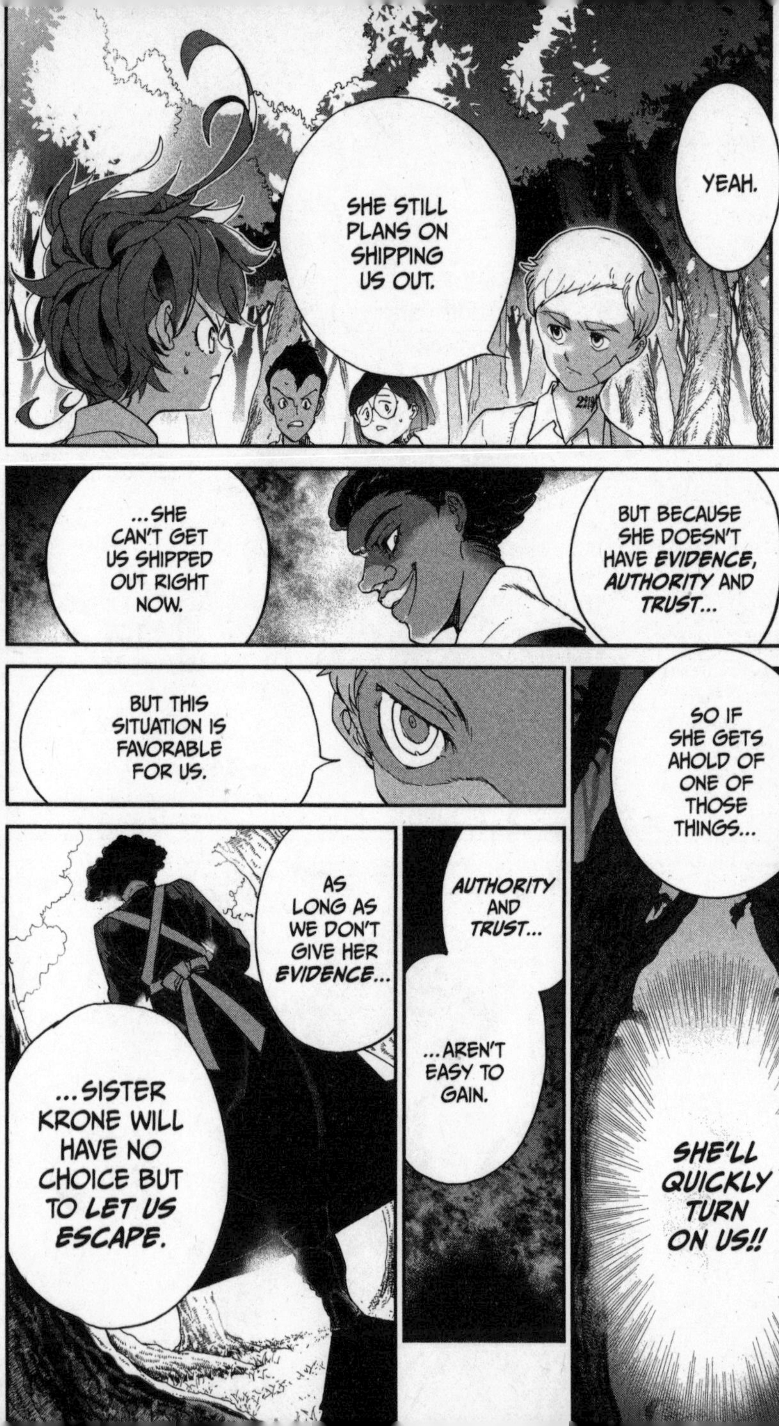
YEAH.
SHE STILL PLANS ON SHIPPING US OUT.
BUT BECAUSE SHE DOESN'T HAVE *EVIDENCE, AUTHORITY* AND *TRUST*...
...SHE CAN'T GET US SHIPPED OUT RIGHT NOW.
SO IF SHE GETS AHOLD OF ONE OF THOSE THINGS...
SHE'LL QUICKLY TURN ON US!!
BUT THIS SITUATION IS FAVORABLE FOR US.
AUTHORITY AND *TRUST*...
...AREN'T EASY TO GAIN.
AS LONG AS WE DON'T GIVE HER *EVIDENCE...*
...SISTER KRONE WILL HAVE NO CHOICE BUT TO *LET US ESCAPE.*

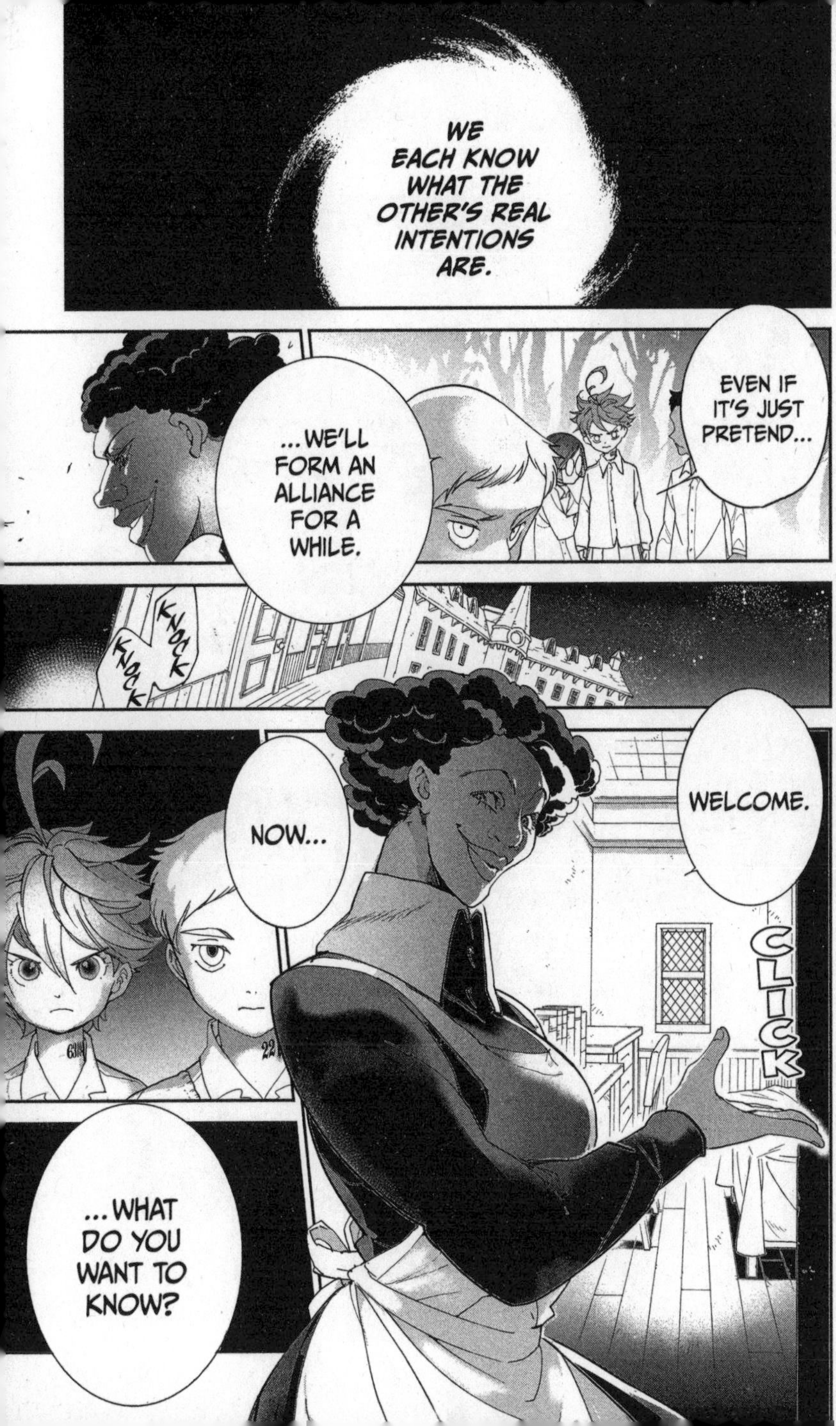
WE EACH KNOW WHAT THE OTHER'S REAL INTENTIONS ARE.
EVEN IF IT'S JUST PRETEND...
...WE'LL FORM AN ALLIANCE FOR A WHILE.
KNOCK
KNOCK
WELCOME.
CLICK
NOW...
...WHAT DO YOU WANT TO KNOW?

THE PROMISED NEVERLAND SIDE SCENE 004

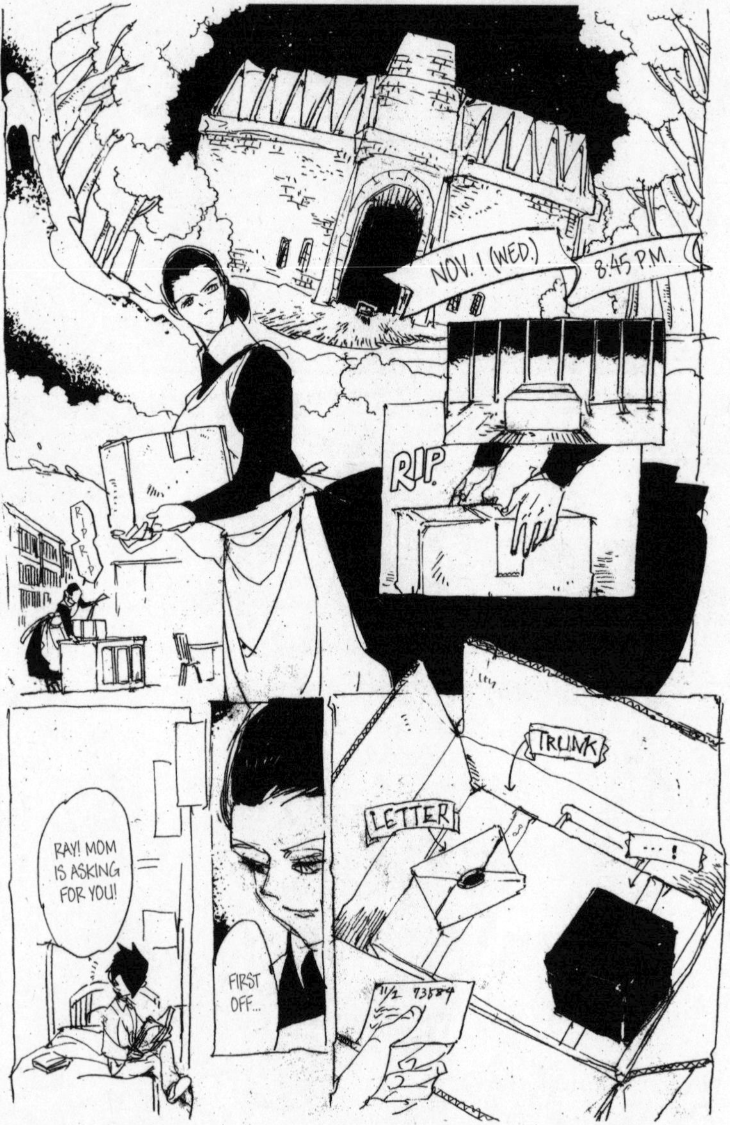

NOV. 1 (WED.)
8:45 P.M.
RIP.
RIP RIP
TRUNK
LETTER
...!
FIRST OFF...
RAY! MOM IS ASKING FOR YOU!

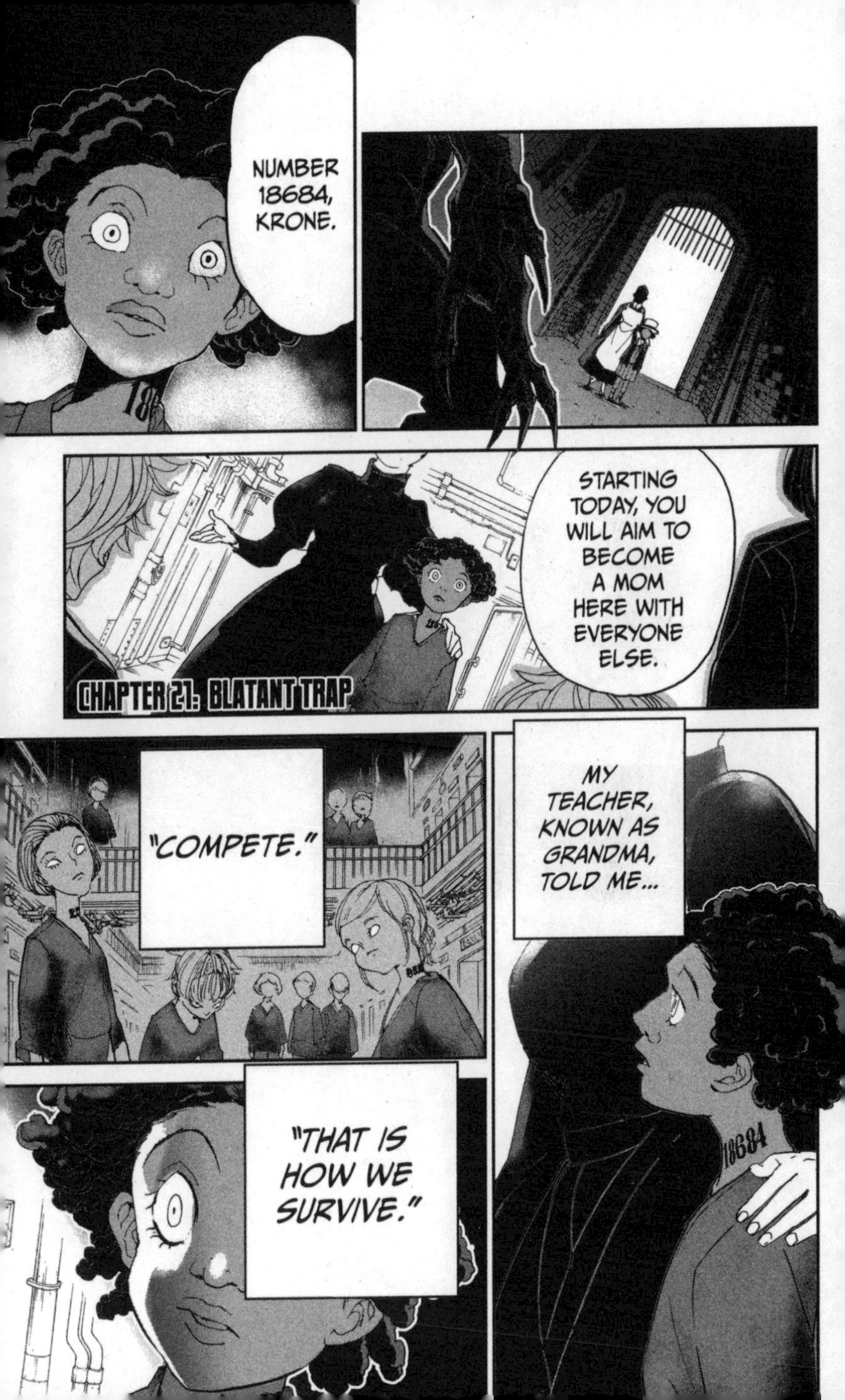
NUMBER 18684, KRONE.
STARTING TODAY, YOU WILL AIM TO BECOME A MOM HERE WITH EVERYONE ELSE.
CHAPTER 21: BLATANT TRAP
MY TEACHER, KNOWN AS GRANDMA, TOLD ME...
18684
"COMPETE."
"THAT IS HOW WE SURVIVE."

CHAPTER 21: BLATANT TRAP

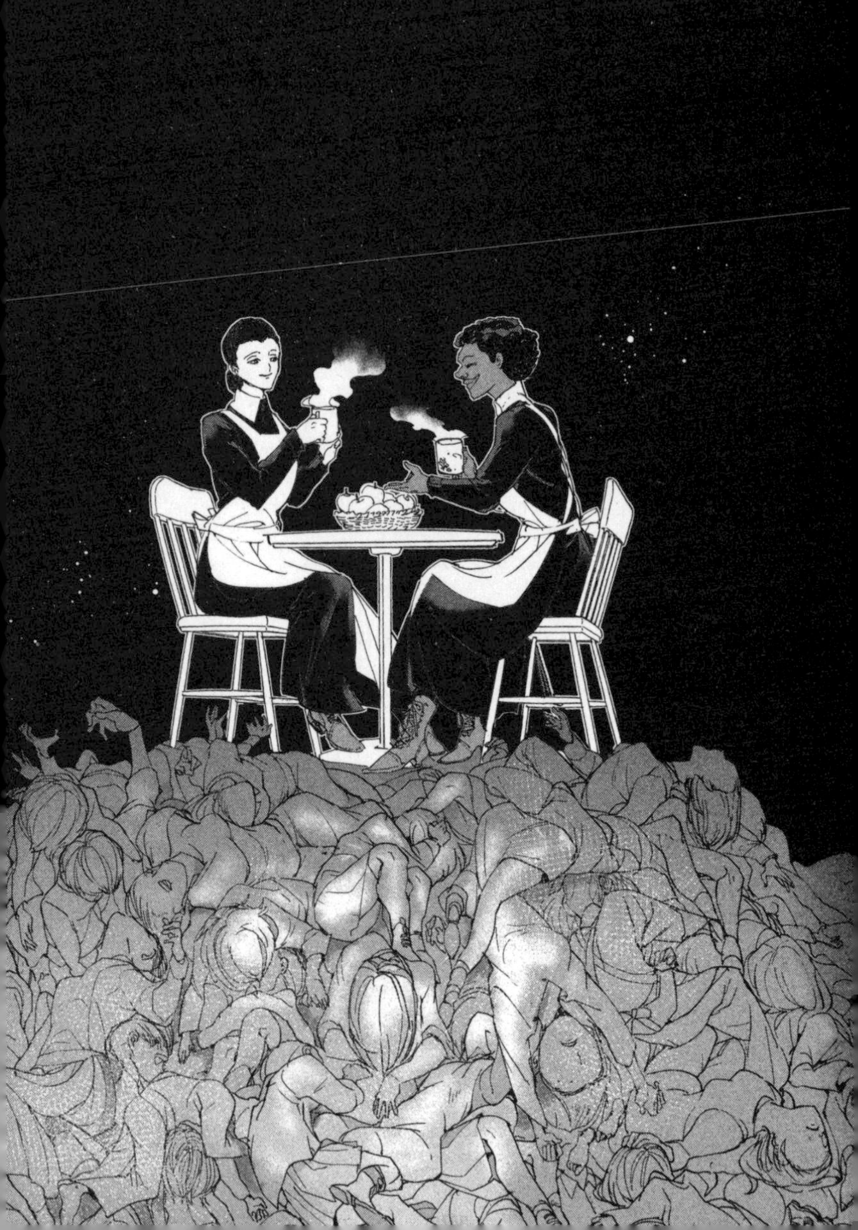

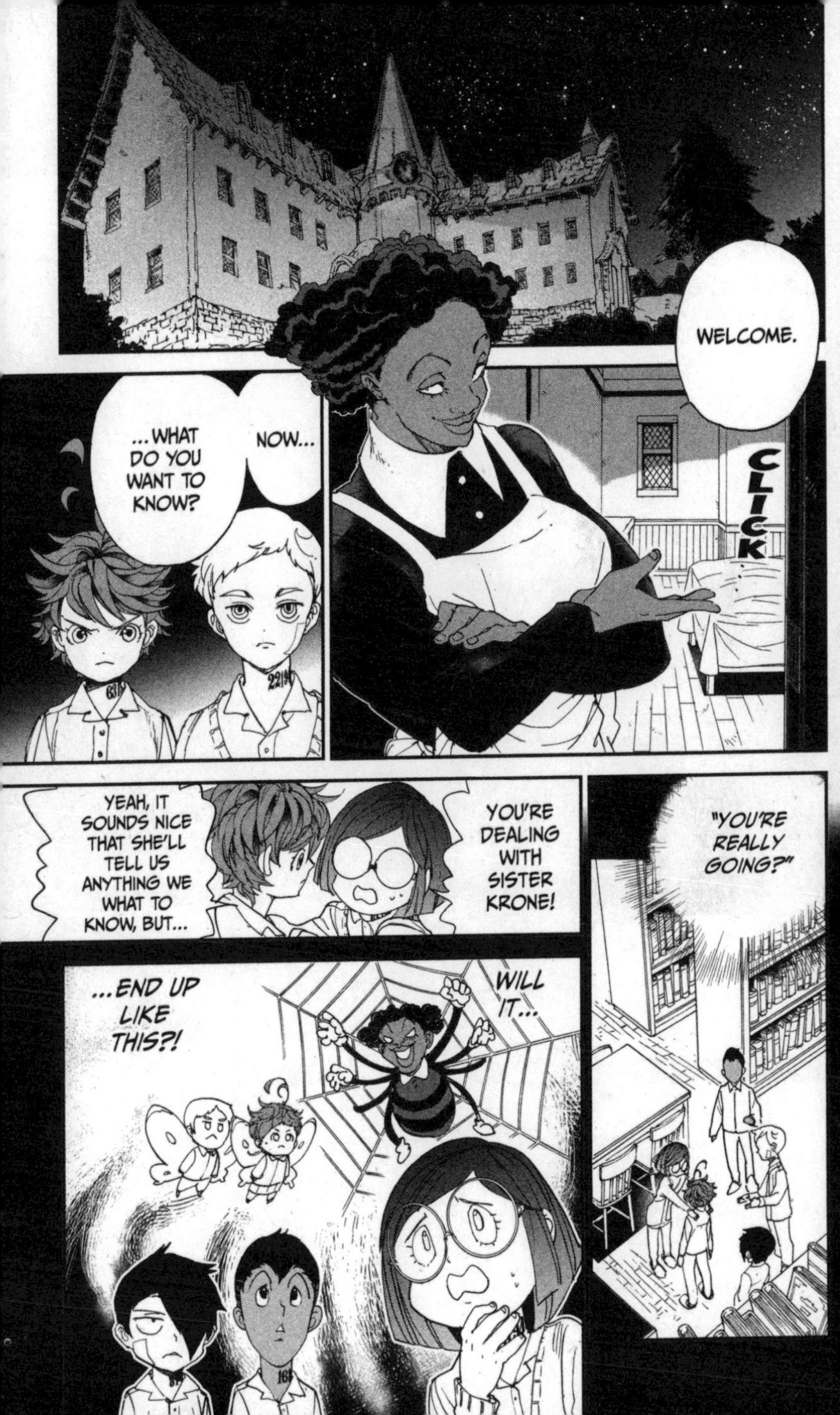
WELCOME.
CLICK
NOW...
...WHAT DO YOU WANT TO KNOW?
"YOU'RE REALLY GOING?"
YOU'RE DEALING WITH SISTER KRONE!
YEAH, IT SOUNDS NICE THAT SHE'LL TELL US ANYTHING WE WHAT TO KNOW, BUT...
WILL IT...
...END UP LIKE THIS?!

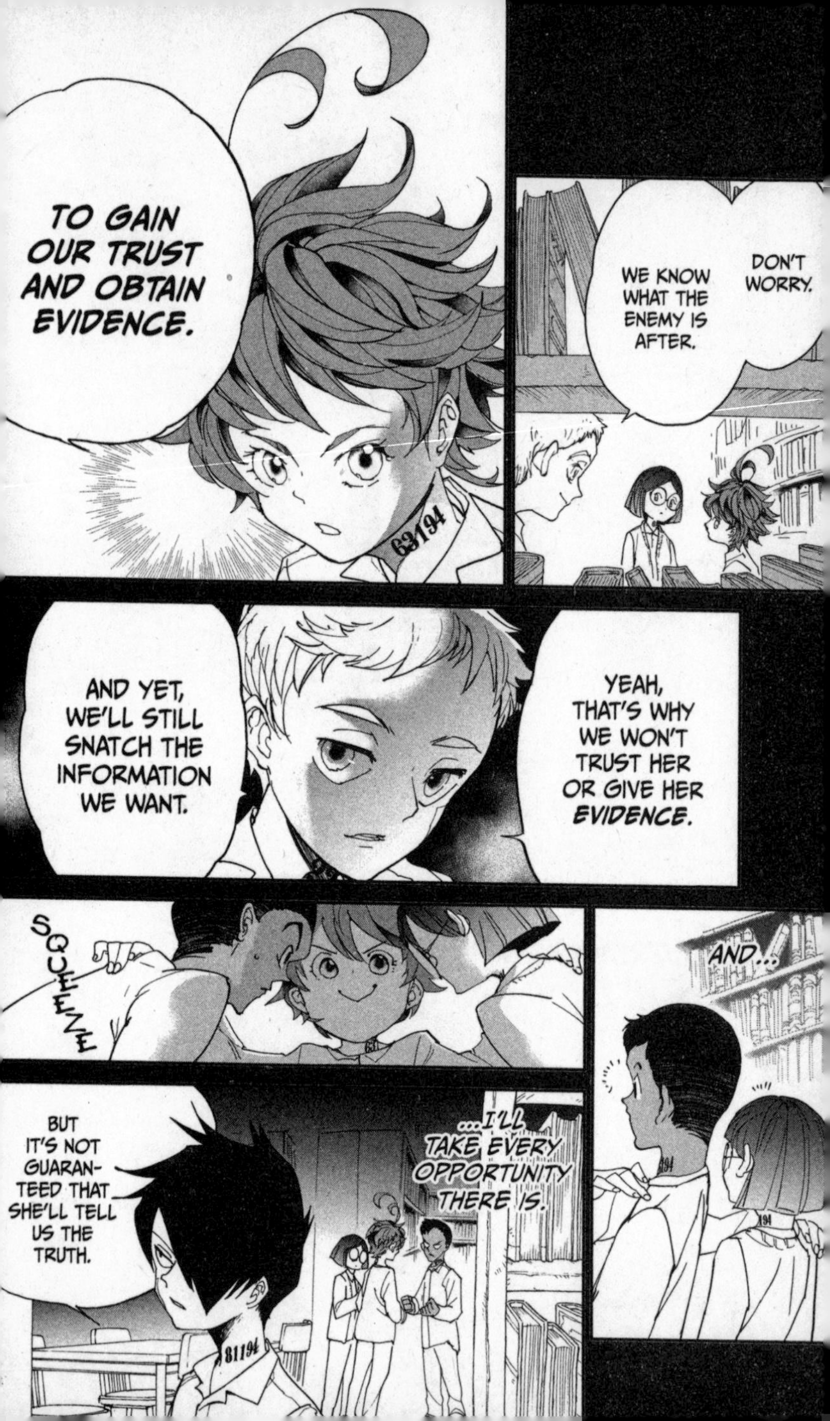
DON'T WORRY.
WE KNOW WHAT THE ENEMY IS AFTER.
TO GAIN OUR TRUST AND OBTAIN EVIDENCE.
YEAH, THAT'S WHY WE WON'T TRUST HER OR GIVE HER EVIDENCE.
AND YET, WE'LL STILL SNATCH THE INFORMATION WE WANT.
AND...
SQUEEZE
...I'LL TAKE EVERY OPPORTUNITY THERE IS.
BUT IT'S NOT GUARAN-TEED THAT SHE'LL TELL US THE TRUTH.

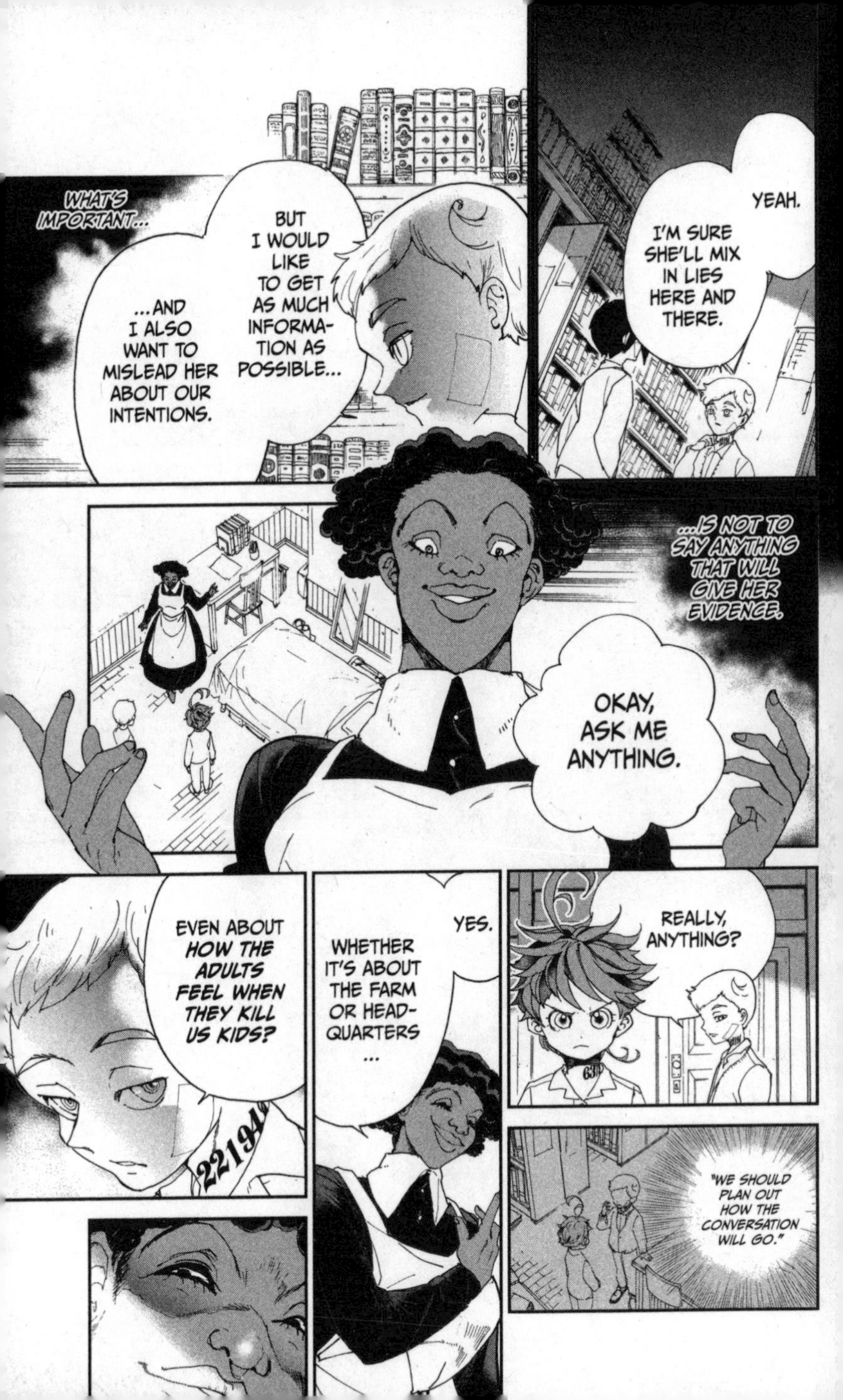
YEAH.
I'M SURE SHE'LL MIX IN LIES HERE AND THERE.
BUT I WOULD LIKE TO GET AS MUCH INFORMATION AS POSSIBLE...
...AND I ALSO WANT TO MISLEAD HER ABOUT OUR INTENTIONS.
WHAT'S IMPORTANT...
...IS NOT TO SAY ANYTHING THAT WILL GIVE HER EVIDENCE.
OKAY, ASK ME ANYTHING.
REALLY, ANYTHING?
"WE SHOULD PLAN OUT HOW THE CONVERSATION WILL GO."
YES.
WHETHER IT'S ABOUT THE FARM OR HEADQUARTERS ...
EVEN ABOUT *HOW THE ADULTS FEEL WHEN THEY KILL US KIDS?*
63
22194

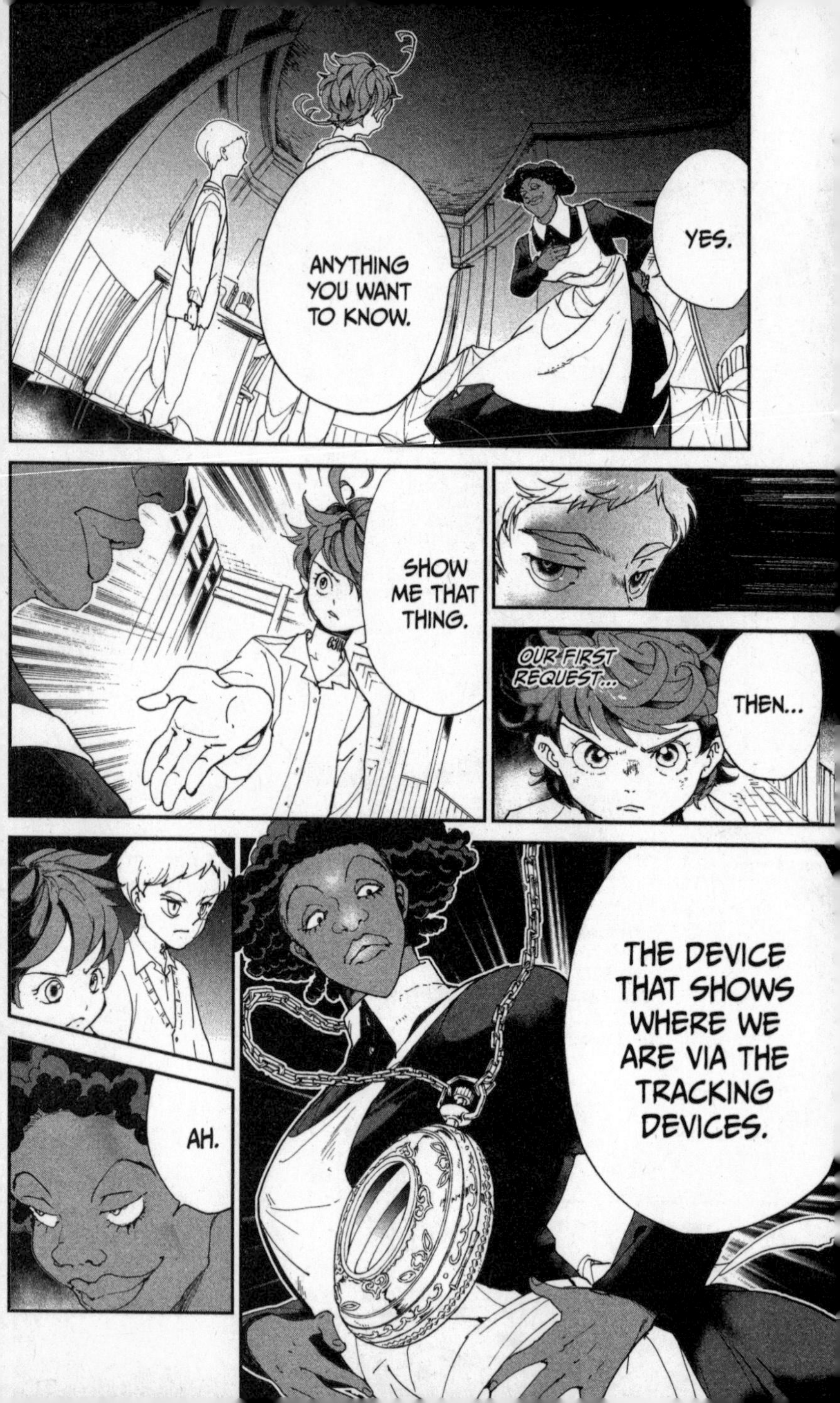

YES.
ANYTHING YOU WANT TO KNOW.
THEN...
OUR FIRST REQUEST...
SHOW ME THAT THING.
THE DEVICE THAT SHOWS WHERE WE ARE VIA THE TRACKING DEVICES.
AH.

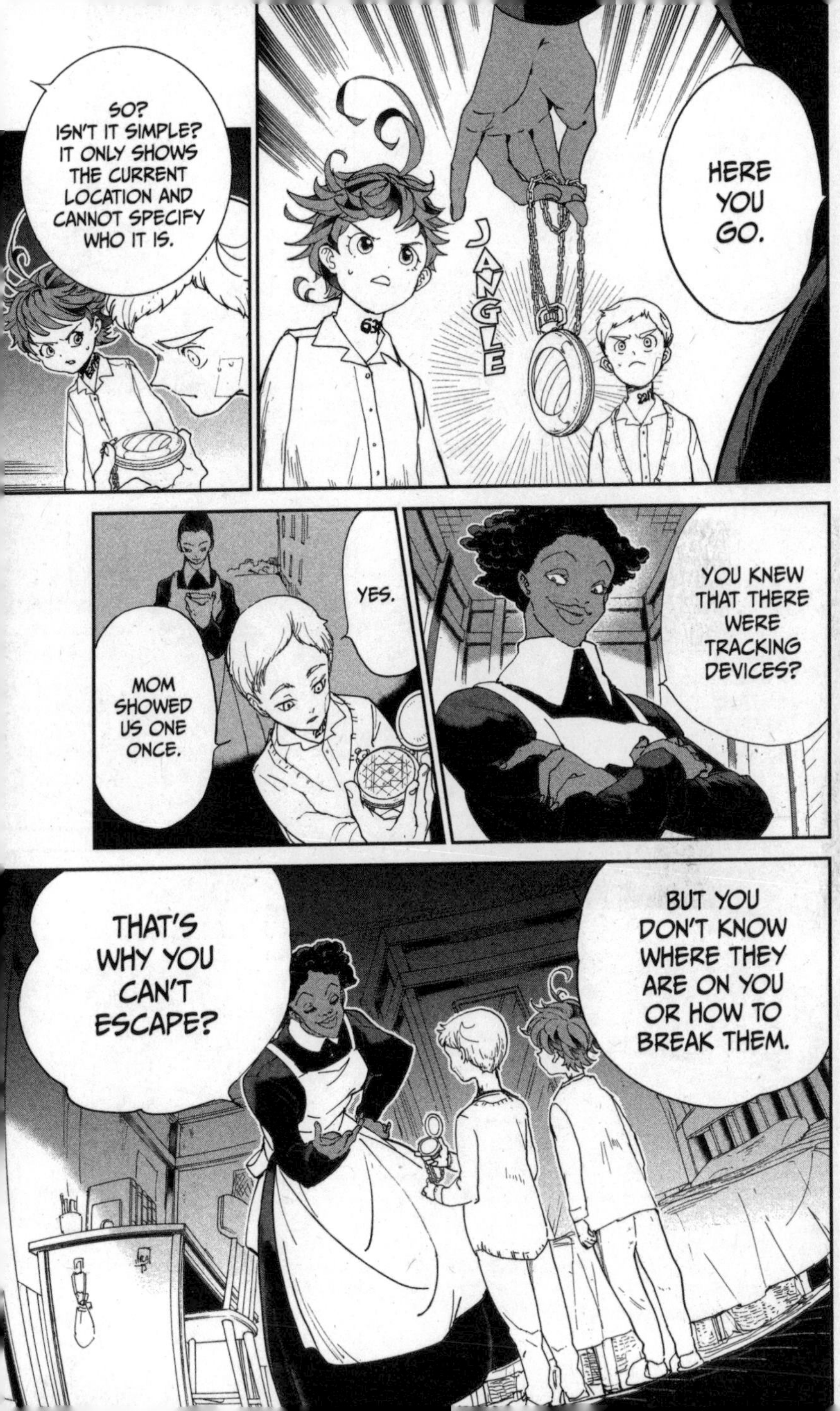
HERE YOU GO.
JANGLE
SO? ISN'T IT SIMPLE? IT ONLY SHOWS THE CURRENT LOCATION AND CANNOT SPECIFY WHO IT IS.
YOU KNEW THAT THERE WERE TRACKING DEVICES?
YES.
MOM SHOWED US ONE ONCE.
BUT YOU DON'T KNOW WHERE THEY ARE ON YOU OR HOW TO BREAK THEM.
THAT'S WHY YOU CAN'T ESCAPE?

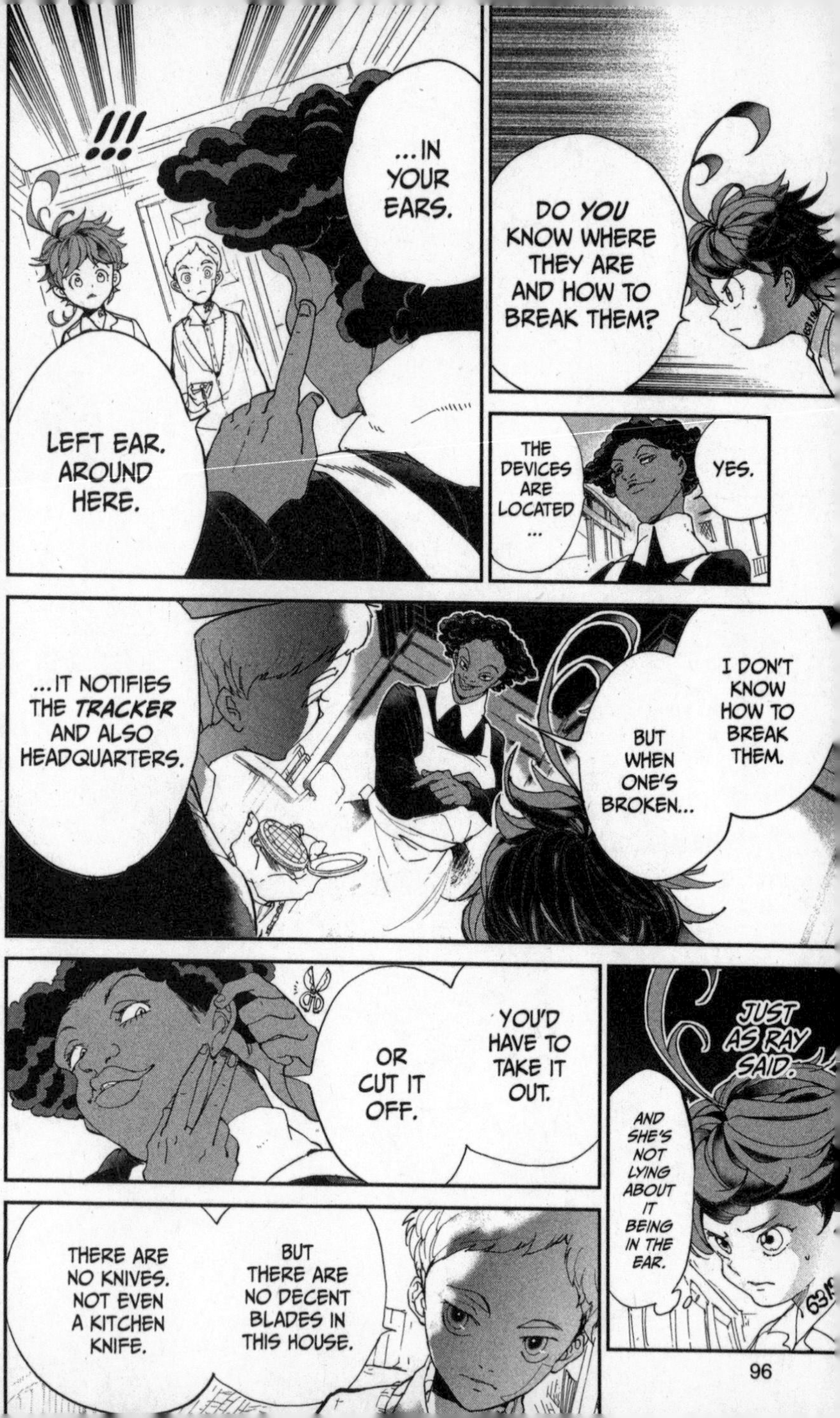
DO *YOU* KNOW WHERE THEY ARE AND HOW TO BREAK THEM?
YES.
THE DEVICES ARE LOCATED...
...IN YOUR EARS.
!!!
LEFT EAR. AROUND HERE.
I DON'T KNOW HOW TO BREAK THEM.
BUT WHEN ONE'S BROKEN...
...IT NOTIFIES THE *TRACKER* AND ALSO HEADQUARTERS.
JUST AS RAY SAID.
AND SHE'S NOT LYING ABOUT IT BEING IN THE EAR.
YOU'D HAVE TO TAKE IT OUT.
OR CUT IT OFF.
BUT THERE ARE NO DECENT BLADES IN THIS HOUSE.
THERE ARE NO KNIVES. NOT EVEN A KITCHEN KNIFE.

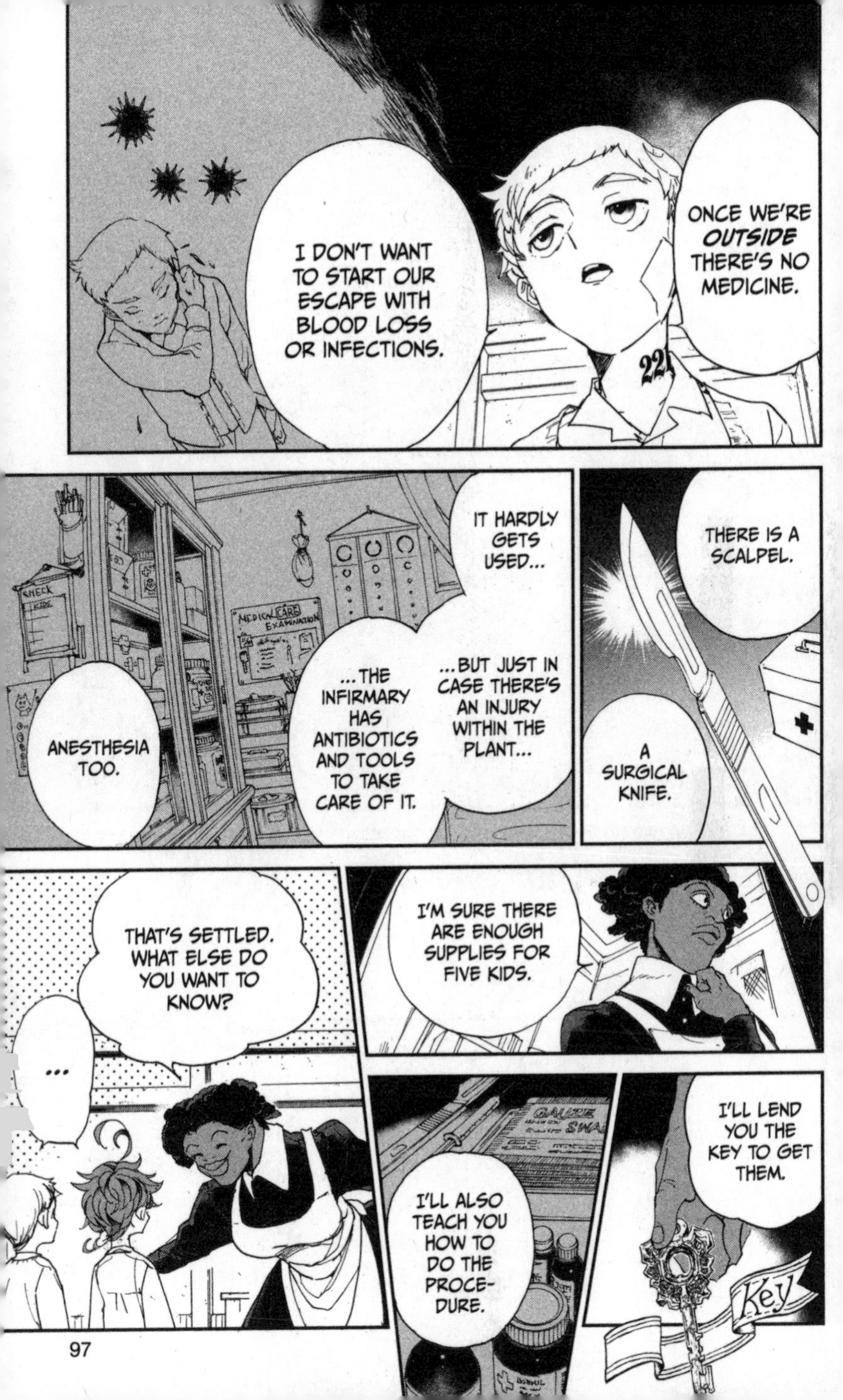
ONCE WE'RE *OUTSIDE* THERE'S NO MEDICINE.
I DON'T WANT TO START OUR ESCAPE WITH BLOOD LOSS OR INFECTIONS.
THERE IS A SCALPEL.
A SURGICAL KNIFE.
IT HARDLY GETS USED...
...BUT JUST IN CASE THERE'S AN INJURY WITHIN THE PLANT...
...THE INFIRMARY HAS ANTIBIOTICS AND TOOLS TO TAKE CARE OF IT.
ANESTHESIA TOO.
I'M SURE THERE ARE ENOUGH SUPPLIES FOR FIVE KIDS.
I'LL LEND YOU THE KEY TO GET THEM.
Key
I'LL ALSO TEACH YOU HOW TO DO THE PROCE-DURE.
THAT'S SETTLED. WHAT ELSE DO YOU WANT TO KNOW?
...

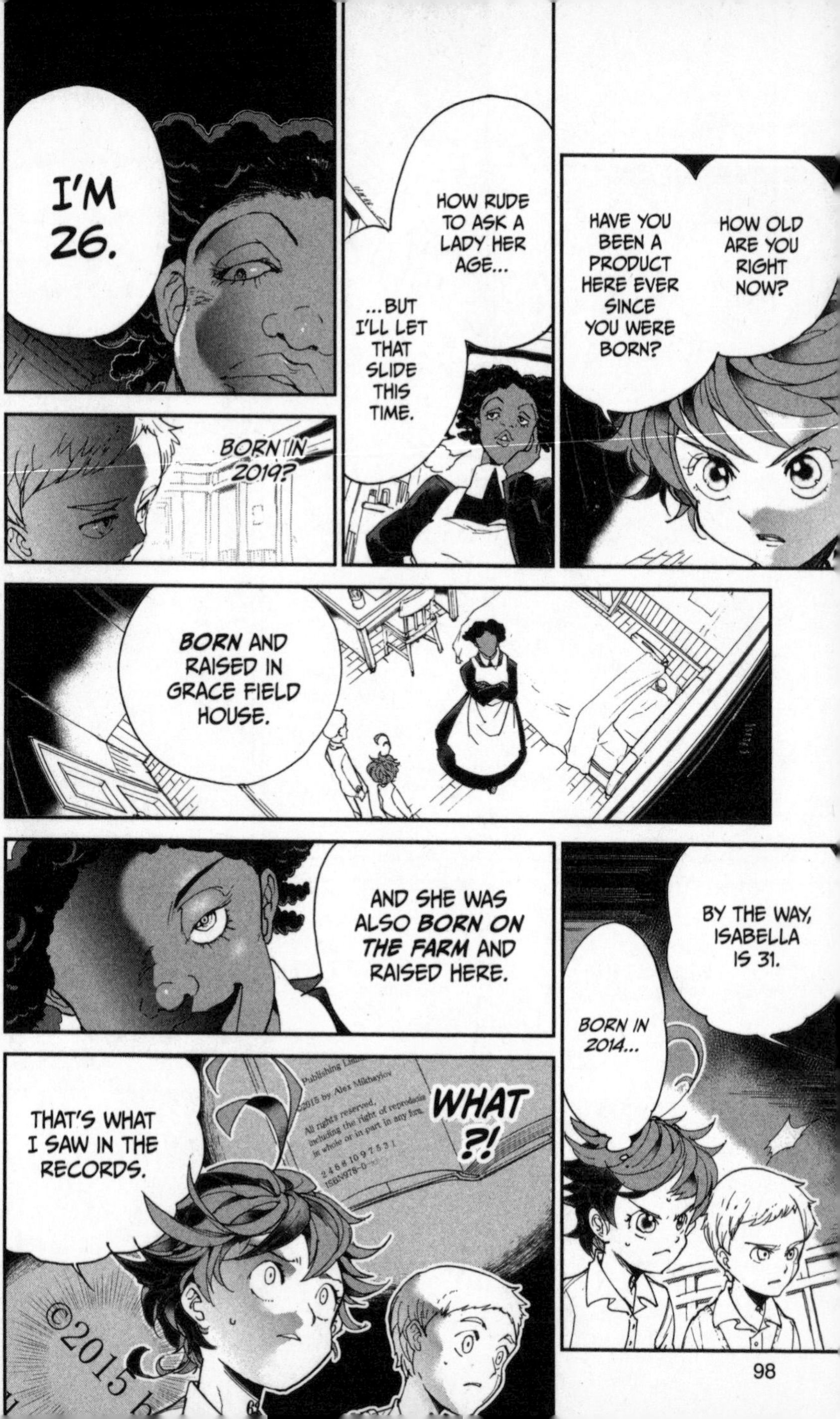
HOW OLD ARE YOU RIGHT NOW?
HAVE YOU BEEN A PRODUCT HERE EVER SINCE YOU WERE BORN?
HOW RUDE TO ASK A LADY HER AGE...
...BUT I'LL LET THAT SLIDE THIS TIME.
I'M 26.
BORN IN 2019?
BORN AND RAISED IN GRACE FIELD HOUSE.
BY THE WAY, ISABELLA IS 31.
BORN IN 2014...
AND SHE WAS ALSO BORN ON THE FARM AND RAISED HERE.
WHAT ?!
THAT'S WHAT I SAW IN THE RECORDS.

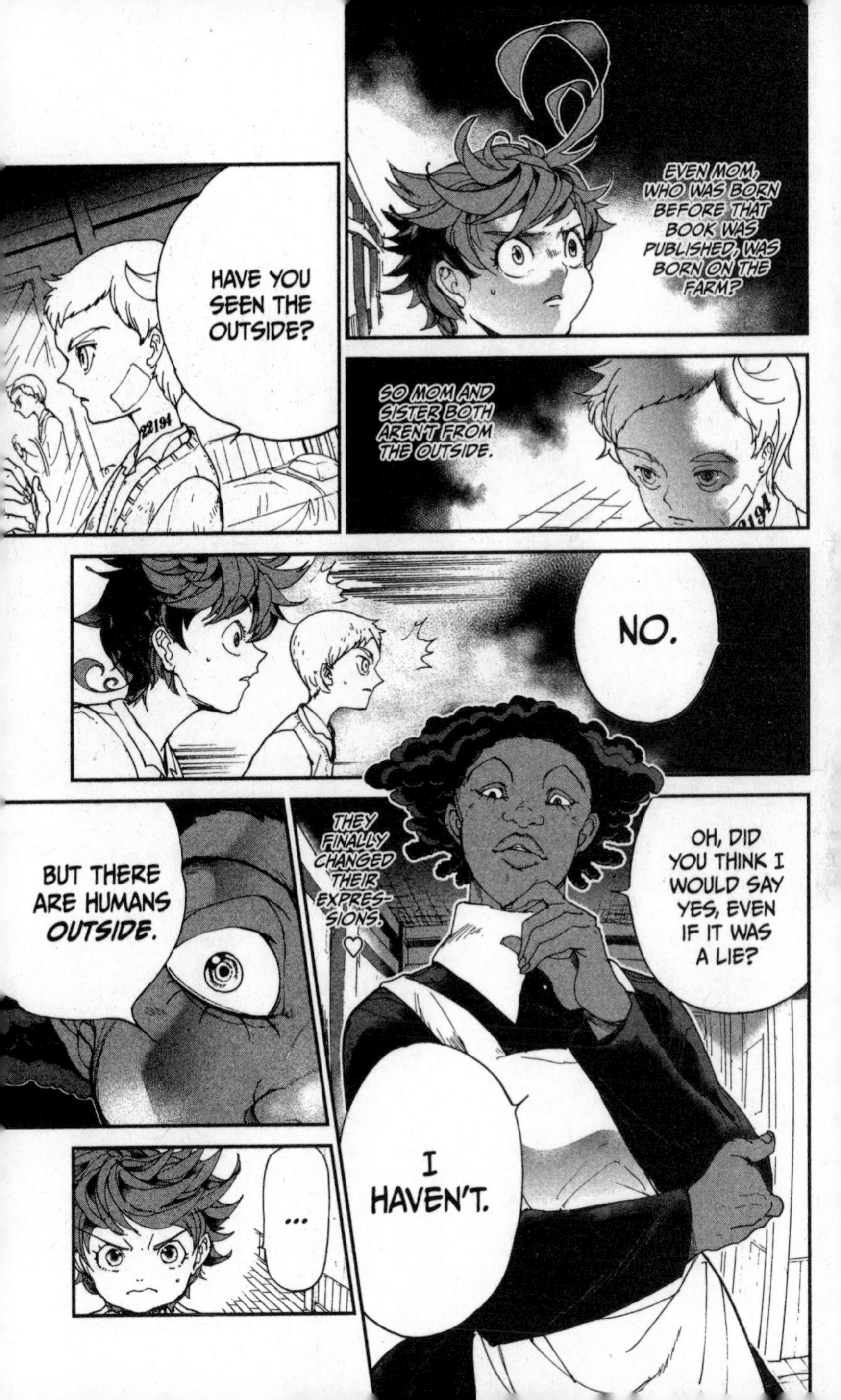
EVEN MOM, WHO WAS BORN BEFORE THAT BOOK WAS PUBLISHED, WAS BORN ON THE FARM?
SO MOM AND SISTER BOTH AREN'T FROM THE OUTSIDE.
HAVE YOU SEEN THE OUTSIDE?
NO.
OH, DID YOU THINK I WOULD SAY YES, EVEN IF IT WAS A LIE?
THEY FINALLY CHANGED THEIR EXPRESSIONS. ♡
I HAVEN'T.
BUT THERE ARE HUMANS OUTSIDE.
...

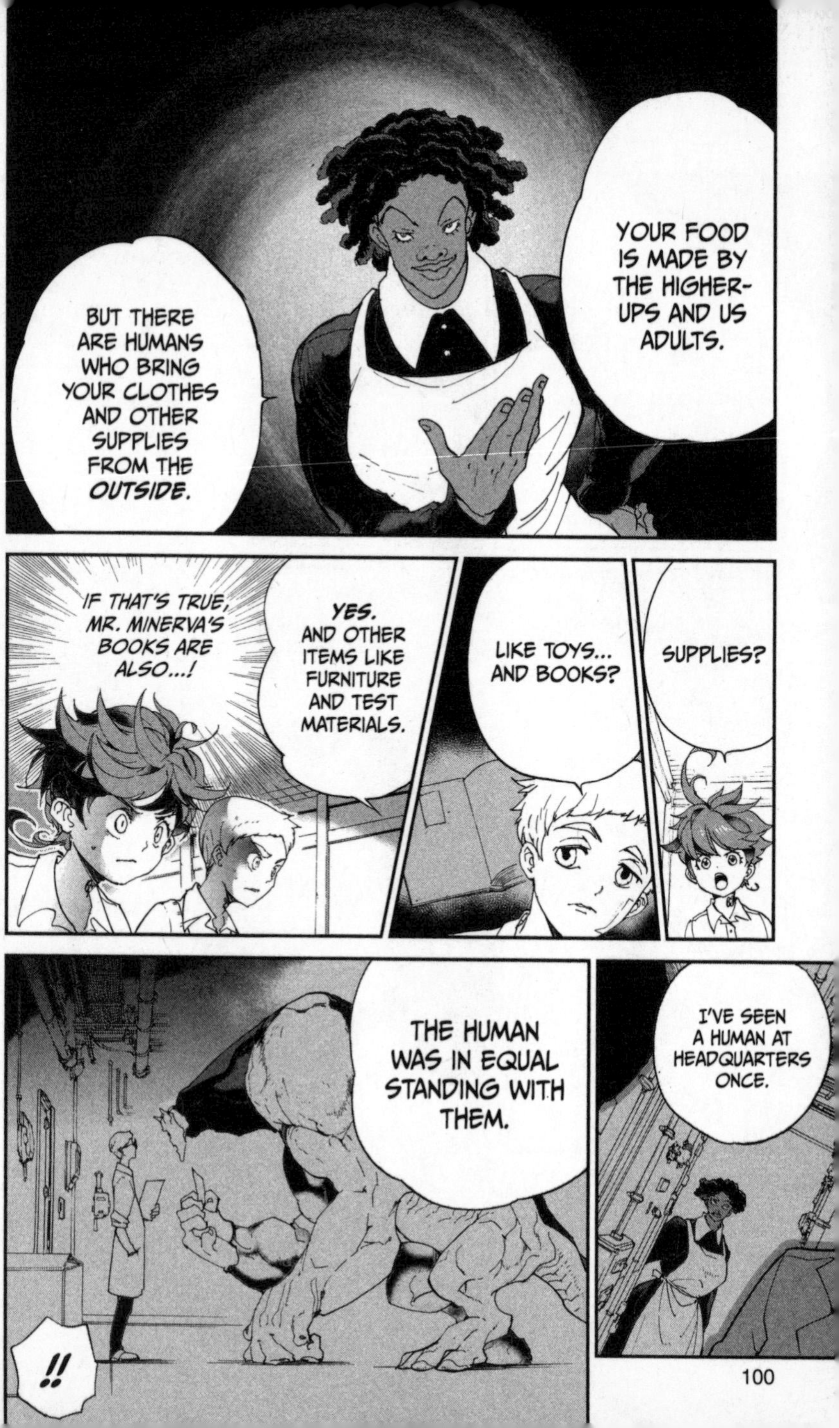
YOUR FOOD IS MADE BY THE HIGHER-UPS AND US ADULTS.
BUT THERE ARE HUMANS WHO BRING YOUR CLOTHES AND OTHER SUPPLIES FROM THE *OUTSIDE*.
SUPPLIES?
LIKE TOYS... AND BOOKS?
YES. AND OTHER ITEMS LIKE FURNITURE AND TEST MATERIALS.
IF THAT'S TRUE, MR. MINERVA'S BOOKS ARE ALSO...!
I'VE SEEN A HUMAN AT HEADQUARTERS ONCE.
THE HUMAN WAS IN EQUAL STANDING WITH THEM.
!!

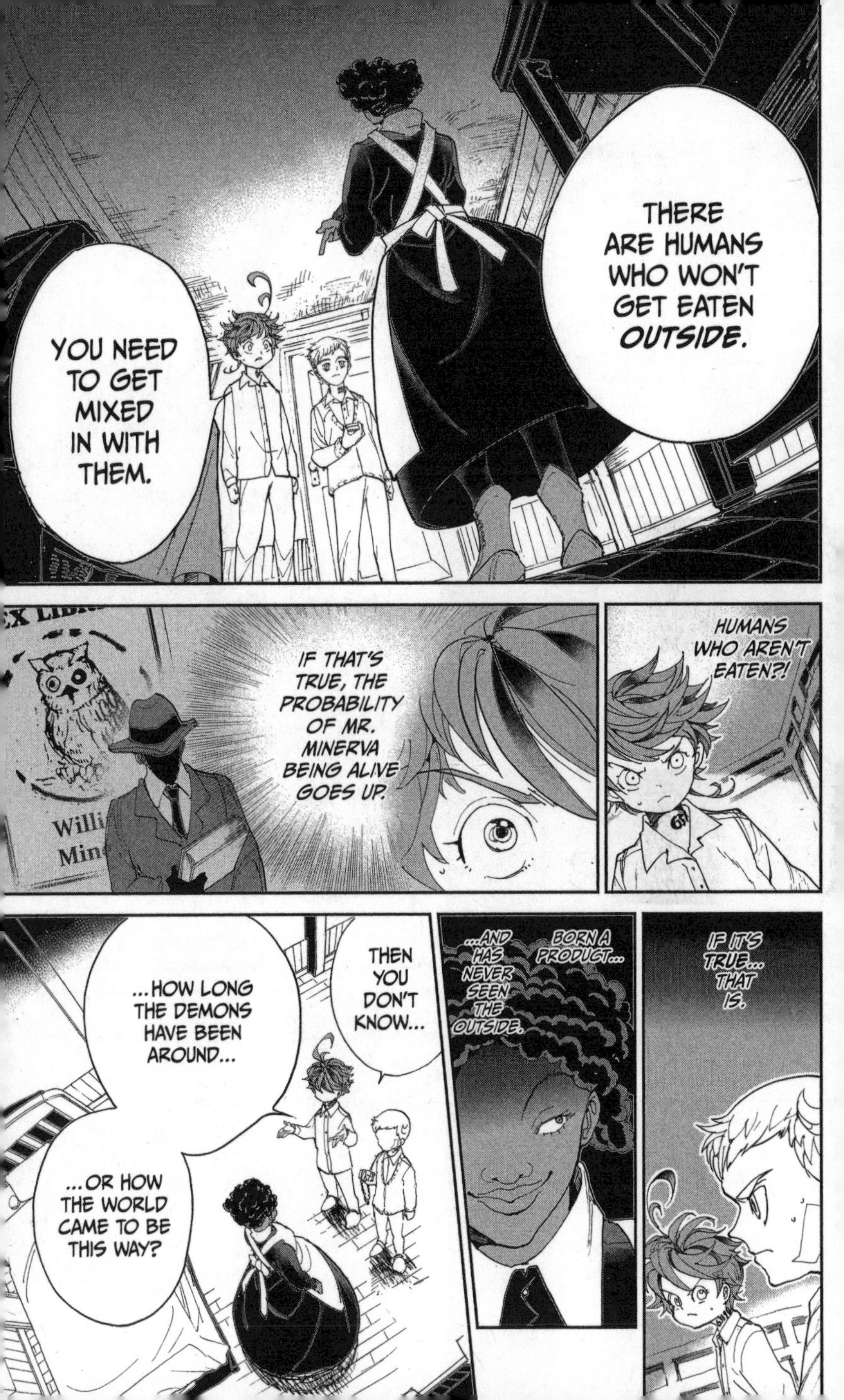
THERE ARE HUMANS WHO WON'T GET EATEN *OUTSIDE*.
YOU NEED TO GET MIXED IN WITH THEM.
HUMANS WHO AREN'T EATEN?!
IF THAT'S TRUE, THE PROBABILITY OF MR. MINERVA BEING ALIVE GOES UP.
IF IT'S TRUE... THAT IS.
BORN A PRODUCT...
...AND HAS NEVER SEEN THE OUTSIDE.
THEN YOU DON'T KNOW...
...HOW LONG THE DEMONS HAVE BEEN AROUND...
...OR HOW THE WORLD CAME TO BE THIS WAY?

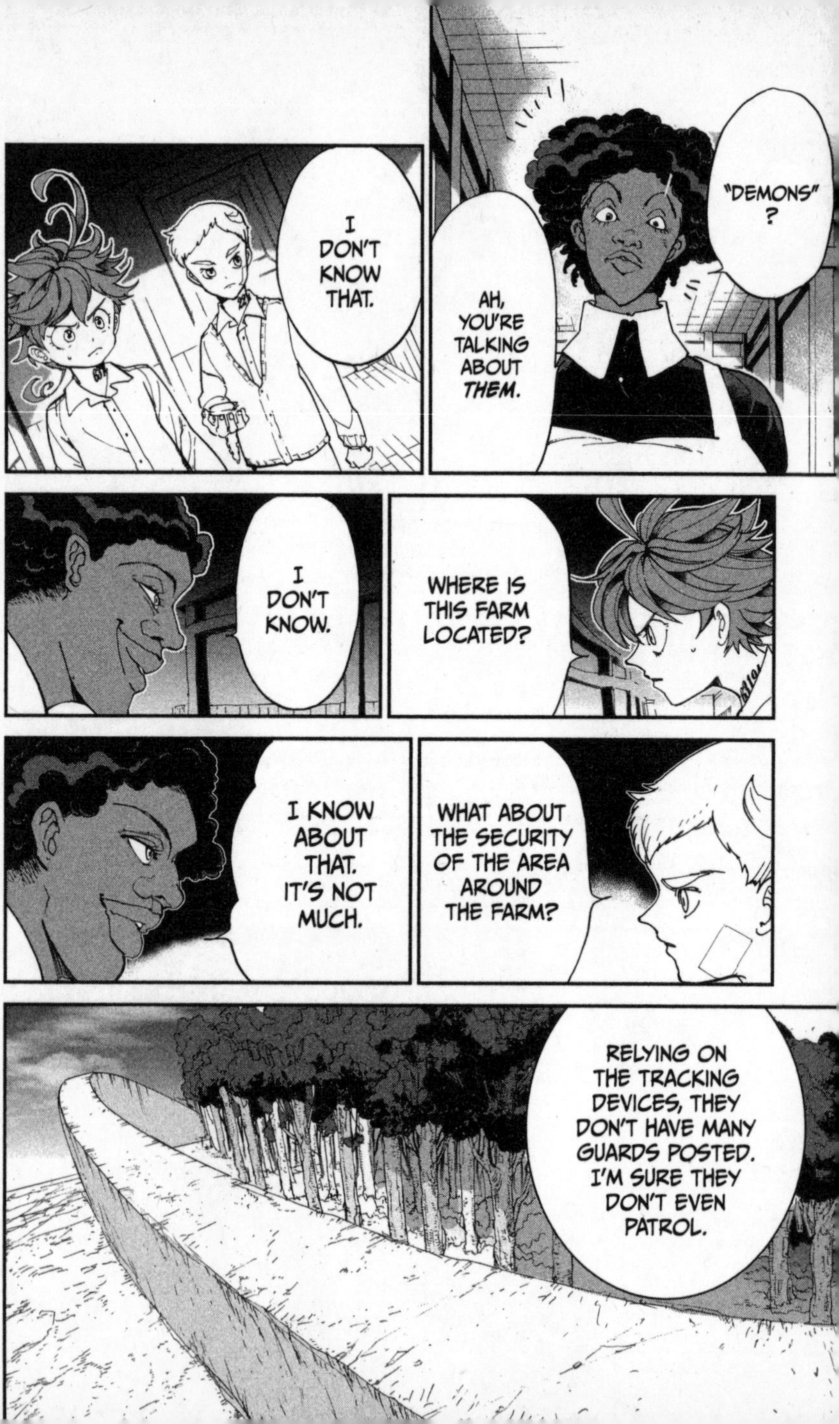
"DEMONS"?
AH, YOU'RE TALKING ABOUT *THEM*.
I DON'T KNOW THAT.
WHERE IS THIS FARM LOCATED?
I DON'T KNOW.
WHAT ABOUT THE SECURITY OF THE AREA AROUND THE FARM?
I KNOW ABOUT THAT. IT'S NOT MUCH.
RELYING ON THE TRACKING DEVICES, THEY DON'T HAVE MANY GUARDS POSTED. I'M SURE THEY DON'T EVEN PATROL.

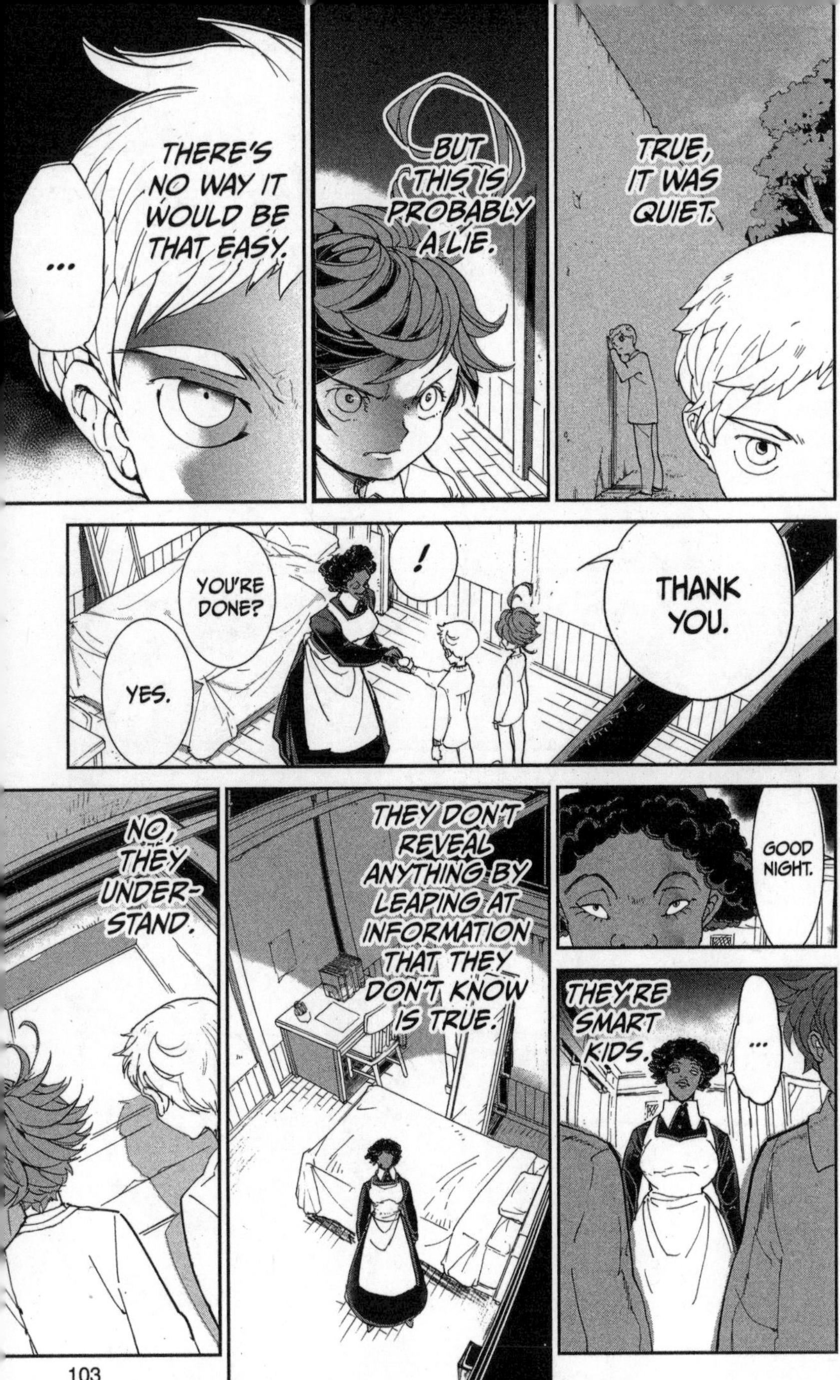
TRUE, IT WAS QUIET.
BUT THIS IS PROBABLY A LIE.
THERE'S NO WAY IT WOULD BE THAT EASY.
...
THANK YOU.
!
YOU'RE DONE?
YES.
GOOD NIGHT.
...
THEY'RE SMART KIDS.
THEY DON'T REVEAL ANYTHING BY LEAPING AT INFORMATION THAT THEY DON'T KNOW IS TRUE.
NO, THEY UNDER-STAND.

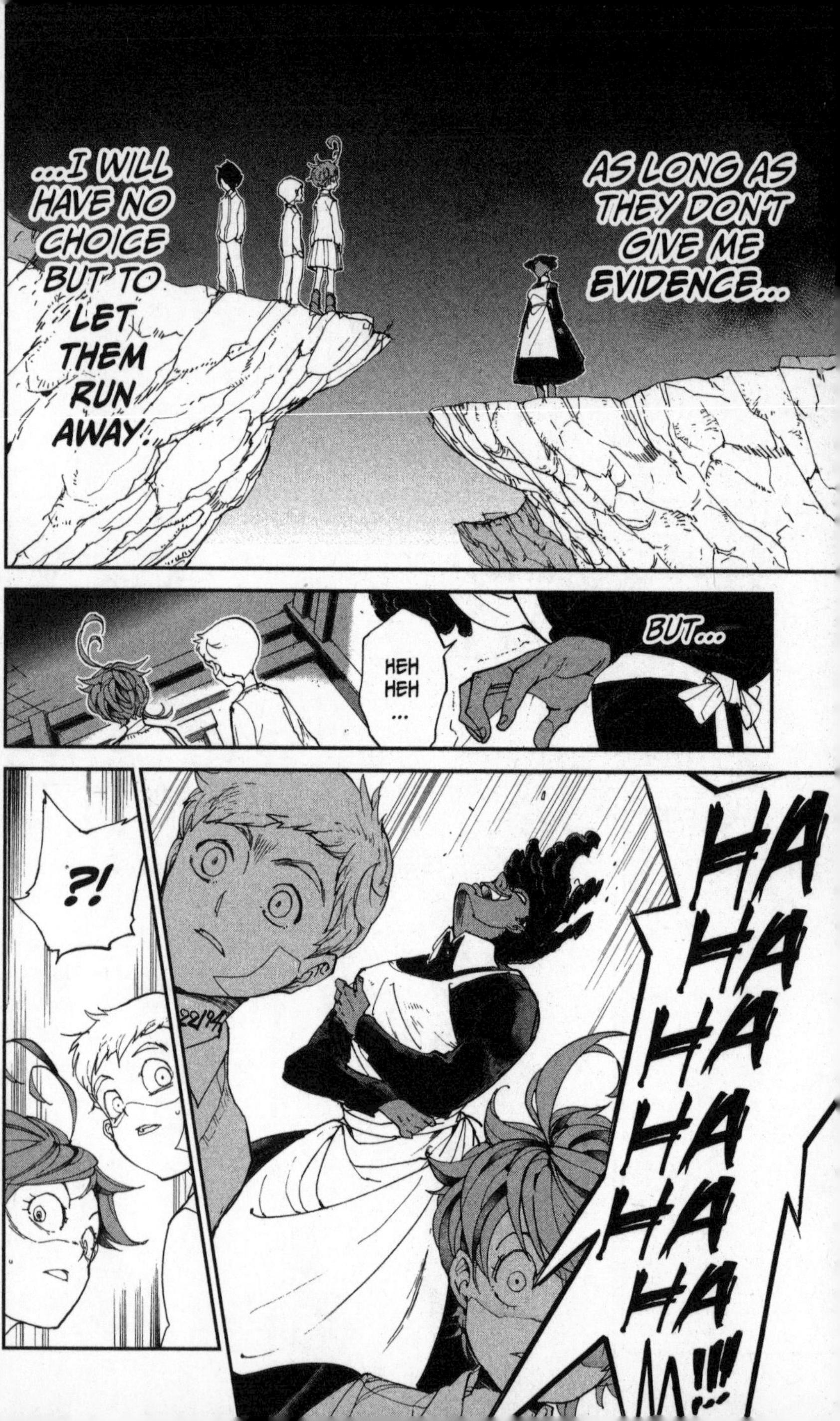
AS LONG AS THEY DON'T GIVE ME EVIDENCE...
...I WILL HAVE NO CHOICE BUT TO LET THEM RUN AWAY.
BUT...
HEH HEH ...
HAHAHAHAHAHAHAHAHAHA!!!
?!
22194

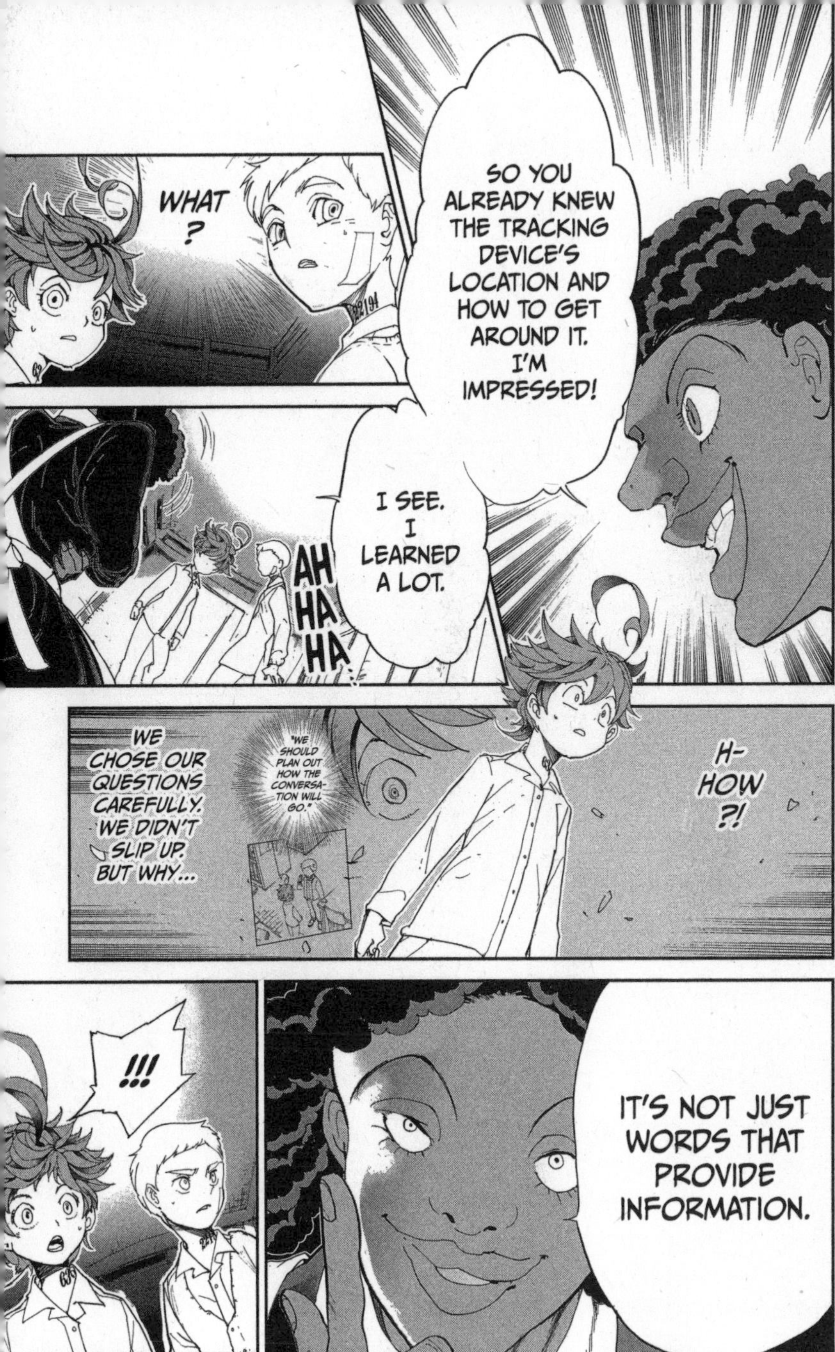
SO YOU ALREADY KNEW THE TRACKING DEVICE'S LOCATION AND HOW TO GET AROUND IT. I'M IMPRESSED!
WHAT ?
I SEE. I LEARNED A LOT.
AH HA HA...
H-HOW ?!
"WE SHOULD PLAN OUT HOW THE CONVERSATION WILL GO."
WE CHOSE OUR QUESTIONS CAREFULLY. WE DIDN'T SLIP UP. BUT WHY...
IT'S NOT JUST WORDS THAT PROVIDE INFORMATION.
!!!

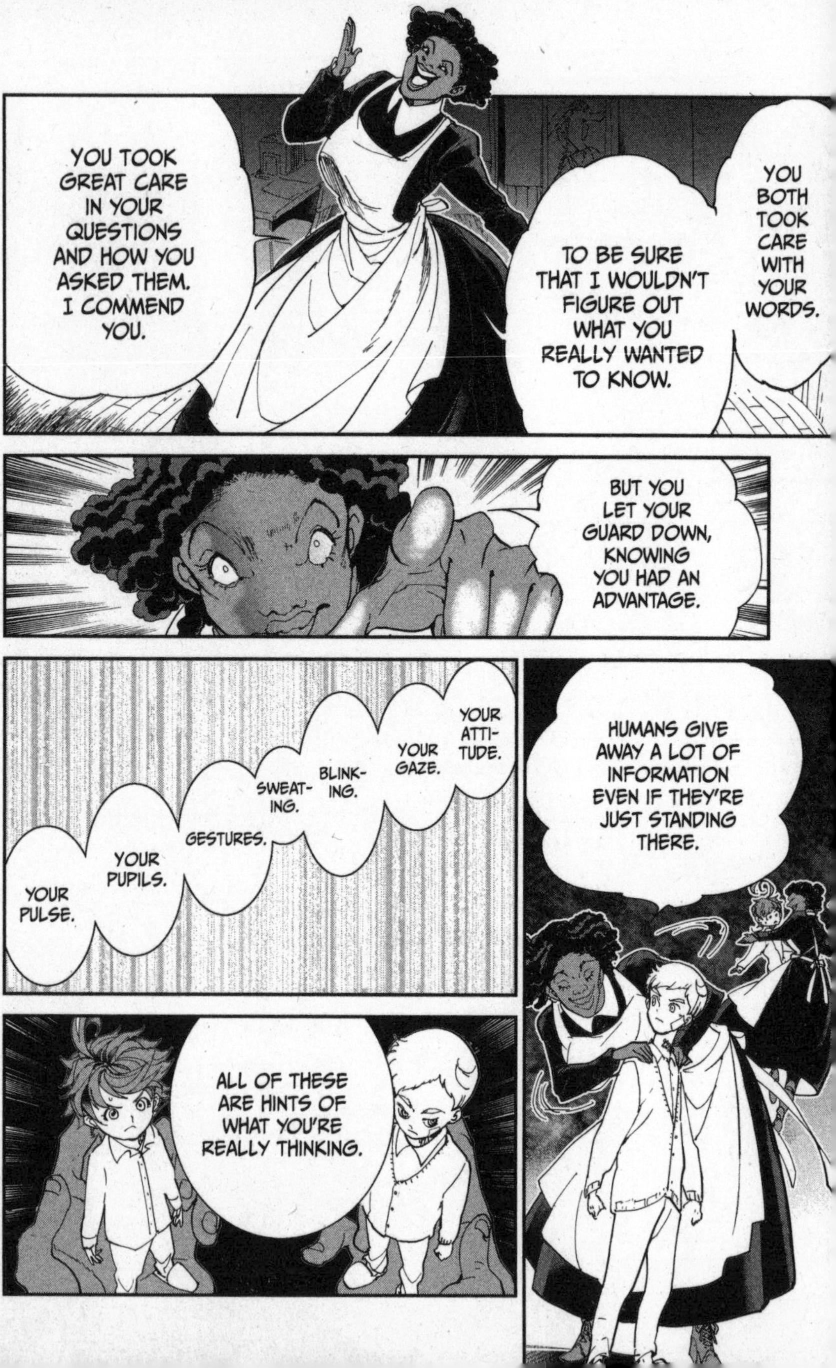
YOU BOTH TOOK CARE WITH YOUR WORDS.
TO BE SURE THAT I WOULDN'T FIGURE OUT WHAT YOU REALLY WANTED TO KNOW.
YOU TOOK GREAT CARE IN YOUR QUESTIONS AND HOW YOU ASKED THEM. I COMMEND YOU.
BUT YOU LET YOUR GUARD DOWN, KNOWING YOU HAD AN ADVANTAGE.
HUMANS GIVE AWAY A LOT OF INFORMATION EVEN IF THEY'RE JUST STANDING THERE.
YOUR ATTI-TUDE.
YOUR GAZE.
BLINK-ING.
SWEAT-ING.
GESTURES.
YOUR PUPILS.
YOUR PULSE.
ALL OF THESE ARE HINTS OF WHAT YOU'RE REALLY THINKING.

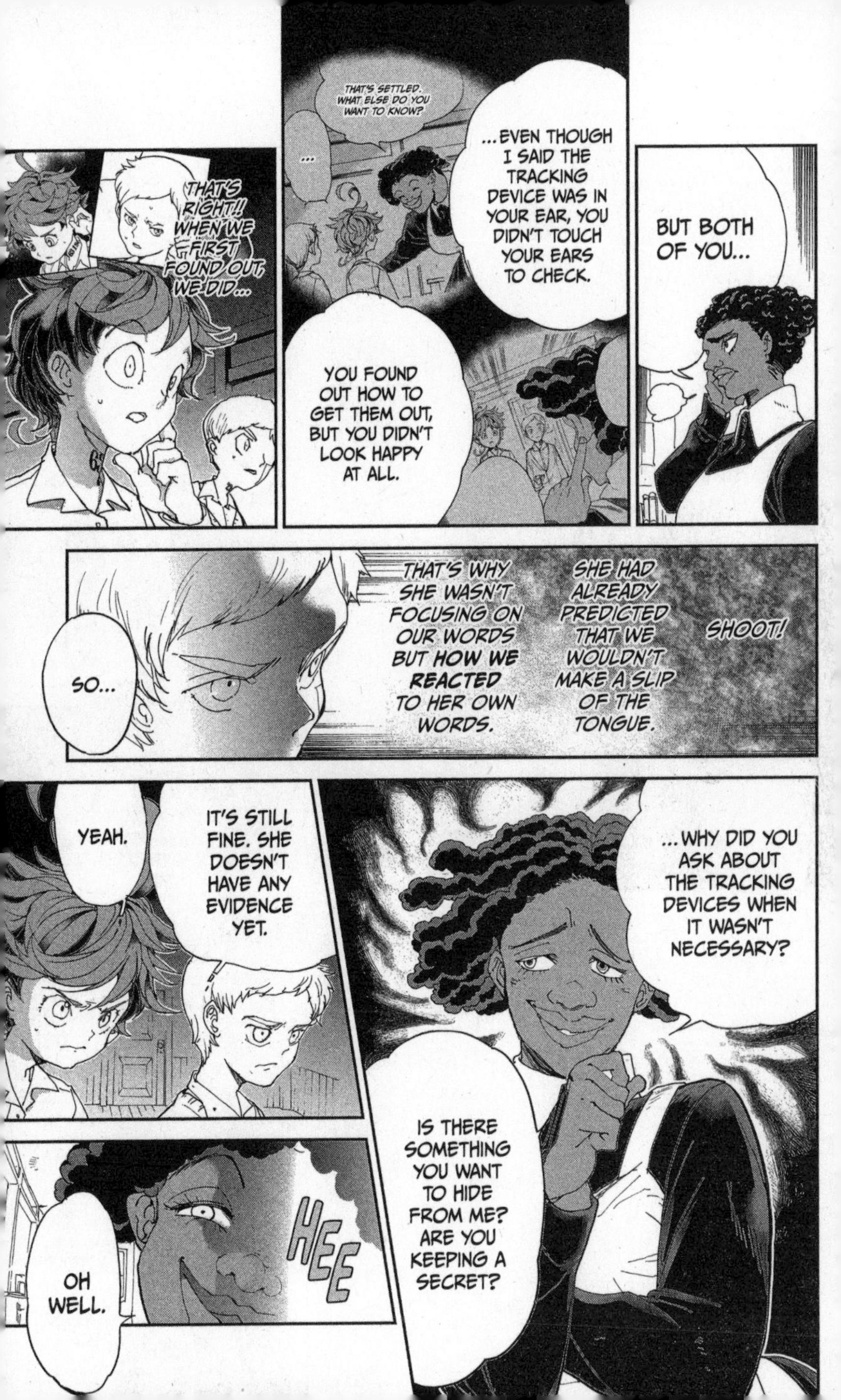
BUT BOTH OF YOU...
THAT'S SETTLED. WHAT ELSE DO YOU WANT TO KNOW?
...
...EVEN THOUGH I SAID THE TRACKING DEVICE WAS IN YOUR EAR, YOU DIDN'T TOUCH YOUR EARS TO CHECK.
YOU FOUND OUT HOW TO GET THEM OUT, BUT YOU DIDN'T LOOK HAPPY AT ALL.
THAT'S RIGHT!! WHEN WE FIRST FOUND OUT, WE DID...
SHOOT!
SHE HAD ALREADY PREDICTED THAT WE WOULDN'T MAKE A SLIP OF THE TONGUE.
THAT'S WHY SHE WASN'T FOCUSING ON OUR WORDS BUT HOW WE REACTED TO HER OWN WORDS.
SO...
...WHY DID YOU ASK ABOUT THE TRACKING DEVICES WHEN IT WASN'T NECESSARY?
IS THERE SOMETHING YOU WANT TO HIDE FROM ME? ARE YOU KEEPING A SECRET?
IT'S STILL FINE. SHE DOESN'T HAVE ANY EVIDENCE YET.
YEAH.
HEE
OH WELL.

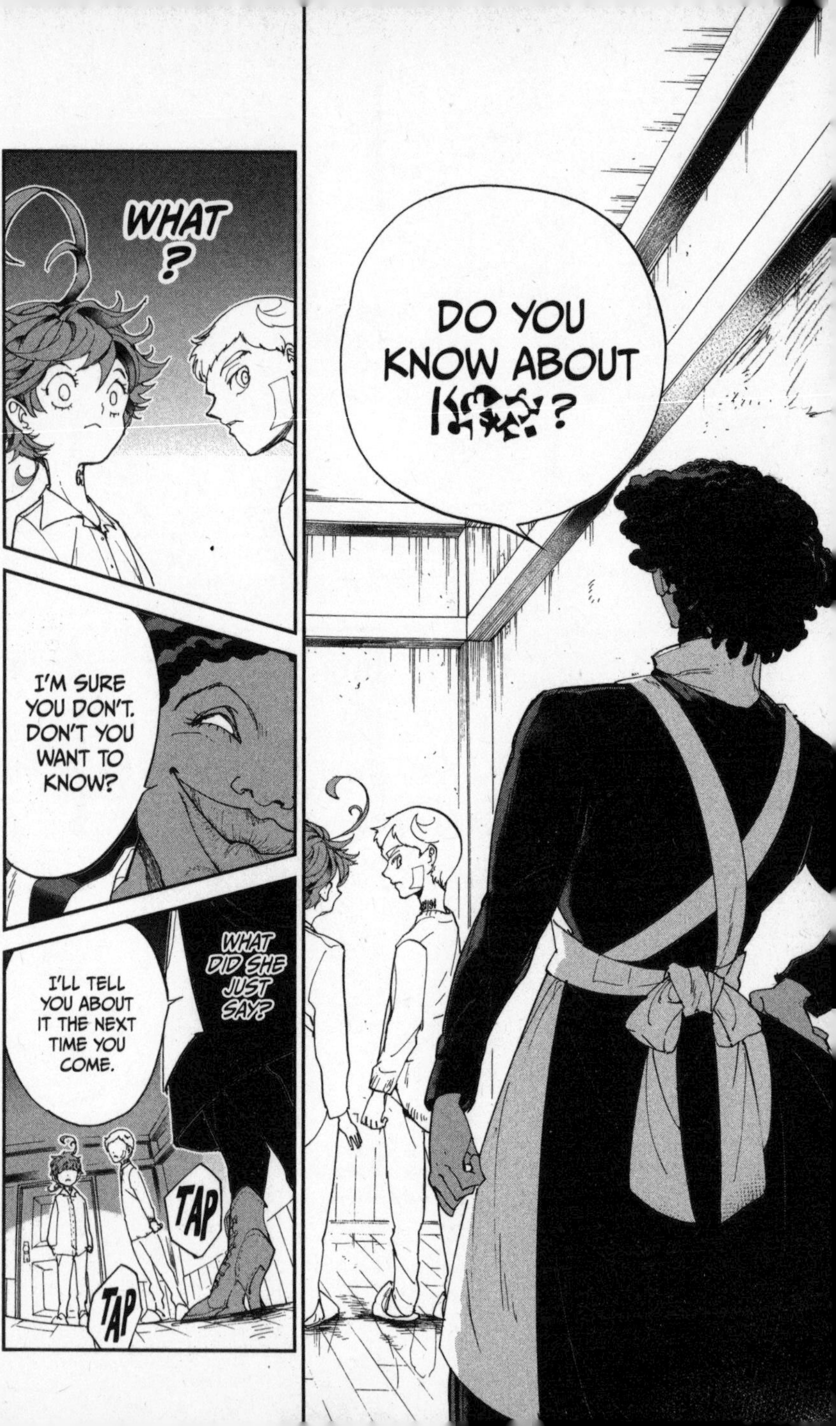
DO YOU KNOW ABOUT ?
WHAT ?
I'M SURE YOU DON'T. DON'T YOU WANT TO KNOW?
WHAT DID SHE JUST SAY?
I'LL TELL YOU ABOUT IT THE NEXT TIME YOU COME.
TAP
TAP

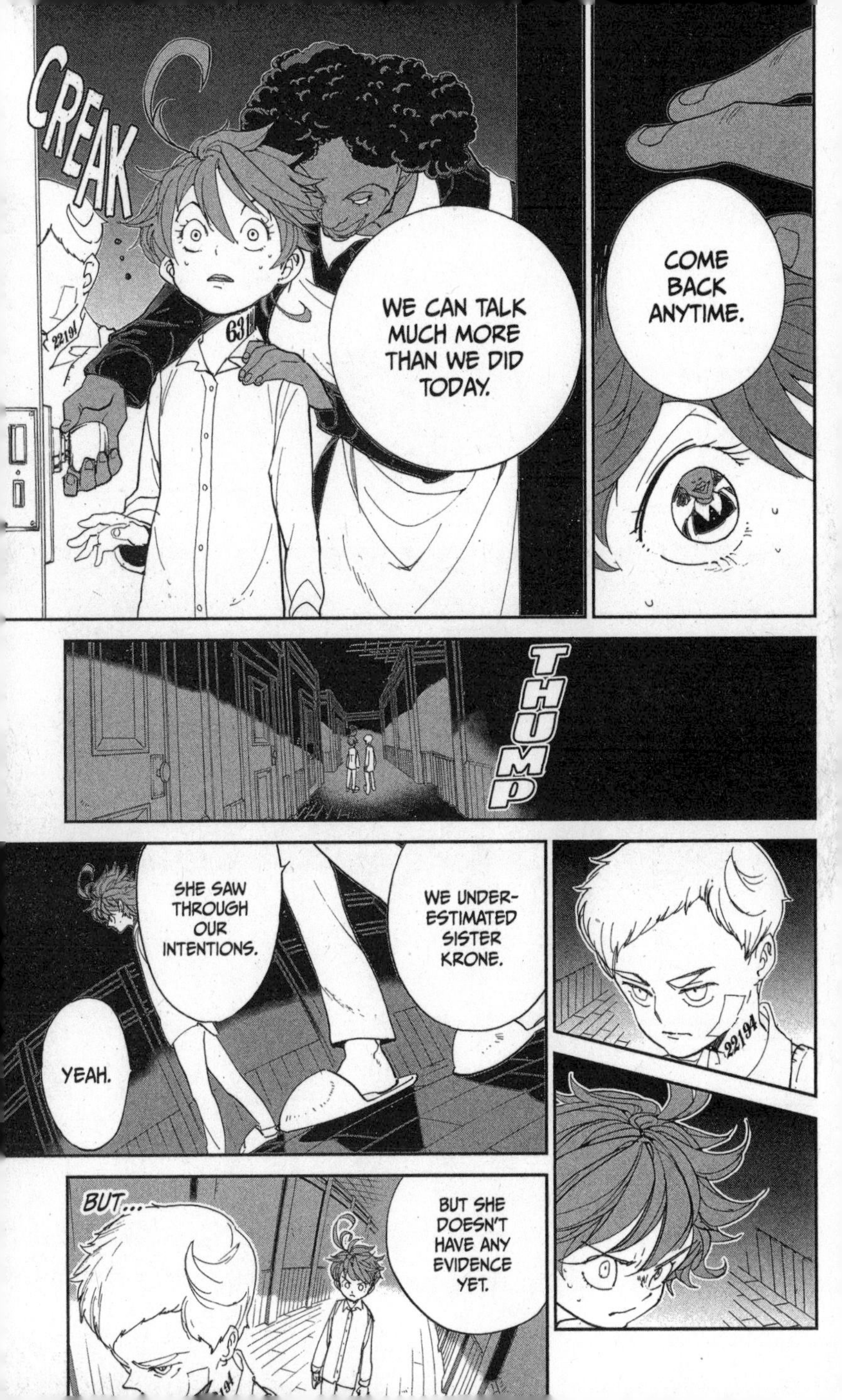
COME BACK ANYTIME.
CREAK
WE CAN TALK MUCH MORE THAN WE DID TODAY.
THUMP
WE UNDER-ESTIMATED SISTER KRONE.
SHE SAW THROUGH OUR INTENTIONS.
YEAH.
BUT...
BUT SHE DOESN'T HAVE ANY EVIDENCE YET.

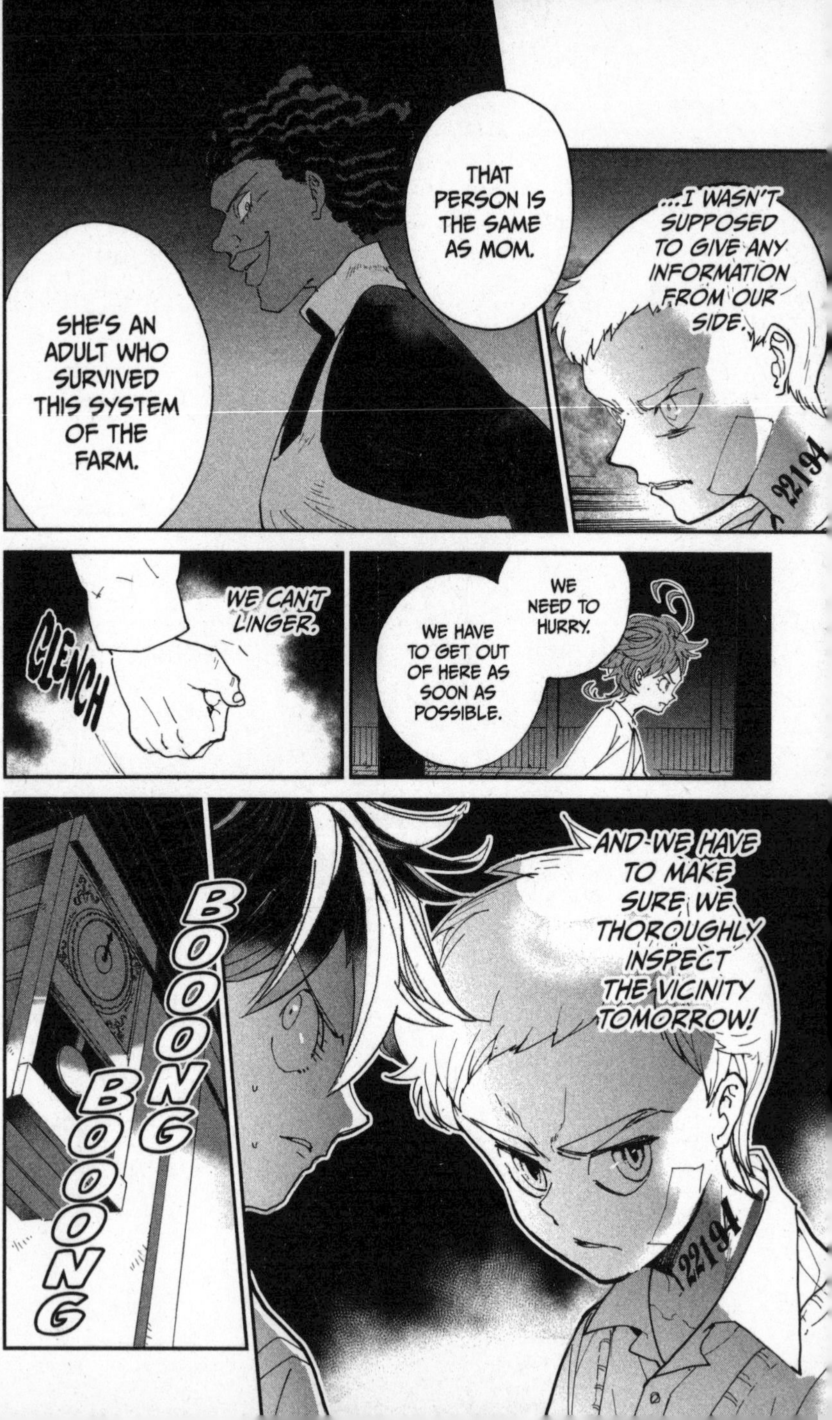
...I WASN'T SUPPOSED TO GIVE ANY INFORMATION FROM OUR SIDE.
22194
THAT PERSON IS THE SAME AS MOM.
SHE'S AN ADULT WHO SURVIVED THIS SYSTEM OF THE FARM.
WE NEED TO HURRY.
WE HAVE TO GET OUT OF HERE AS SOON AS POSSIBLE.
WE CAN'T LINGER.
CLENCH
AND WE HAVE TO MAKE SURE WE THOROUGHLY INSPECT THE VICINITY TOMORROW!
22194
BOOOONG
BOOOONG

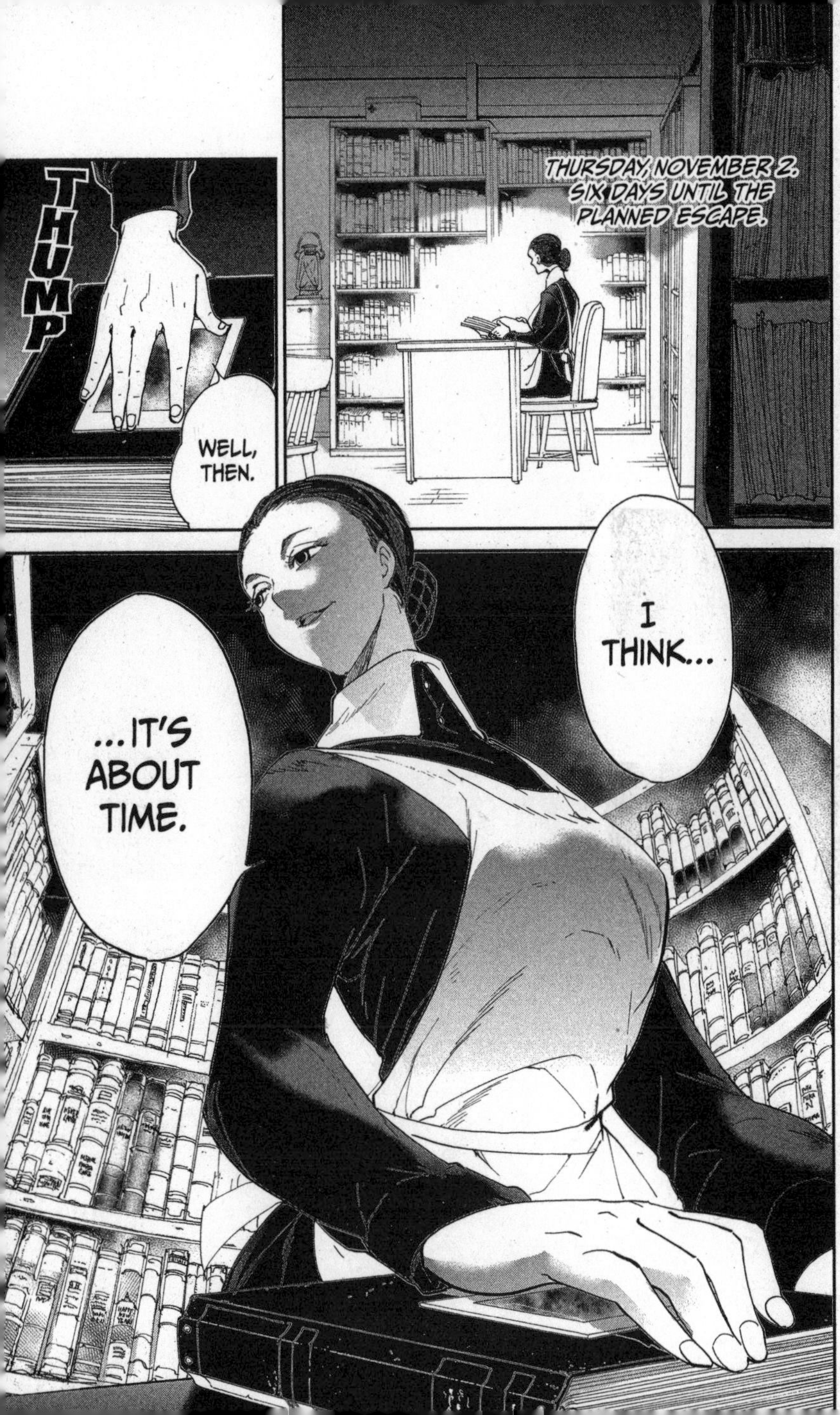
THURSDAY, NOVEMBER 2. SIX DAYS UNTIL THE PLANNED ESCAPE.
THUMP
WELL, THEN.
I THINK...
...IT'S ABOUT TIME.

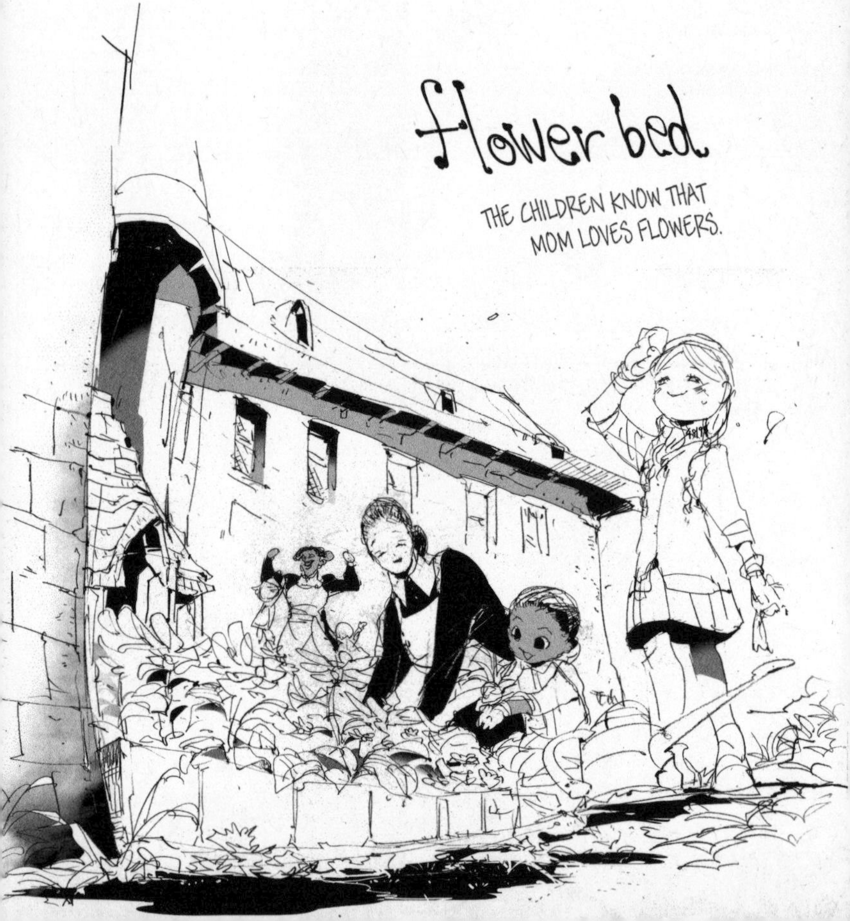
flower bed
THE CHILDREN KNOW THAT
MOM LOVES FLOWERS.

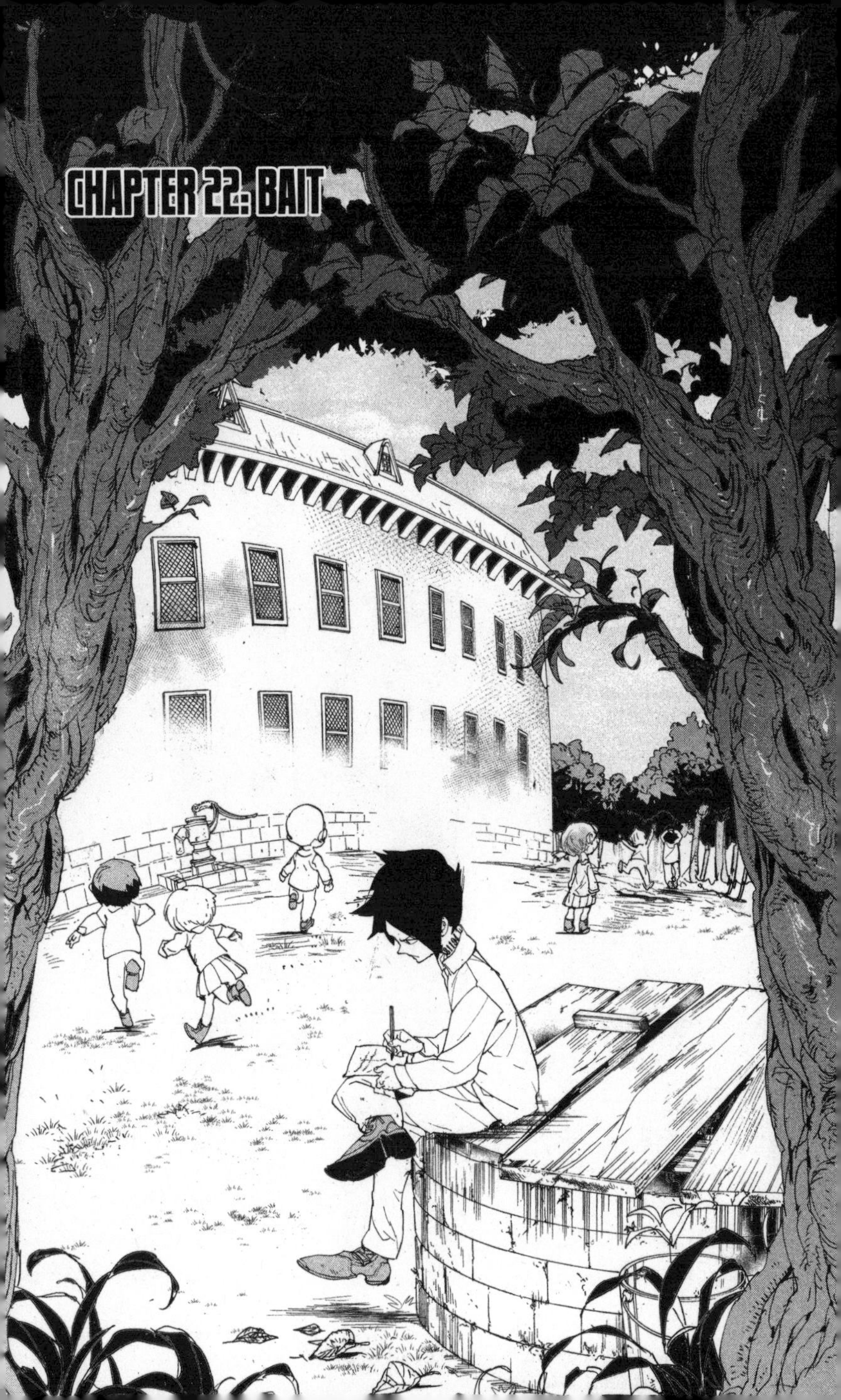
CHAPTER 22. BAIT

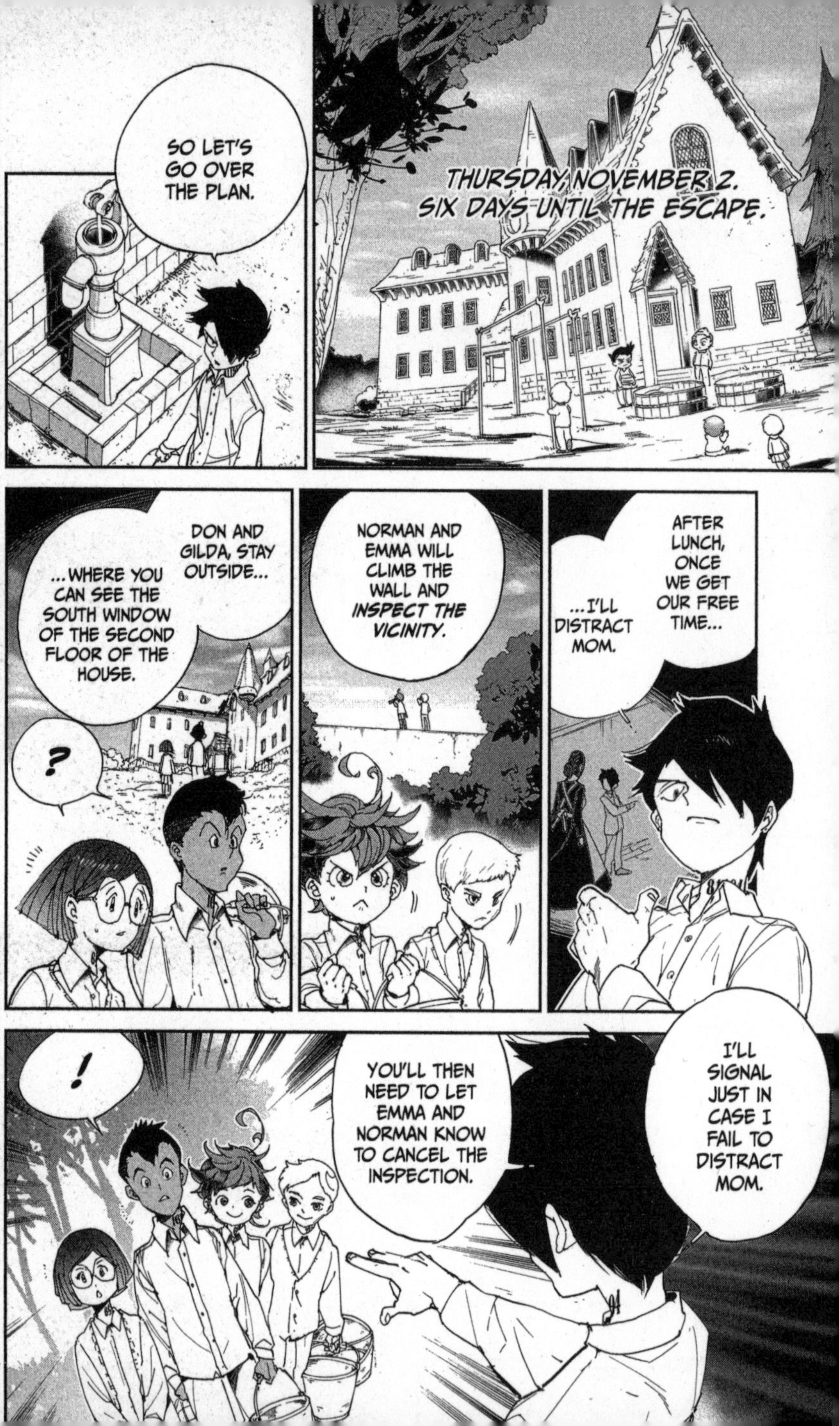
THURSDAY, NOVEMBER 2.
SIX DAYS UNTIL THE ESCAPE.
SO LET'S GO OVER THE PLAN.
AFTER LUNCH, ONCE WE GET OUR FREE TIME...
...I'LL DISTRACT MOM.
NORMAN AND EMMA WILL CLIMB THE WALL AND *INSPECT THE VICINITY.*
DON AND GILDA, STAY OUTSIDE...
...WHERE YOU CAN SEE THE SOUTH WINDOW OF THE SECOND FLOOR OF THE HOUSE.
?
I'LL SIGNAL JUST IN CASE I FAIL TO DISTRACT MOM.
YOU'LL THEN NEED TO LET EMMA AND NORMAN KNOW TO CANCEL THE INSPECTION.
!

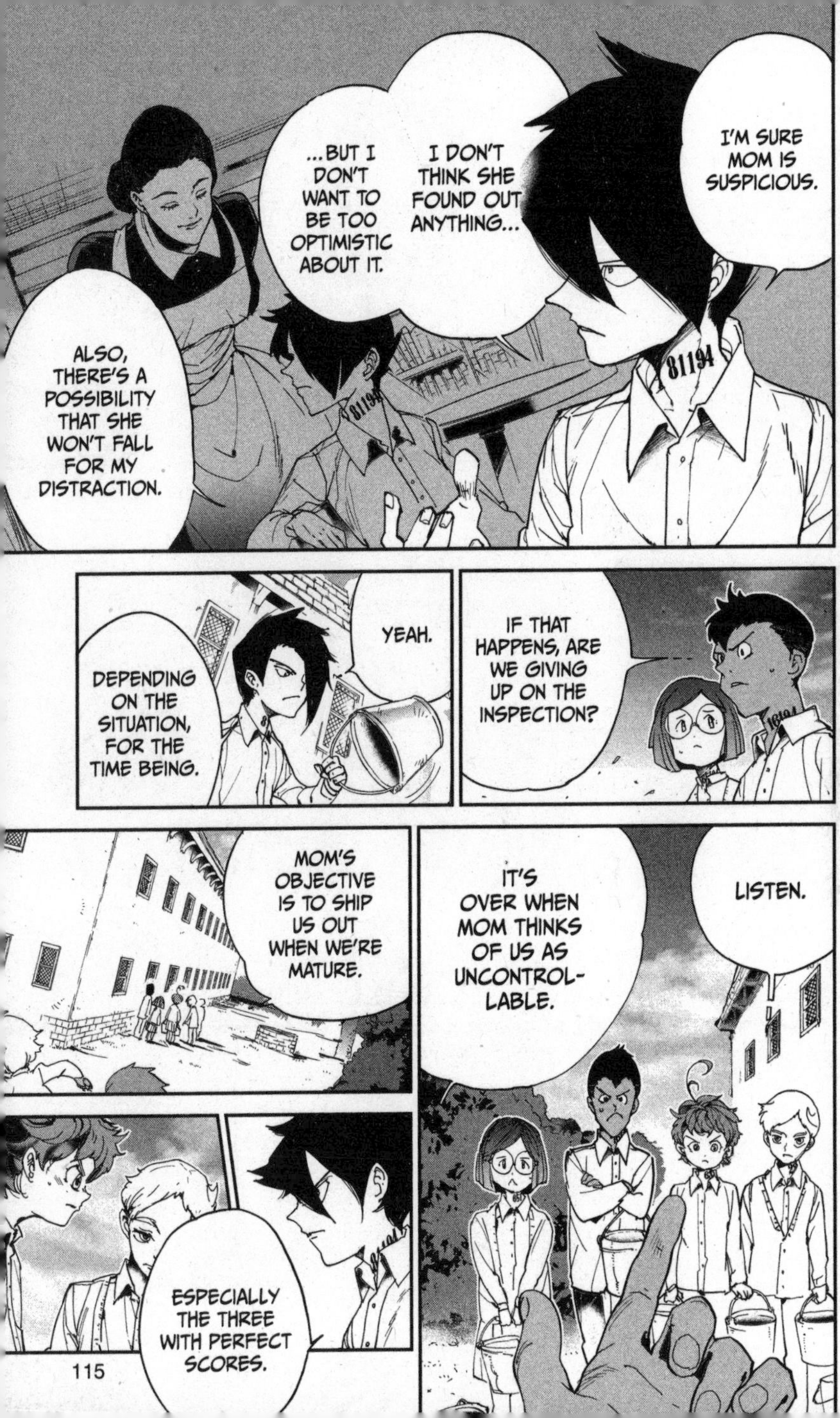
I'M SURE MOM IS SUSPICIOUS.
I DON'T THINK SHE FOUND OUT ANYTHING...
...BUT I DON'T WANT TO BE TOO OPTIMISTIC ABOUT IT.
ALSO, THERE'S A POSSIBILITY THAT SHE WON'T FALL FOR MY DISTRACTION.
IF THAT HAPPENS, ARE WE GIVING UP ON THE INSPECTION?
YEAH.
DEPENDING ON THE SITUATION, FOR THE TIME BEING.
LISTEN.
IT'S OVER WHEN MOM THINKS OF US AS UNCONTROL-LABLE.
MOM'S OBJECTIVE IS TO SHIP US OUT WHEN WE'RE MATURE.
ESPECIALLY THE THREE WITH PERFECT SCORES.

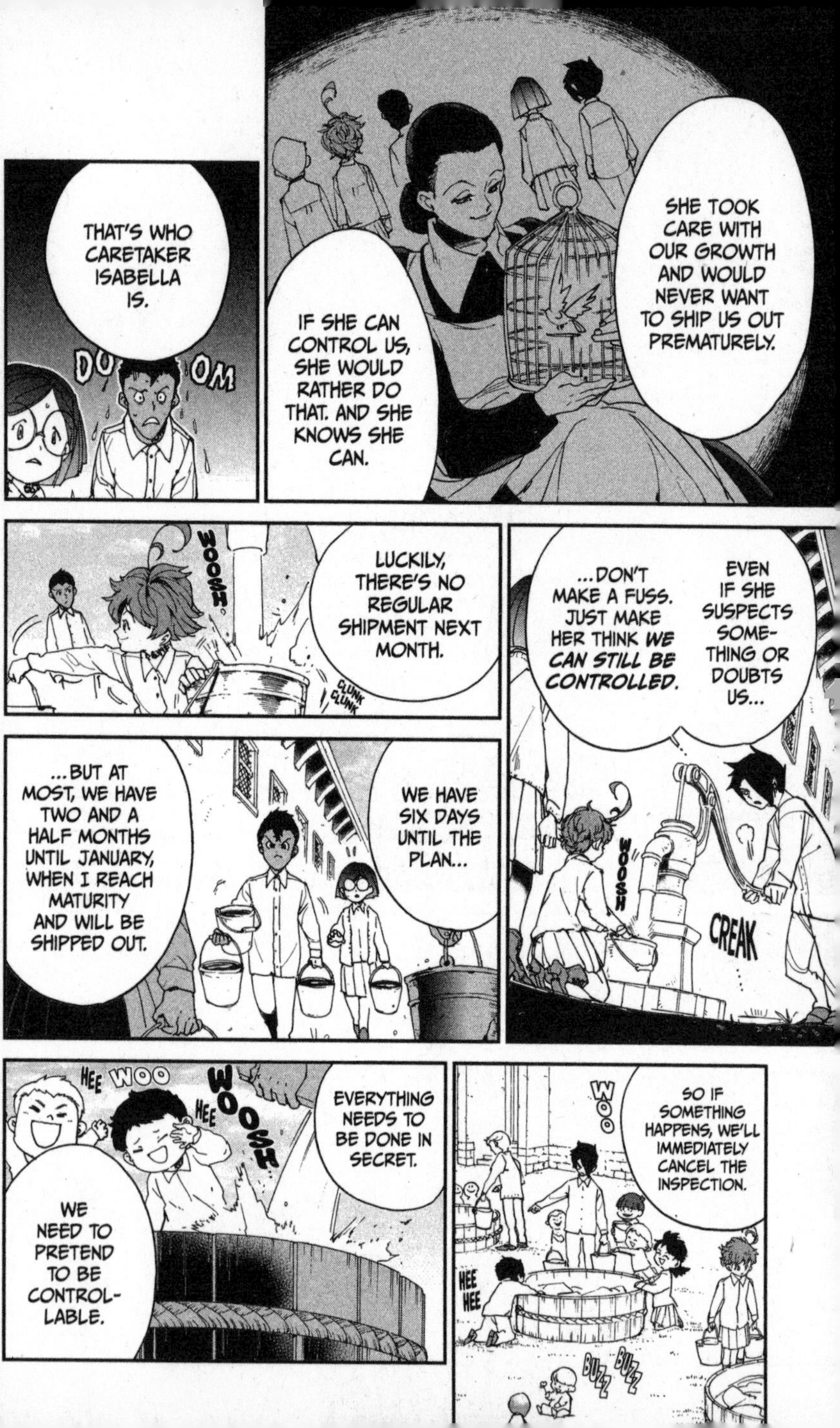
SHE TOOK CARE WITH OUR GROWTH AND WOULD NEVER WANT TO SHIP US OUT PREMATURELY.
IF SHE CAN CONTROL US, SHE WOULD RATHER DO THAT. AND SHE KNOWS SHE CAN.
THAT'S WHO CARETAKER ISABELLA IS.
DO OM
EVEN IF SHE SUSPECTS SOME-THING OR DOUBTS US...
...DON'T MAKE A FUSS. JUST MAKE HER THINK *WE CAN STILL BE CONTROLLED.*
WOOSH
CREAK
WOOSH
LUCKILY, THERE'S NO REGULAR SHIPMENT NEXT MONTH.
CLUNK CLUNK
WE HAVE SIX DAYS UNTIL THE PLAN...
...BUT AT MOST, WE HAVE TWO AND A HALF MONTHS UNTIL JANUARY, WHEN I REACH MATURITY AND WILL BE SHIPPED OUT.
WOO
SO IF SOMETHING HAPPENS, WE'LL IMMEDIATELY CANCEL THE INSPECTION.
HEE HEE
BUZZ BUZZ
EVERYTHING NEEDS TO BE DONE IN SECRET.
WOOSH
HEE WOO
HEE
WE NEED TO PRETEND TO BE CONTROL-LABLE.

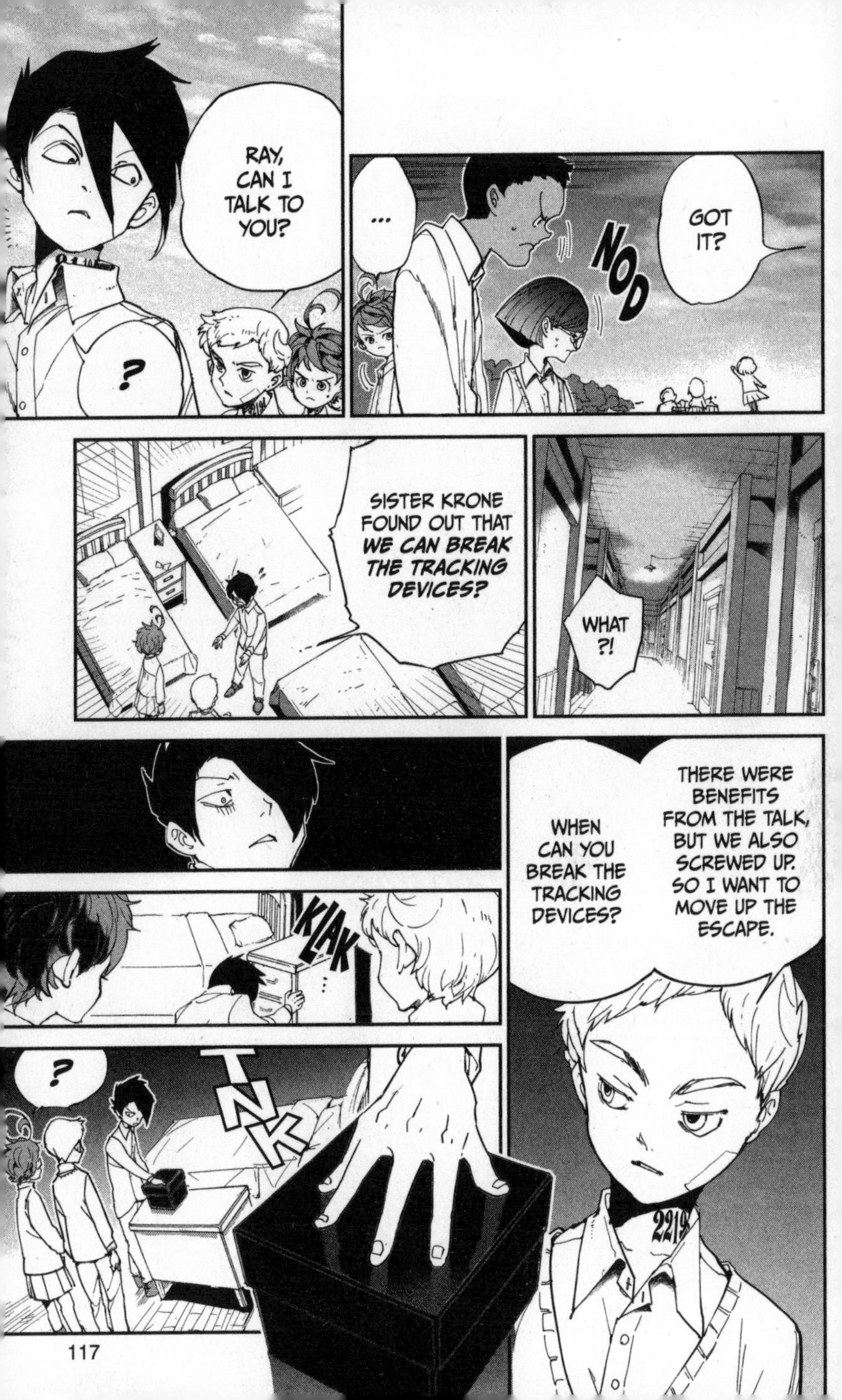
GOT IT?
...
NOD
RAY, CAN I TALK TO YOU?
?
WHAT?!
SISTER KRONE FOUND OUT THAT ***WE CAN BREAK THE TRACKING DEVICES?***
THERE WERE BENEFITS FROM THE TALK, BUT WE ALSO SCREWED UP. SO I WANT TO MOVE UP THE ESCAPE.
WHEN CAN YOU BREAK THE TRACKING DEVICES?
KLAK
...
?
TNK

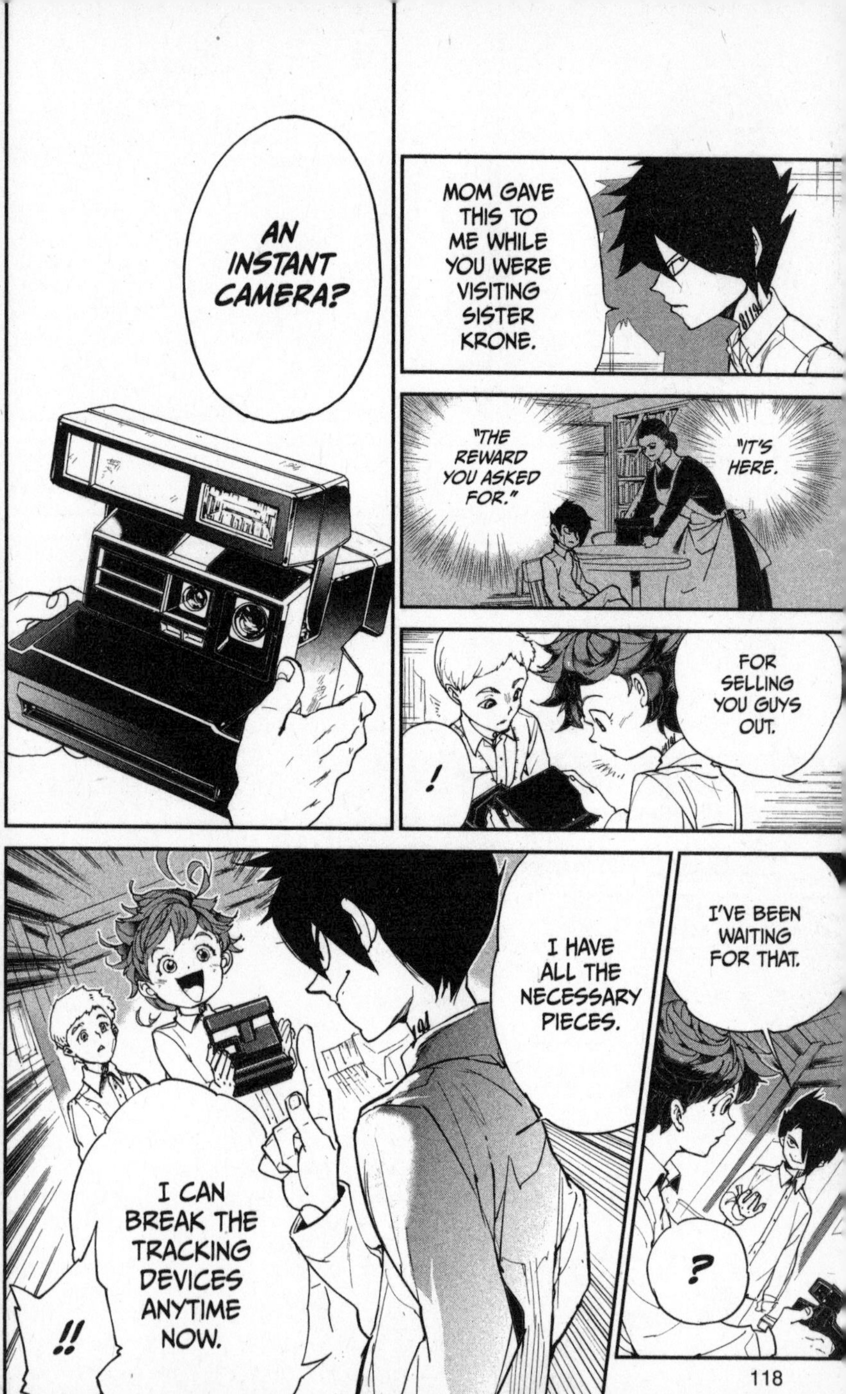

MOM GAVE THIS TO ME WHILE YOU WERE VISITING SISTER KRONE.
"IT'S HERE.
"THE REWARD YOU ASKED FOR."
FOR SELLING YOU GUYS OUT.
!
AN INSTANT CAMERA?
I'VE BEEN WAITING FOR THAT.
?
I HAVE ALL THE NECESSARY PIECES.
I CAN BREAK THE TRACKING DEVICES ANYTIME NOW.
!!

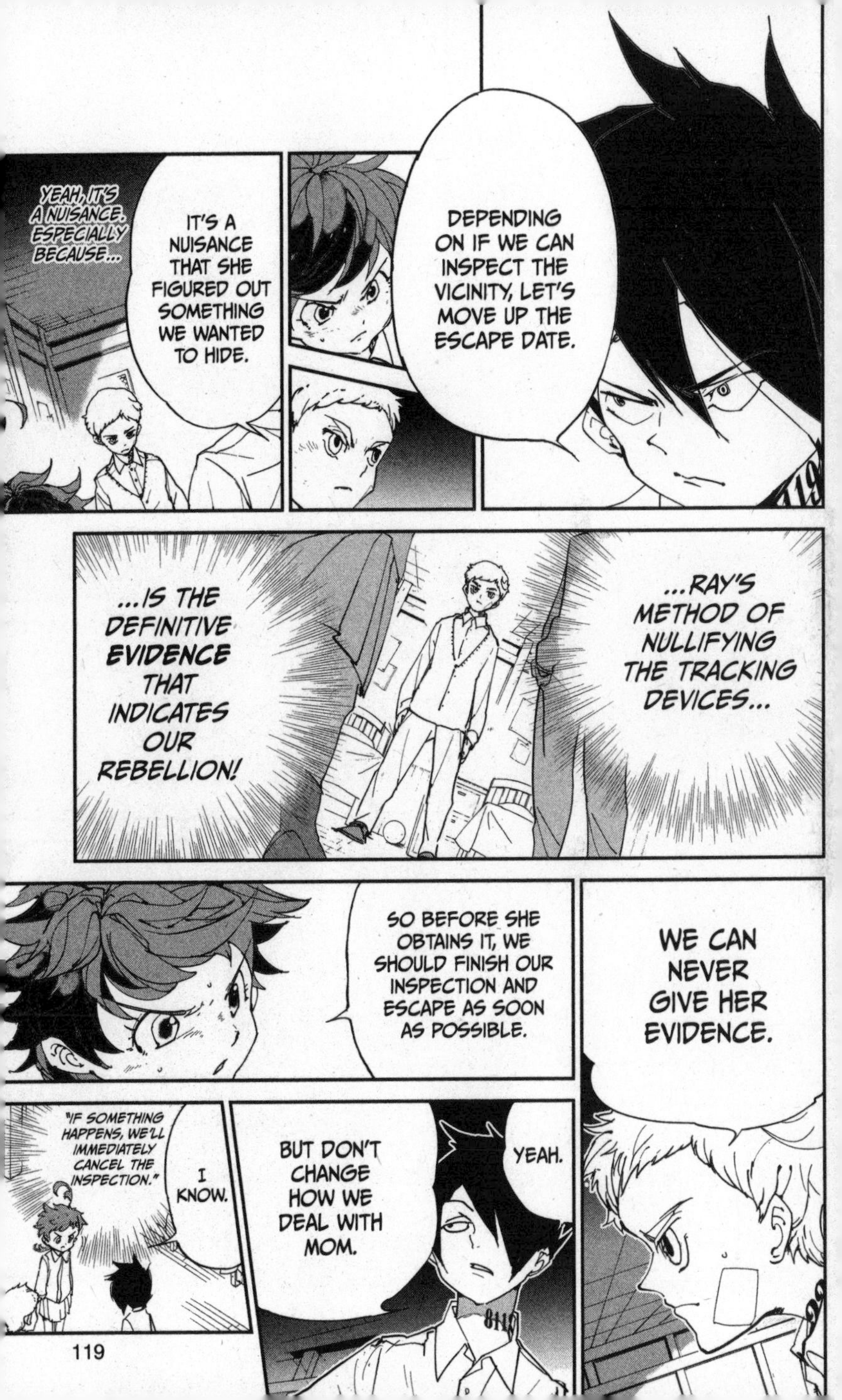

DEPENDING ON IF WE CAN INSPECT THE VICINITY, LET'S MOVE UP THE ESCAPE DATE.
IT'S A NUISANCE THAT SHE FIGURED OUT SOMETHING WE WANTED TO HIDE.
YEAH, IT'S A NUISANCE. ESPECIALLY BECAUSE...
...RAY'S METHOD OF NULLIFYING THE TRACKING DEVICES...
...IS THE DEFINITIVE EVIDENCE THAT INDICATES OUR REBELLION!
WE CAN NEVER GIVE HER EVIDENCE.
SO BEFORE SHE OBTAINS IT, WE SHOULD FINISH OUR INSPECTION AND ESCAPE AS SOON AS POSSIBLE.
YEAH.
BUT DON'T CHANGE HOW WE DEAL WITH MOM.
I KNOW.
"IF SOMETHING HAPPENS, WE'LL IMMEDIATELY CANCEL THE INSPECTION."

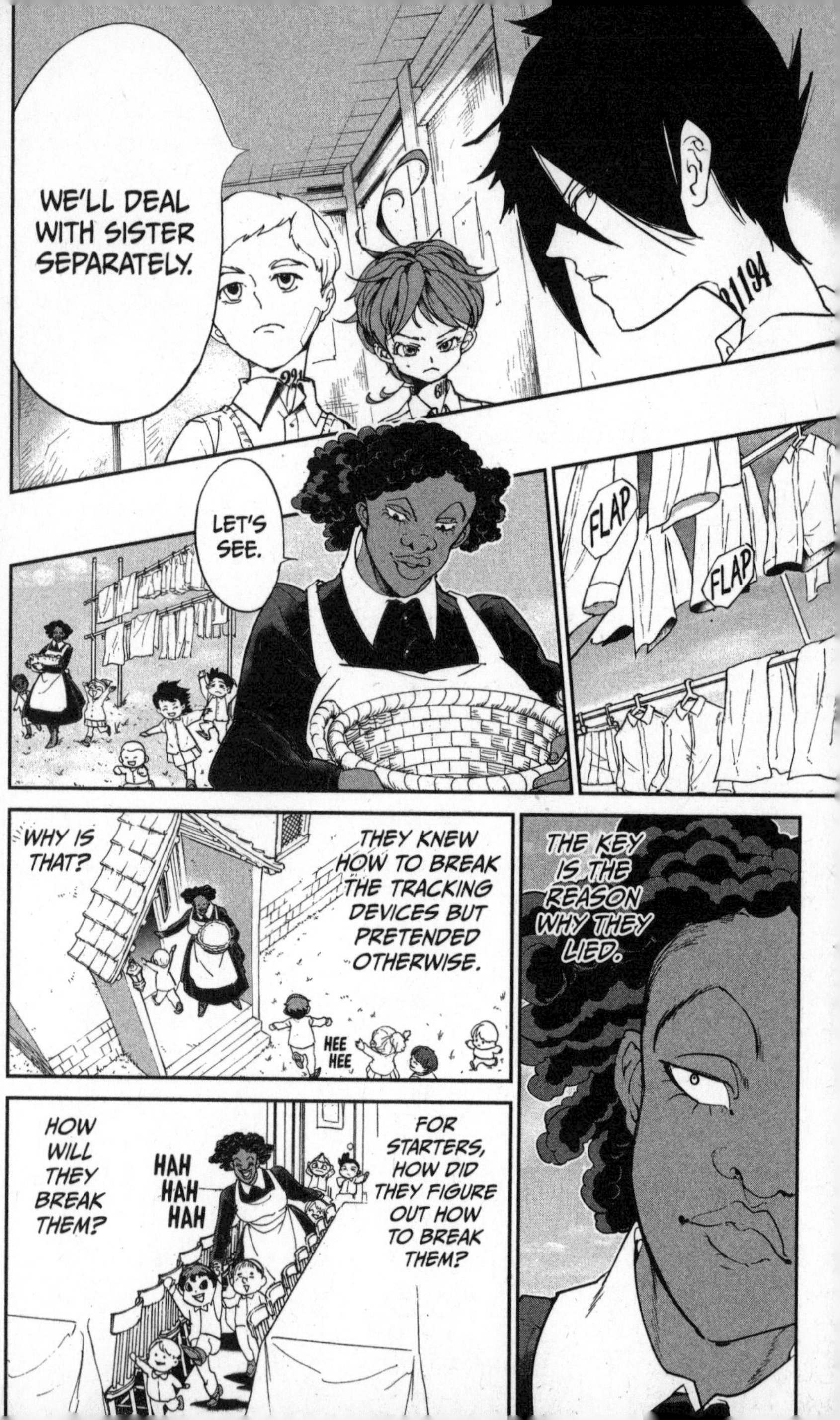
WE'LL DEAL WITH SISTER SEPARATELY.
FLAP
FLAP
LET'S SEE.
THE KEY IS THE REASON WHY THEY LIED.
THEY KNEW HOW TO BREAK THE TRACKING DEVICES BUT PRETENDED OTHERWISE.
WHY IS THAT?
HEE HEE
FOR STARTERS, HOW DID THEY FIGURE OUT HOW TO BREAK THEM?
HAH HAH HAH
HOW WILL THEY BREAK THEM?

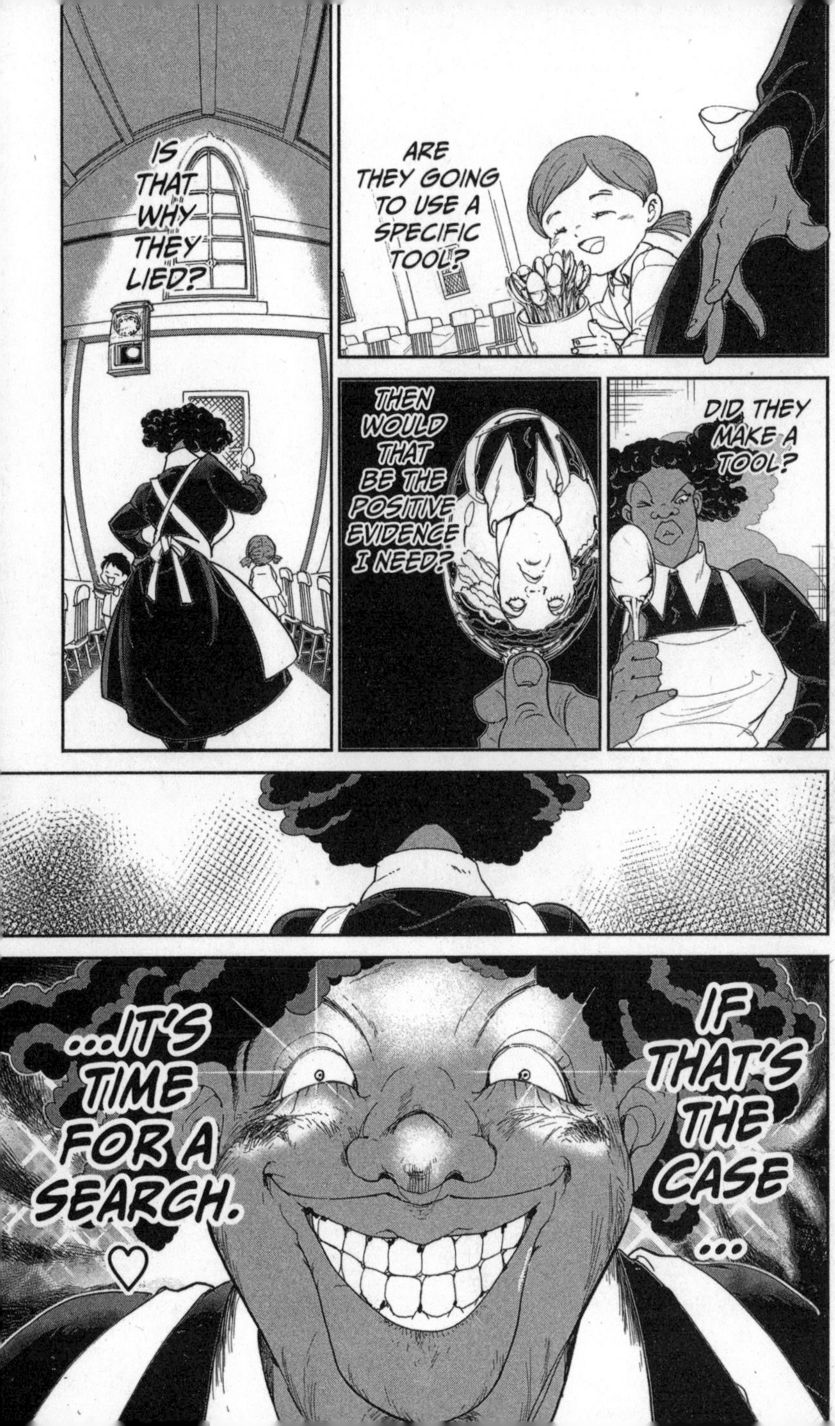
ARE THEY GOING TO USE A SPECIFIC TOOL?
DID THEY MAKE A TOOL?
THEN WOULD THAT BE THE POSITIVE EVIDENCE I NEED?
IS THAT WHY THEY LIED?
IF THAT'S THE CASE...
...IT'S TIME FOR A SEARCH. ♡

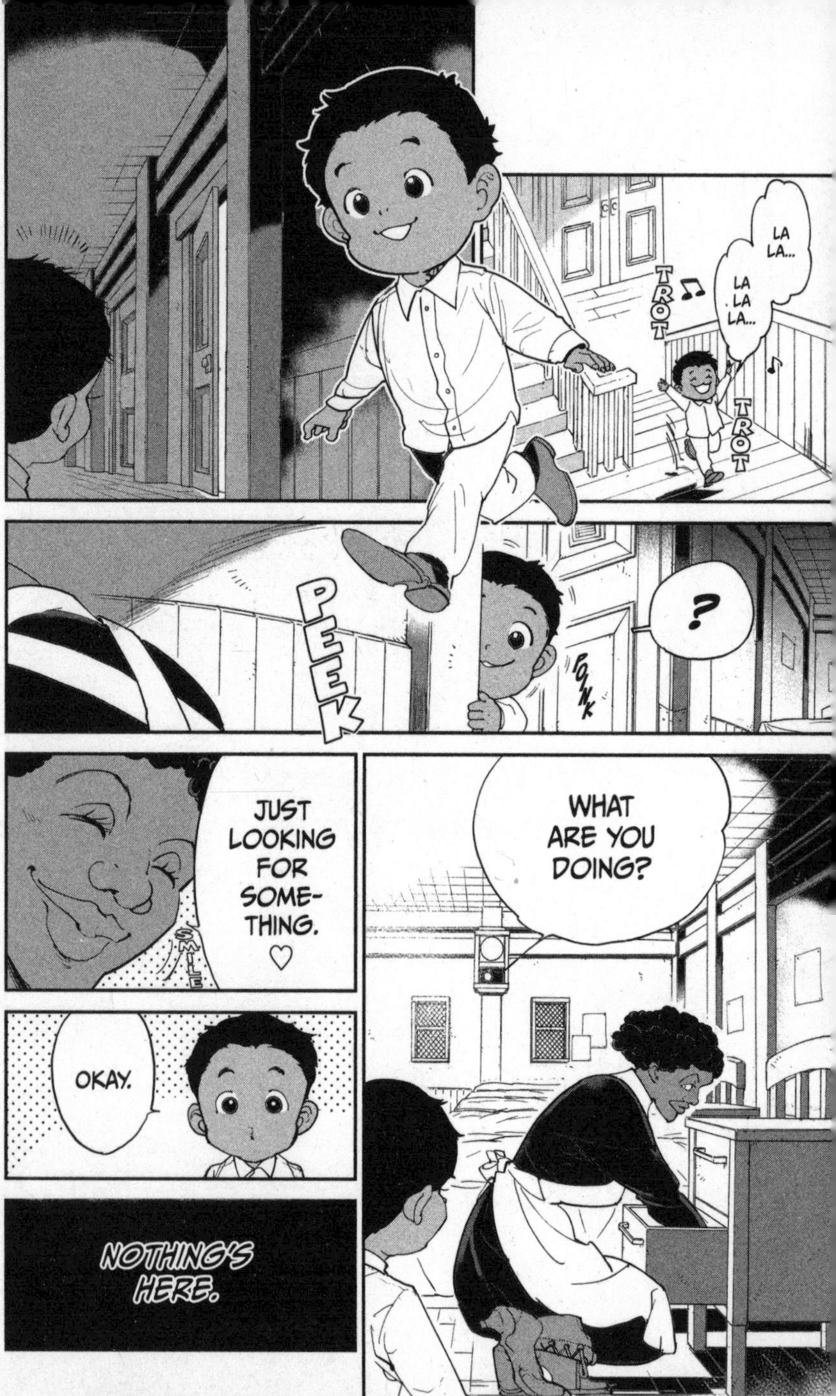
TROT
LA LA...
LA LA LA...
TROT
?
POINK
PEEK
WHAT ARE YOU DOING?
JUST LOOKING FOR SOME-THING. ♡
SMILE
OKAY.
NOTHING'S HERE.

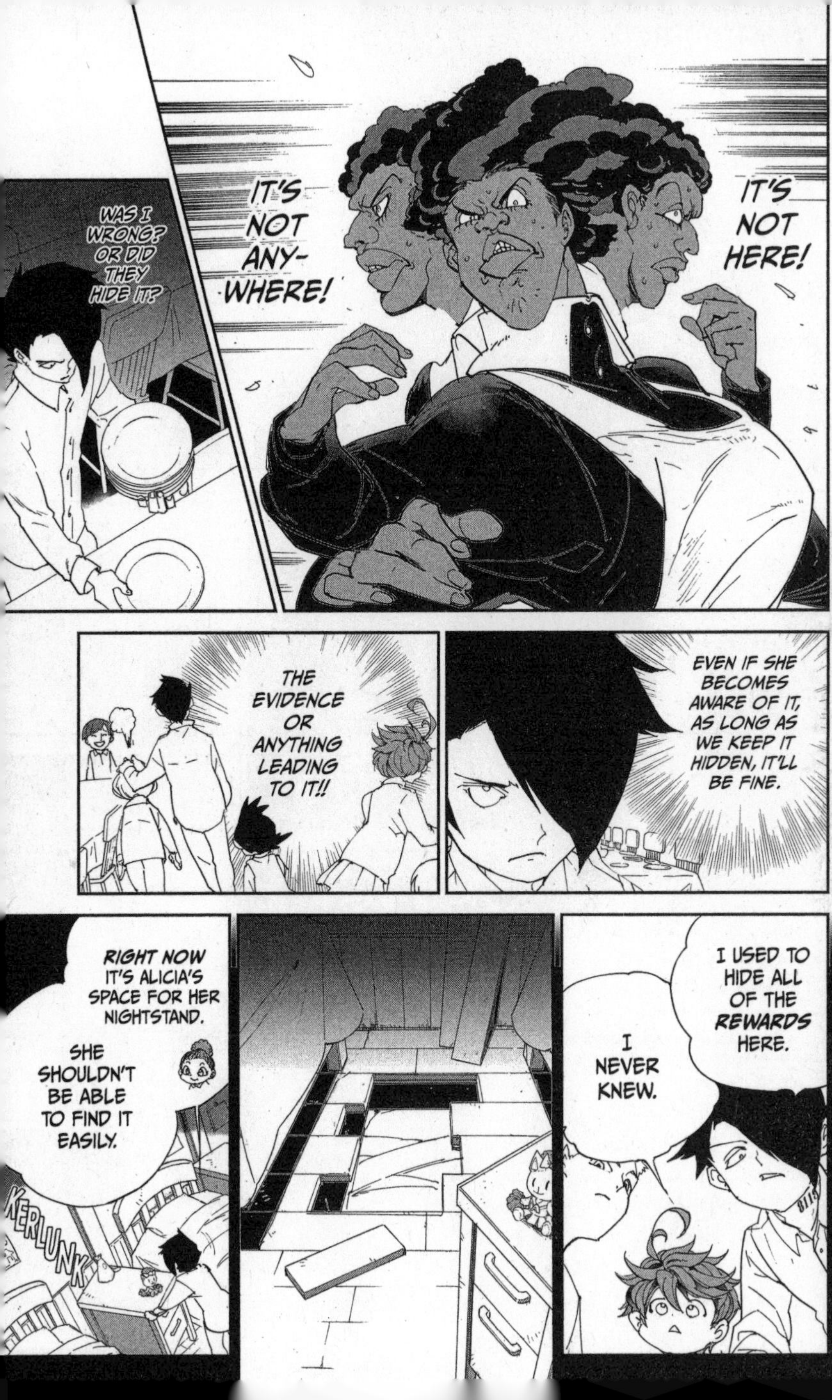
IT'S NOT HERE!
IT'S NOT ANY-WHERE!
WAS I WRONG? OR DID THEY HIDE IT?
EVEN IF SHE BECOMES AWARE OF IT, AS LONG AS WE KEEP IT HIDDEN, IT'LL BE FINE.
THE EVIDENCE OR ANYTHING LEADING TO IT!!
I USED TO HIDE ALL OF THE *REWARDS* HERE.
I NEVER KNEW.
RIGHT NOW IT'S ALICIA'S SPACE FOR HER NIGHTSTAND.
SHE SHOULDN'T BE ABLE TO FIND IT EASILY.
KERLUNK

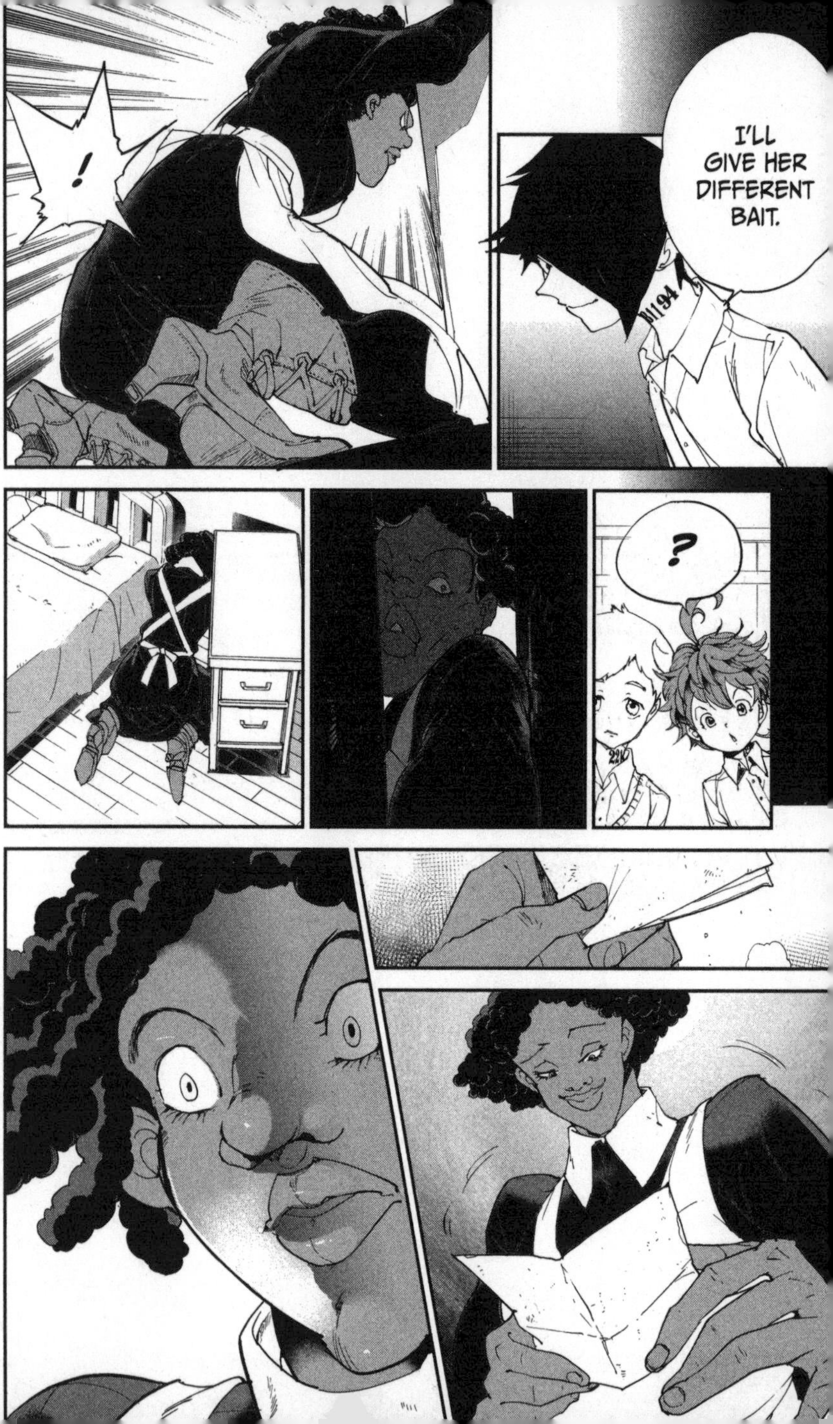
I'LL GIVE HER DIFFERENT BAIT.
!
?

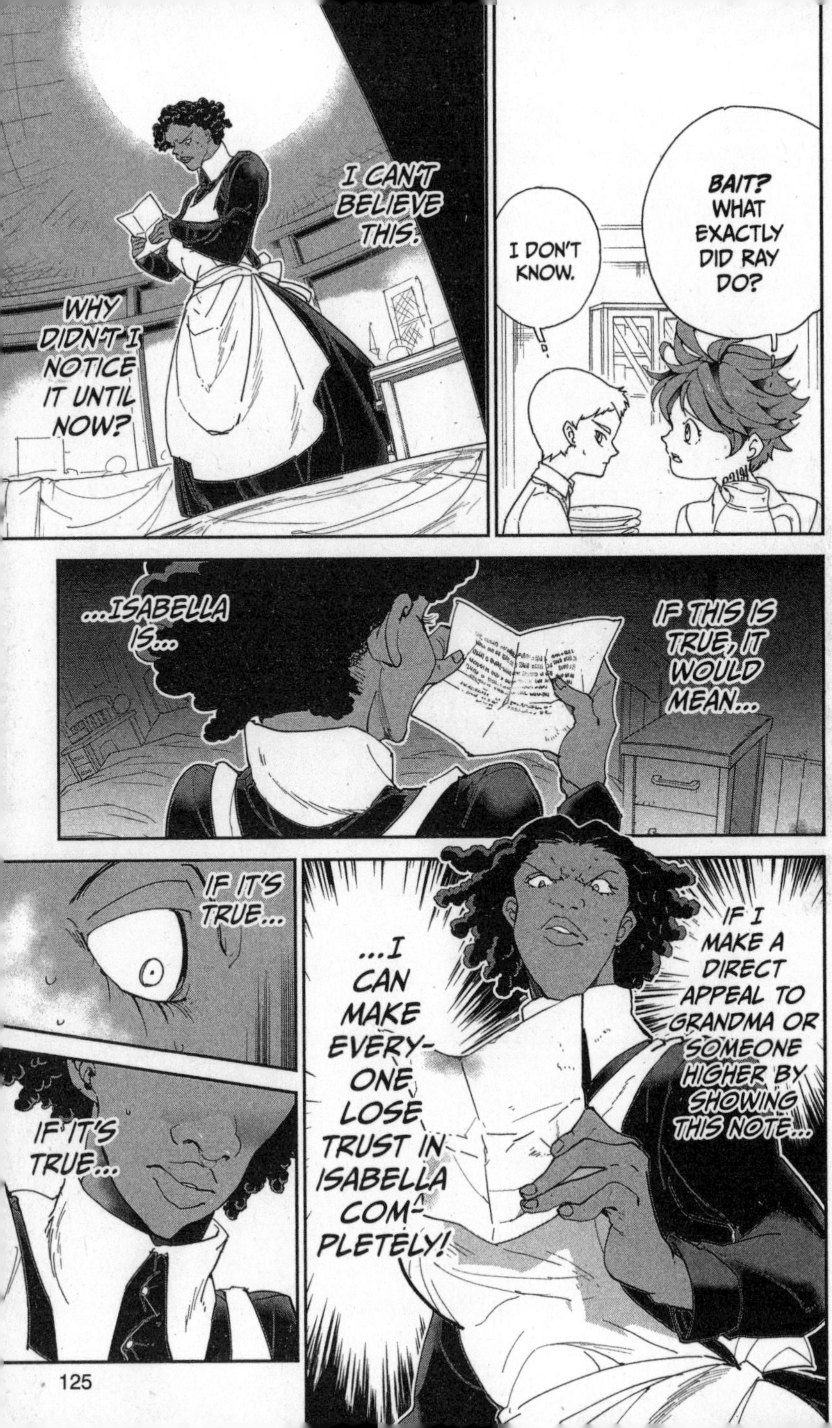
BAIT? WHAT EXACTLY DID RAY DO?
I DON'T KNOW.
I CAN'T BELIEVE THIS.
WHY DIDN'T I NOTICE IT UNTIL NOW?
IF THIS IS TRUE, IT WOULD MEAN...
...ISABELLA IS...
IF I MAKE A DIRECT APPEAL TO GRANDMA OR SOMEONE HIGHER BY SHOWING THIS NOTE...
...I CAN MAKE EVERY-ONE LOSE TRUST IN ISABELLA COM-PLETELY!
IF IT'S TRUE...
IF IT'S TRUE...

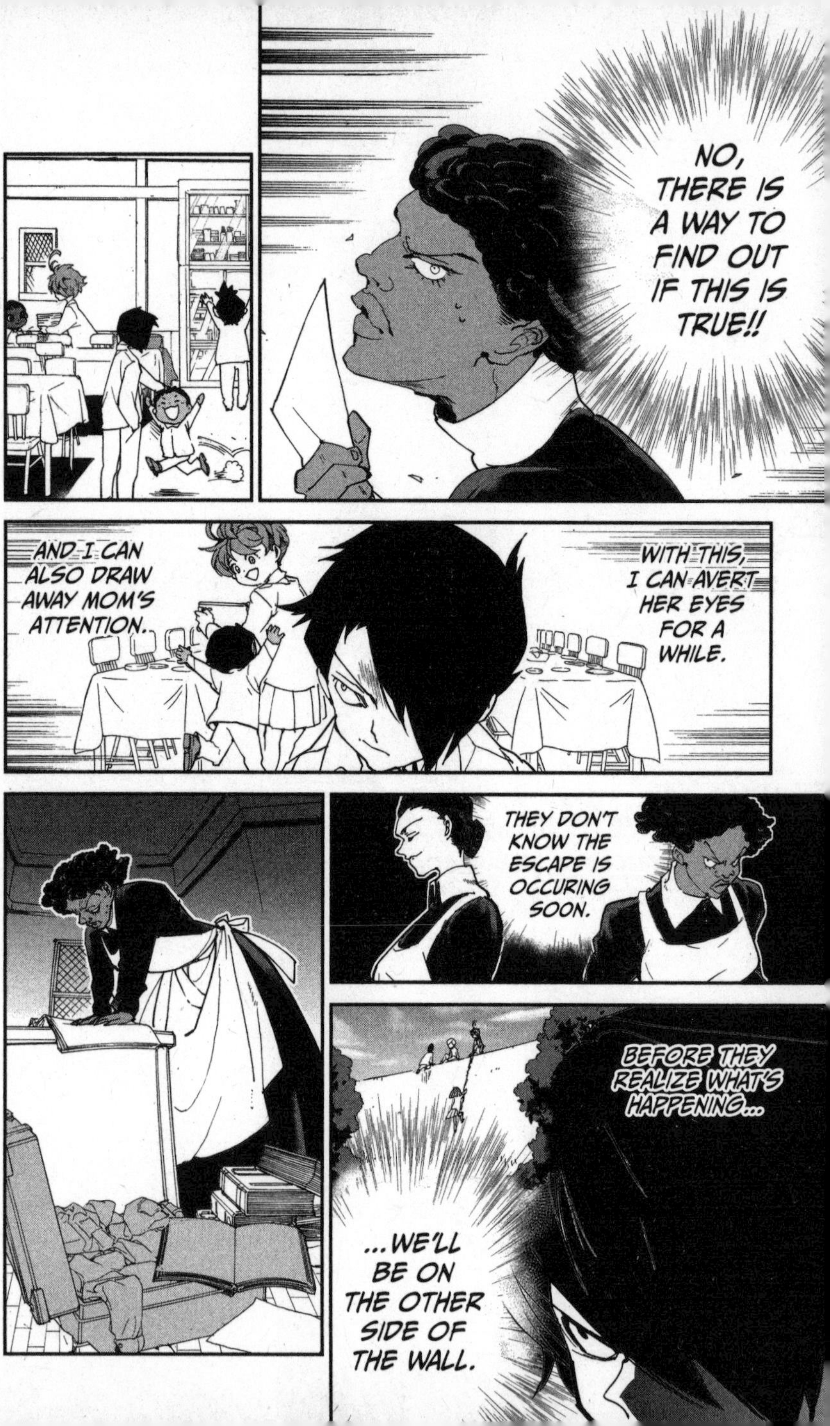
NO, THERE IS A WAY TO FIND OUT IF THIS IS TRUE!!
WITH THIS, I CAN AVERT HER EYES FOR A WHILE.
AND I CAN ALSO DRAW AWAY MOM'S ATTENTION.
THEY DON'T KNOW THE ESCAPE IS OCCURING SOON.
BEFORE THEY REALIZE WHAT'S HAPPENING...
...WE'LL BE ON THE OTHER SIDE OF THE WALL.

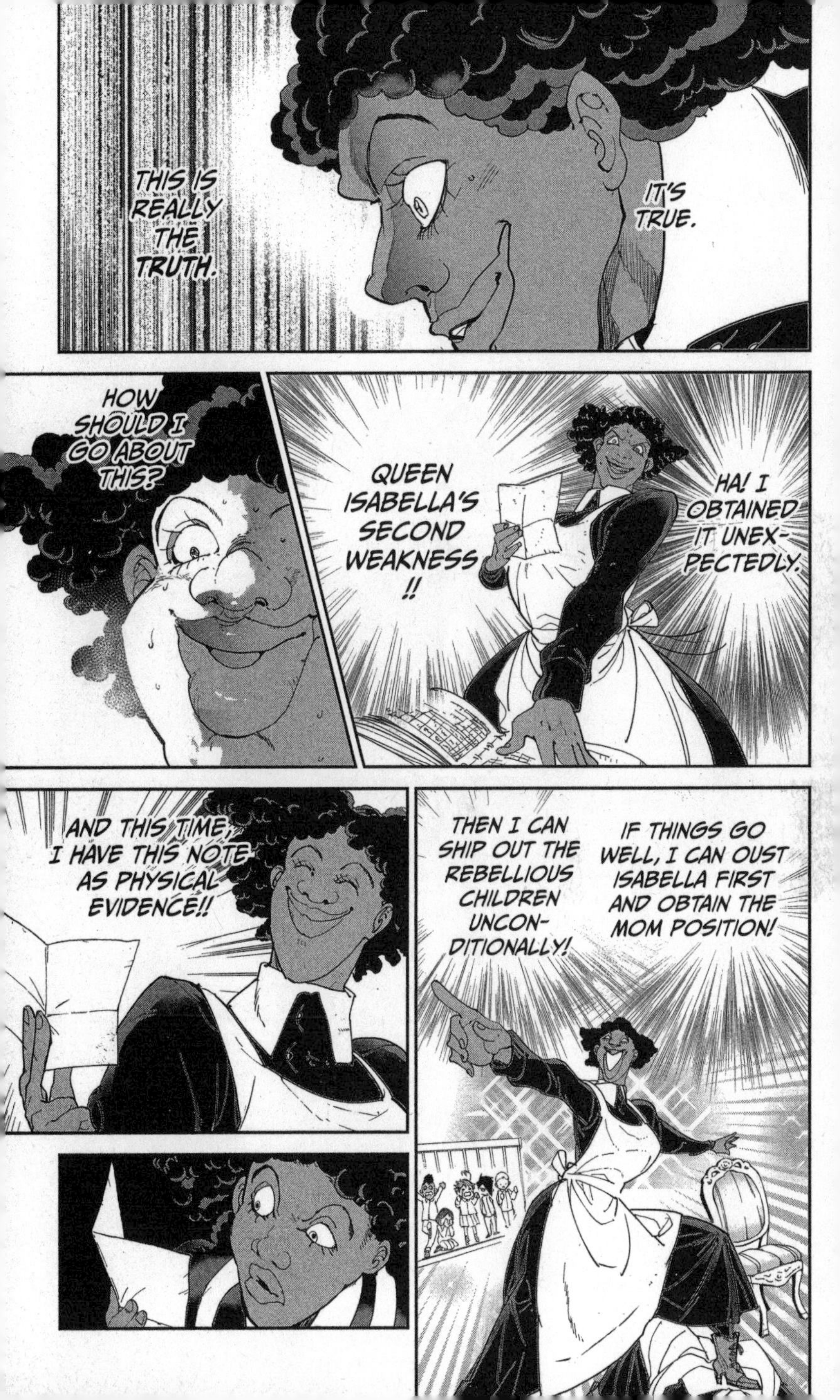
IT'S TRUE.
THIS IS REALLY THE TRUTH.
HA! I OBTAINED IT UNEX-PECTEDLY.
QUEEN ISABELLA'S SECOND WEAKNESS!!
HOW SHOULD I GO ABOUT THIS?
IF THINGS GO WELL, I CAN OUST ISABELLA FIRST AND OBTAIN THE MOM POSITION!
THEN I CAN SHIP OUT THE REBELLIOUS CHILDREN UNCON-DITIONALLY!
AND THIS TIME, I HAVE THIS NOTE AS PHYSICAL EVIDENCE!!

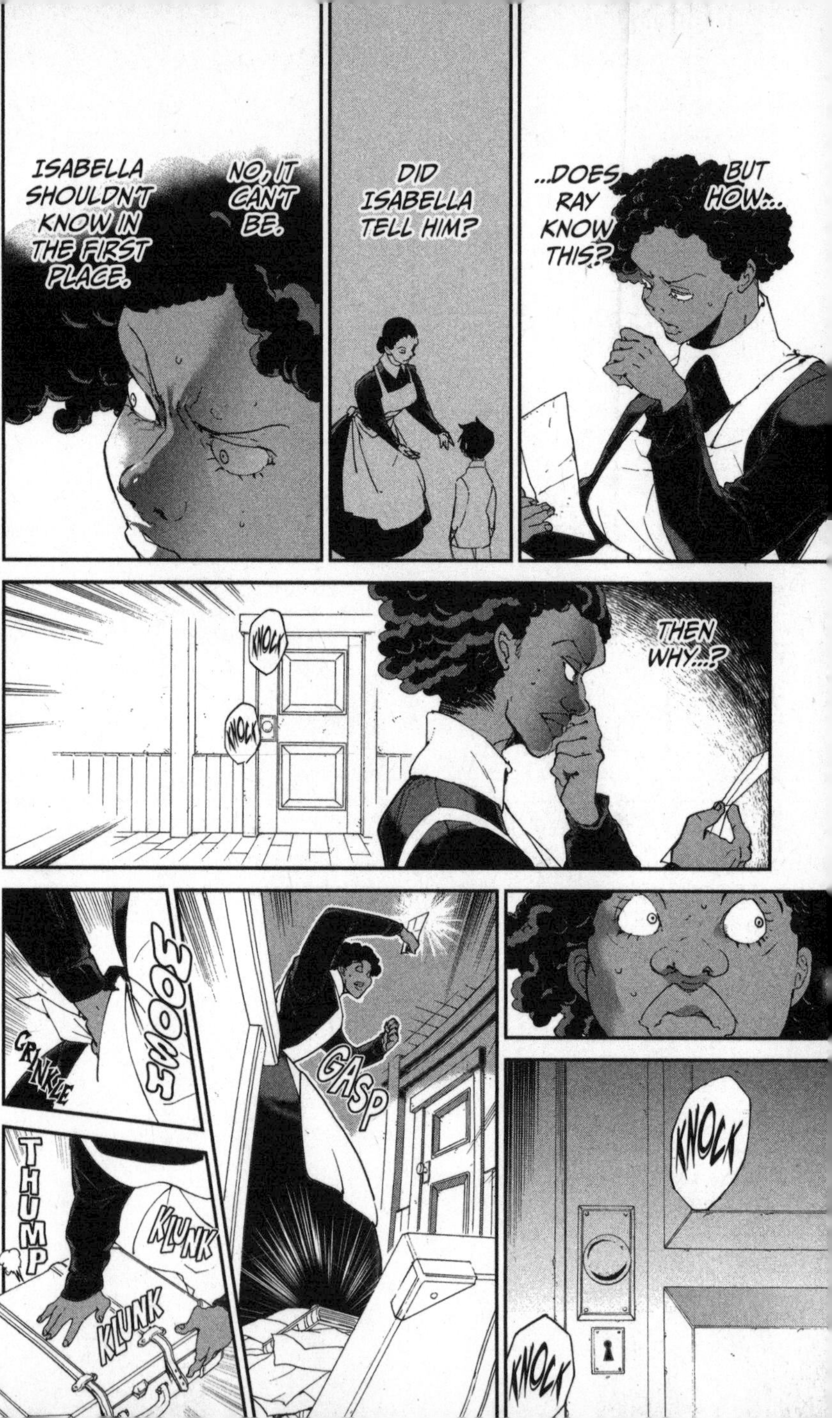

BUT HOW...
...DOES RAY KNOW THIS?
DID ISABELLA TELL HIM?
NO, IT CAN'T BE.
ISABELLA SHOULDN'T KNOW IN THE FIRST PLACE.
THEN WHY...?
KNOCK
KNOCK
KNOCK
KNOCK
GASP
WOOSH
CRINKLE
KLUNK
THUMP
KLUNK

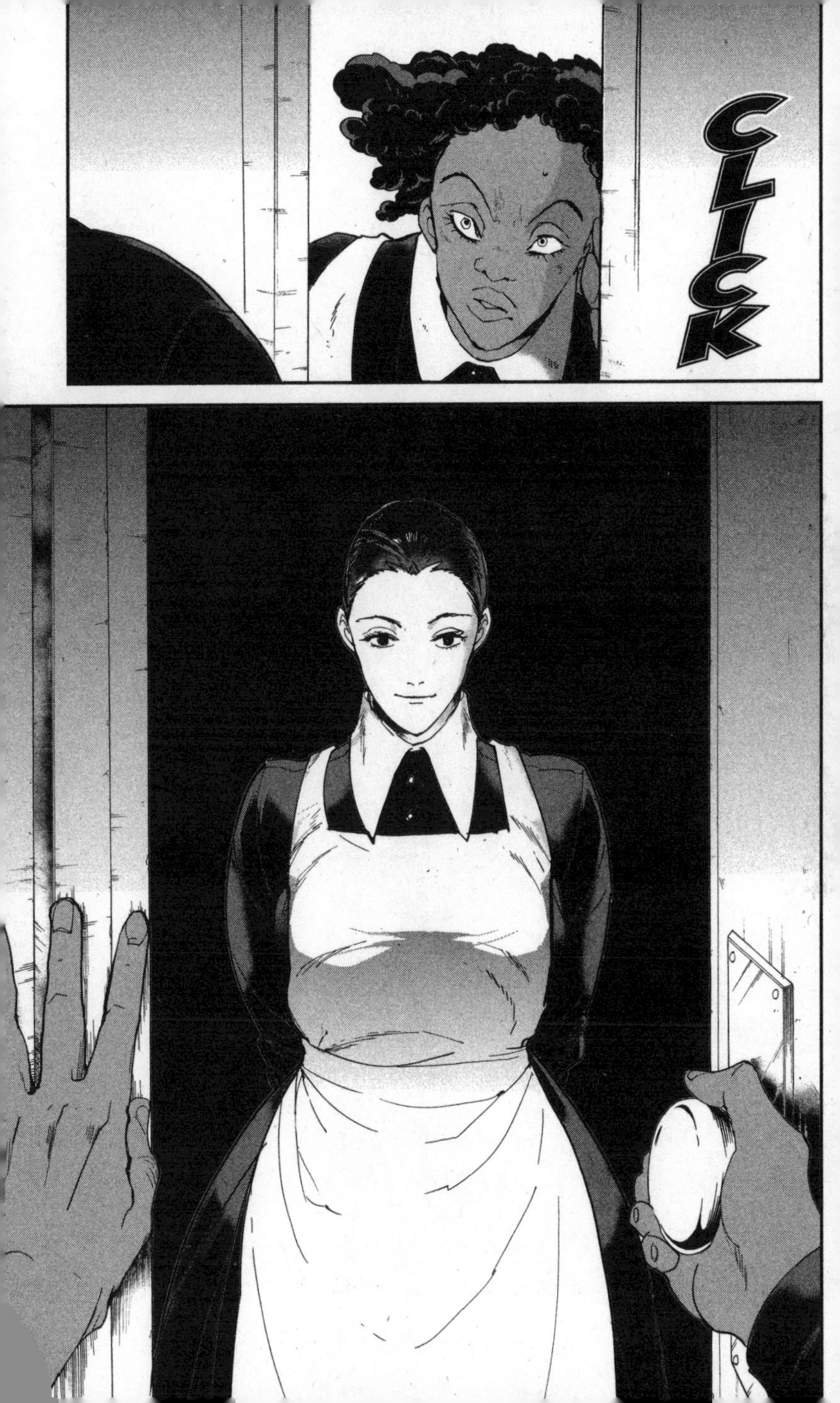
CLICK

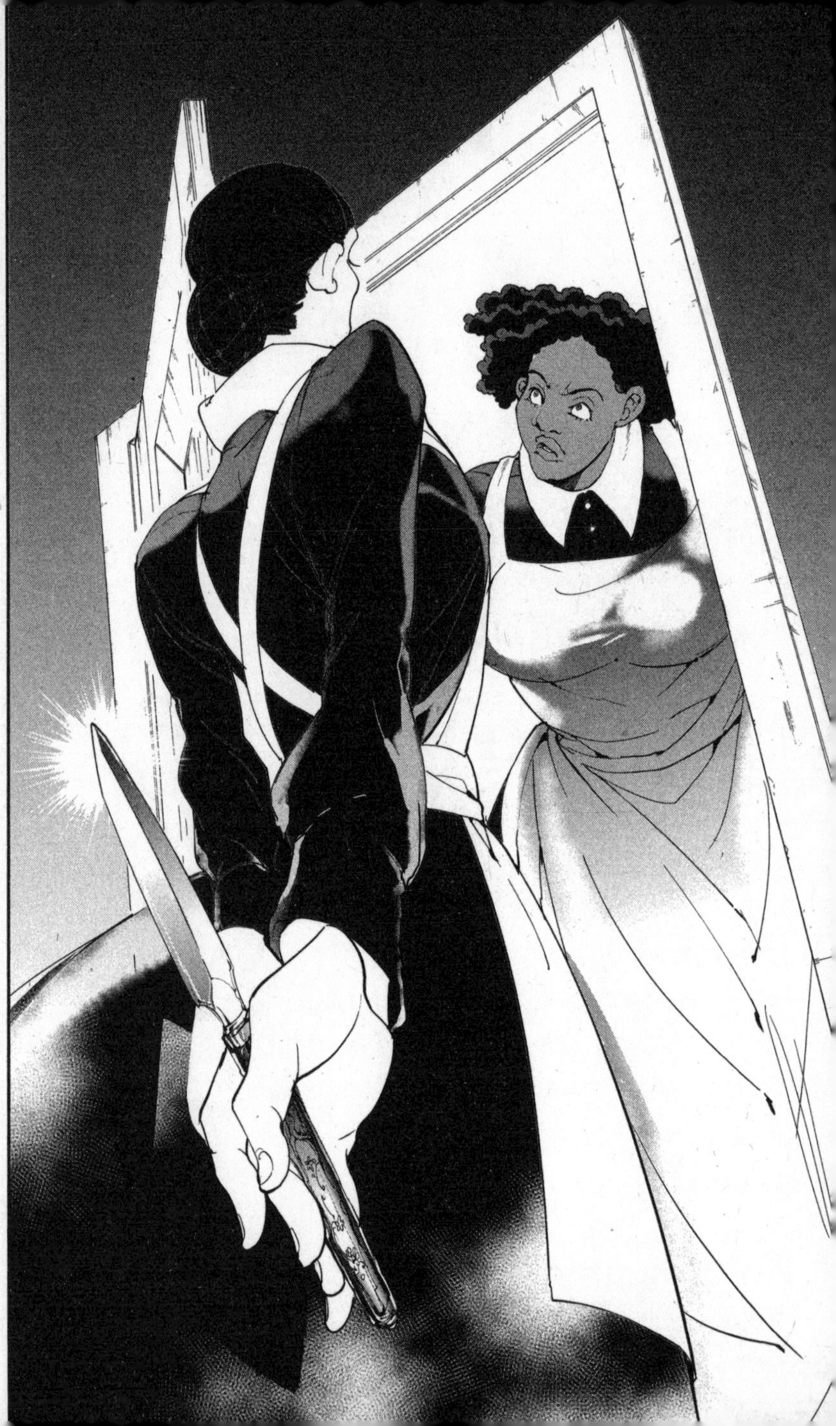

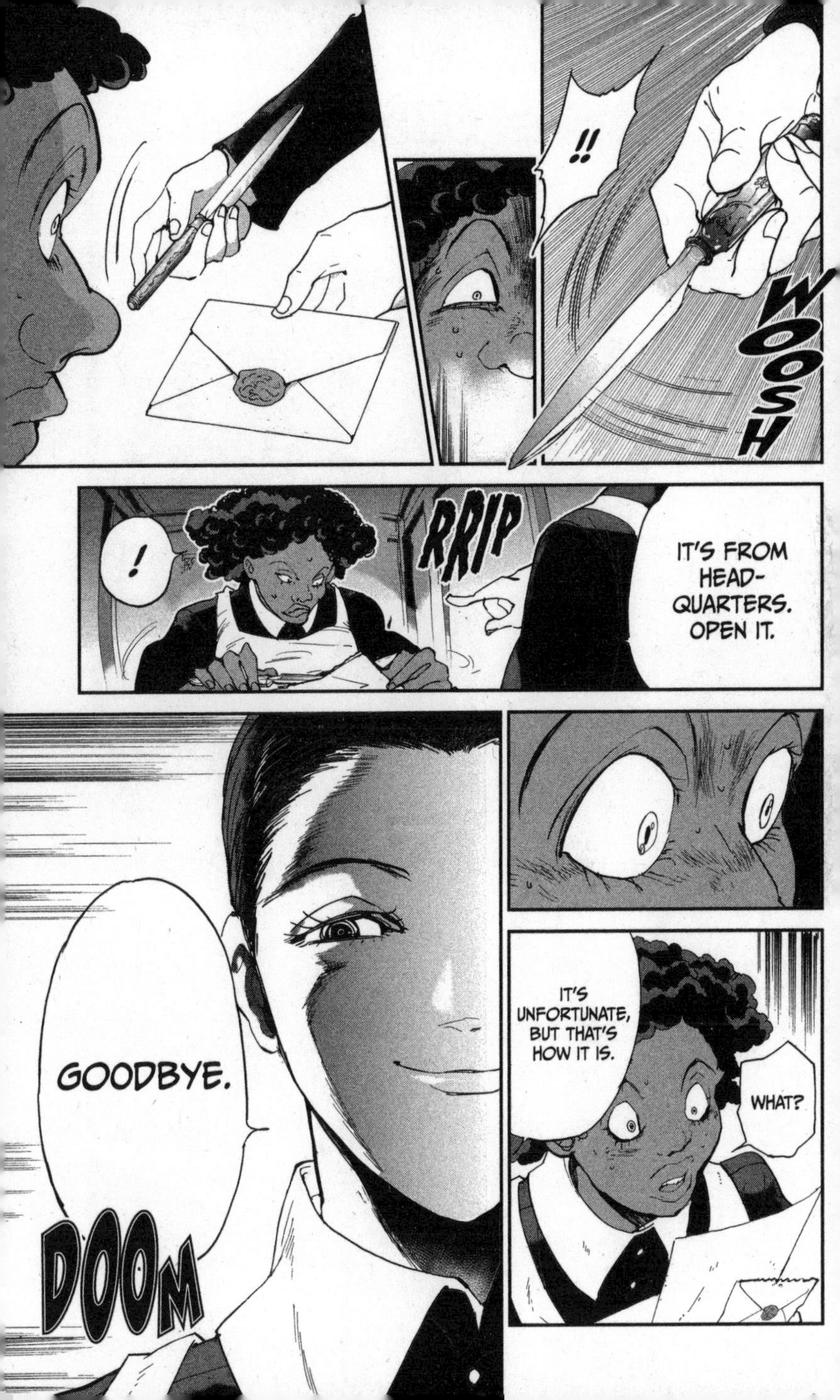
!!
WOOSH
IT'S FROM HEAD-QUARTERS. OPEN IT.
RRIP
!
WHAT?
IT'S UNFORTUNATE, BUT THAT'S HOW IT IS.
GOODBYE.
DOOM

THE PROMISED NEVERLAND SIDE SCENE 005

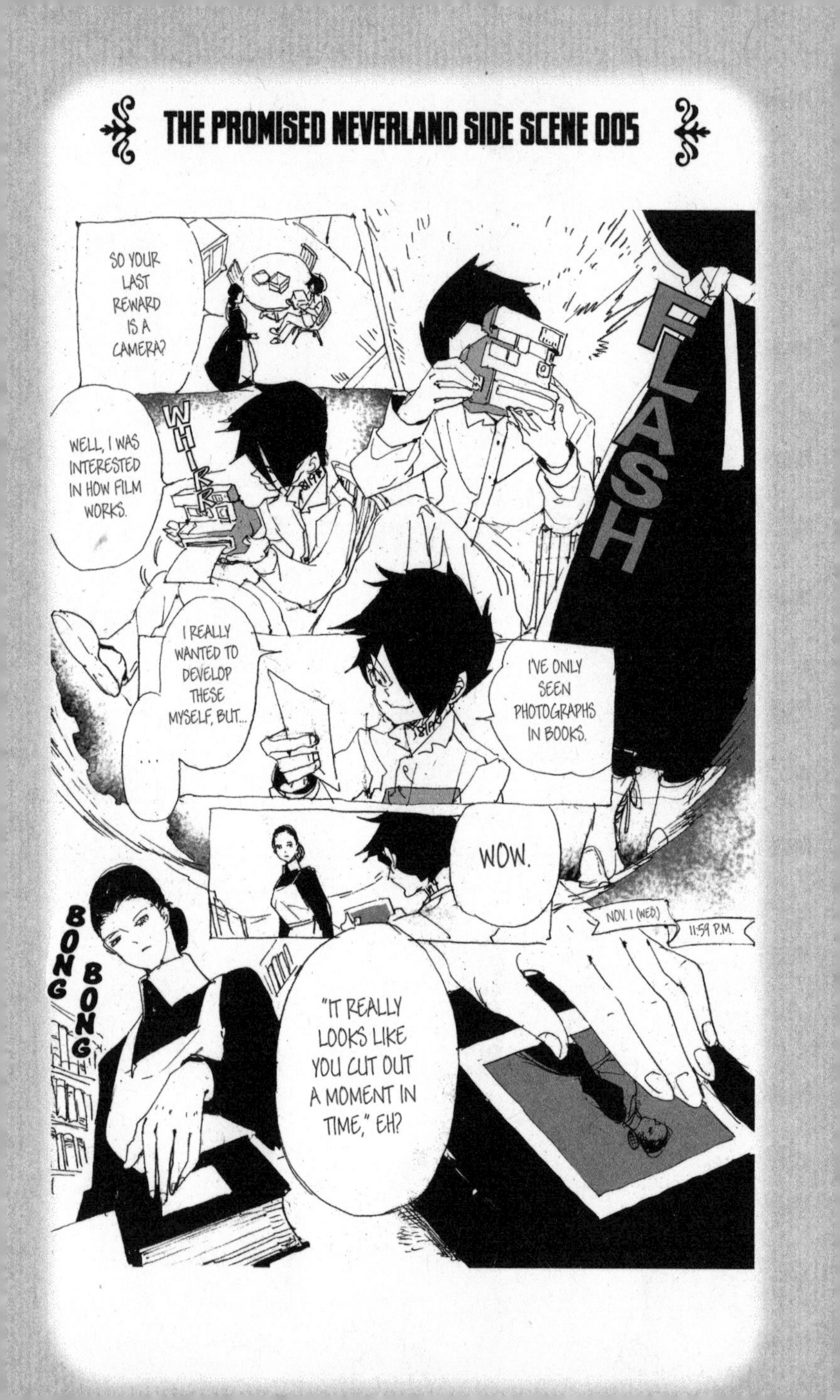
FLASH
SO YOUR LAST REWARD IS A CAMERA?
WHIRR
WELL, I WAS INTERESTED IN HOW FILM WORKS.
I'VE ONLY SEEN PHOTOGRAPHS IN BOOKS.
I REALLY WANTED TO DEVELOP THESE MYSELF, BUT...
...
WOW.
NOV. 1 (WED.)
11:59 P.M.
"IT REALLY LOOKS LIKE YOU CUT OUT A MOMENT IN TIME," EH?
BONG
BONG

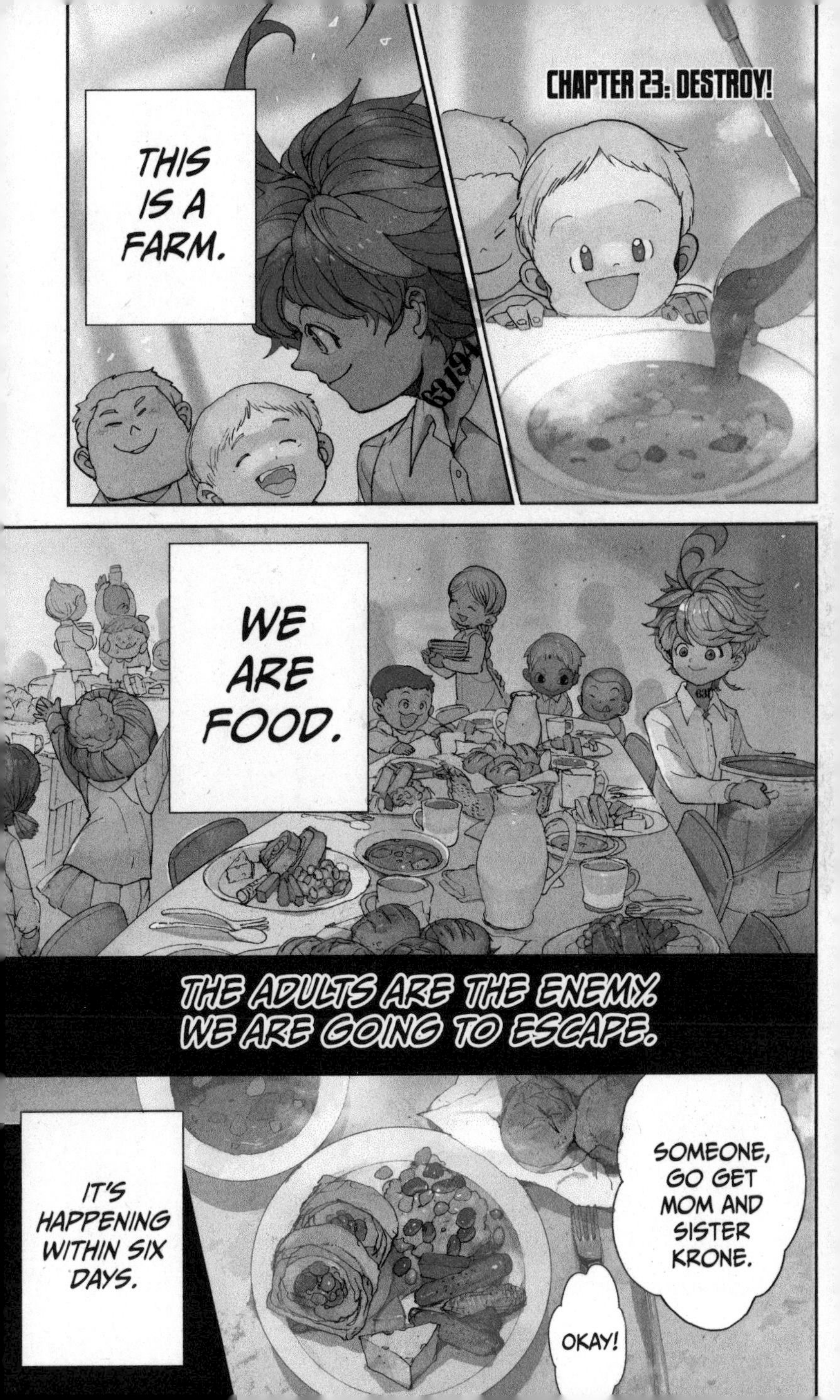
CHAPTER 23: DESTROY!
THIS IS A FARM.
63194
WE ARE FOOD.
THE ADULTS ARE THE ENEMY. WE ARE GOING TO ESCAPE.
SOMEONE, GO GET MOM AND SISTER KRONE.
IT'S HAPPENING WITHIN SIX DAYS.
OKAY!

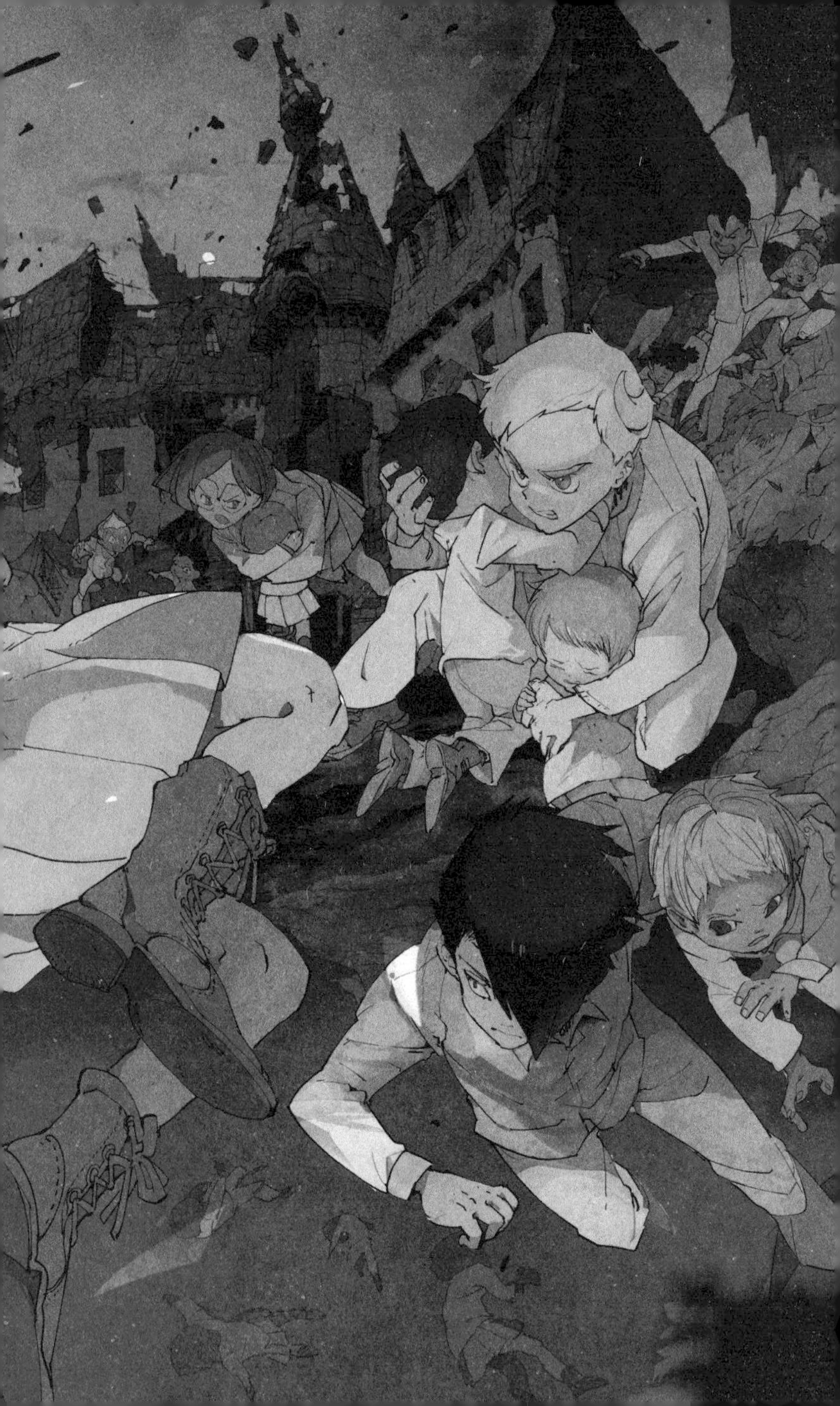

CHAPTER 23: DESTROY!

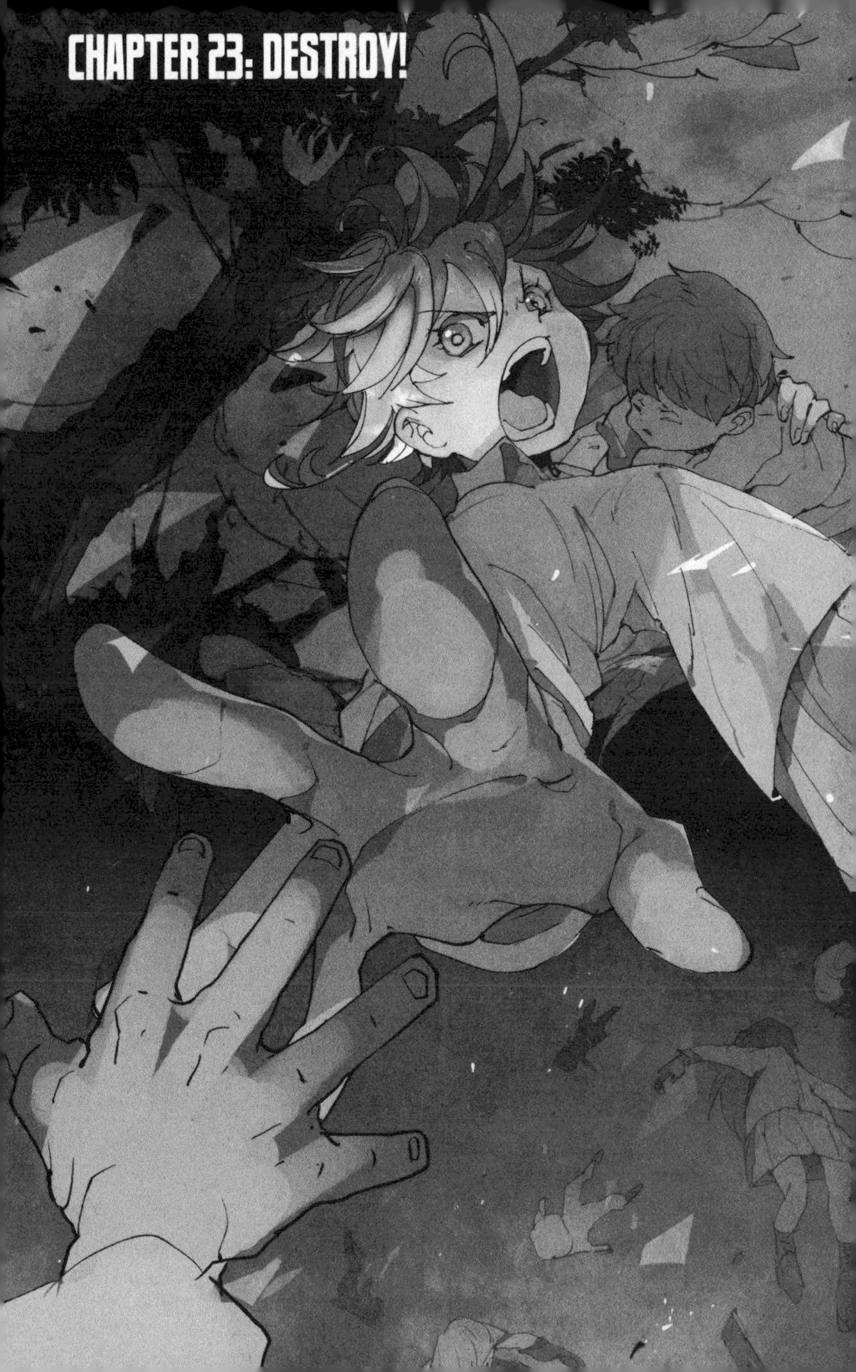

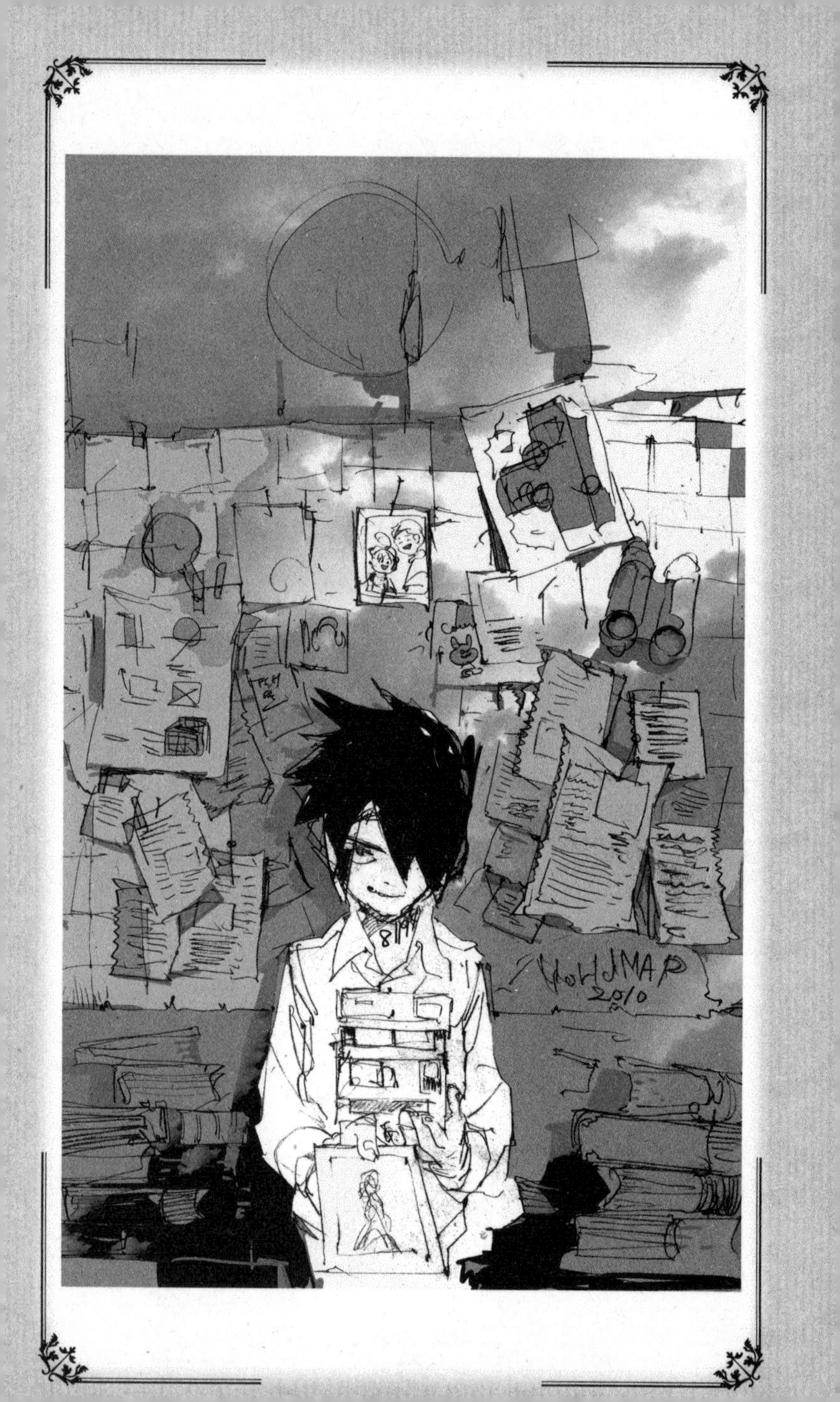

WorldMAP
2010

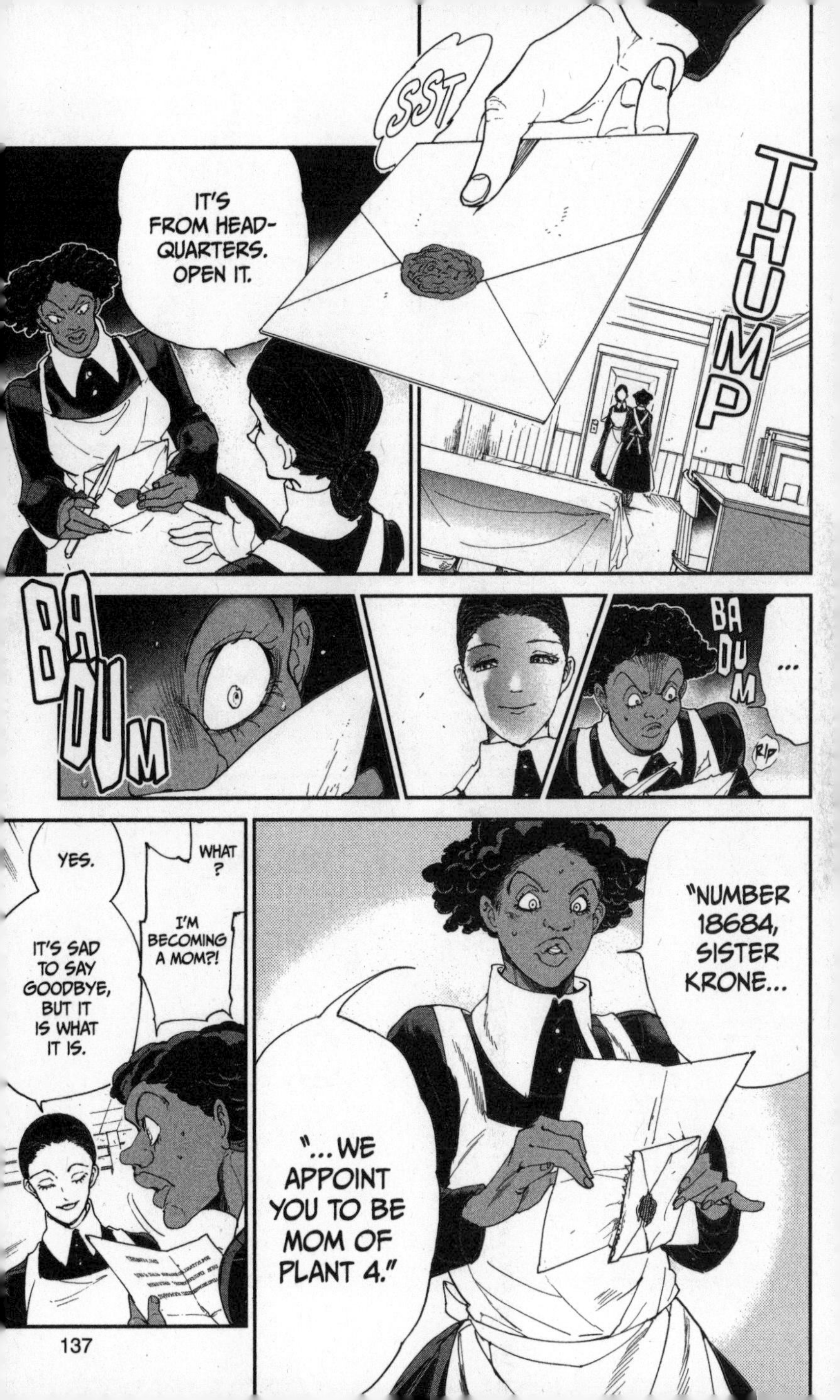
SST
THUMP
IT'S FROM HEAD-QUARTERS. OPEN IT.
BA DUM
...
RIP
BA DUM
"NUMBER 18684, SISTER KRONE...
"...WE APPOINT YOU TO BE MOM OF PLANT 4."
WHAT?
I'M BECOMING A MOM?!
YES.
IT'S SAD TO SAY GOODBYE, BUT IT IS WHAT IT IS.

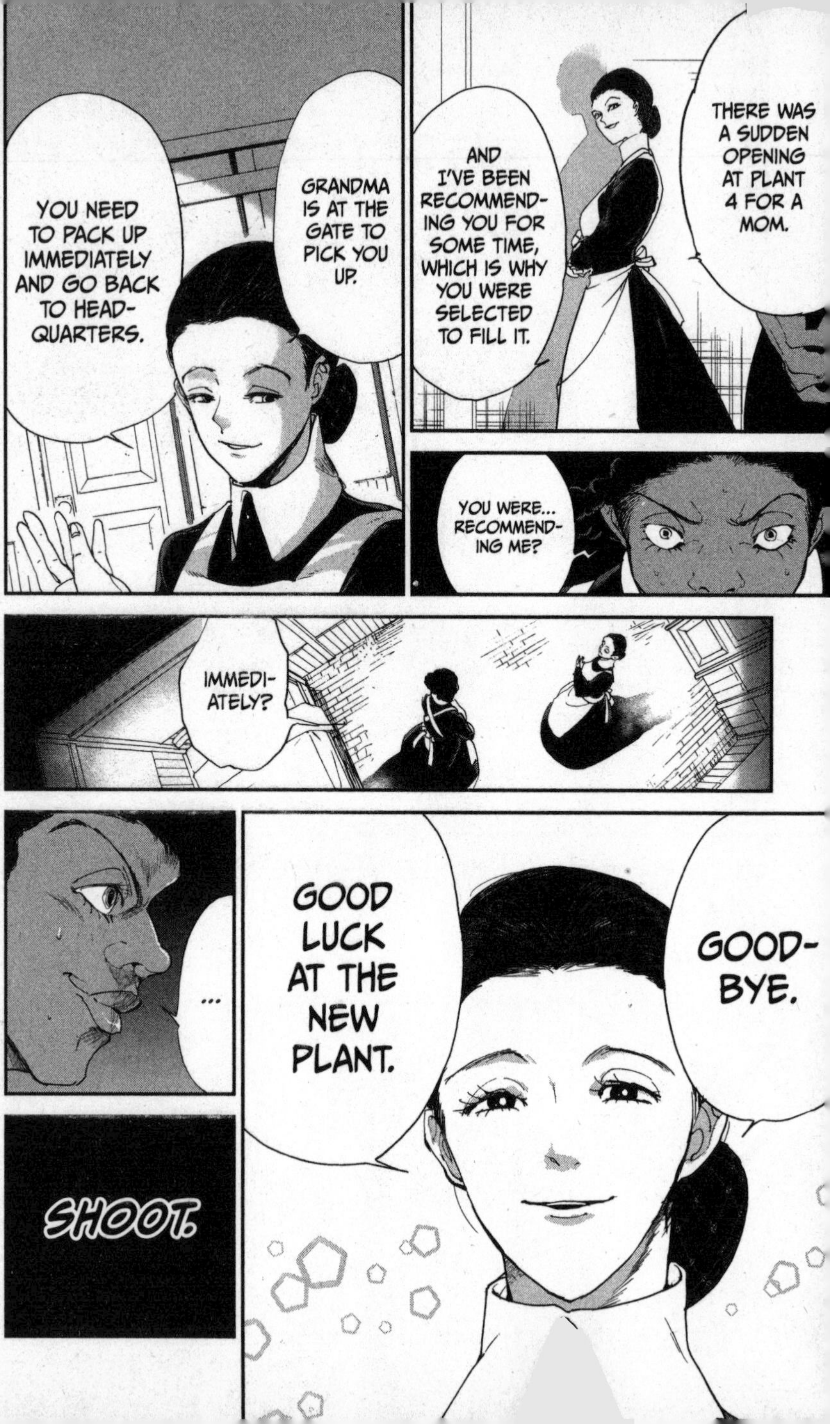
THERE WAS A SUDDEN OPENING AT PLANT 4 FOR A MOM.
AND I'VE BEEN RECOMMENDING YOU FOR SOME TIME, WHICH IS WHY YOU WERE SELECTED TO FILL IT.
YOU WERE... RECOMMENDING ME?
GRANDMA IS AT THE GATE TO PICK YOU UP.
YOU NEED TO PACK UP IMMEDIATELY AND GO BACK TO HEADQUARTERS.
IMMEDIATELY?
GOOD-BYE.
GOOD LUCK AT THE NEW PLANT.
...
SHOOT.

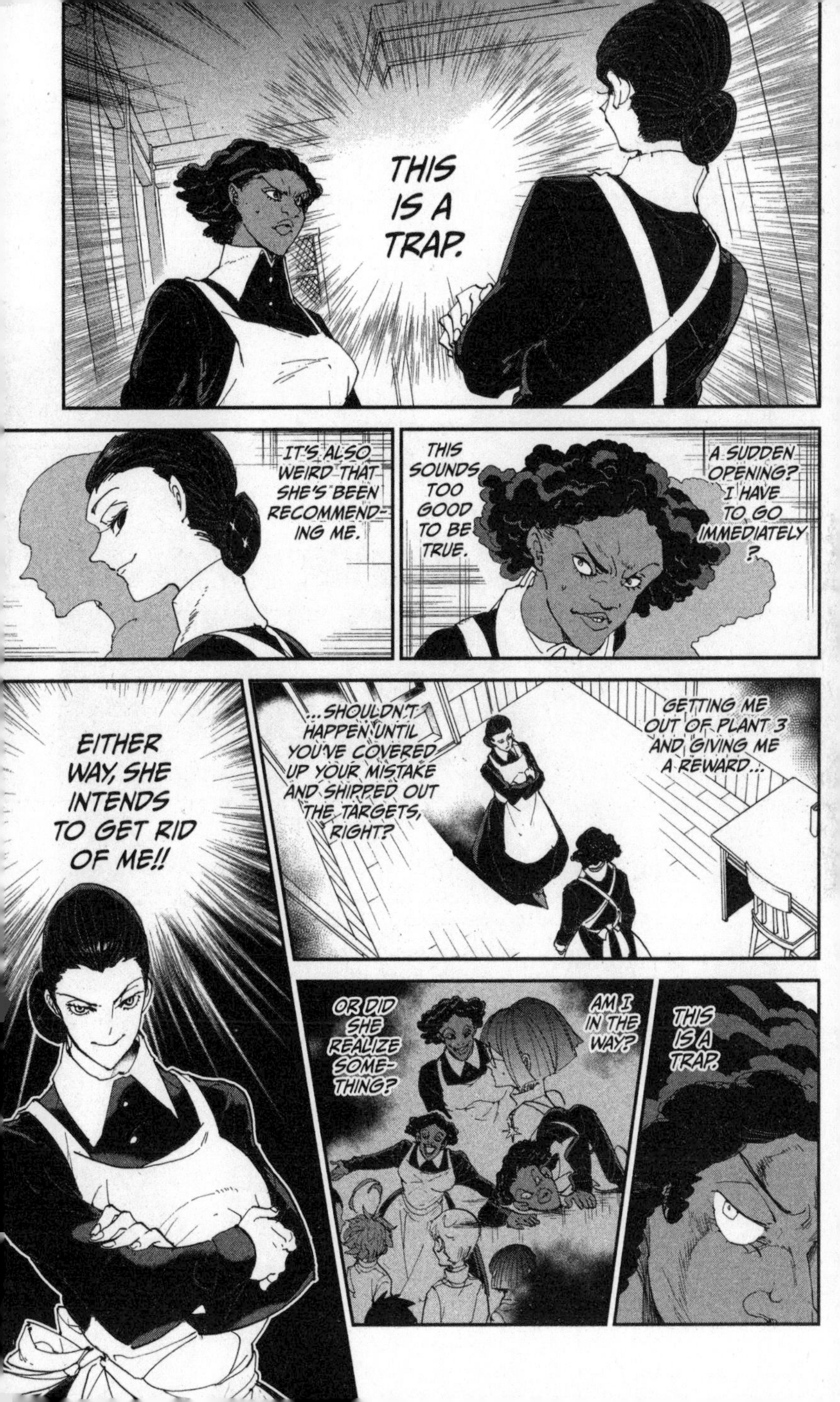
THIS IS A TRAP.
A SUDDEN OPENING? I HAVE TO GO IMMEDIATELY?
THIS SOUNDS TOO GOOD TO BE TRUE.
IT'S ALSO WEIRD THAT SHE'S BEEN RECOMMEND-ING ME.
GETTING ME OUT OF PLANT 3 AND GIVING ME A REWARD...
...SHOULDN'T HAPPEN UNTIL YOU'VE COVERED UP YOUR MISTAKE AND SHIPPED OUT THE TARGETS, RIGHT?
THIS IS A TRAP.
AM I IN THE WAY?
OR DID SHE REALIZE SOME-THING?
EITHER WAY, SHE INTENDS TO GET RID OF ME!!

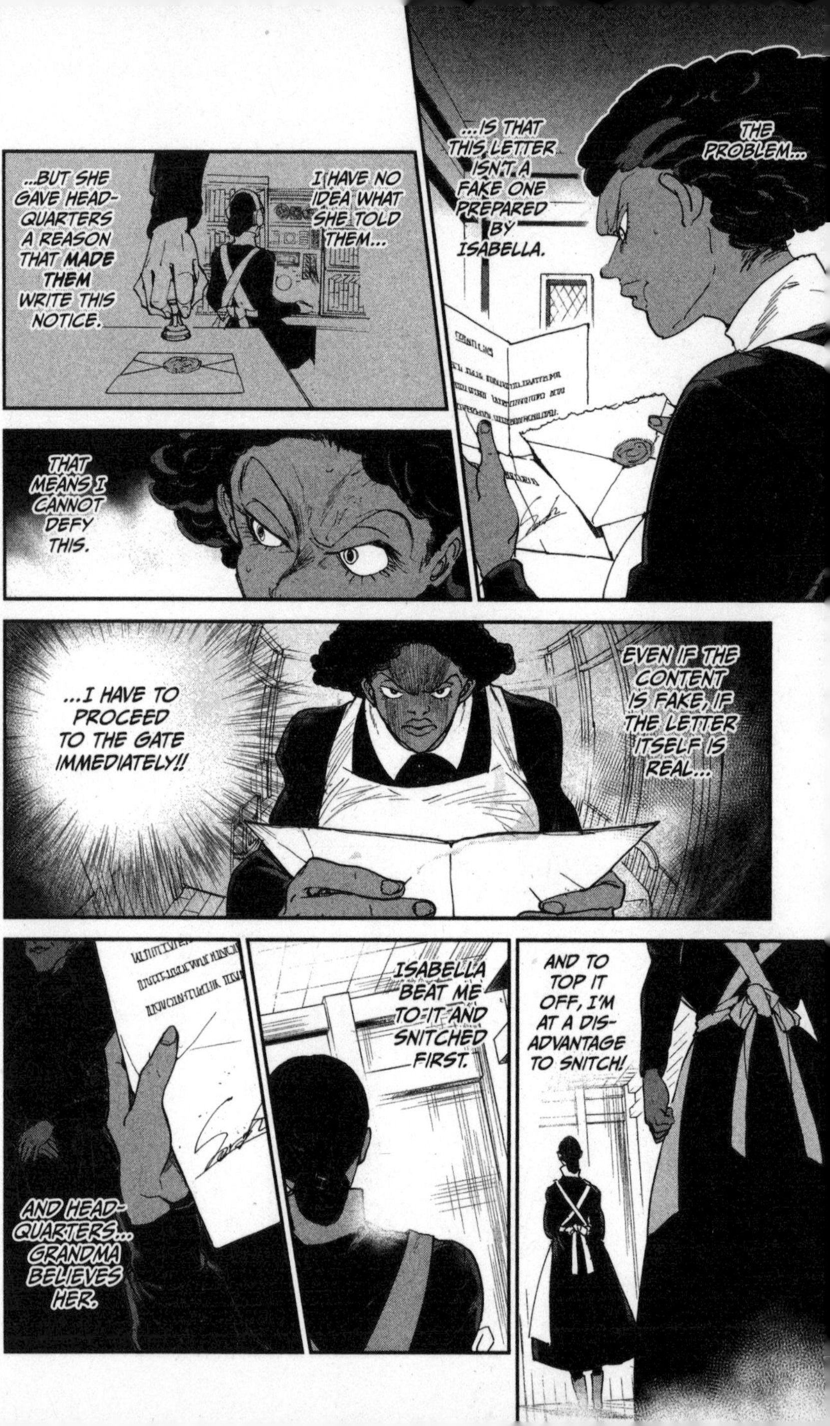
THE PROBLEM...
...IS THAT THIS LETTER ISN'T A FAKE ONE PREPARED BY ISABELLA.
I HAVE NO IDEA WHAT SHE TOLD THEM...
...BUT SHE GAVE HEAD-QUARTERS A REASON THAT MADE THEM WRITE THIS NOTICE.
THAT MEANS I CANNOT DEFY THIS.
EVEN IF THE CONTENT IS FAKE, IF THE LETTER ITSELF IS REAL...
...I HAVE TO PROCEED TO THE GATE IMMEDIATELY!!
AND TO TOP IT OFF, I'M AT A DIS-ADVANTAGE TO SNITCH!
ISABELLA BEAT ME TO IT AND SNITCHED FIRST.
AND HEAD-QUARTERS... GRANDMA BELIEVES HER.

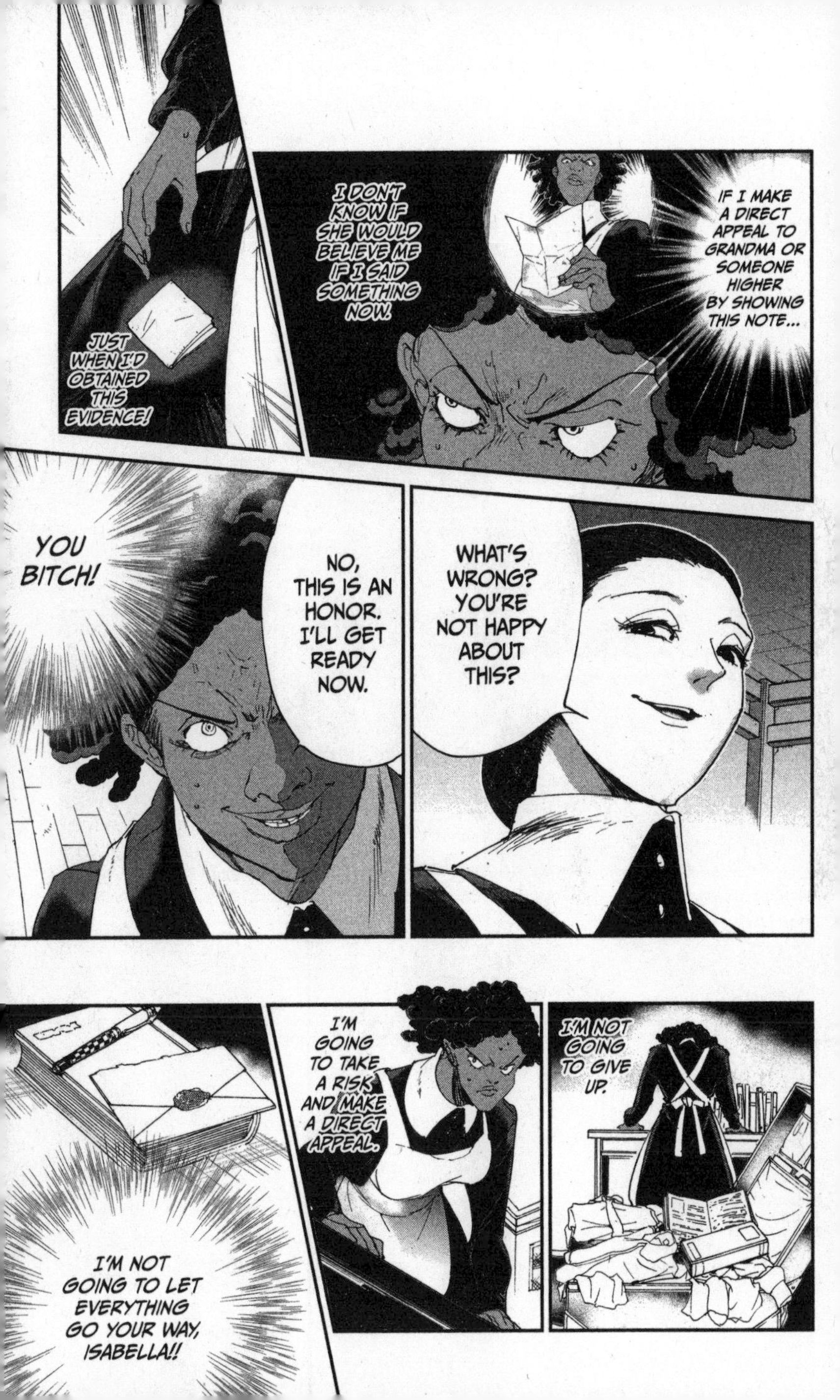
IF I MAKE A DIRECT APPEAL TO GRANDMA OR SOMEONE HIGHER BY SHOWING THIS NOTE...
I DON'T KNOW IF SHE WOULD BELIEVE ME IF I SAID SOMETHING NOW.
JUST WHEN I'D OBTAINED THIS EVIDENCE!
WHAT'S WRONG? YOU'RE NOT HAPPY ABOUT THIS?
NO, THIS IS AN HONOR. I'LL GET READY NOW.
YOU BITCH!
I'M NOT GOING TO GIVE UP.
I'M GOING TO TAKE A RISK AND MAKE A DIRECT APPEAL.
I'M NOT GOING TO LET EVERYTHING GO YOUR WAY, ISABELLA!!

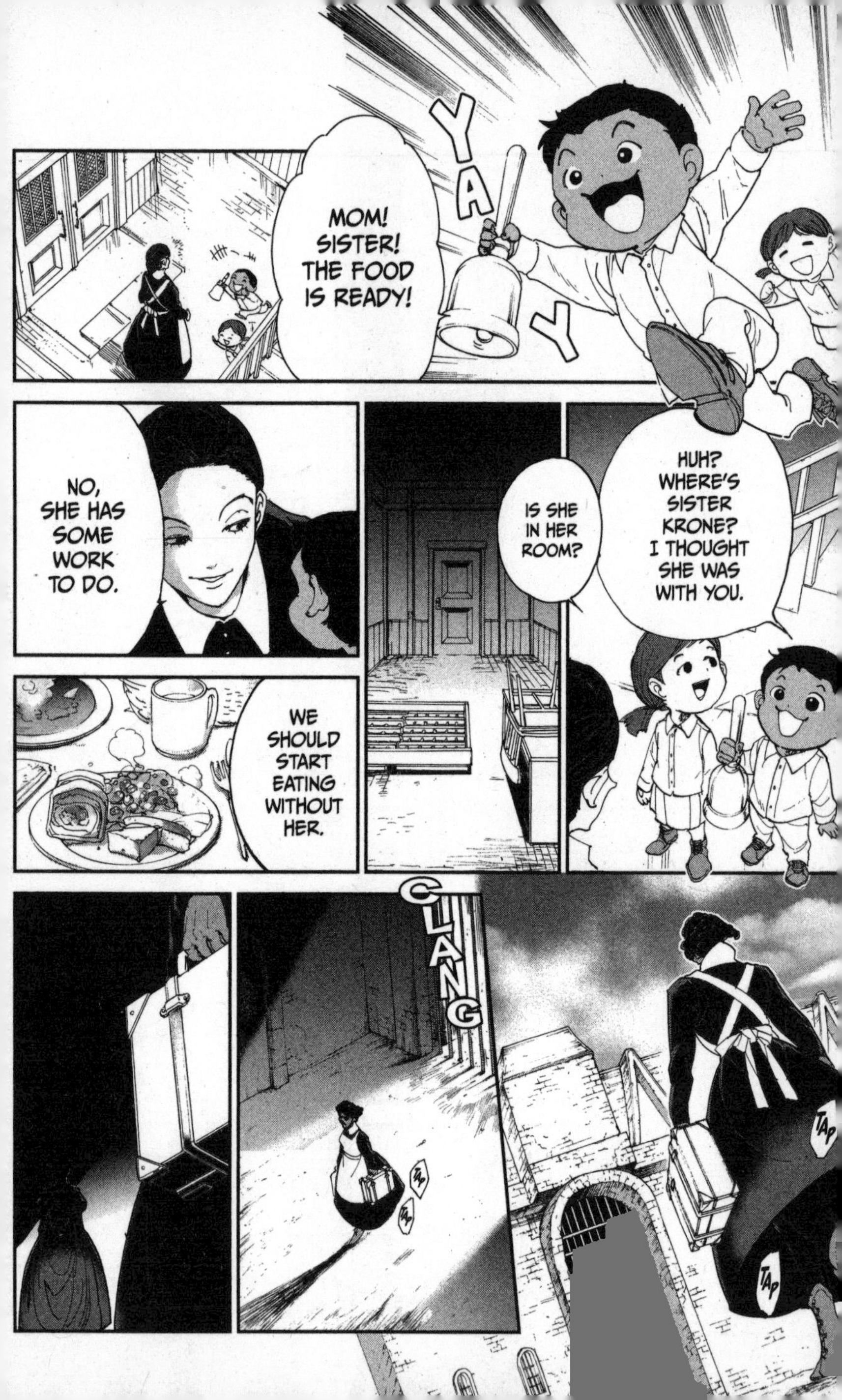
YAY
MOM! SISTER! THE FOOD IS READY!
HUH? WHERE'S SISTER KRONE? I THOUGHT SHE WAS WITH YOU.
IS SHE IN HER ROOM?
NO, SHE HAS SOME WORK TO DO.
WE SHOULD START EATING WITHOUT HER.
TAP
TAP
CLANG
TAP
TAP

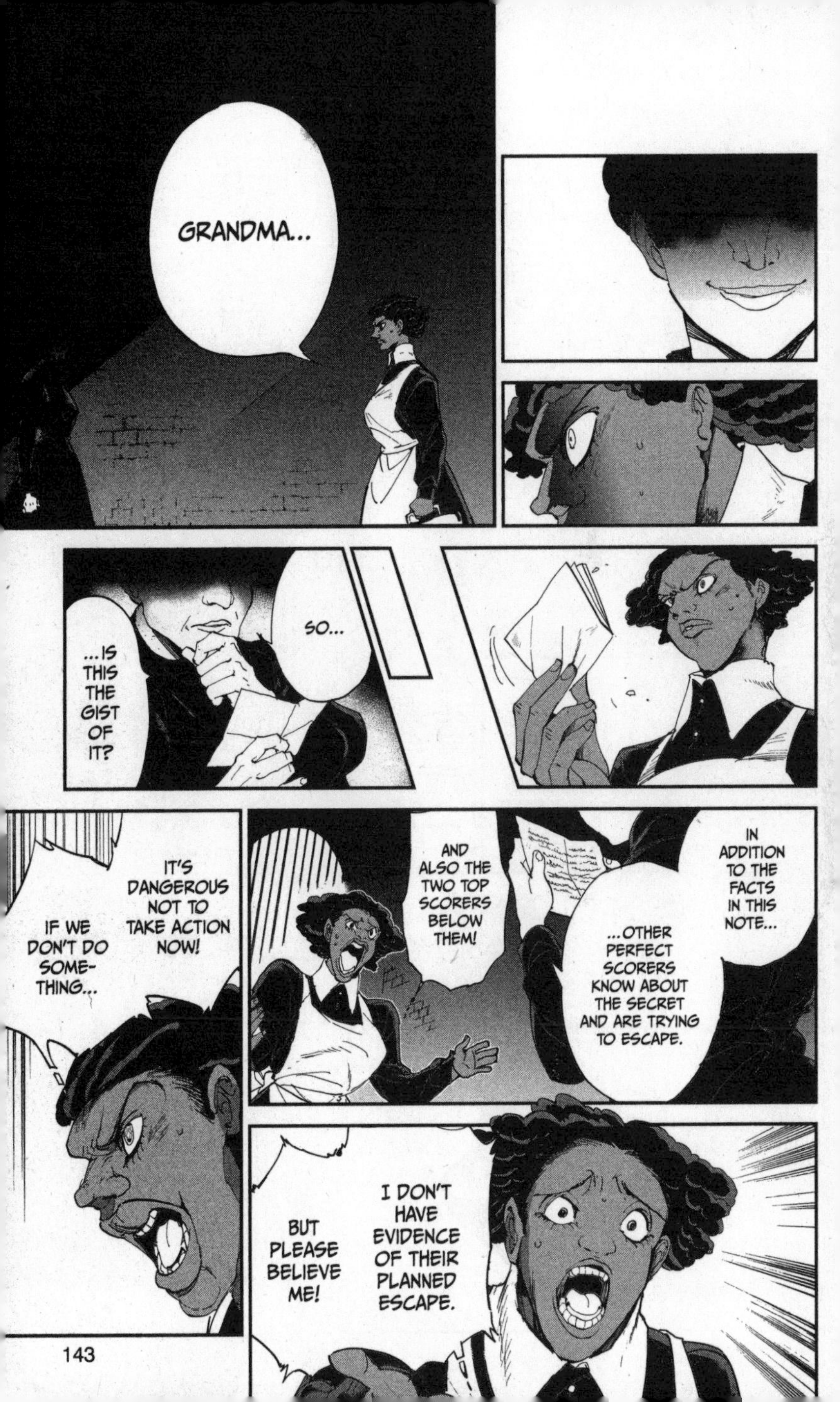
GRANDMA...
SO...
...IS THIS THE GIST OF IT?
IN ADDITION TO THE FACTS IN THIS NOTE...
...OTHER PERFECT SCORERS KNOW ABOUT THE SECRET AND ARE TRYING TO ESCAPE.
AND ALSO THE TWO TOP SCORERS BELOW THEM!
I DON'T HAVE EVIDENCE OF THEIR PLANNED ESCAPE.
BUT PLEASE BELIEVE ME!
IT'S DANGEROUS NOT TO TAKE ACTION NOW!
IF WE DON'T DO SOMETHING...

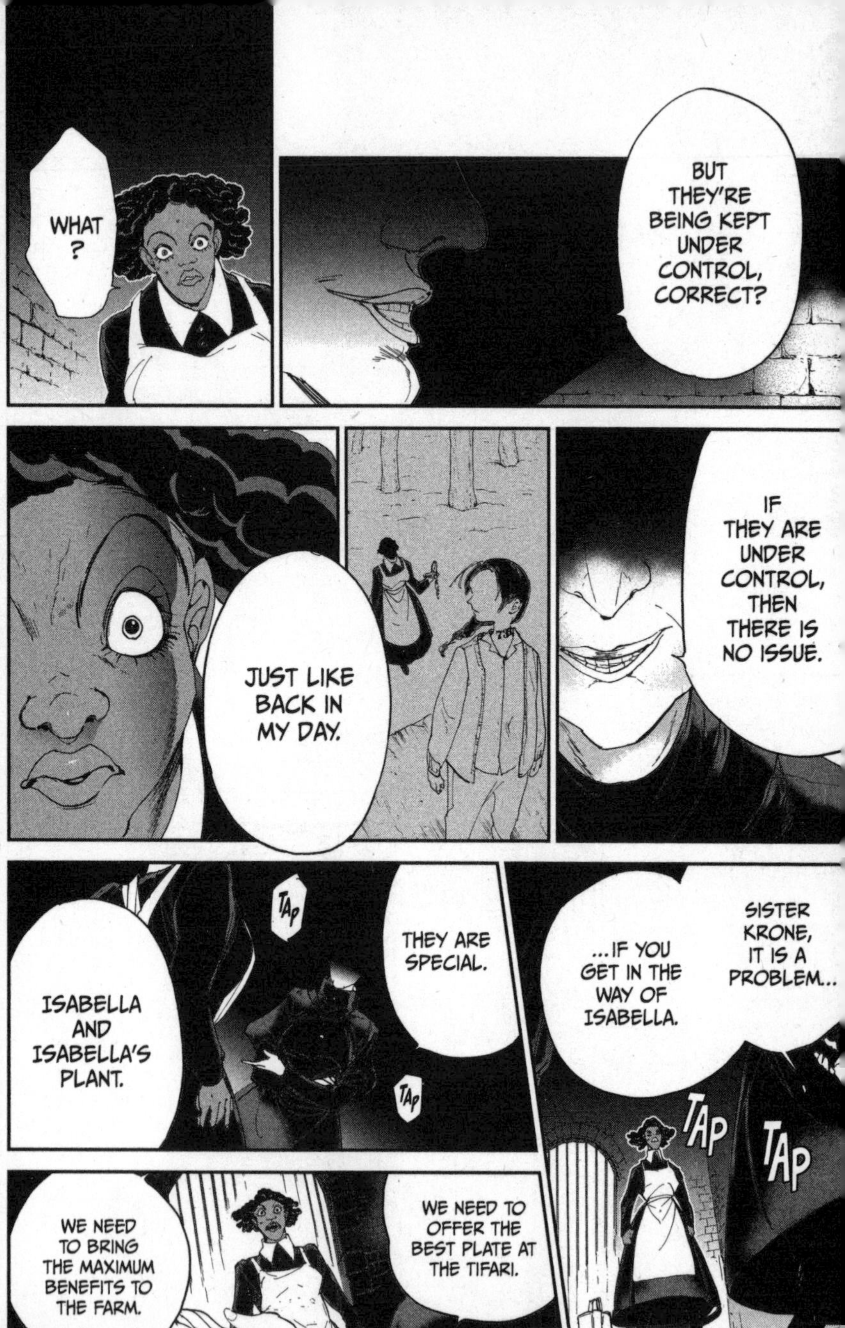
BUT THEY'RE BEING KEPT UNDER CONTROL, CORRECT?
WHAT ?
IF THEY ARE UNDER CONTROL, THEN THERE IS NO ISSUE.
JUST LIKE BACK IN MY DAY.
SISTER KRONE, IT IS A PROBLEM...
...IF YOU GET IN THE WAY OF ISABELLA.
TAP
TAP
THEY ARE SPECIAL.
TAP
ISABELLA AND ISABELLA'S PLANT.
TAP
WE NEED TO OFFER THE BEST PLATE AT THE TIFARI.
WE NEED TO BRING THE MAXIMUM BENEFITS TO THE FARM.

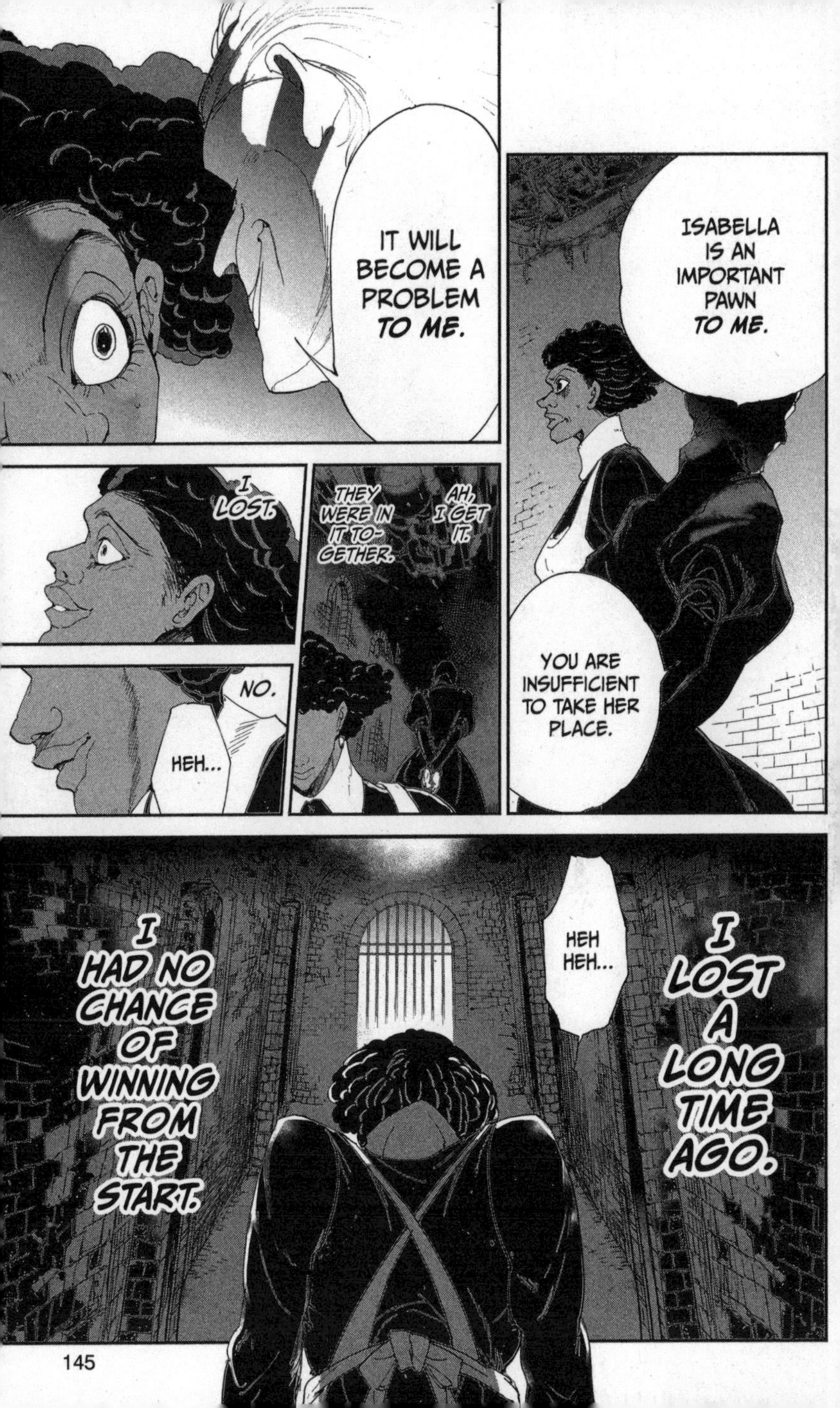
IT WILL BECOME A PROBLEM TO ME.
ISABELLA IS AN IMPORTANT PAWN TO ME.
YOU ARE INSUFFICIENT TO TAKE HER PLACE.
AH, I GET IT.
THEY WERE IN IT TO-GETHER.
I LOST.
NO.
HEH...
I LOST A LONG TIME AGO.
HEH HEH...
I HAD NO CHANCE OF WINNING FROM THE START.

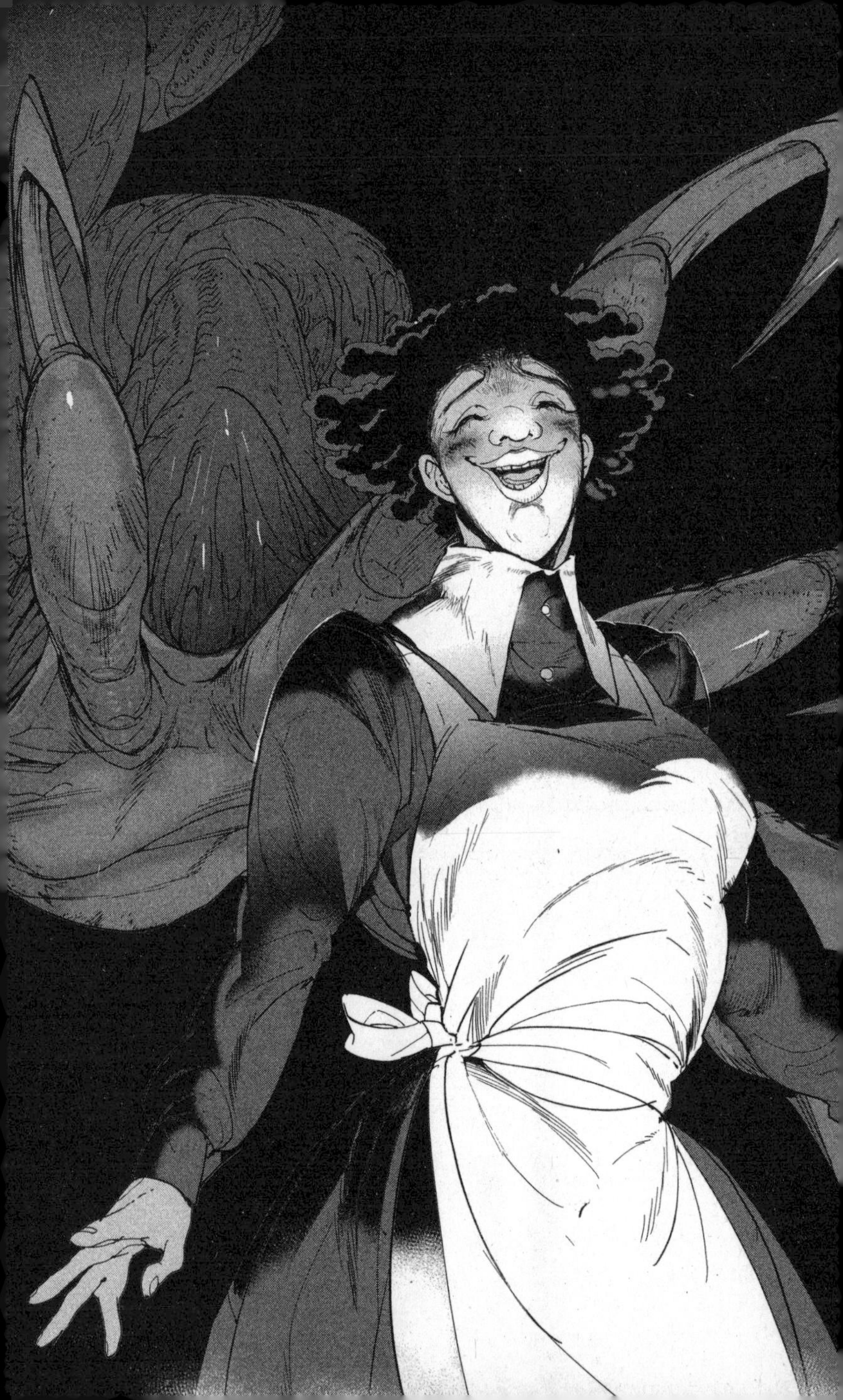

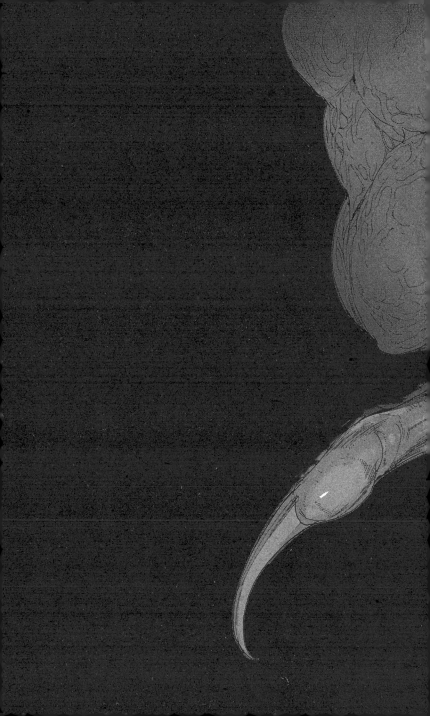

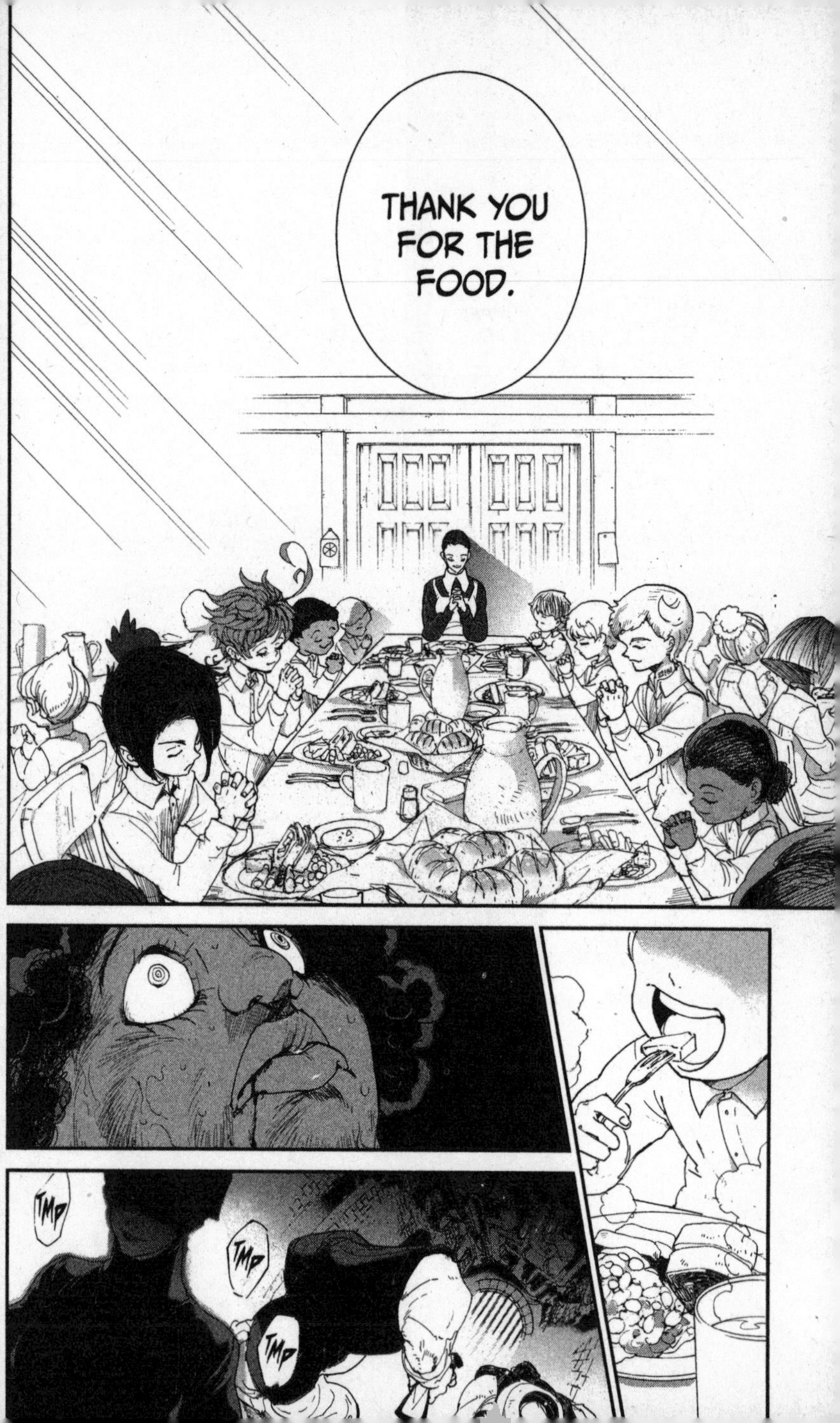
THANK YOU FOR THE FOOD.
TMP
TMP
TMP

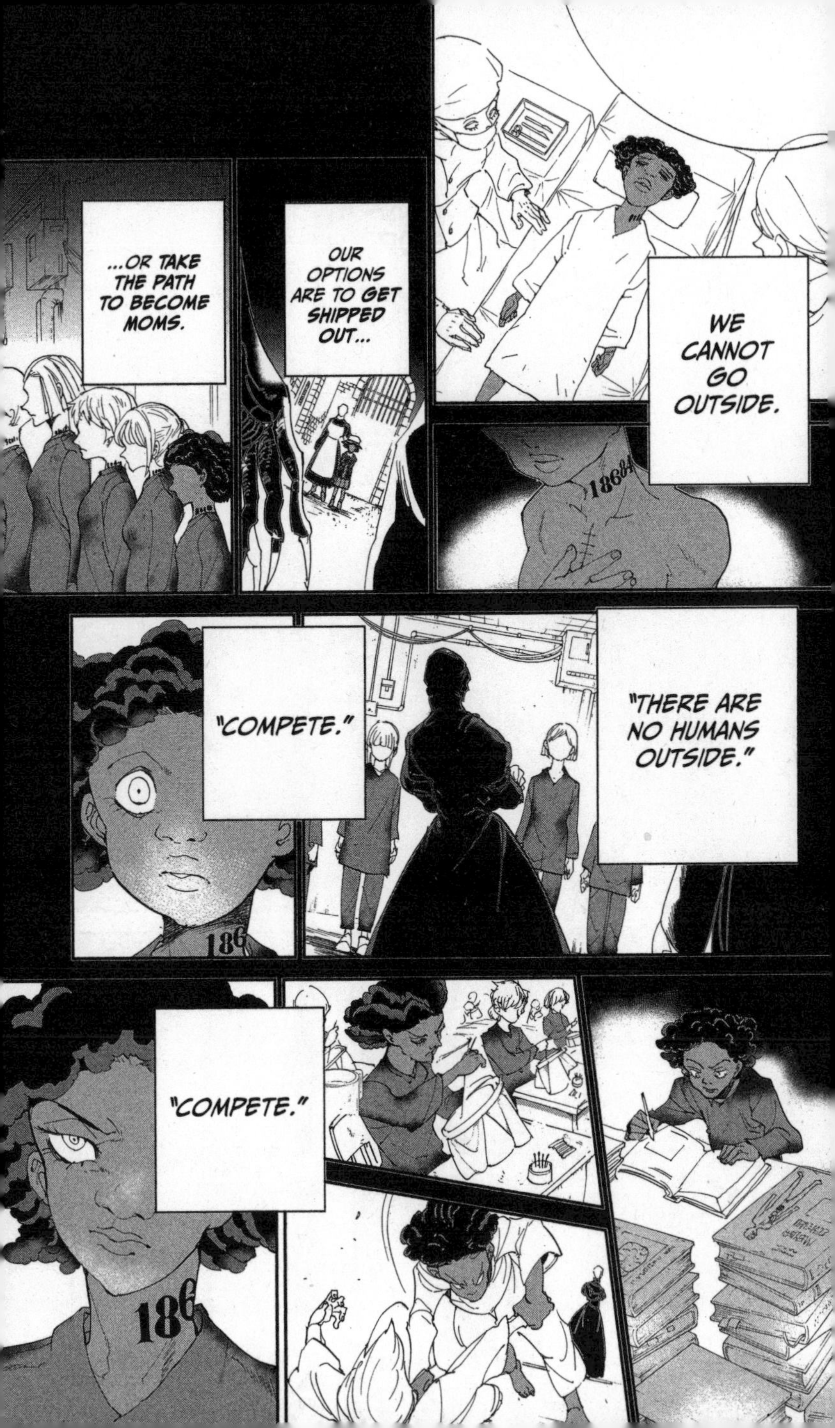
WE CANNOT GO OUTSIDE.
OUR OPTIONS ARE TO GET SHIPPED OUT...
...OR TAKE THE PATH TO BECOME MOMS.
"THERE ARE NO HUMANS OUTSIDE."
"COMPETE."
"COMPETE."

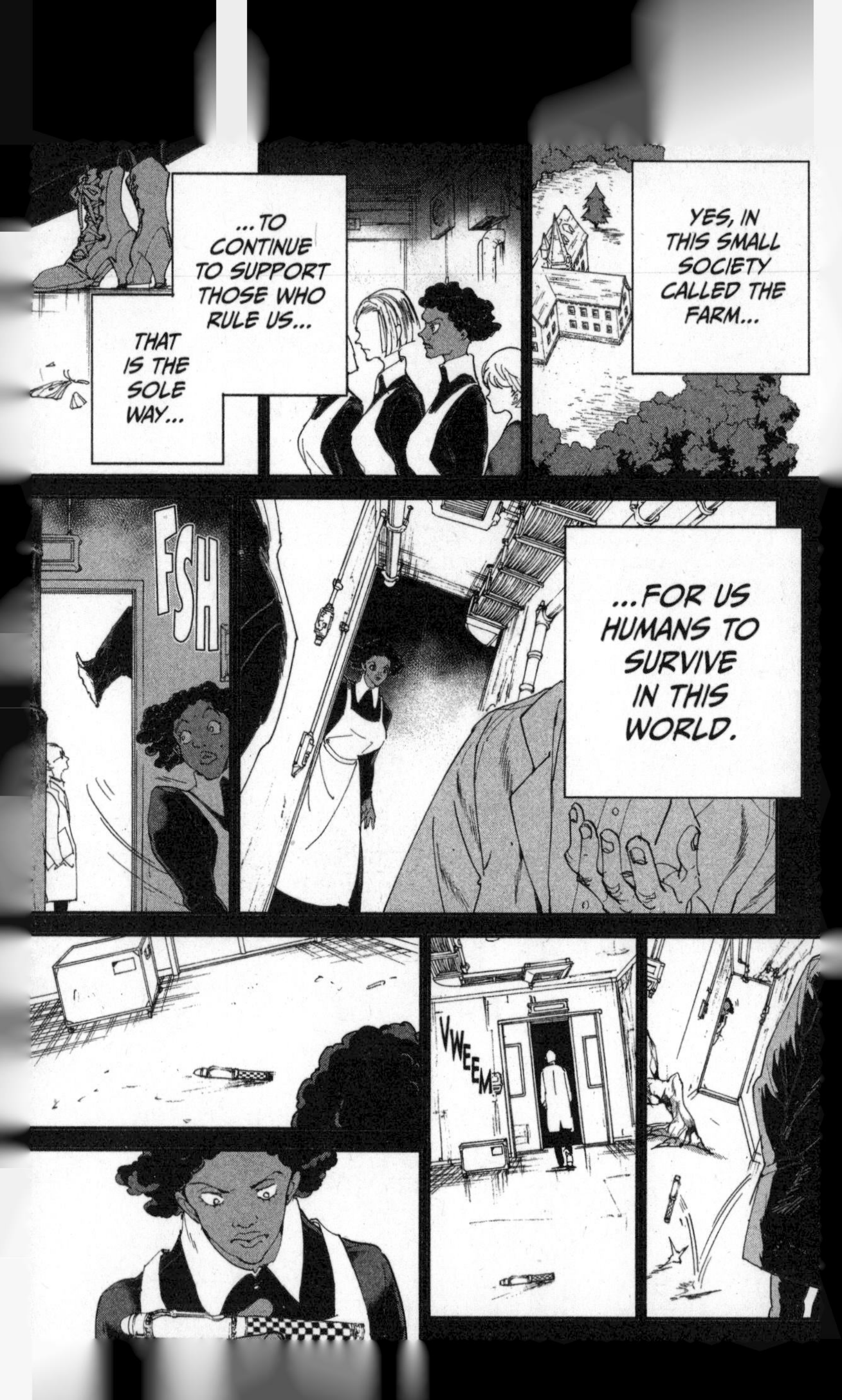
YES, IN THIS SMALL SOCIETY CALLED THE FARM...
...TO CONTINUE TO SUPPORT THOSE WHO RULE US...
THAT IS THE SOLE WAY...
...FOR US HUMANS TO SURVIVE IN THIS WORLD.
FSH
VWEEM

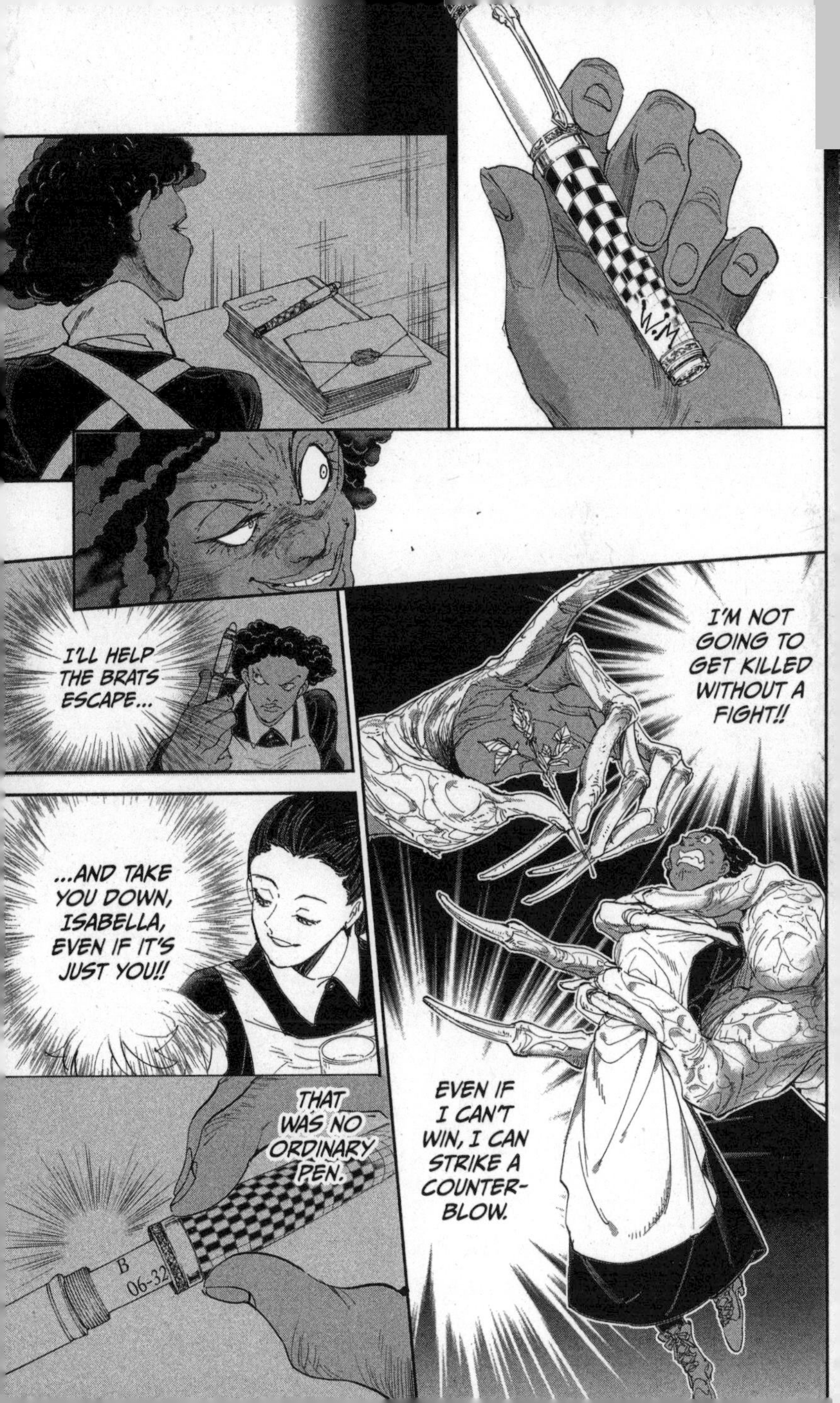
I'M NOT GOING TO GET KILLED WITHOUT A FIGHT!!
EVEN IF I CAN'T WIN, I CAN STRIKE A COUNTER-BLOW.
I'LL HELP THE BRATS ESCAPE...
...AND TAKE YOU DOWN, ISABELLA, EVEN IF IT'S JUST YOU!!
THAT WAS NO ORDINARY PEN.
B
06-32

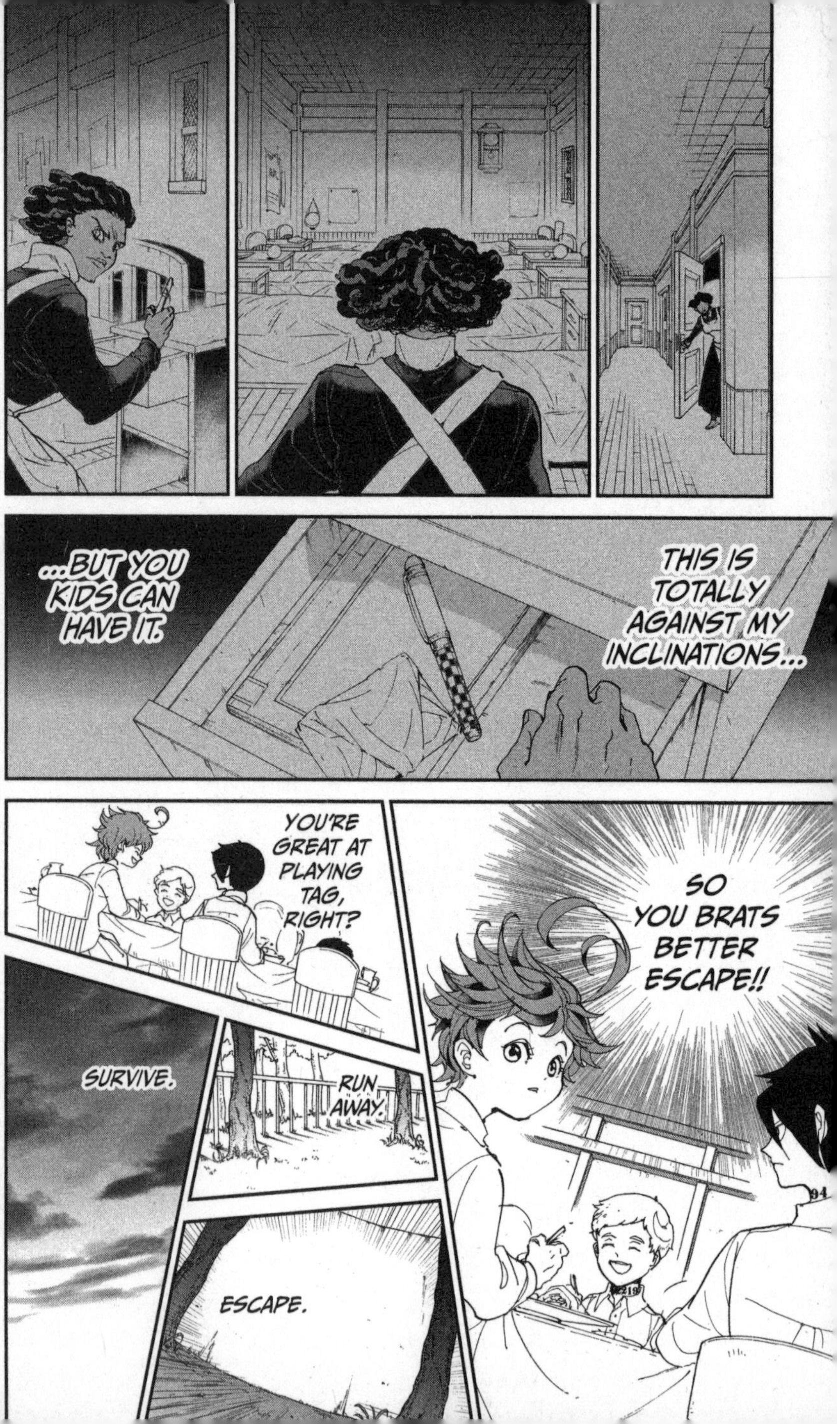
THIS IS TOTALLY AGAINST MY INCLINATIONS...
...BUT YOU KIDS CAN HAVE IT.
SO YOU BRATS BETTER ESCAPE!!
YOU'RE GREAT AT PLAYING TAG, RIGHT?
RUN AWAY.
SURVIVE.
ESCAPE.

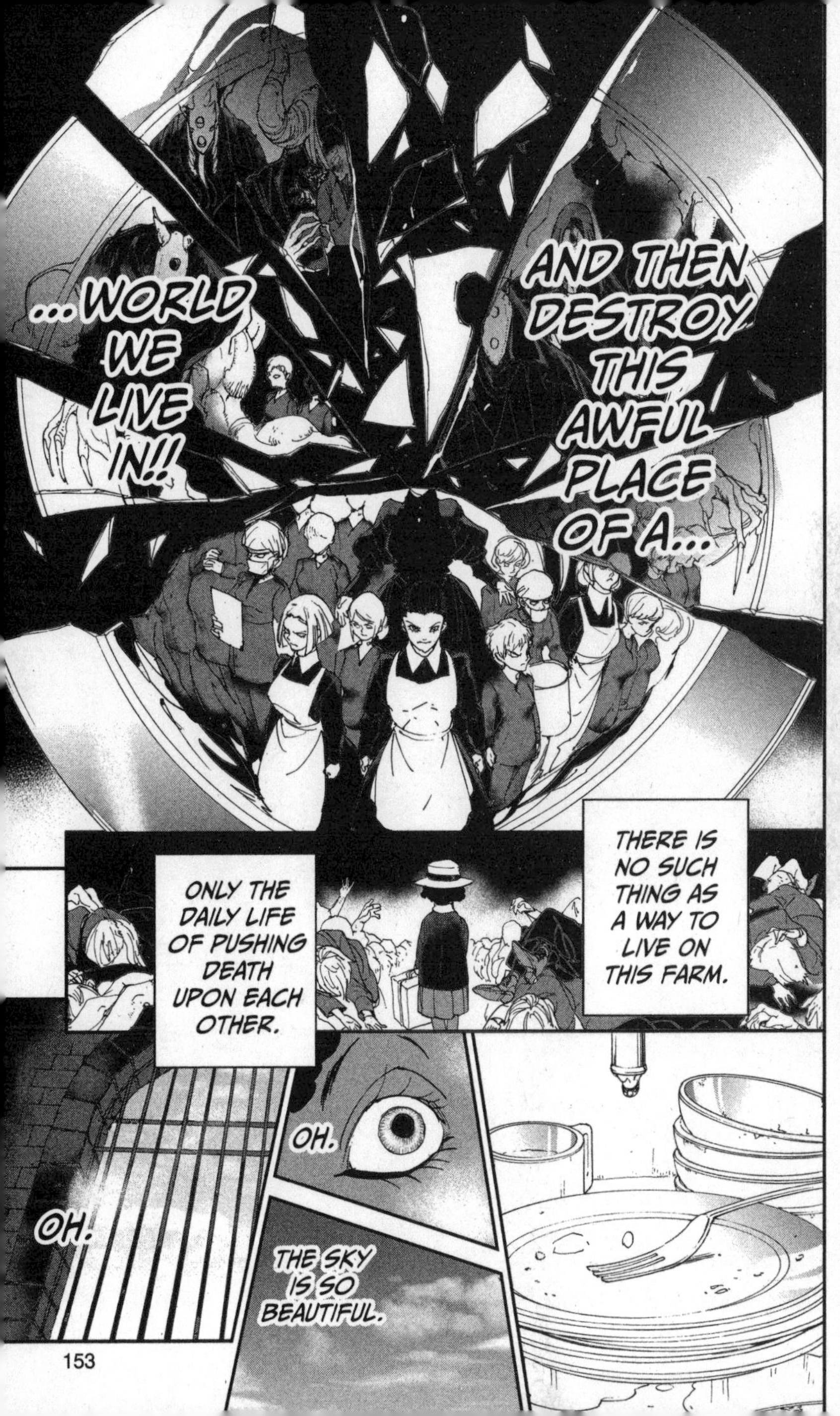
AND THEN DESTROY THIS AWFUL PLACE OF A...
...WORLD WE LIVE IN!!
THERE IS NO SUCH THING AS A WAY TO LIVE ON THIS FARM.
ONLY THE DAILY LIFE OF PUSHING DEATH UPON EACH OTHER.
OH.
THE SKY IS SO BEAUTIFUL.
OH.

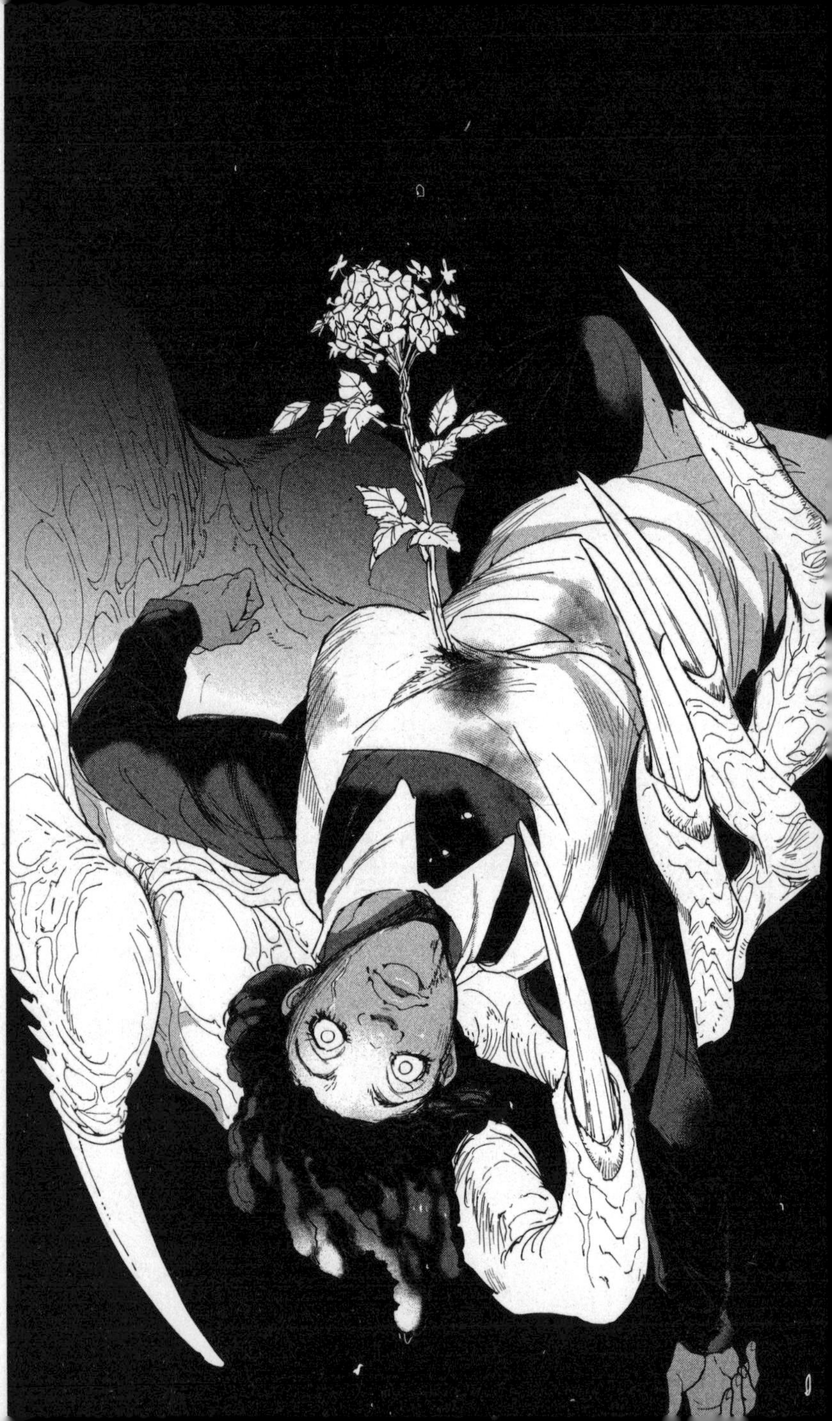

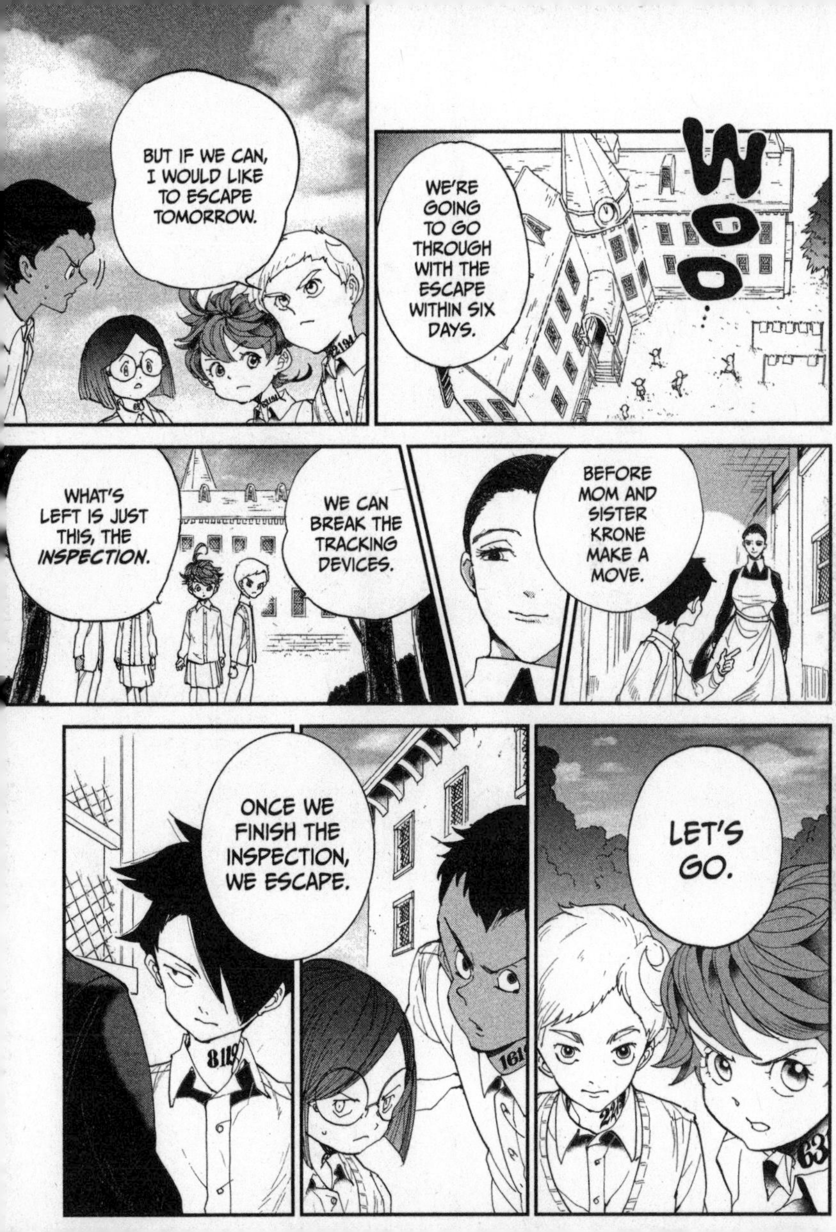
WOO...
WE'RE GOING TO GO THROUGH WITH THE ESCAPE WITHIN SIX DAYS.
BUT IF WE CAN, I WOULD LIKE TO ESCAPE TOMORROW.
BEFORE MOM AND SISTER KRONE MAKE A MOVE.
WE CAN BREAK THE TRACKING DEVICES.
WHAT'S LEFT IS JUST THIS, THE *INSPECTION*.
LET'S GO.
ONCE WE FINISH THE INSPECTION, WE ESCAPE.

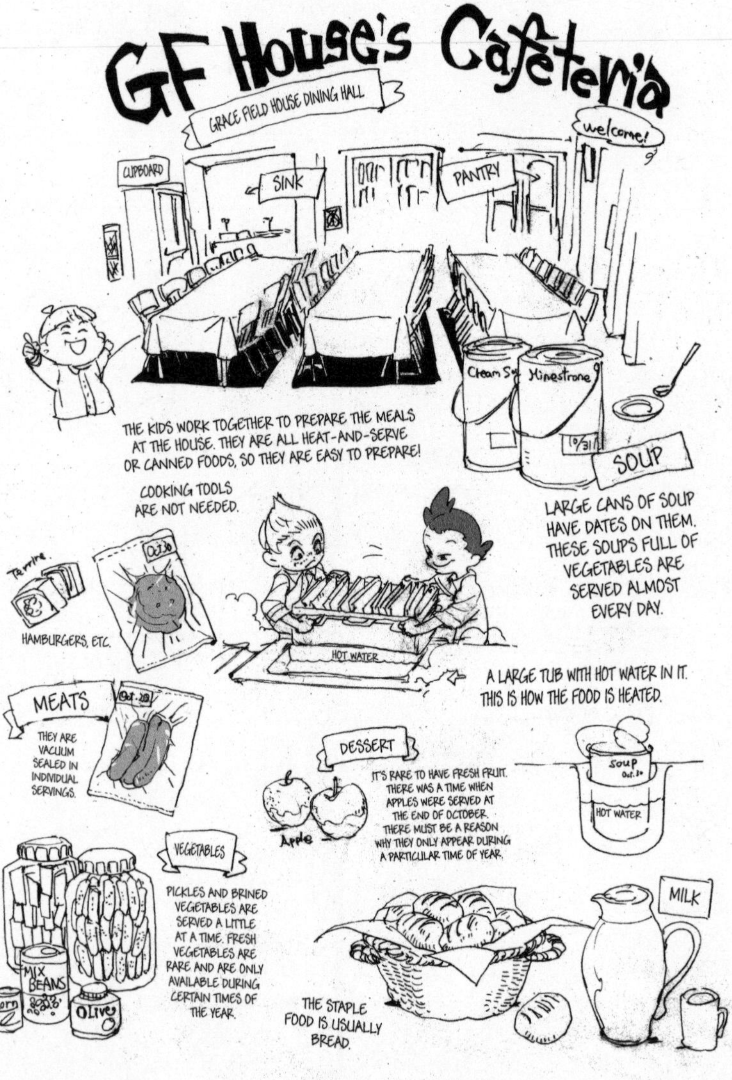
GF House's Cafeteria
GRACE FIELD HOUSE DINING HALL
welcome!
CUPBOARD
SINK
PANTRY
Cream So
Minestrone
10/31
SOUP
THE KIDS WORK TOGETHER TO PREPARE THE MEALS AT THE HOUSE. THEY ARE ALL HEAT-AND-SERVE OR CANNED FOODS, SO THEY ARE EASY TO PREPARE!
COOKING TOOLS ARE NOT NEEDED.
LARGE CANS OF SOUP HAVE DATES ON THEM. THESE SOUPS FULL OF VEGETABLES ARE SERVED ALMOST EVERY DAY.
Terrine
Oct.30
HAMBURGERS, ETC.
HOT WATER
A LARGE TUB WITH HOT WATER IN IT. THIS IS HOW THE FOOD IS HEATED.
MEATS
Oct.29
THEY ARE VACUUM SEALED IN INDIVIDUAL SERVINGS.
DESSERT
IT'S RARE TO HAVE FRESH FRUIT. THERE WAS A TIME WHEN APPLES WERE SERVED AT THE END OF OCTOBER. THERE MUST BE A REASON WHY THEY ONLY APPEAR DURING A PARTICULAR TIME OF YEAR.
Apple
Soup
Oct.30
HOT WATER
VEGETABLES
PICKLES AND BRINED VEGETABLES ARE SERVED A LITTLE AT A TIME. FRESH VEGETABLES ARE RARE AND ARE ONLY AVAILABLE DURING CERTAIN TIMES OF THE YEAR.
MIX BEANS
Corn
Olive
THE STAPLE FOOD IS USUALLY BREAD.
MILK

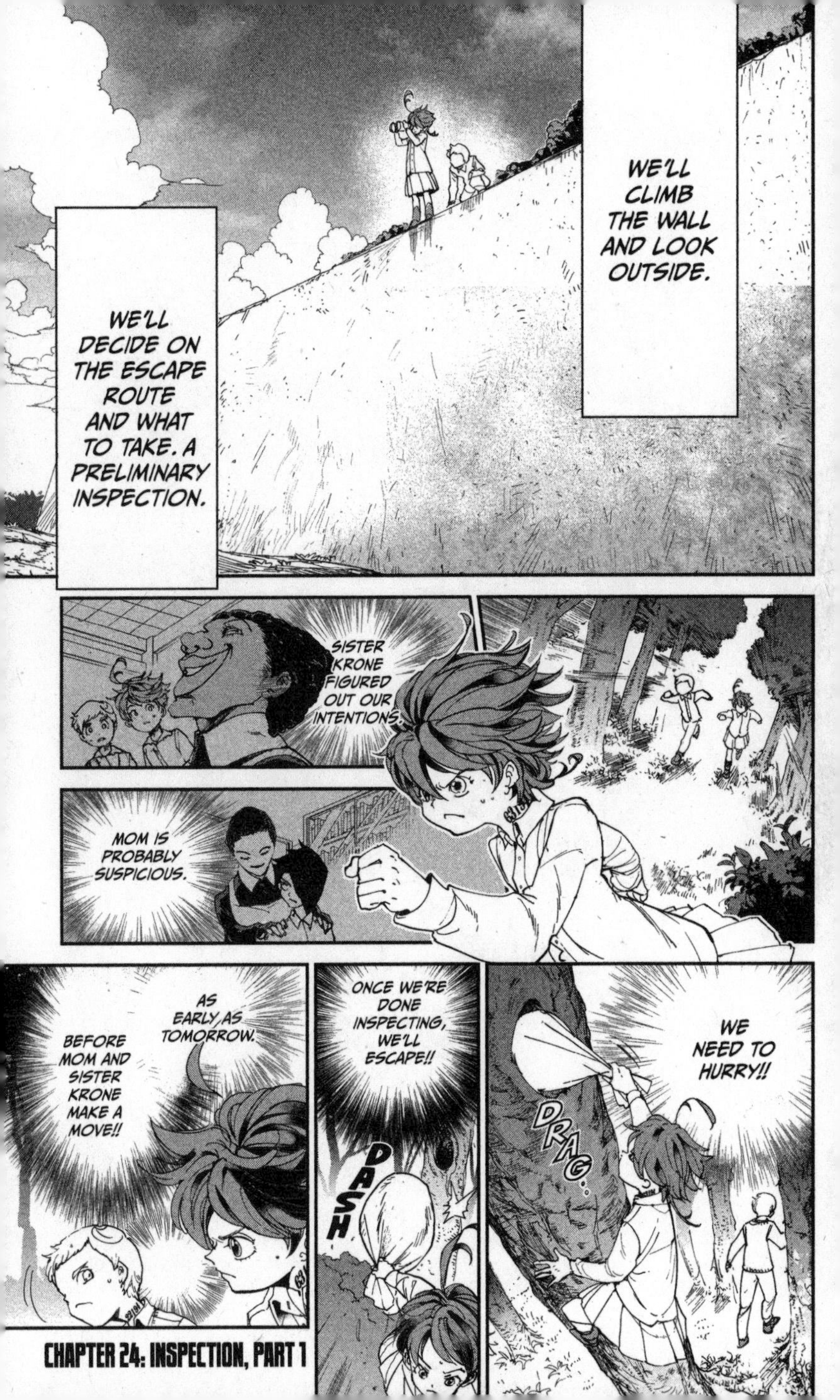
WE'LL CLIMB THE WALL AND LOOK OUTSIDE.
WE'LL DECIDE ON THE ESCAPE ROUTE AND WHAT TO TAKE. A PRELIMINARY INSPECTION.
SISTER KRONE FIGURED OUT OUR INTENTIONS.
MOM IS PROBABLY SUSPICIOUS.
WE NEED TO HURRY!!
DRAG...
ONCE WE'RE DONE INSPECTING, WE'LL ESCAPE!!
DASH
AS EARLY AS TOMORROW.
BEFORE MOM AND SISTER KRONE MAKE A MOVE!!

CHAPTER 24: INSPECTION, PART 1

CHAPTER 24: INSPECTION, PART 1

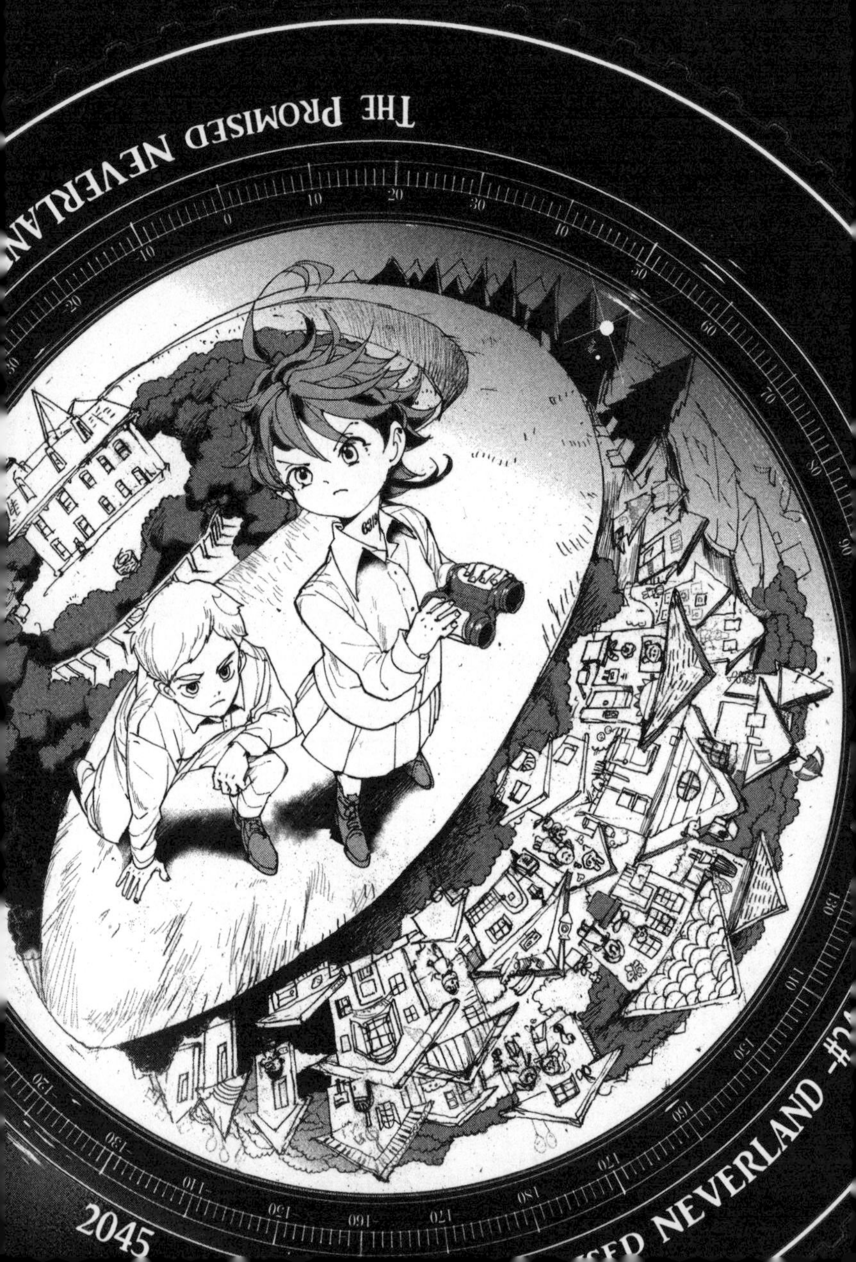
THE PROMISED NEVERLAN
2045
SED NEVERLAND

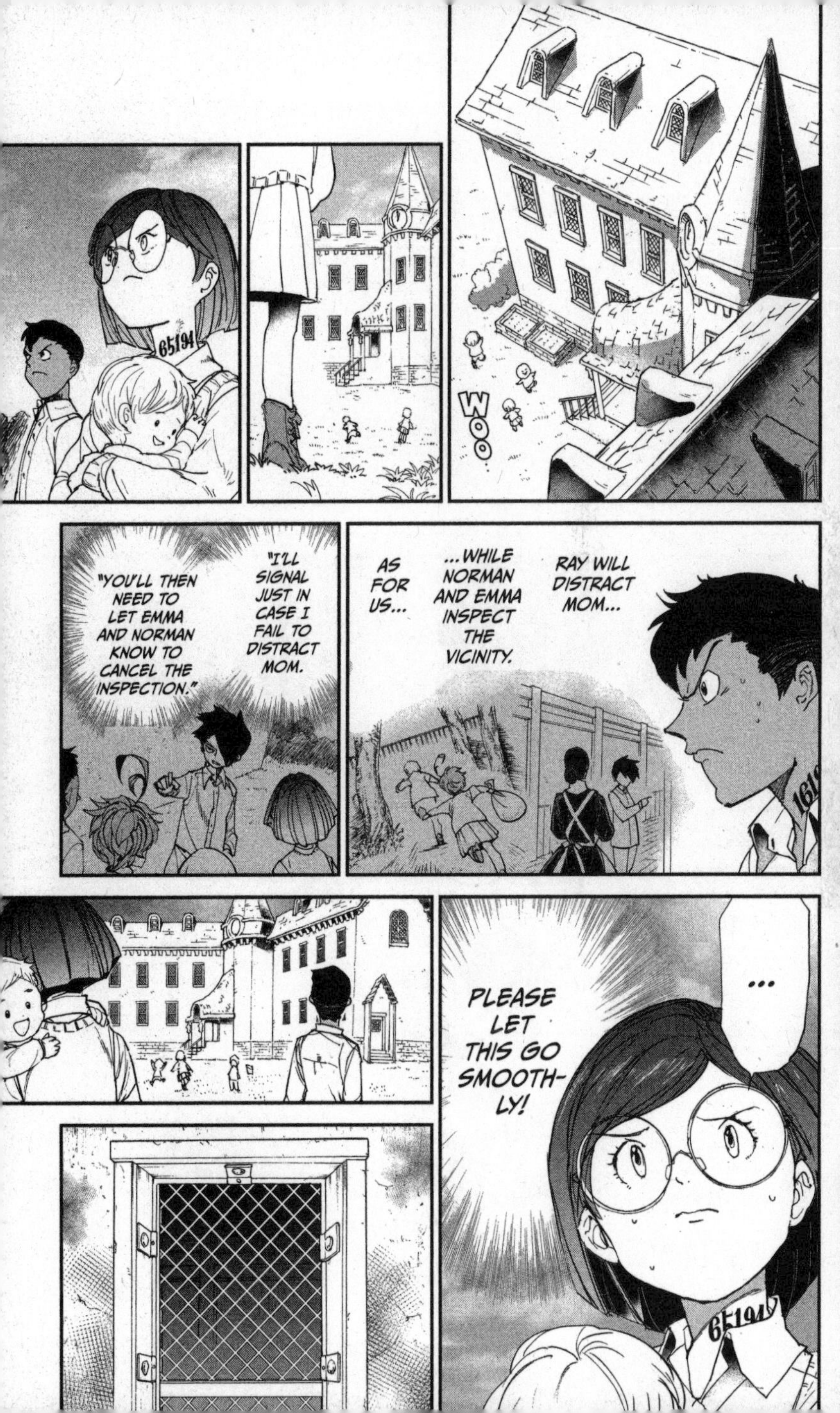
WOO
RAY WILL DISTRACT MOM...
...WHILE NORMAN AND EMMA INSPECT THE VICINITY.
AS FOR US...
"I'LL SIGNAL JUST IN CASE I FAIL TO DISTRACT MOM.
"YOU'LL THEN NEED TO LET EMMA AND NORMAN KNOW TO CANCEL THE INSPECTION."
...
PLEASE LET THIS GO SMOOTH-LY!

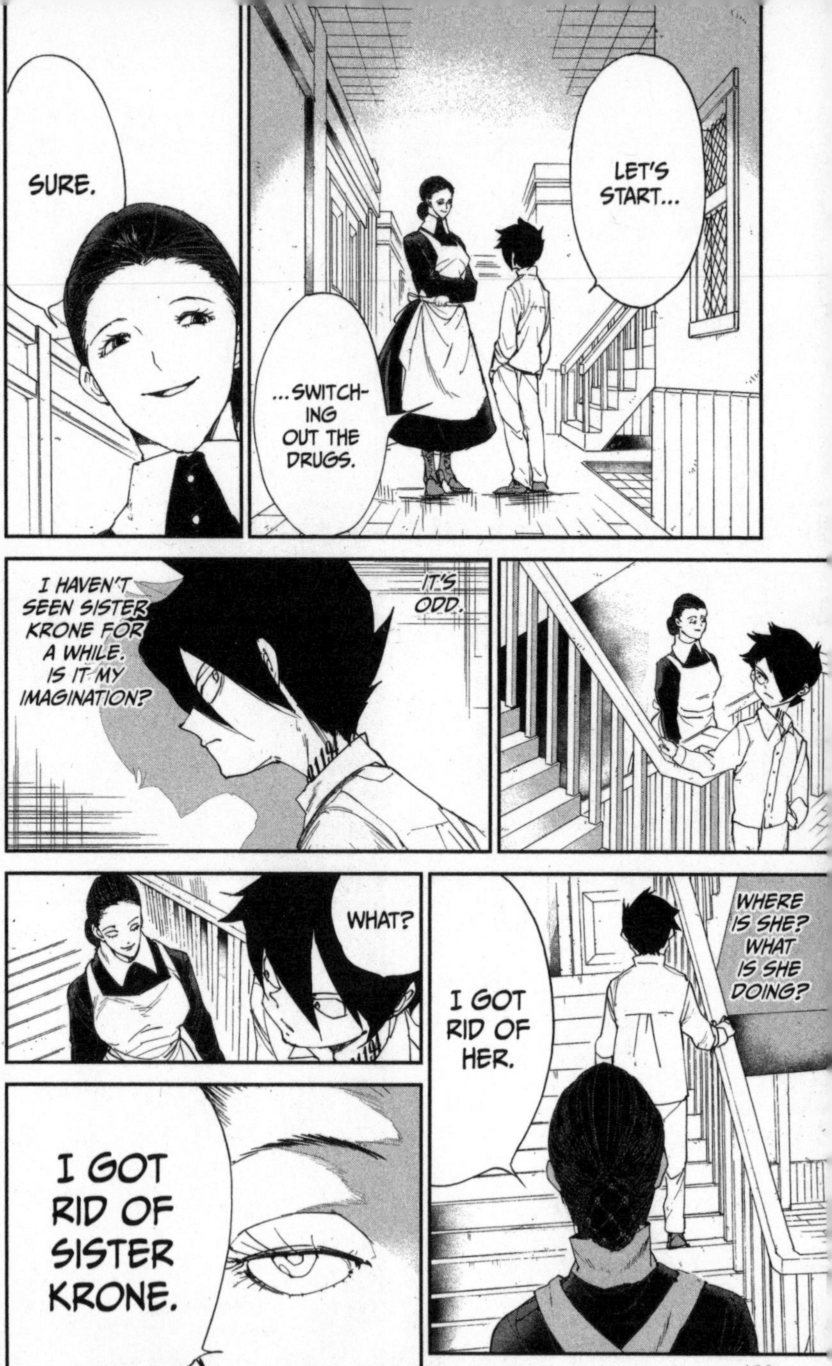
LET'S START...
...SWITCHING OUT THE DRUGS.
SURE.
IT'S ODD.
I HAVEN'T SEEN SISTER KRONE FOR A WHILE. IS IT MY IMAGINATION?
WHERE IS SHE? WHAT IS SHE DOING?
I GOT RID OF HER.
WHAT?
I GOT RID OF SISTER KRONE.

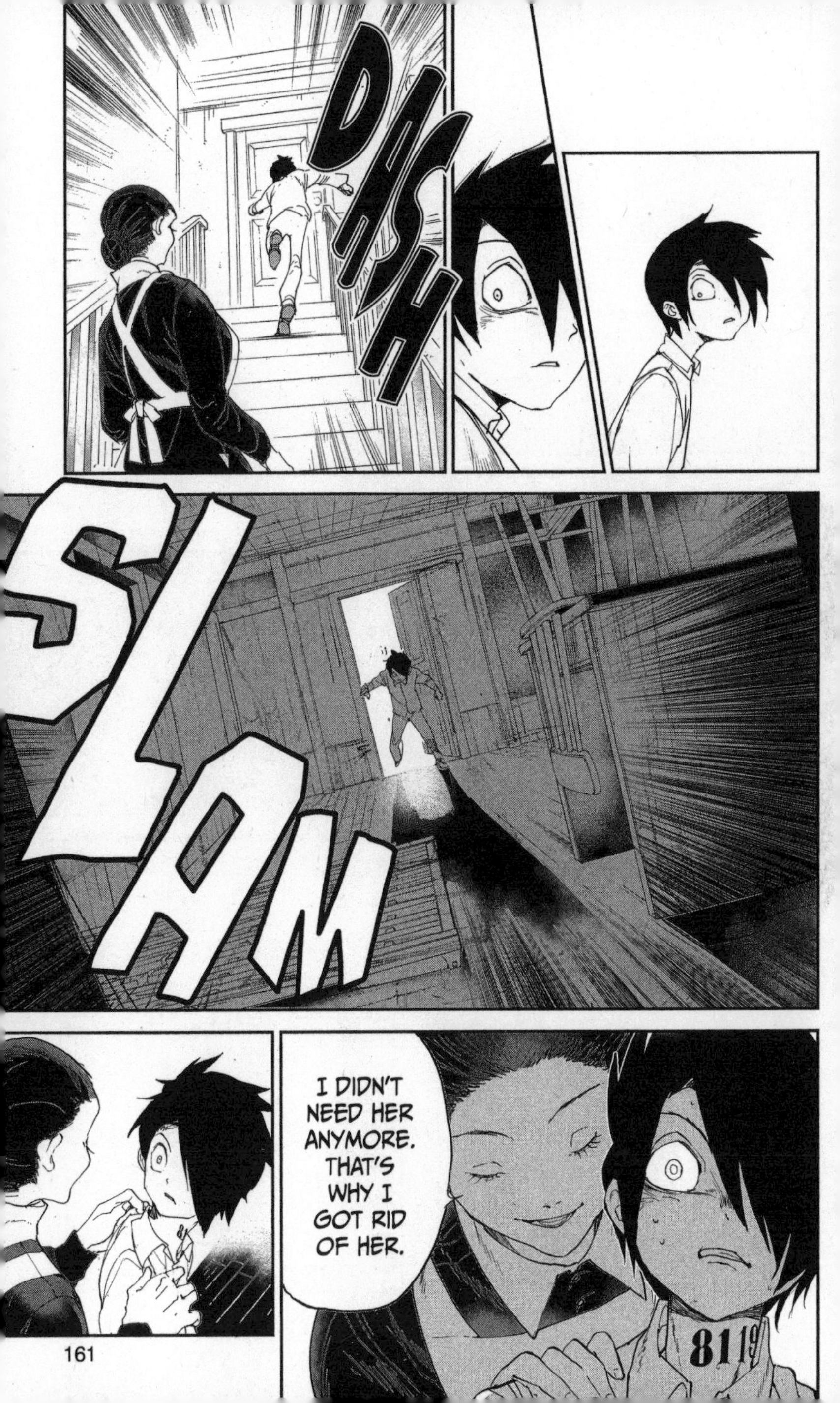
DASHH
SLAM
I DIDN'T NEED HER ANYMORE. THAT'S WHY I GOT RID OF HER.
81

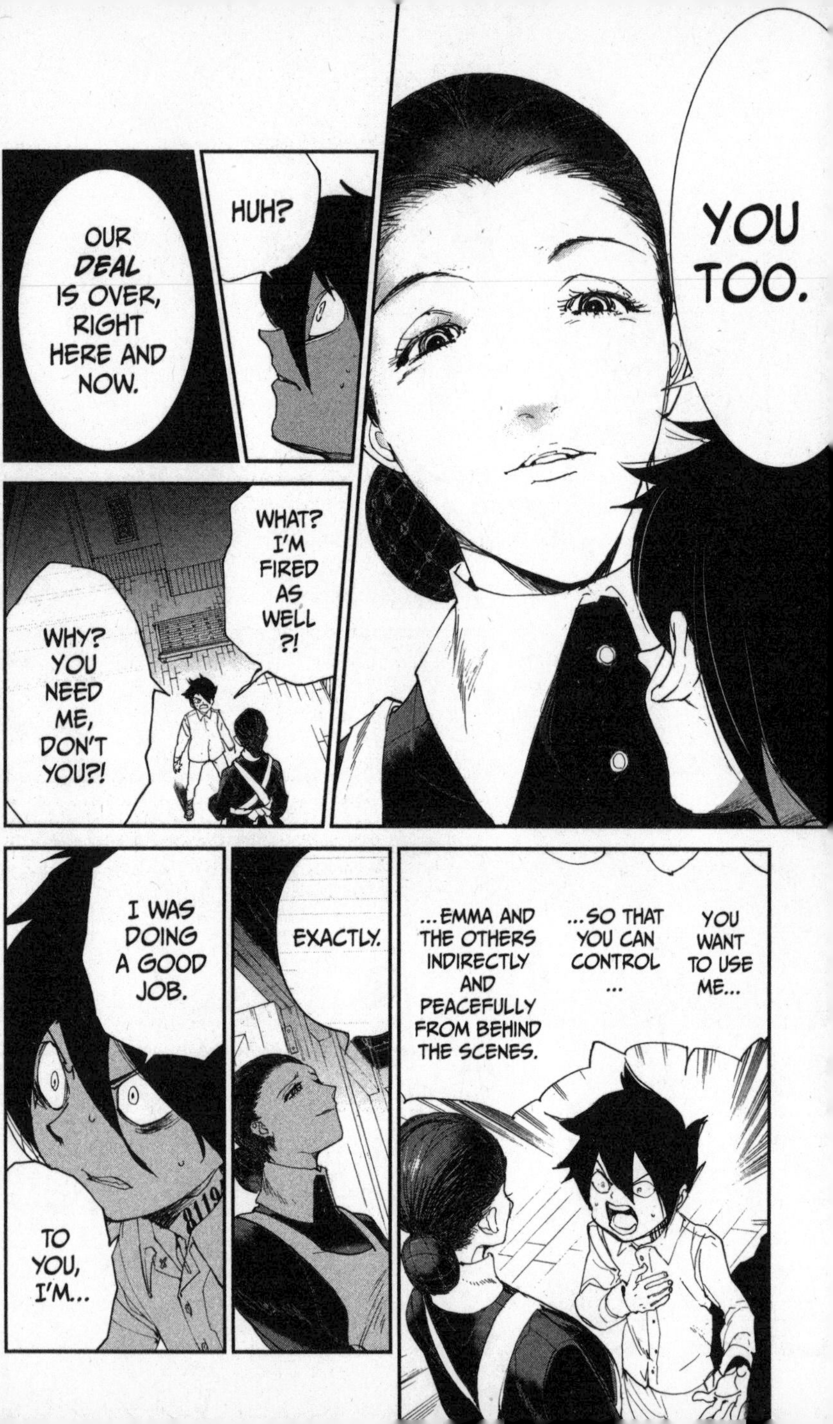
YOU TOO.
HUH?
OUR *DEAL* IS OVER, RIGHT HERE AND NOW.
WHAT? I'M FIRED AS WELL?!
WHY? YOU NEED ME, DON'T YOU?!
YOU WANT TO USE ME...
...SO THAT YOU CAN CONTROL ...
...EMMA AND THE OTHERS INDIRECTLY AND PEACEFULLY FROM BEHIND THE SCENES.
EXACTLY.
I WAS DOING A GOOD JOB.
TO YOU, I'M...

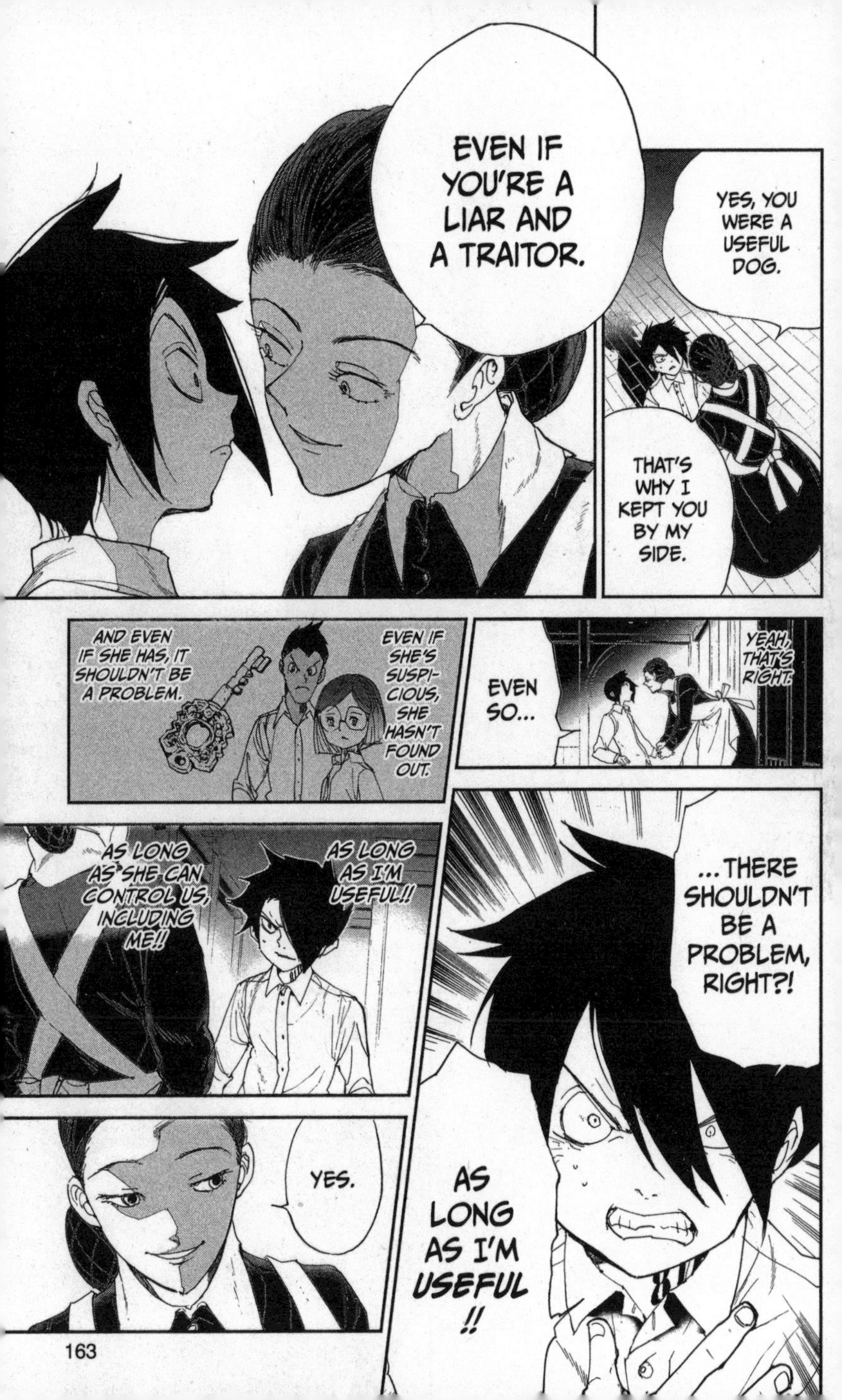

YES, YOU WERE A USEFUL DOG.
THAT'S WHY I KEPT YOU BY MY SIDE.
EVEN IF YOU'RE A LIAR AND A TRAITOR.
YEAH, THAT'S RIGHT.
EVEN SO...
EVEN IF SHE'S SUSPICIOUS, SHE HASN'T FOUND OUT.
AND EVEN IF SHE HAS, IT SHOULDN'T BE A PROBLEM.
...THERE SHOULDN'T BE A PROBLEM, RIGHT?!
AS LONG AS I'M USEFUL!!
AS LONG AS I'M USEFUL!!
AS LONG AS SHE CAN CONTROL US, INCLUDING ME!!
YES.

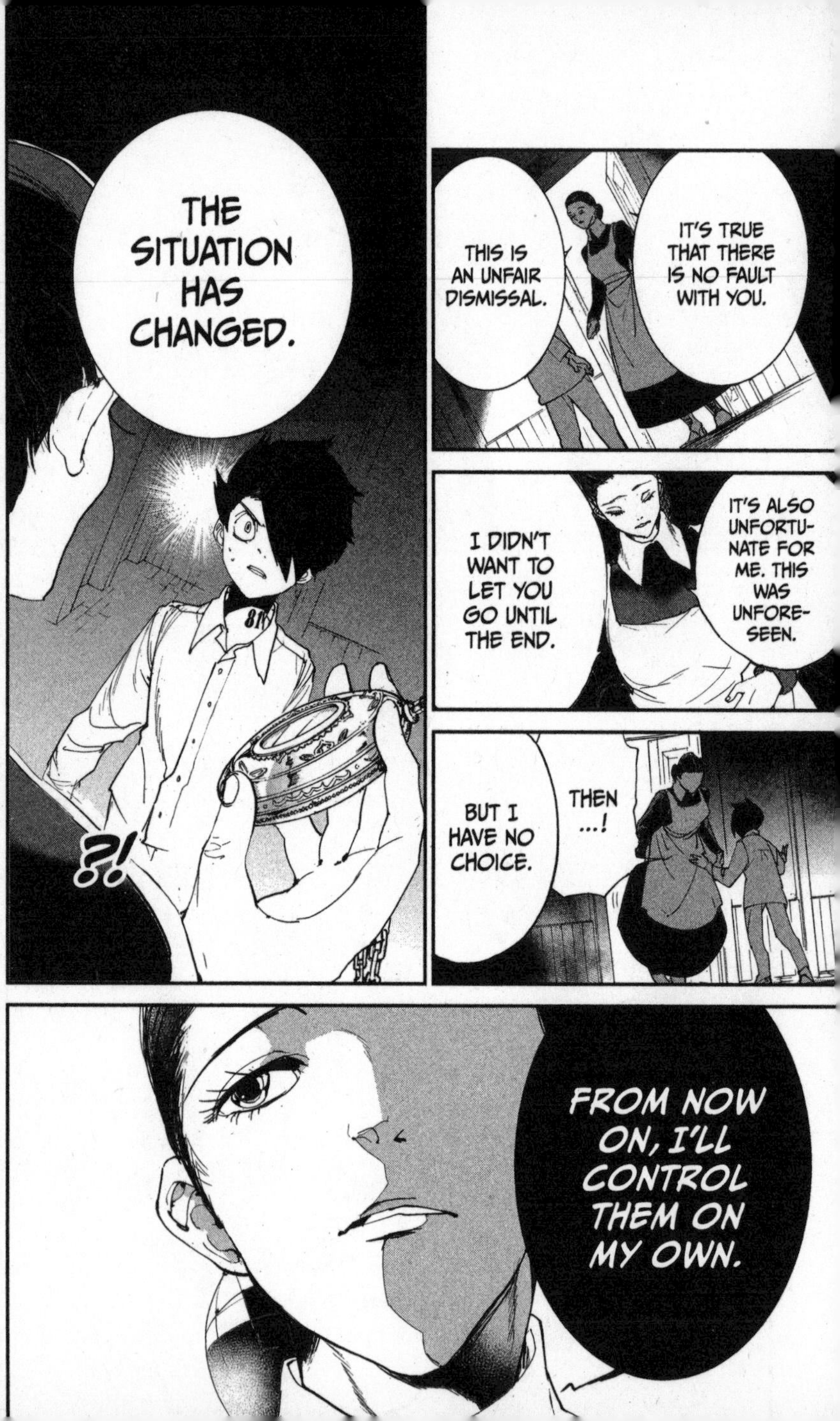
IT'S TRUE THAT THERE IS NO FAULT WITH YOU.
THIS IS AN UNFAIR DISMISSAL.
IT'S ALSO UNFORTUNATE FOR ME. THIS WAS UNFORESEEN.
I DIDN'T WANT TO LET YOU GO UNTIL THE END.
THEN ...!
BUT I HAVE NO CHOICE.
THE SITUATION HAS CHANGED.
?!
FROM NOW ON, I'LL CONTROL THEM ON MY OWN.

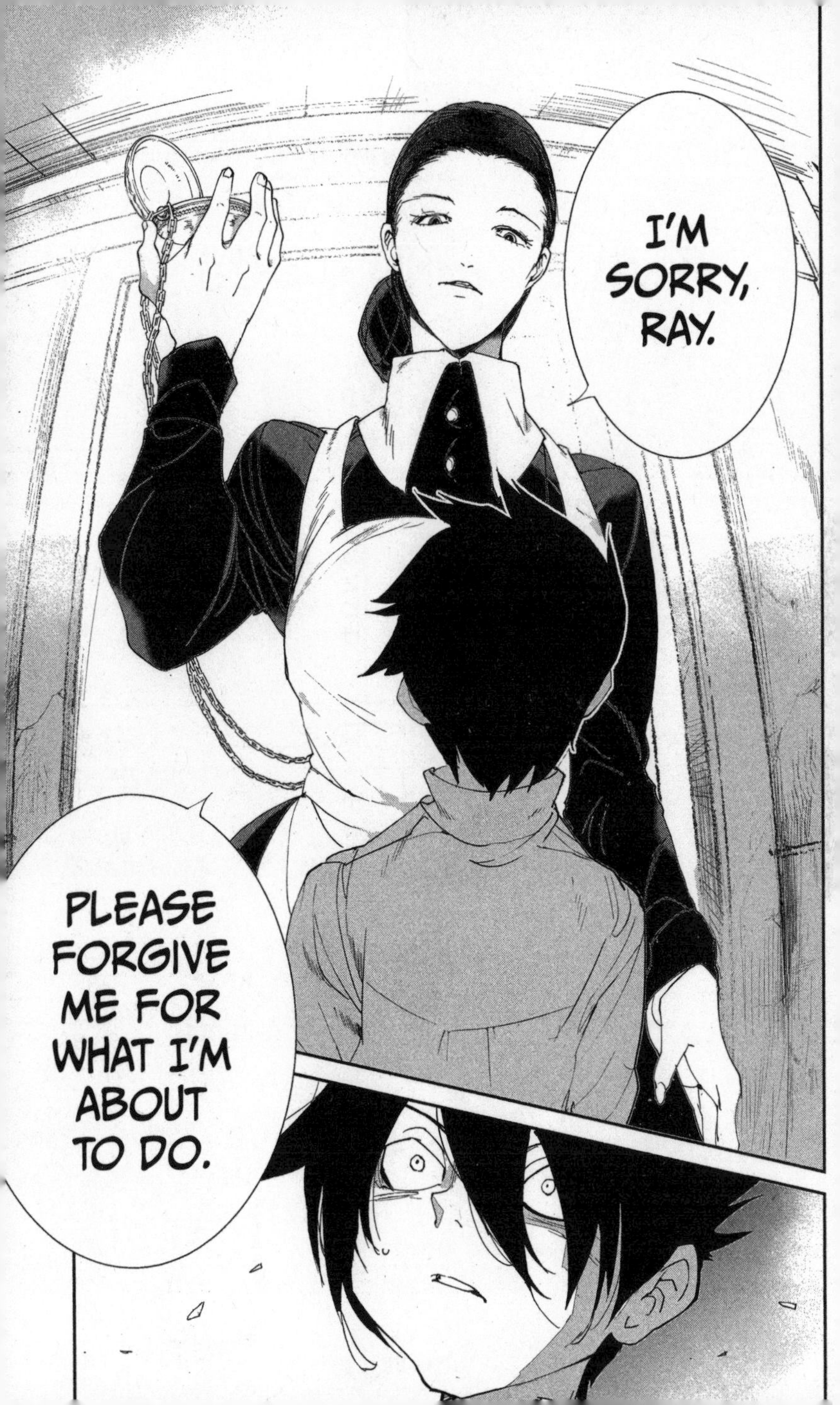
I'M SORRY, RAY.
PLEASE FORGIVE ME FOR WHAT I'M ABOUT TO DO.

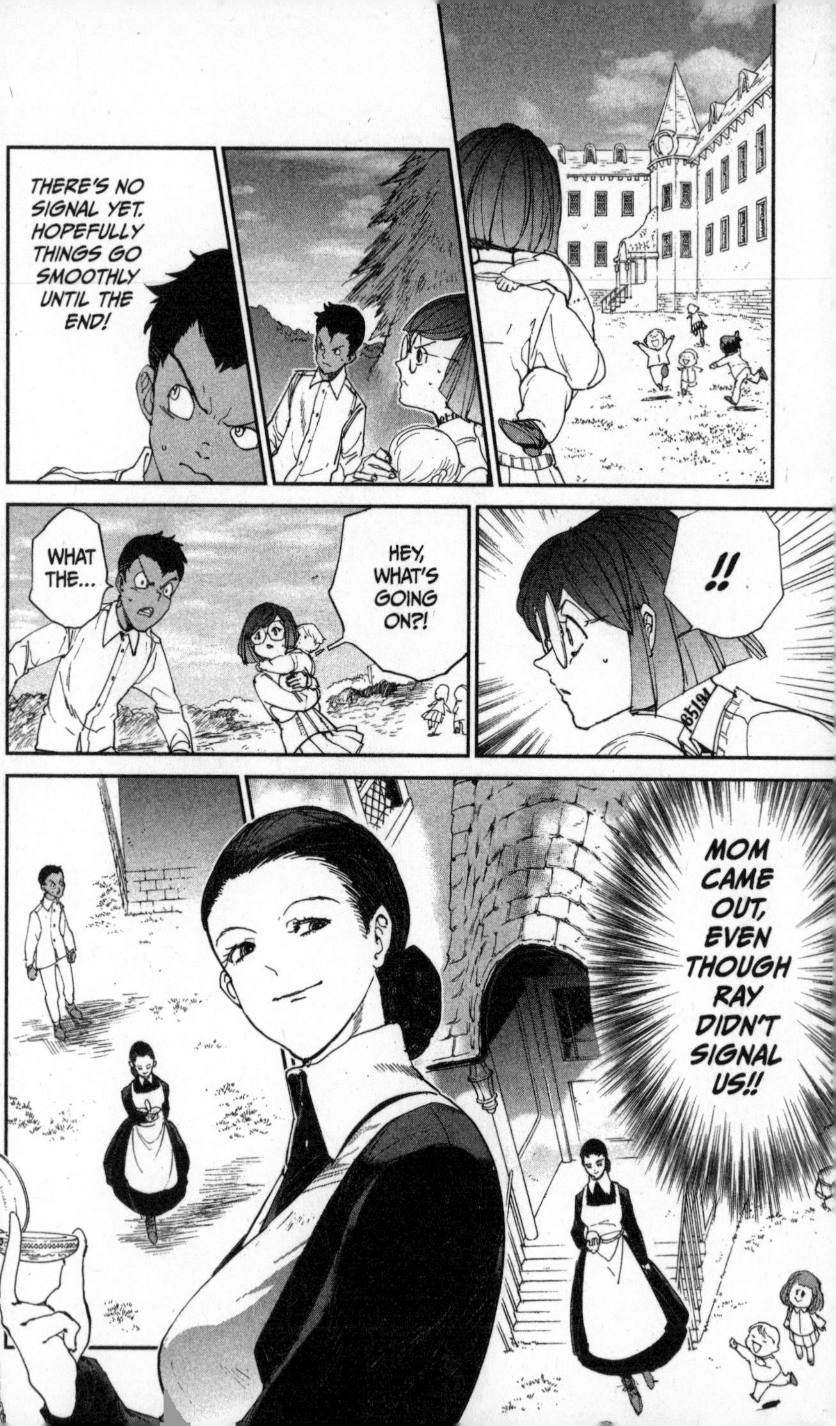
THERE'S NO SIGNAL YET. HOPEFULLY THINGS GO SMOOTHLY UNTIL THE END!
!!
HEY, WHAT'S GOING ON?!
WHAT THE...
MOM CAME OUT, EVEN THOUGH RAY DIDN'T SIGNAL US!!

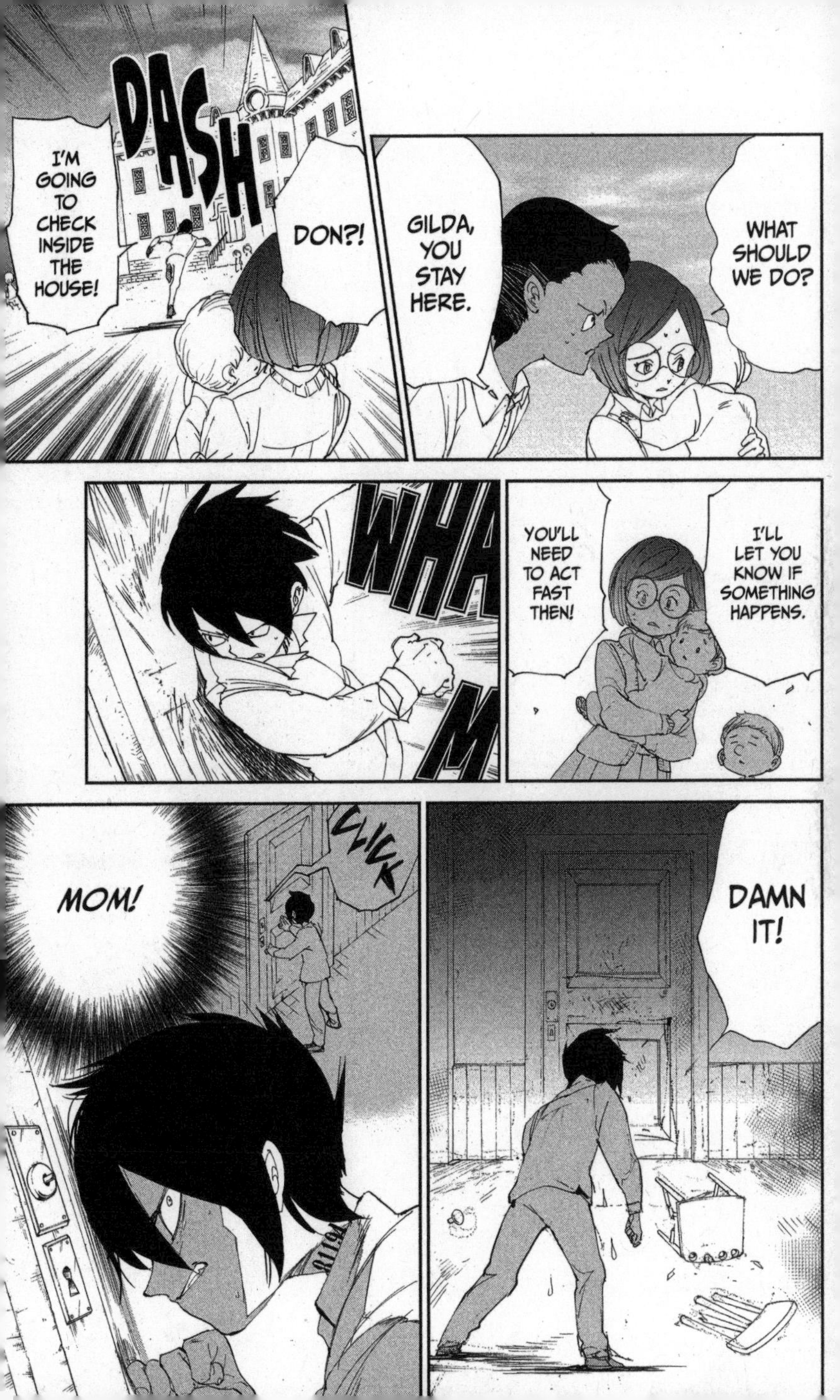
WHAT SHOULD WE DO?
GILDA, YOU STAY HERE.
DON?!
DASH
I'M GOING TO CHECK INSIDE THE HOUSE!
I'LL LET YOU KNOW IF SOMETHING HAPPENS.
YOU'LL NEED TO ACT FAST THEN!
WHAM
DAMN IT!
CLICK
MOM!

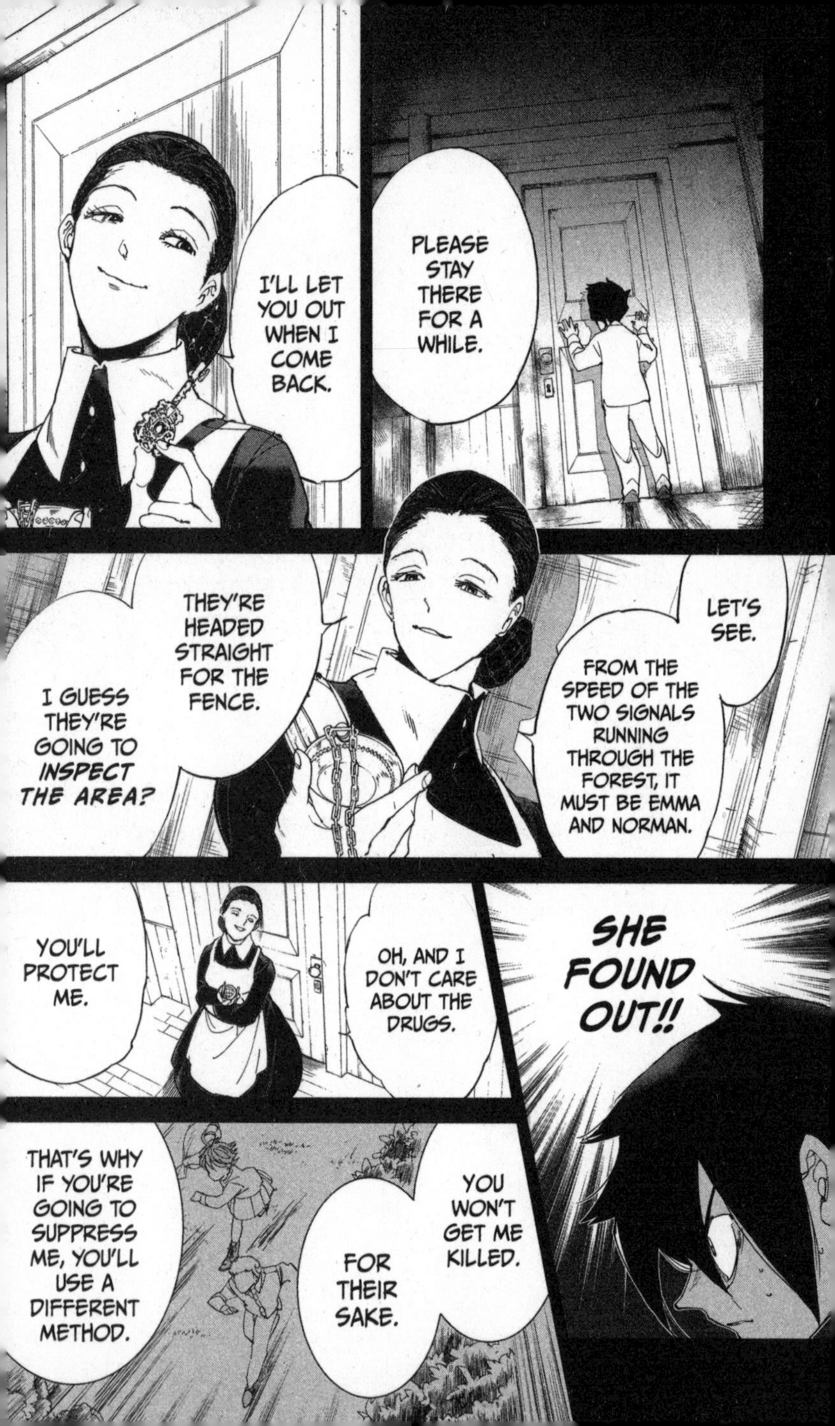
PLEASE STAY THERE FOR A WHILE.
I'LL LET YOU OUT WHEN I COME BACK.
LET'S SEE.
FROM THE SPEED OF THE TWO SIGNALS RUNNING THROUGH THE FOREST, IT MUST BE EMMA AND NORMAN.
THEY'RE HEADED STRAIGHT FOR THE FENCE.
I GUESS THEY'RE GOING TO *INSPECT THE AREA?*
SHE FOUND OUT!!
OH, AND I DON'T CARE ABOUT THE DRUGS.
YOU'LL PROTECT ME.
YOU WON'T GET ME KILLED.
FOR THEIR SAKE.
THAT'S WHY IF YOU'RE GOING TO SUPPRESS ME, YOU'LL USE A DIFFERENT METHOD.

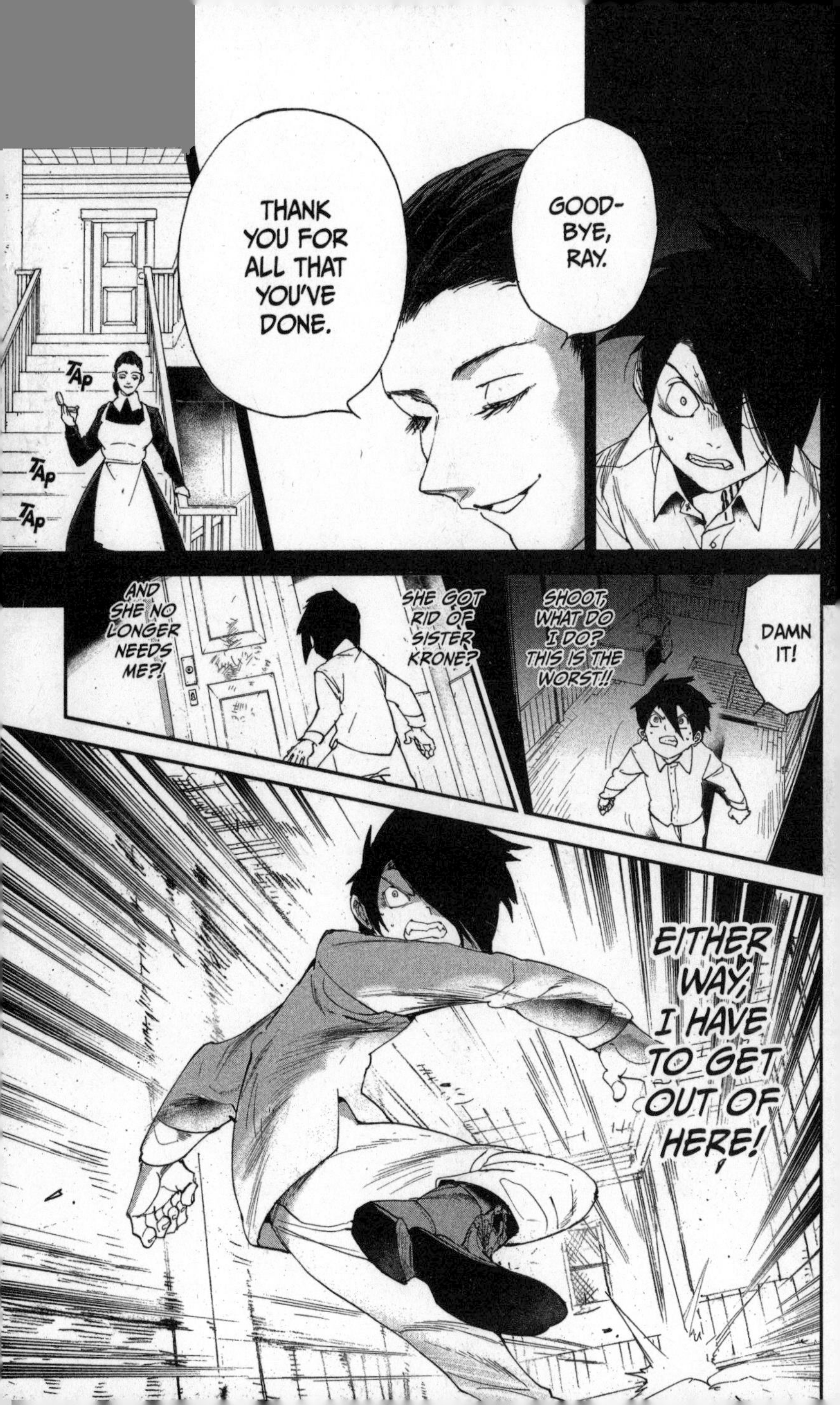
GOOD-BYE, RAY.
THANK YOU FOR ALL THAT YOU'VE DONE.
TAP
TAP
TAP
DAMN IT!
SHOOT, WHAT DO I DO? THIS IS THE WORST!!
SHE GOT RID OF SISTER KRONE?
AND SHE NO LONGER NEEDS ME?!
EITHER WAY, I HAVE TO GET OUT OF HERE!

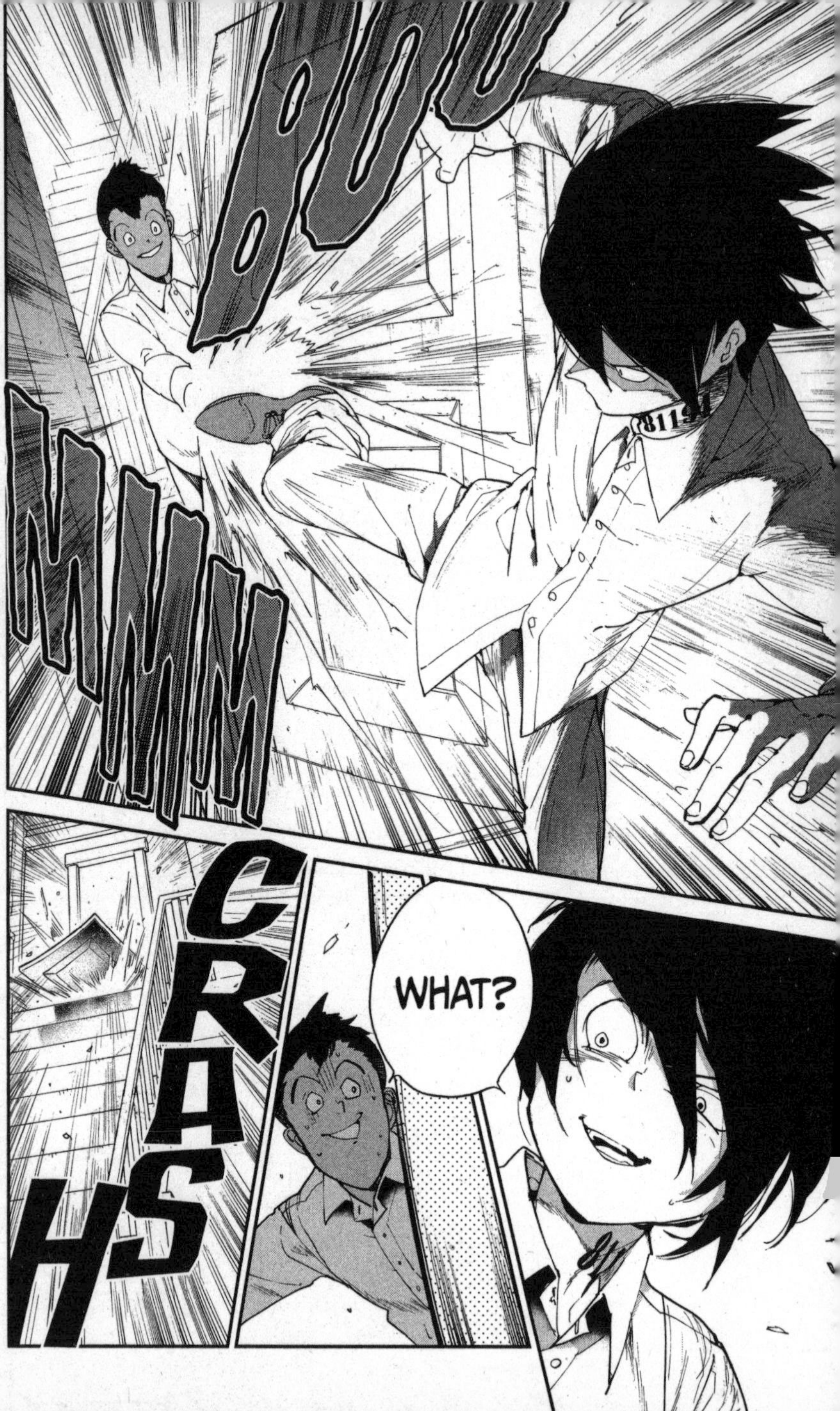
WHAT?
CRASH

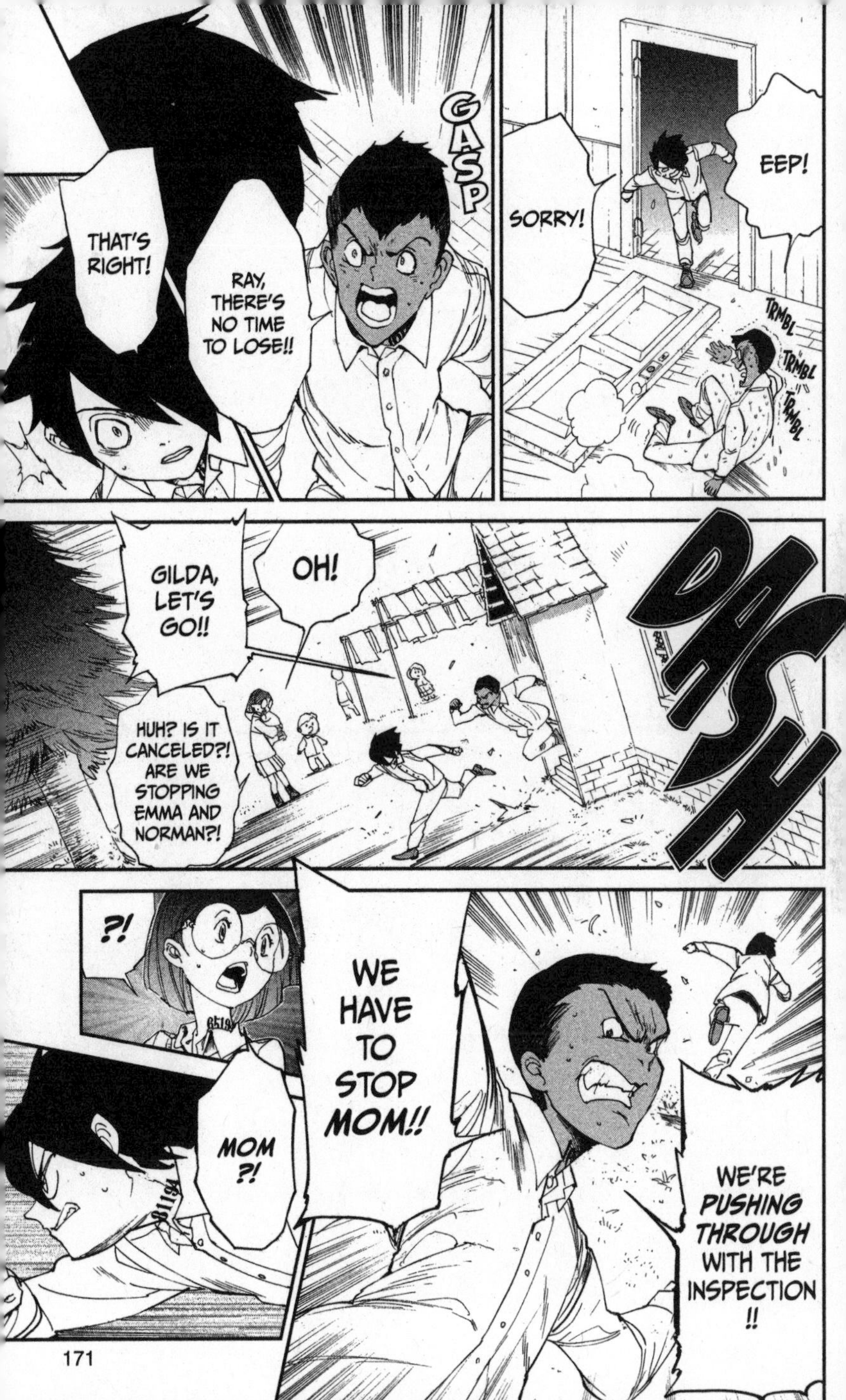

EEP!
SORRY!
TRMBL
TRMBL
TRMBL
GASP
RAY, THERE'S NO TIME TO LOSE!!
THAT'S RIGHT!
DASH
OH!
GILDA, LET'S GO!!
HUH? IS IT CANCELED?! ARE WE STOPPING EMMA AND NORMAN?!
WE HAVE TO STOP MOM!!
WE'RE PUSHING THROUGH WITH THE INSPECTION!!
?!
MOM?!

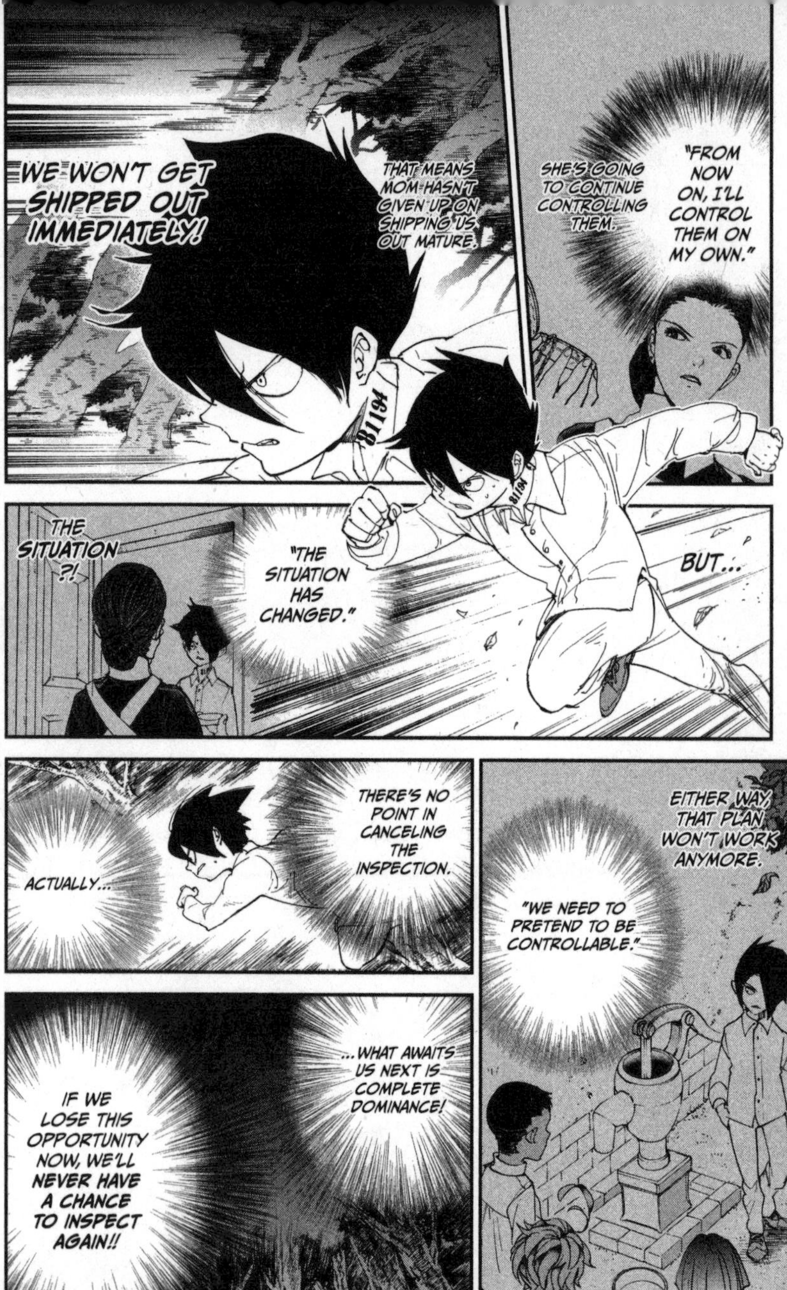
"FROM NOW ON, I'LL CONTROL THEM ON MY OWN."
SHE'S GOING TO CONTINUE CONTROLLING THEM.
THAT MEANS MOM HASN'T GIVEN UP ON SHIPPING US OUT MATURE.
WE WON'T GET SHIPPED OUT IMMEDIATELY!
BUT...
"THE SITUATION HAS CHANGED."
THE SITUATION?!
EITHER WAY, THAT PLAN WON'T WORK ANYMORE.
"WE NEED TO PRETEND TO BE CONTROLLABLE."
THERE'S NO POINT IN CANCELING THE INSPECTION.
ACTUALLY...
...WHAT AWAITS US NEXT IS COMPLETE DOMINANCE!
IF WE LOSE THIS OPPORTUNITY NOW, WE'LL NEVER HAVE A CHANCE TO INSPECT AGAIN!!

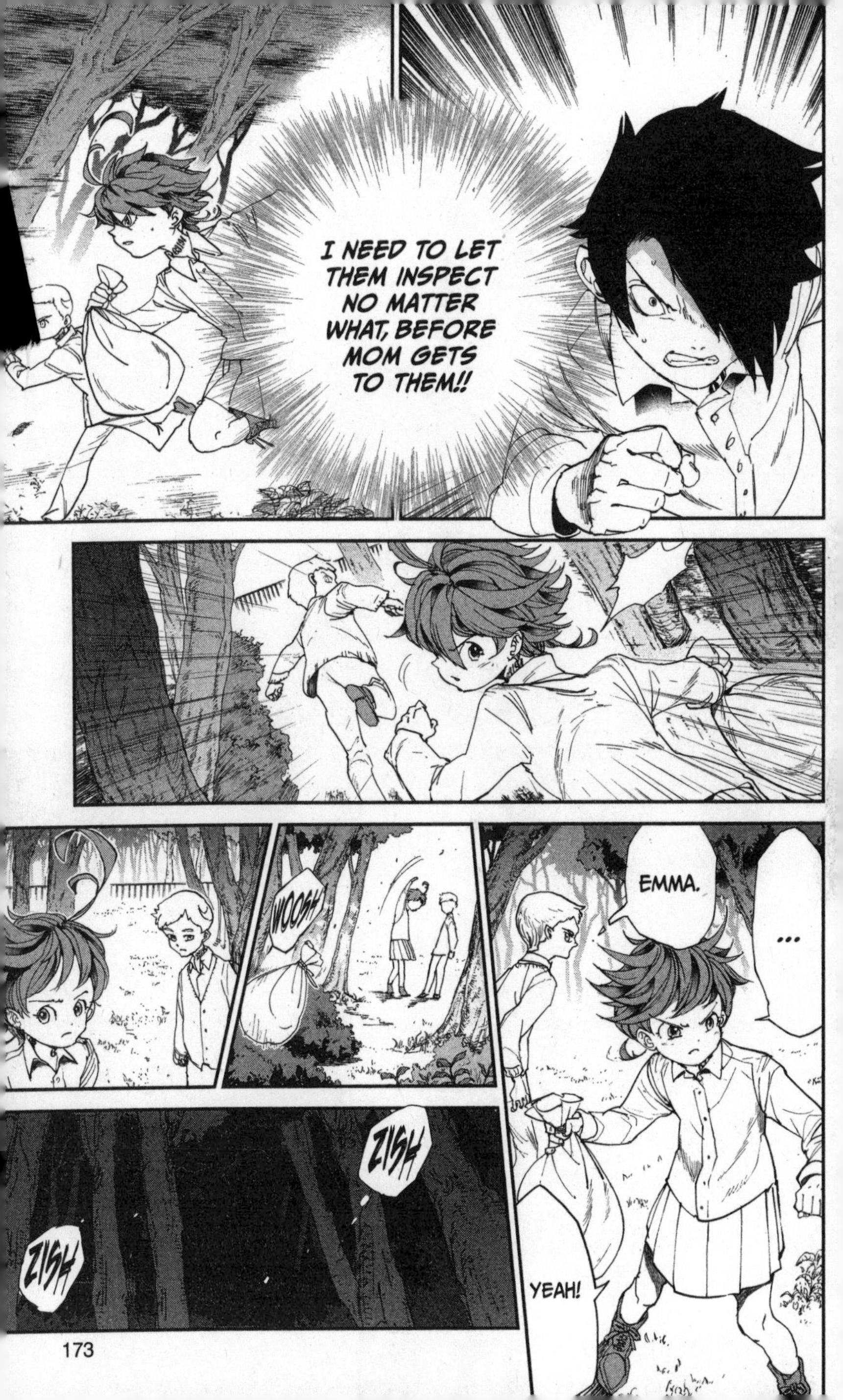
I NEED TO LET THEM INSPECT NO MATTER WHAT, BEFORE MOM GETS TO THEM!!
EMMA.
...
YEAH!
WOOSH
ZISH
ZISH

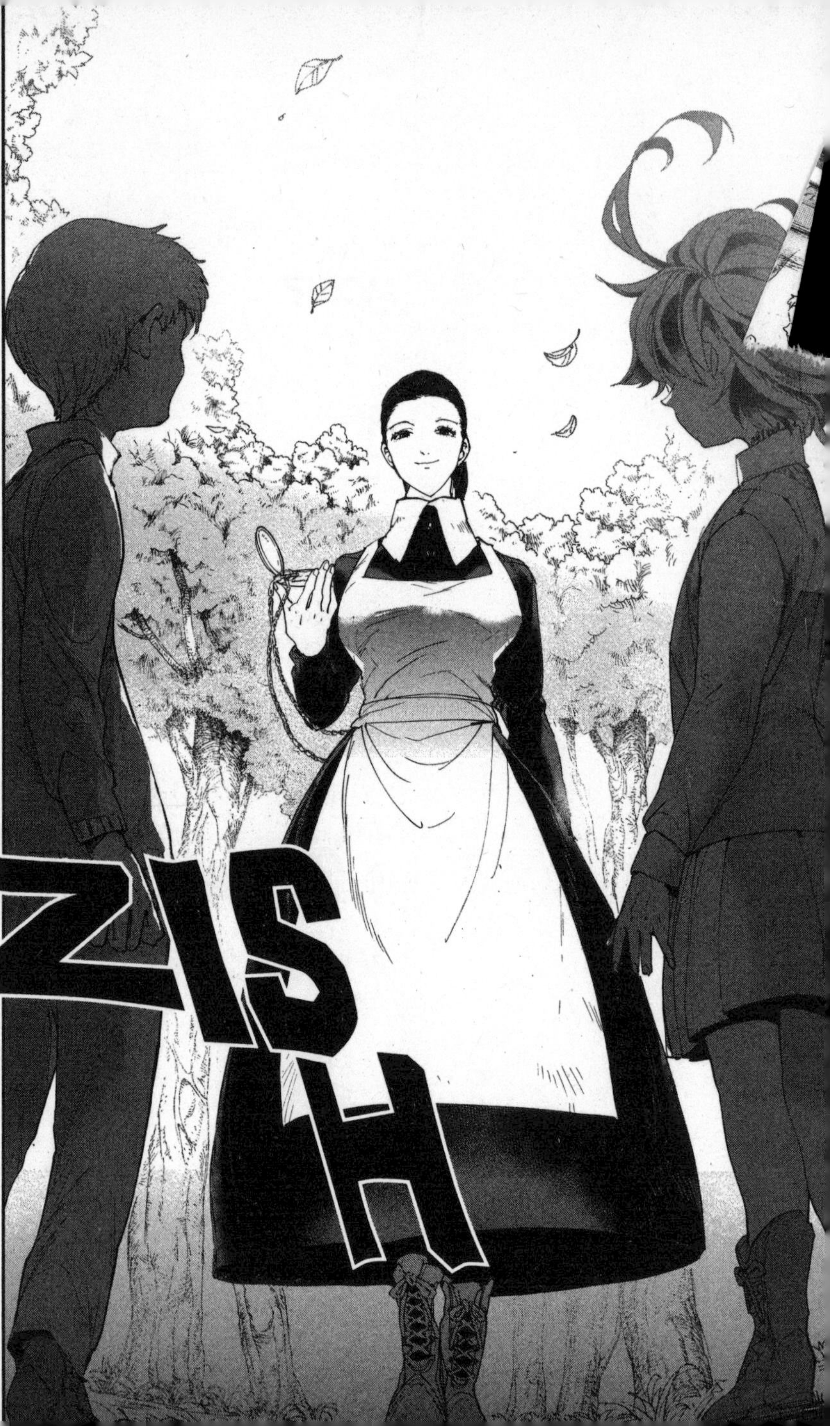
ZISH

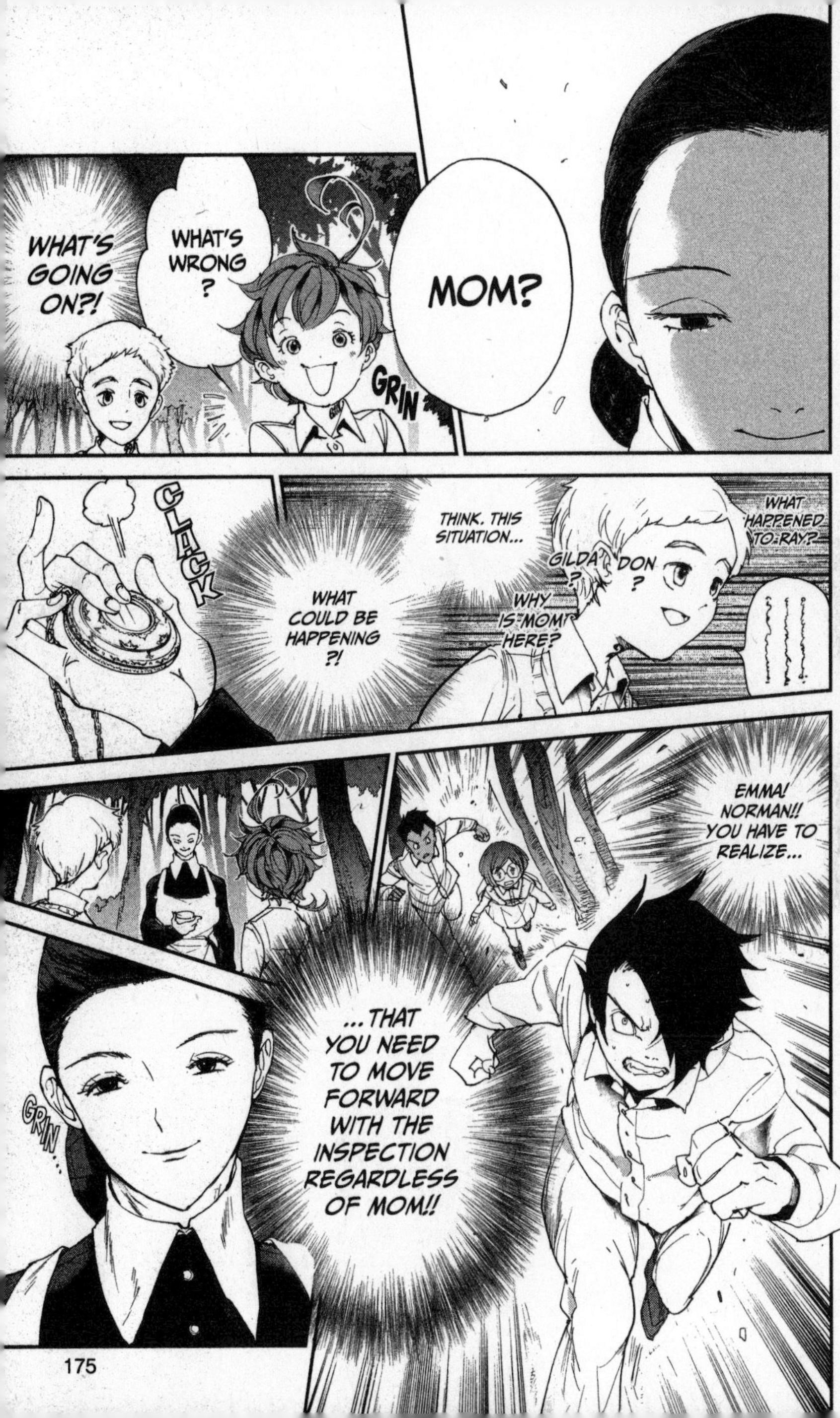

MOM?
WHAT'S WRONG?
WHAT'S GOING ON?!
GRIN
WHAT HAPPENED TO RAY?
DON?
GILDA?
WHY IS MOM HERE?
THINK. THIS SITUATION...
WHAT COULD BE HAPPENING?!
CLACK
EMMA! NORMAN!! YOU HAVE TO REALIZE...
...THAT YOU NEED TO MOVE FORWARD WITH THE INSPECTION REGARDLESS OF MOM!!
GRIN...

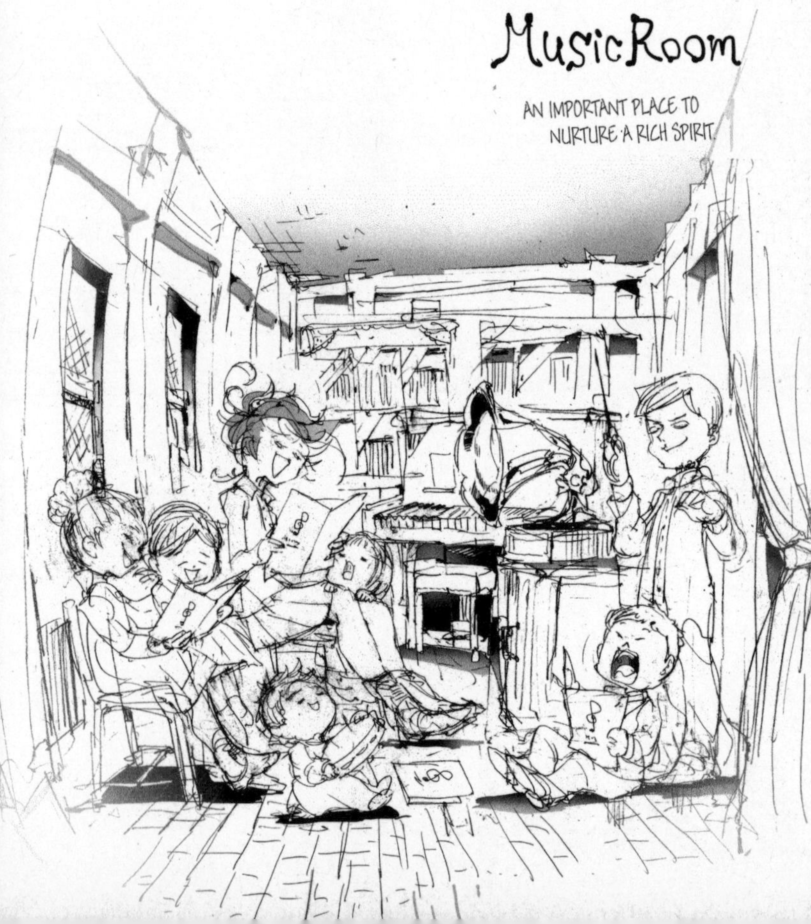
Music Room
AN IMPORTANT PLACE TO
NURTURE A RICH SPIRIT.

CHAPTER 25: INSPECTION, PART 2

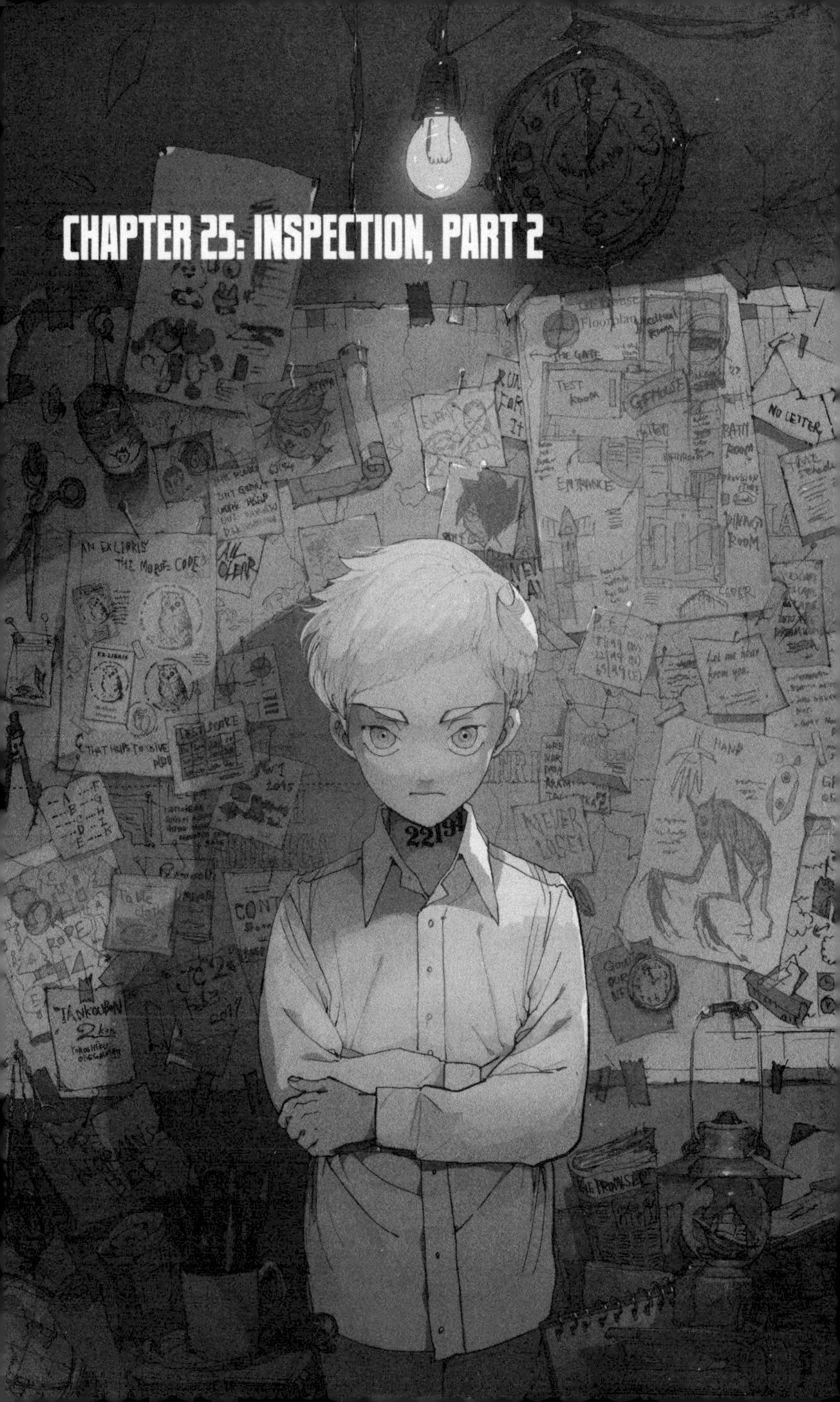

NO LETTER
TEST room
ENTRANCE
BATH ROOM
DINING ROOM
AN EX LIBRIS
THE MORSE CODE
ALL CLEAR
Let me hear from you.
HAND
NEVER FORGET
22194
ROPE

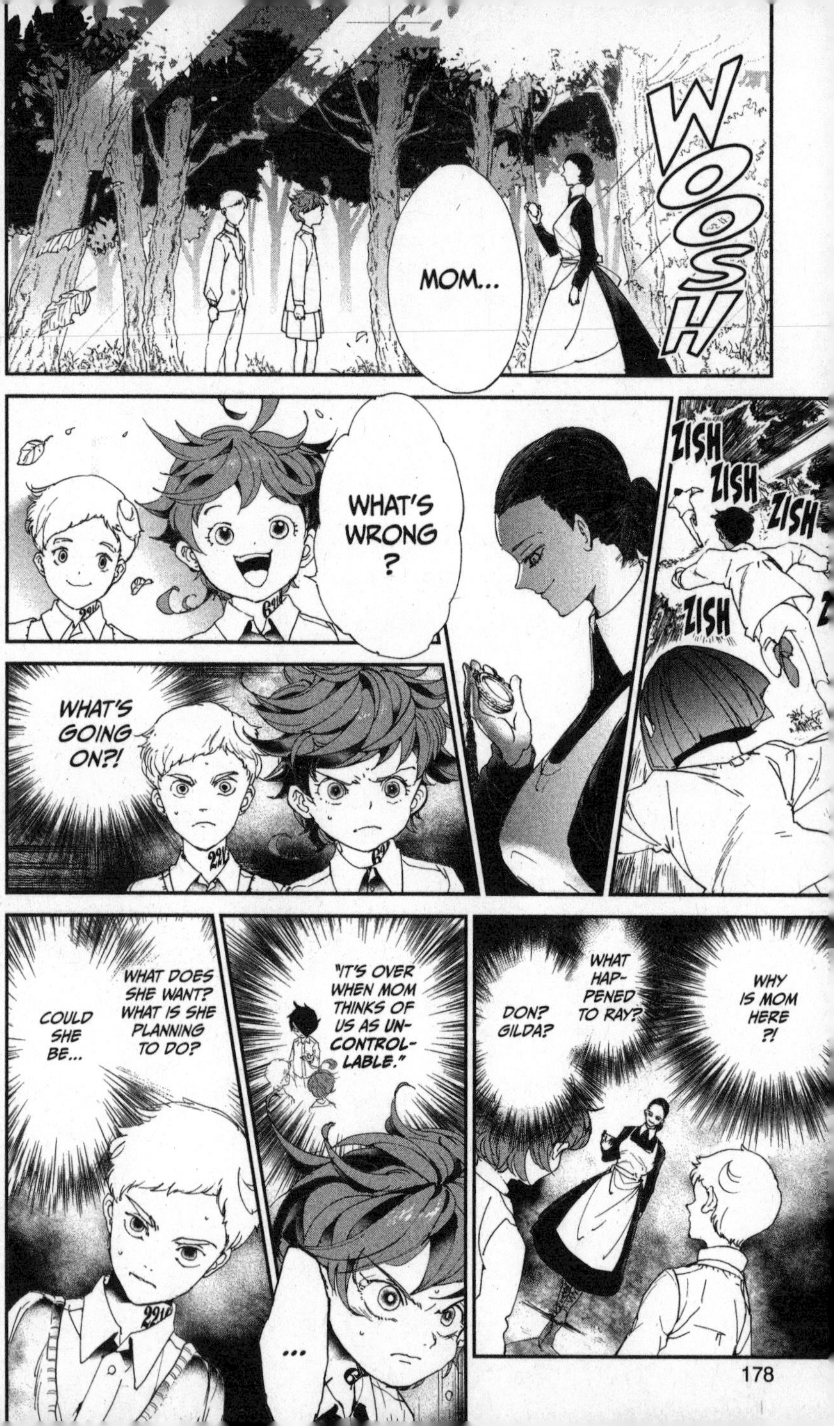
WOOSH
MOM...
ZISH ZISH ZISH
ZISH
WHAT'S WRONG?
WHAT'S GOING ON?!
WHY IS MOM HERE?!
WHAT HAPPENED TO RAY?
DON? GILDA?
"IT'S OVER WHEN MOM THINKS OF US AS UNCONTROLLABLE."
...
WHAT DOES SHE WANT? WHAT IS SHE PLANNING TO DO?
COULD SHE BE...

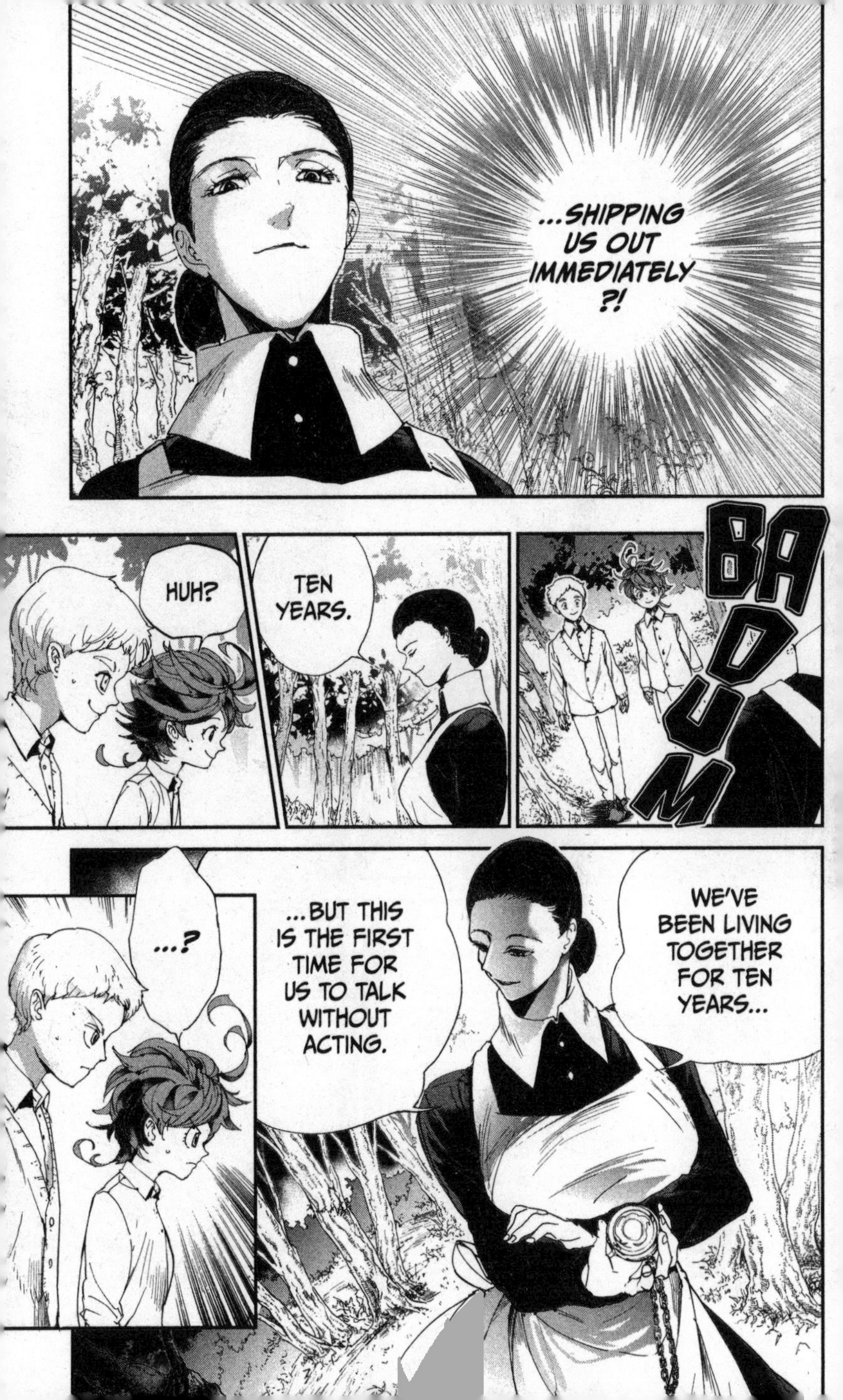
...SHIPPING US OUT IMMEDIATELY ?!
BADUM
TEN YEARS.
HUH?
WE'VE BEEN LIVING TOGETHER FOR TEN YEARS...
...BUT THIS IS THE FIRST TIME FOR US TO TALK WITHOUT ACTING.
...?

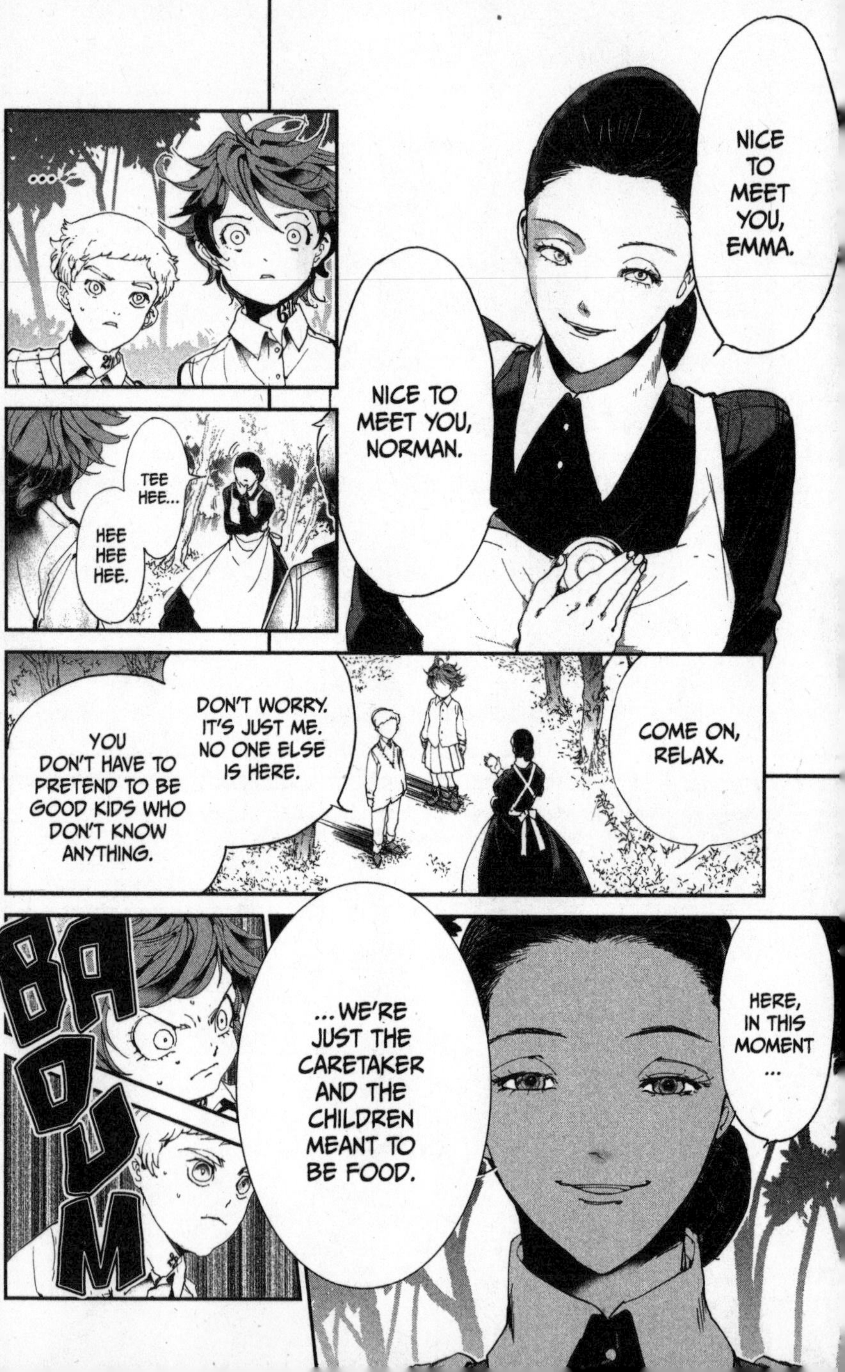
NICE TO MEET YOU, EMMA.
NICE TO MEET YOU, NORMAN.
...
TEE HEE...
HEE HEE HEE.
COME ON, RELAX.
DON'T WORRY. IT'S JUST ME. NO ONE ELSE IS HERE.
YOU DON'T HAVE TO PRETEND TO BE GOOD KIDS WHO DON'T KNOW ANYTHING.
HERE, IN THIS MOMENT...
...WE'RE JUST THE CARETAKER AND THE CHILDREN MEANT TO BE FOOD.
BA-DUM

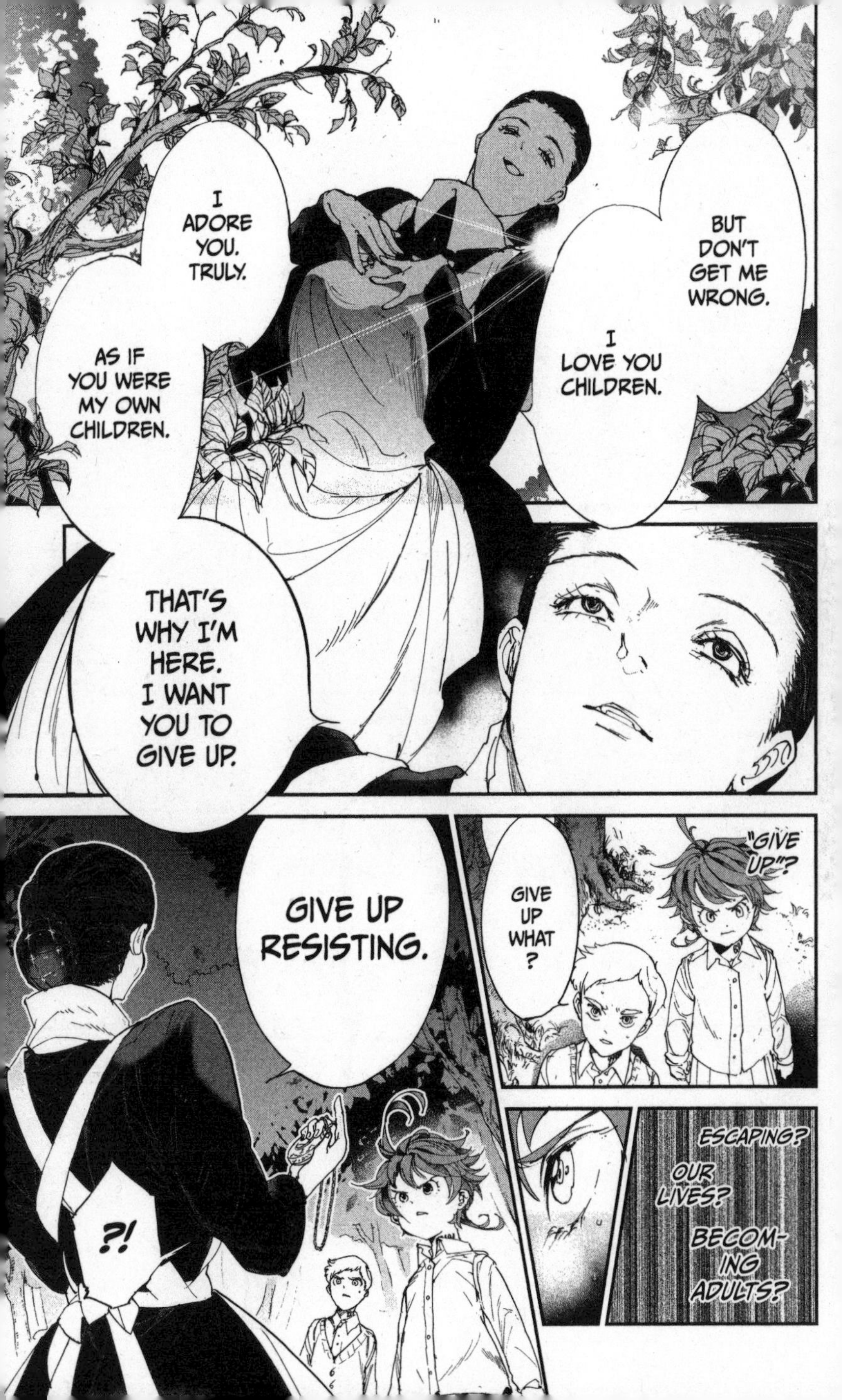

BUT DON'T GET ME WRONG.
I LOVE YOU CHILDREN.
I ADORE YOU. TRULY.
AS IF YOU WERE MY OWN CHILDREN.
THAT'S WHY I'M HERE. I WANT YOU TO GIVE UP.
"GIVE UP"?
GIVE UP WHAT?
ESCAPING?
OUR LIVES?
BECOM-ING ADULTS?
GIVE UP RESISTING.
?!

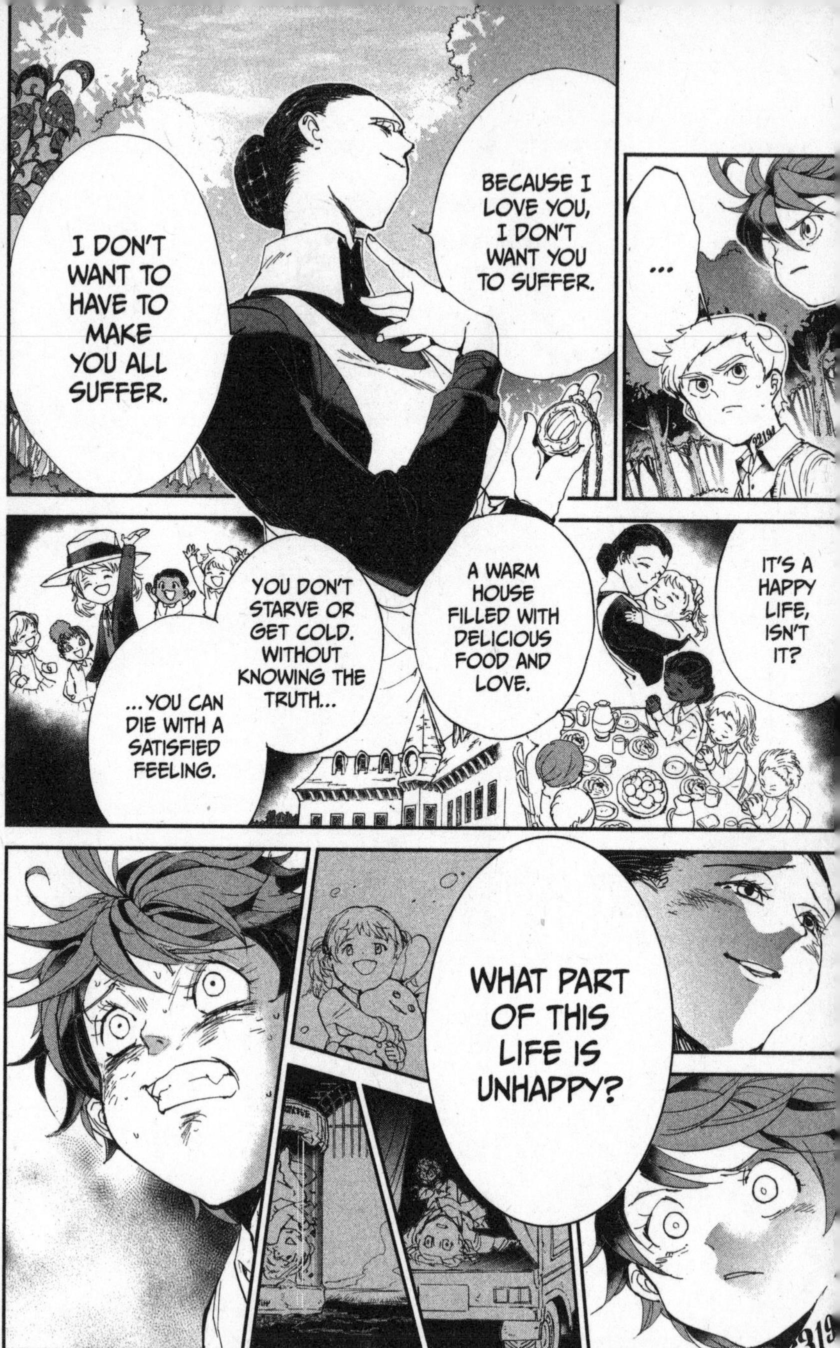
...
BECAUSE I LOVE YOU, I DON'T WANT YOU TO SUFFER.
I DON'T WANT TO HAVE TO MAKE YOU ALL SUFFER.
IT'S A HAPPY LIFE, ISN'T IT?
A WARM HOUSE FILLED WITH DELICIOUS FOOD AND LOVE.
YOU DON'T STARVE OR GET COLD. WITHOUT KNOWING THE TRUTH...
...YOU CAN DIE WITH A SATISFIED FEELING.
WHAT PART OF THIS LIFE IS UNHAPPY?

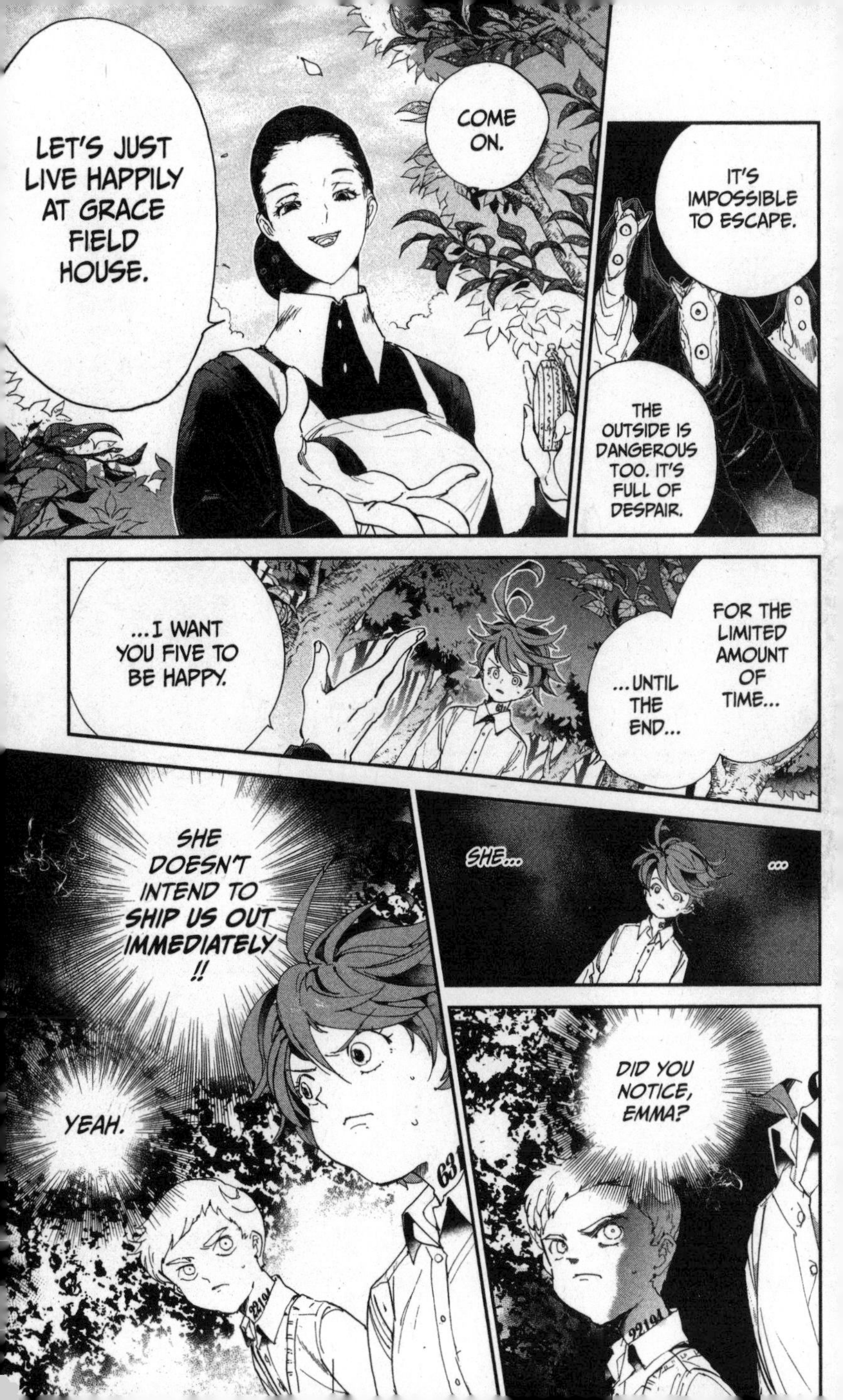
IT'S IMPOSSIBLE TO ESCAPE.
THE OUTSIDE IS DANGEROUS TOO. IT'S FULL OF DESPAIR.
COME ON.
LET'S JUST LIVE HAPPILY AT GRACE FIELD HOUSE.
FOR THE LIMITED AMOUNT OF TIME...
...UNTIL THE END...
...I WANT YOU FIVE TO BE HAPPY.
SHE...
...
DID YOU NOTICE, EMMA?
SHE DOESN'T INTEND TO SHIP US OUT IMMEDIATELY !!
YEAH.

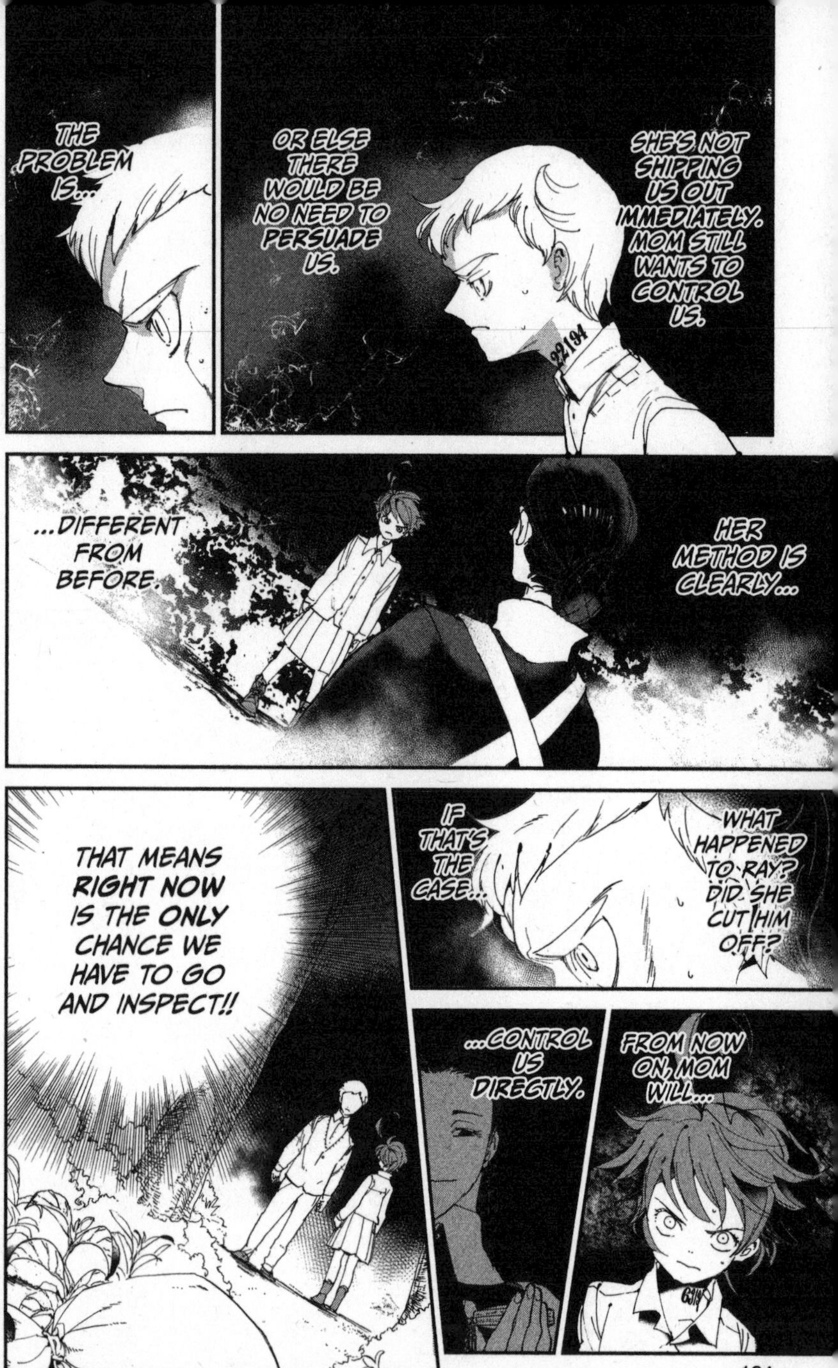
SHE'S NOT SHIPPING US OUT IMMEDIATELY. MOM STILL WANTS TO CONTROL US.
OR ELSE THERE WOULD BE NO NEED TO PERSUADE US.
THE PROBLEM IS...
HER METHOD IS CLEARLY...
...DIFFERENT FROM BEFORE.
WHAT HAPPENED TO RAY? DID SHE CUT HIM OFF?
IF THAT'S THE CASE...
FROM NOW ON, MOM WILL...
...CONTROL US DIRECTLY.
THAT MEANS RIGHT NOW IS THE ONLY CHANCE WE HAVE TO GO AND INSPECT!!

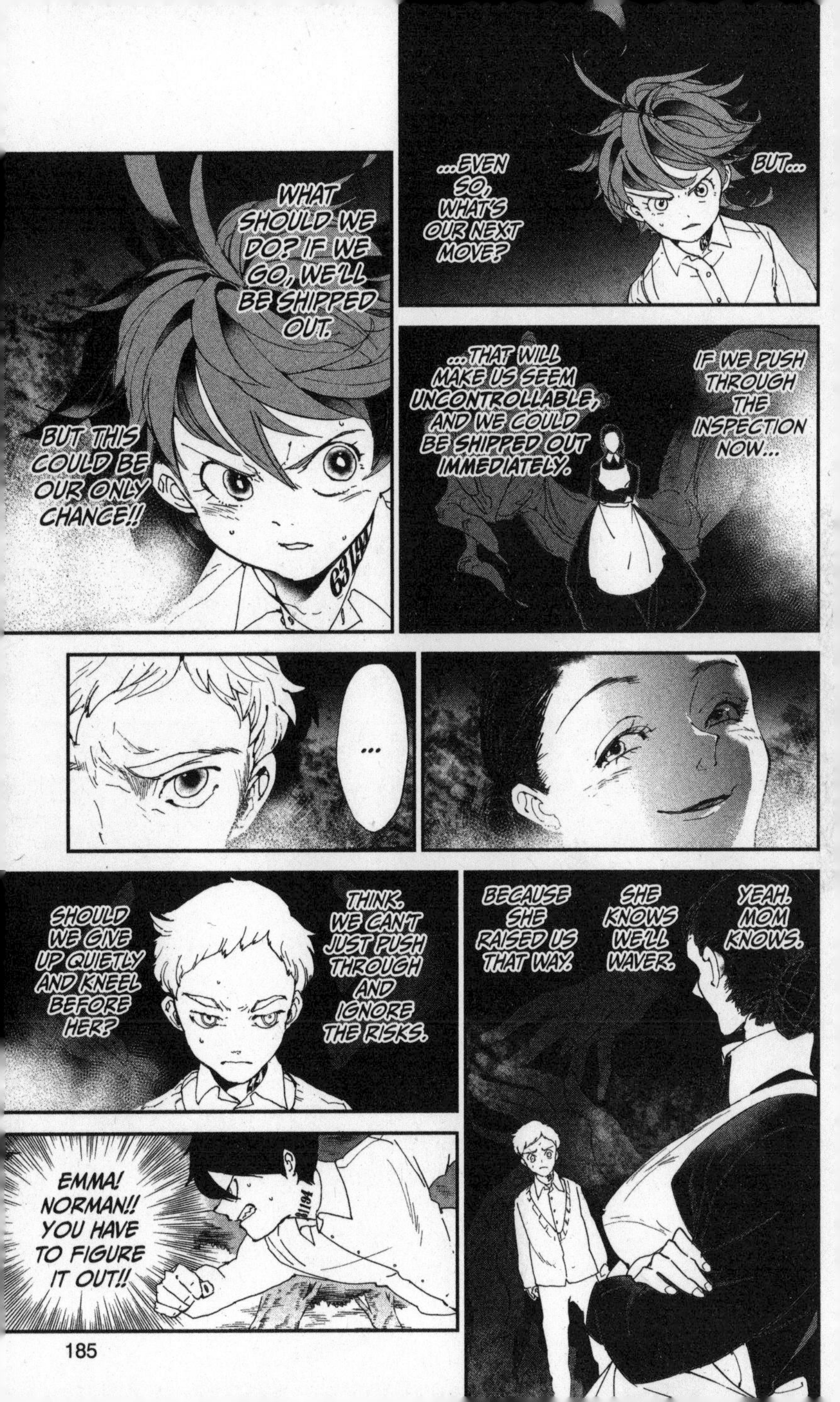
BUT...
...EVEN SO, WHAT'S OUR NEXT MOVE?
IF WE PUSH THROUGH THE INSPECTION NOW...
...THAT WILL MAKE US SEEM UNCONTROLLABLE, AND WE COULD BE SHIPPED OUT IMMEDIATELY.
WHAT SHOULD WE DO? IF WE GO, WE'LL BE SHIPPED OUT.
BUT THIS COULD BE OUR ONLY CHANCE!!
...
YEAH. MOM KNOWS.
SHE KNOWS WE'LL WAVER.
BECAUSE SHE RAISED US THAT WAY.
THINK. WE CAN'T JUST PUSH THROUGH AND IGNORE THE RISKS.
SHOULD WE GIVE UP QUIETLY AND KNEEL BEFORE HER?
EMMA! NORMAN!! YOU HAVE TO FIGURE IT OUT!!

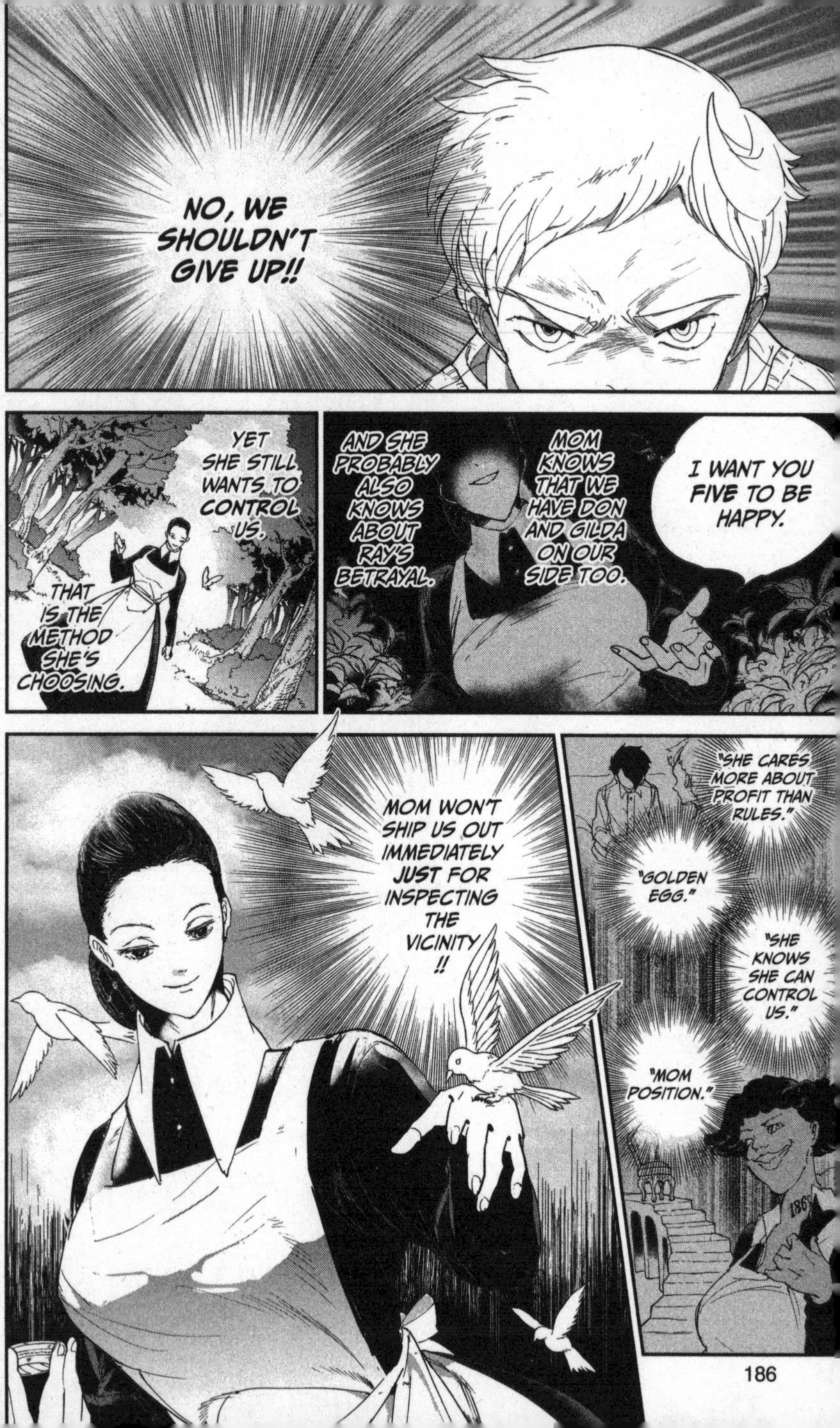
NO, WE SHOULDN'T GIVE UP!!
I WANT YOU FIVE TO BE HAPPY.
MOM KNOWS THAT WE HAVE DON AND GILDA ON OUR SIDE TOO.
AND SHE PROBABLY ALSO KNOWS ABOUT RAY'S BETRAYAL.
YET SHE STILL WANTS TO CONTROL US.
THAT IS THE METHOD SHE'S CHOOSING.
"SHE CARES MORE ABOUT PROFIT THAN RULES."
"GOLDEN EGG."
"SHE KNOWS SHE CAN CONTROL US."
"MOM POSITION."
MOM WON'T SHIP US OUT IMMEDIATELY JUST FOR INSPECTING THE VICINITY!!

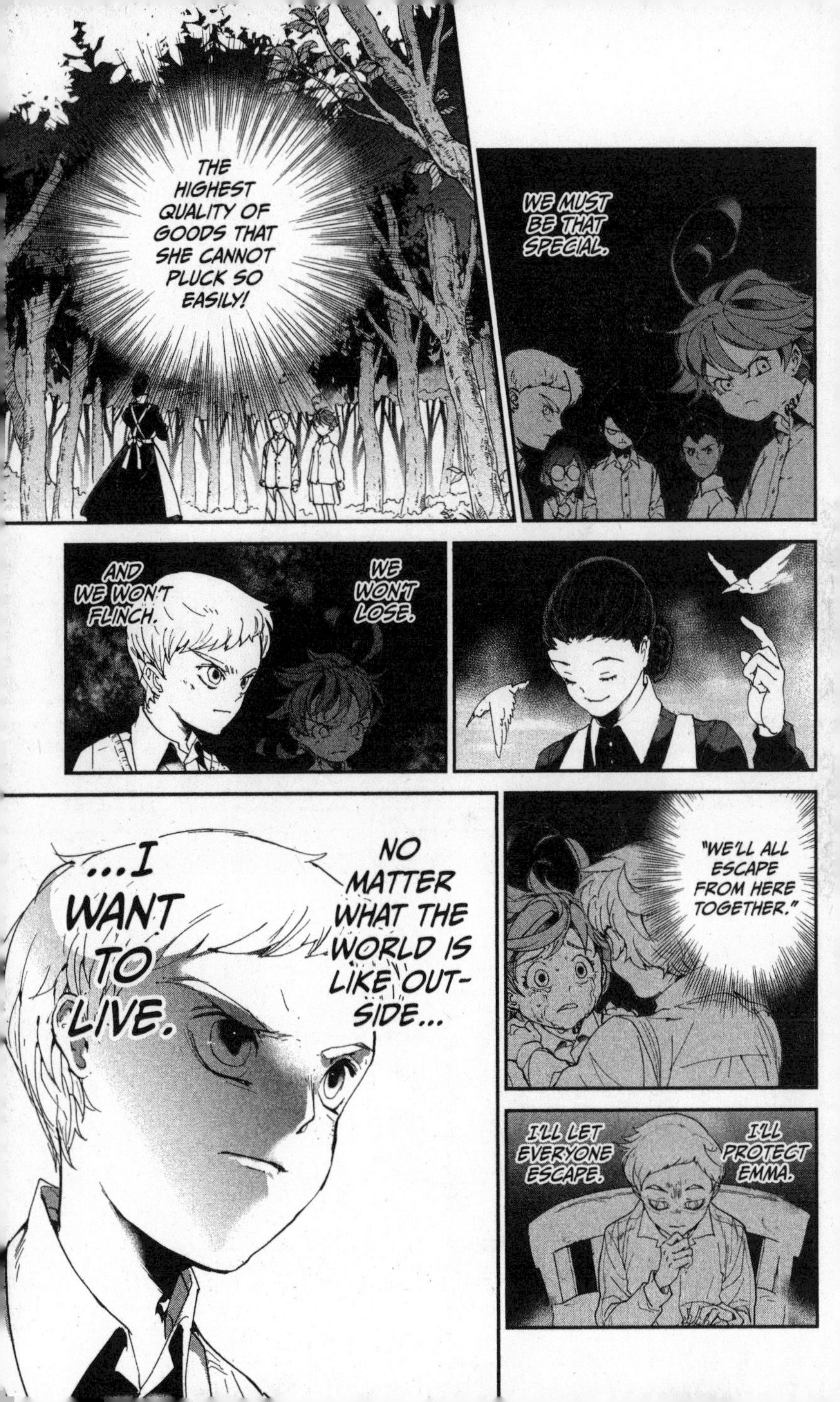
WE MUST BE THAT SPECIAL.
THE HIGHEST QUALITY OF GOODS THAT SHE CANNOT PLUCK SO EASILY!
WE WON'T LOSE.
AND WE WON'T FLINCH.
"WE'LL ALL ESCAPE FROM HERE TOGETHER."
I'LL PROTECT EMMA.
I'LL LET EVERYONE ESCAPE.
NO MATTER WHAT THE WORLD IS LIKE OUT-SIDE...
...I WANT TO LIVE.

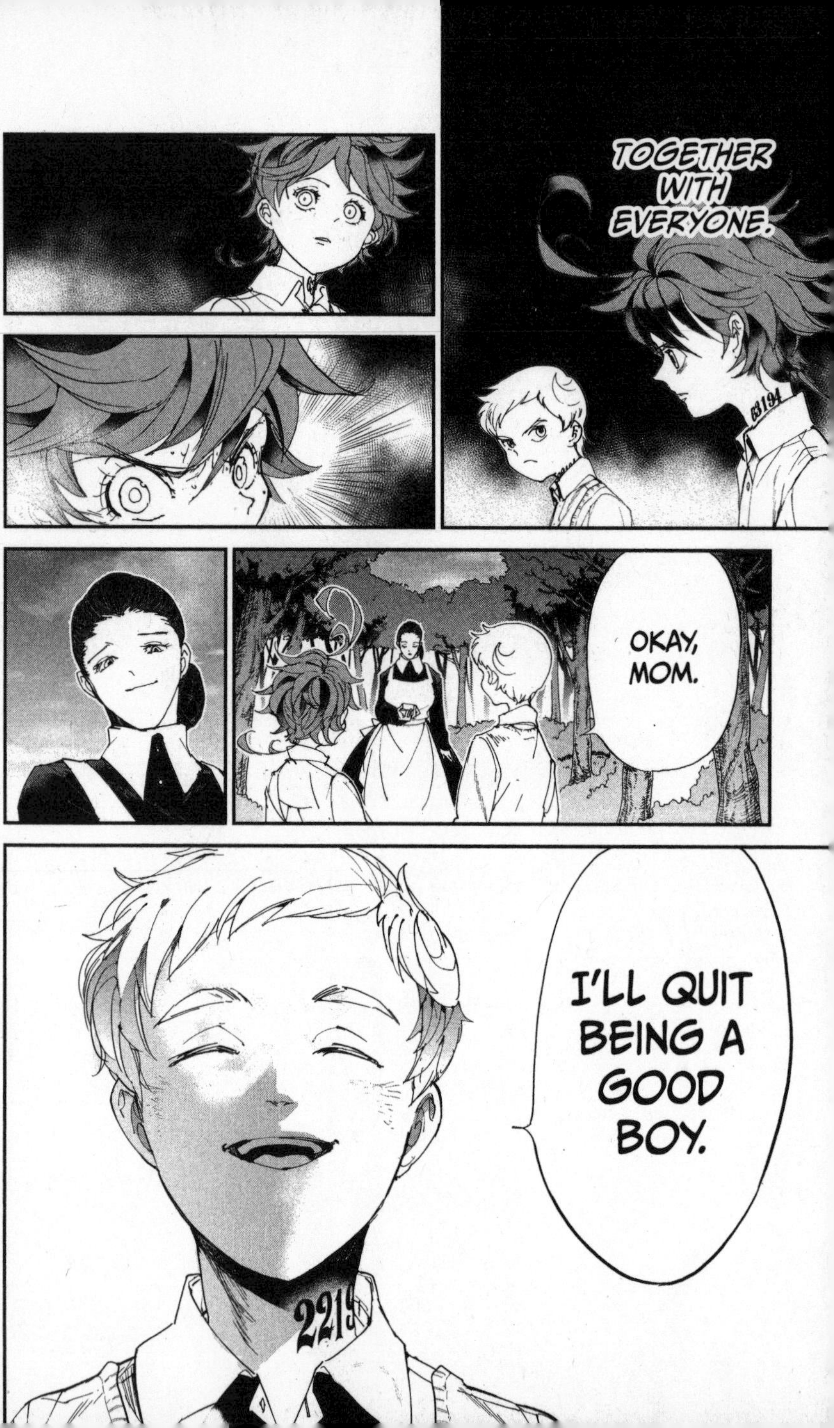
TOGETHER WITH EVERYONE.
OKAY, MOM.
I'LL QUIT BEING A GOOD BOY.

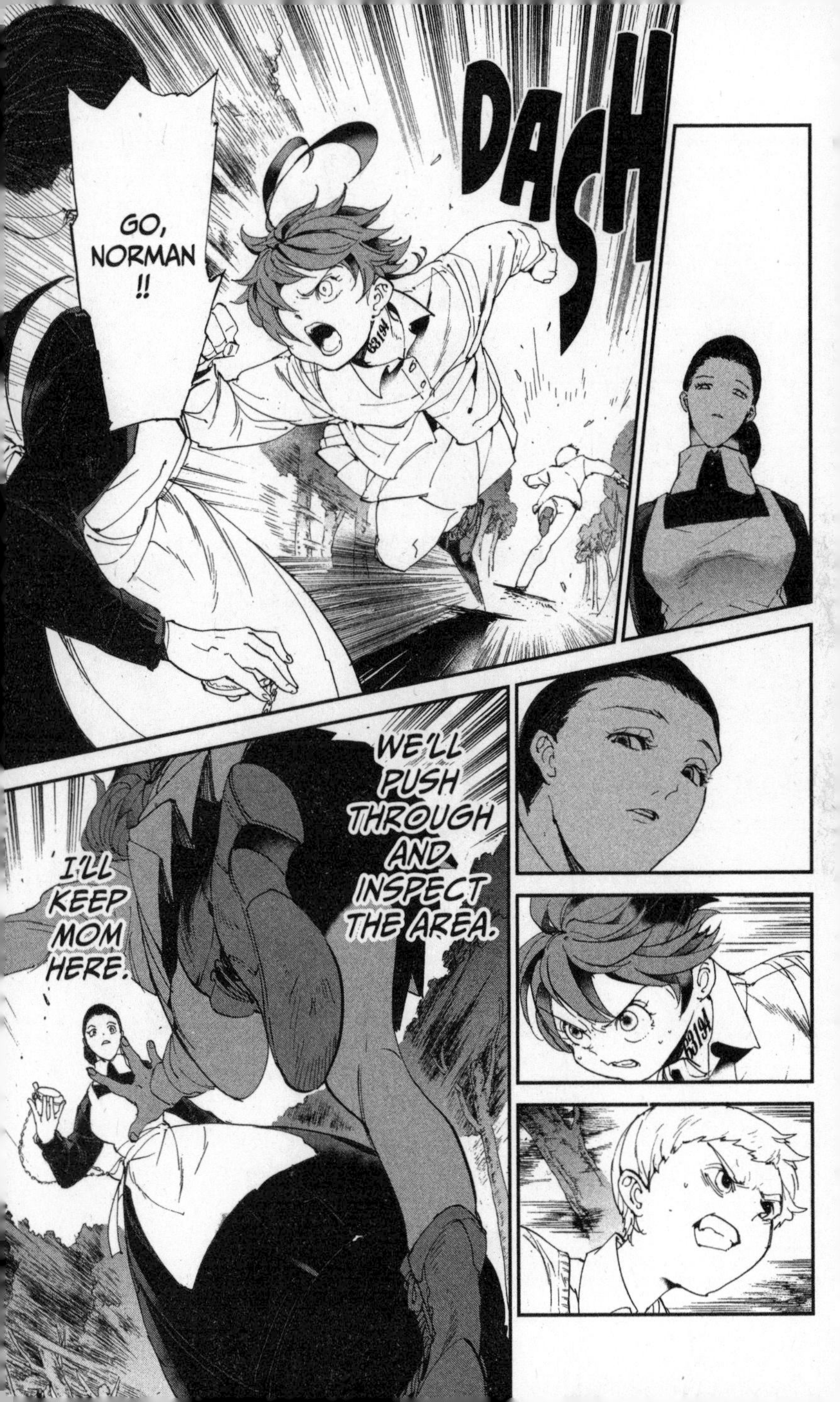
DASH
GO, NORMAN !!
WE'LL PUSH THROUGH AND INSPECT THE AREA.
I'LL KEEP MOM HERE.

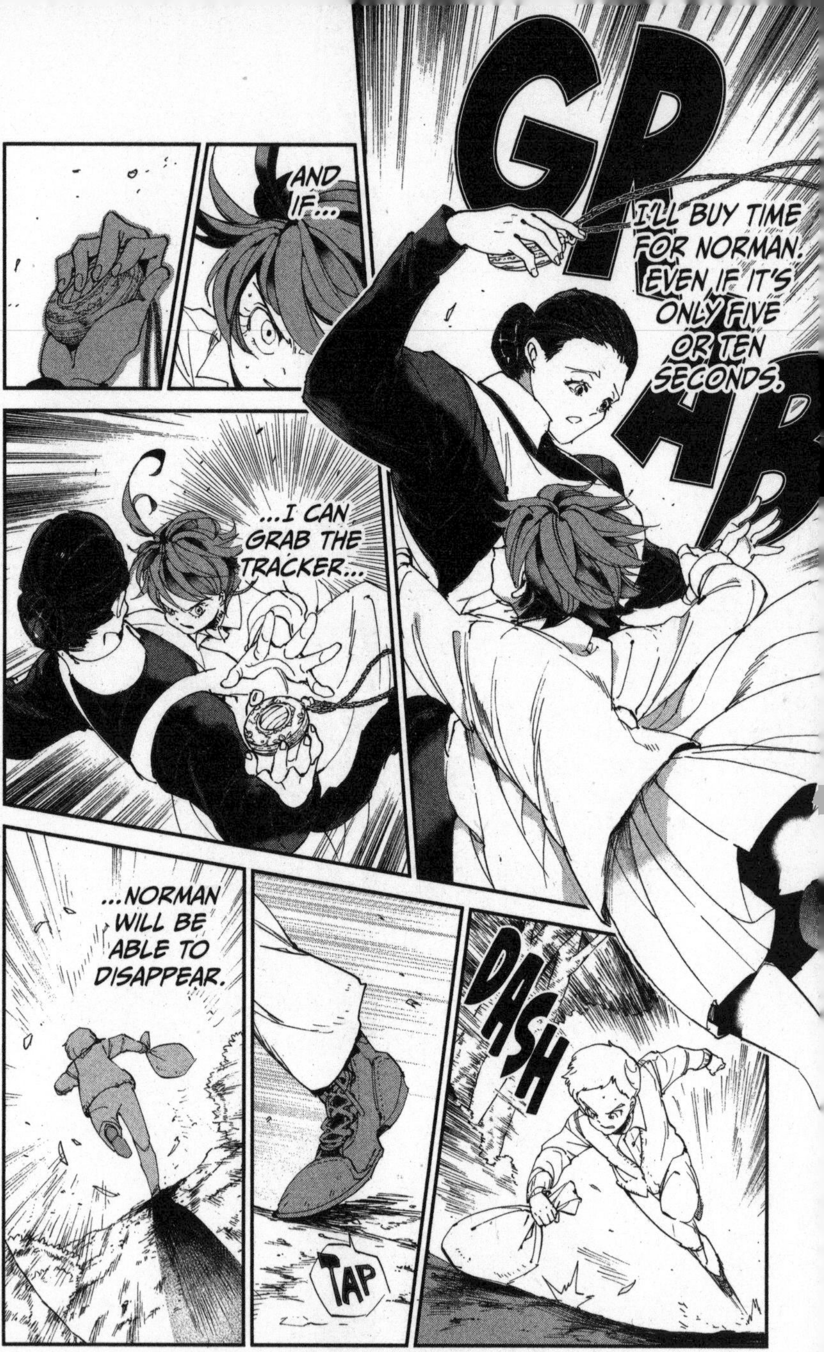
GRAB
I'LL BUY TIME FOR NORMAN. EVEN IF IT'S ONLY FIVE OR TEN SECONDS.
AND IF...
...I CAN GRAB THE TRACKER...
DASH
TAP
...NORMAN WILL BE ABLE TO DISAPPEAR.

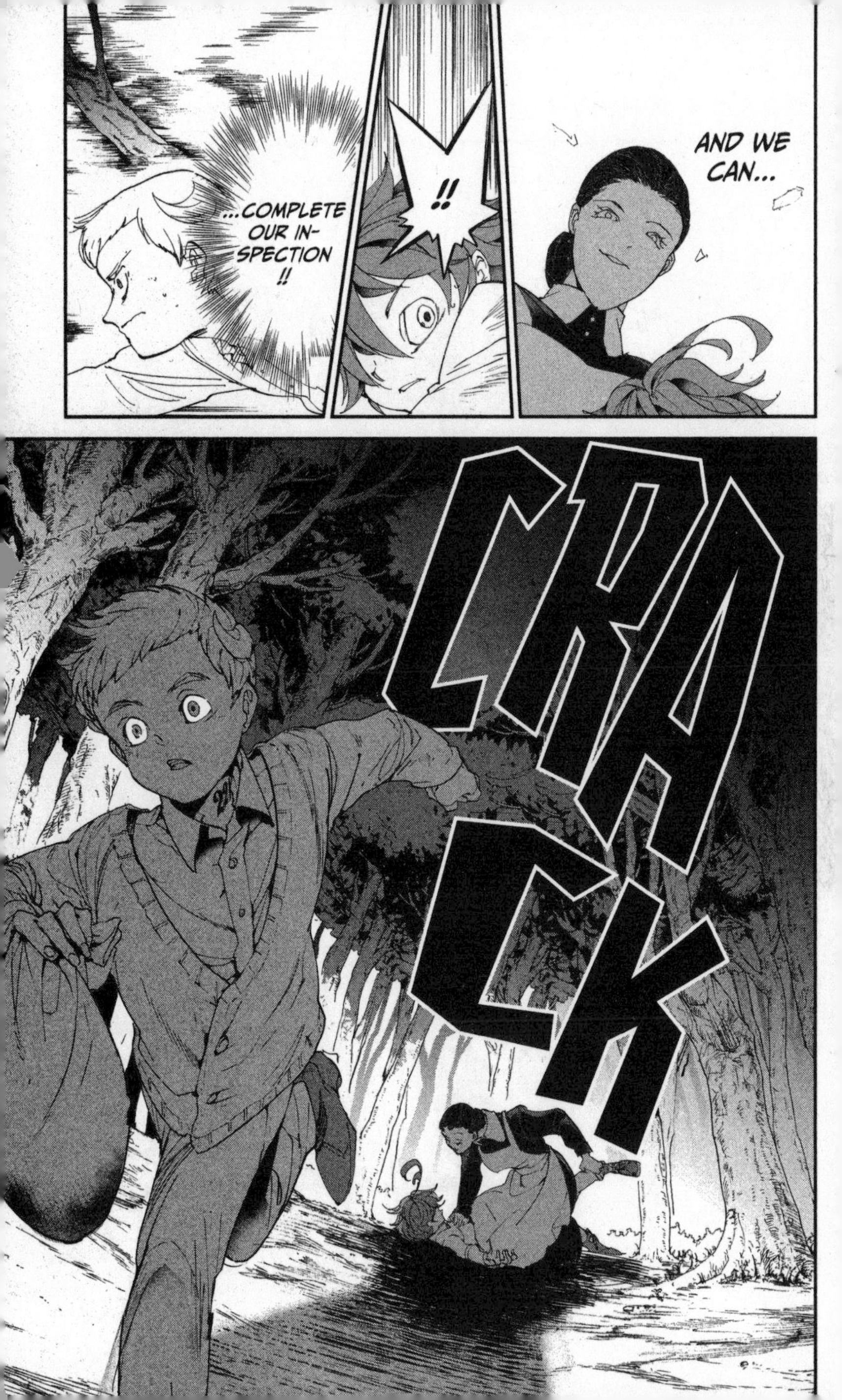
AND WE CAN...
!!
...COMPLETE OUR IN-SPECTION !!
CRACK

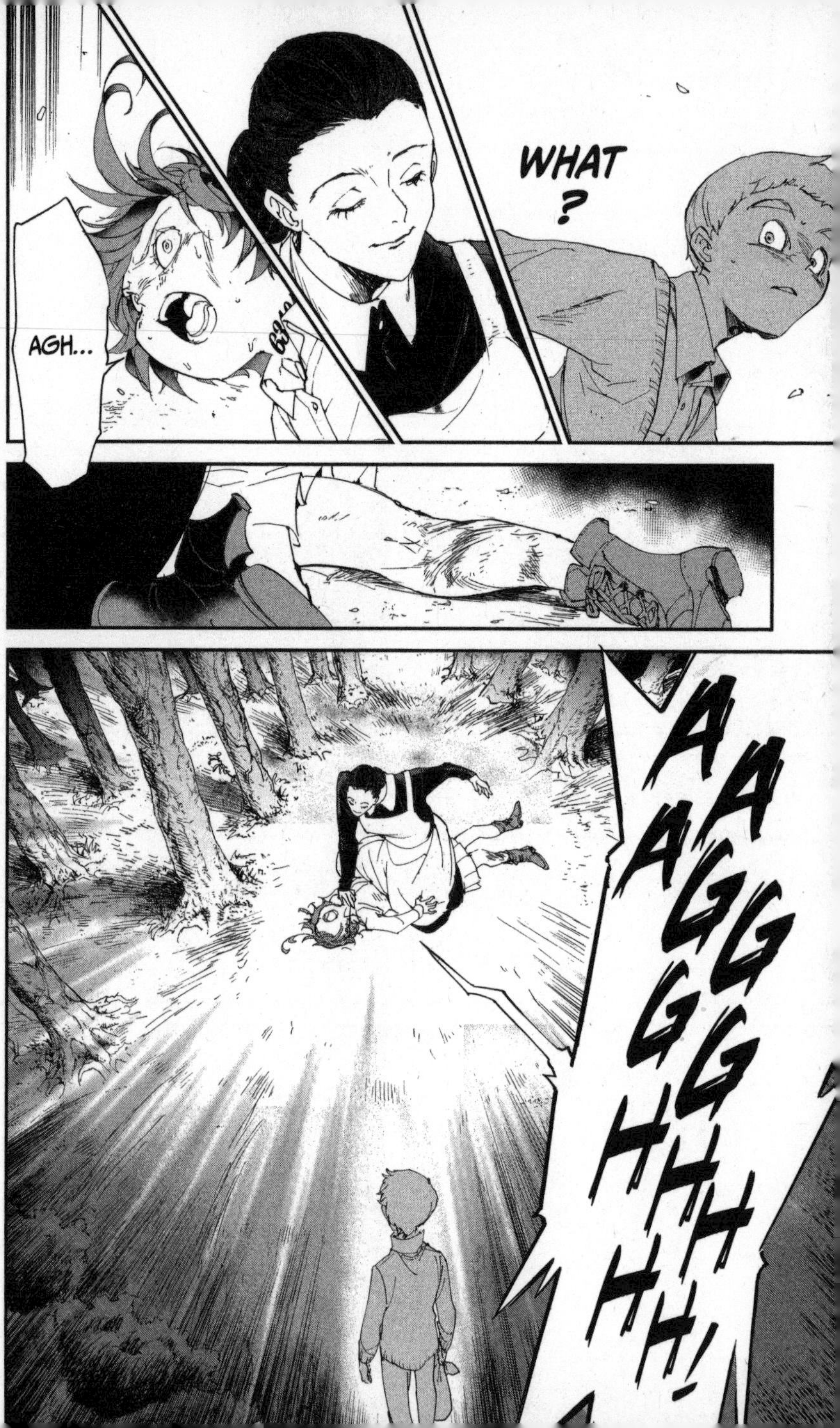
WHAT ?
AGH...
AAAGGGHHHHHH!

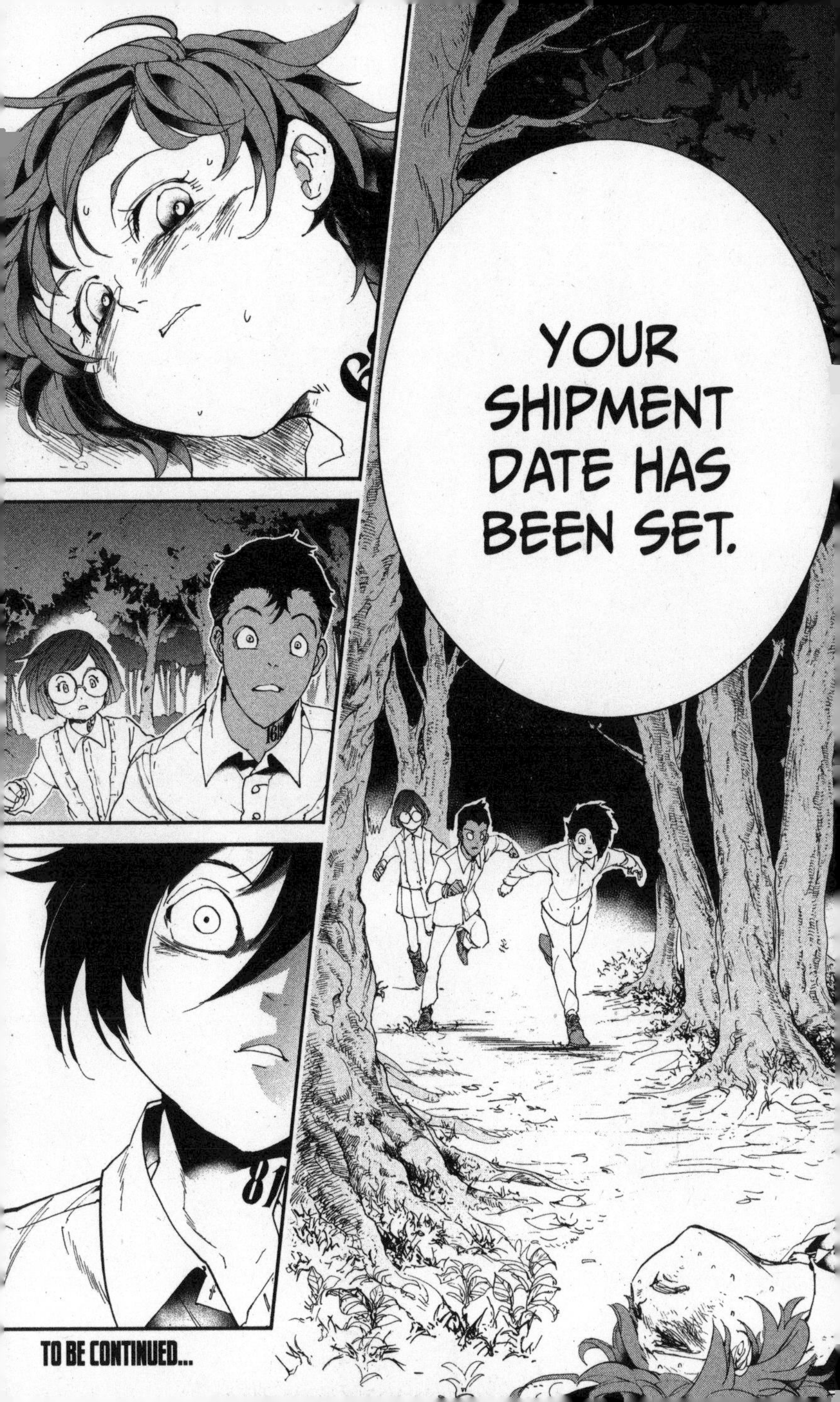
YOUR SHIPMENT DATE HAS BEEN SET.

TO BE CONTINUED...

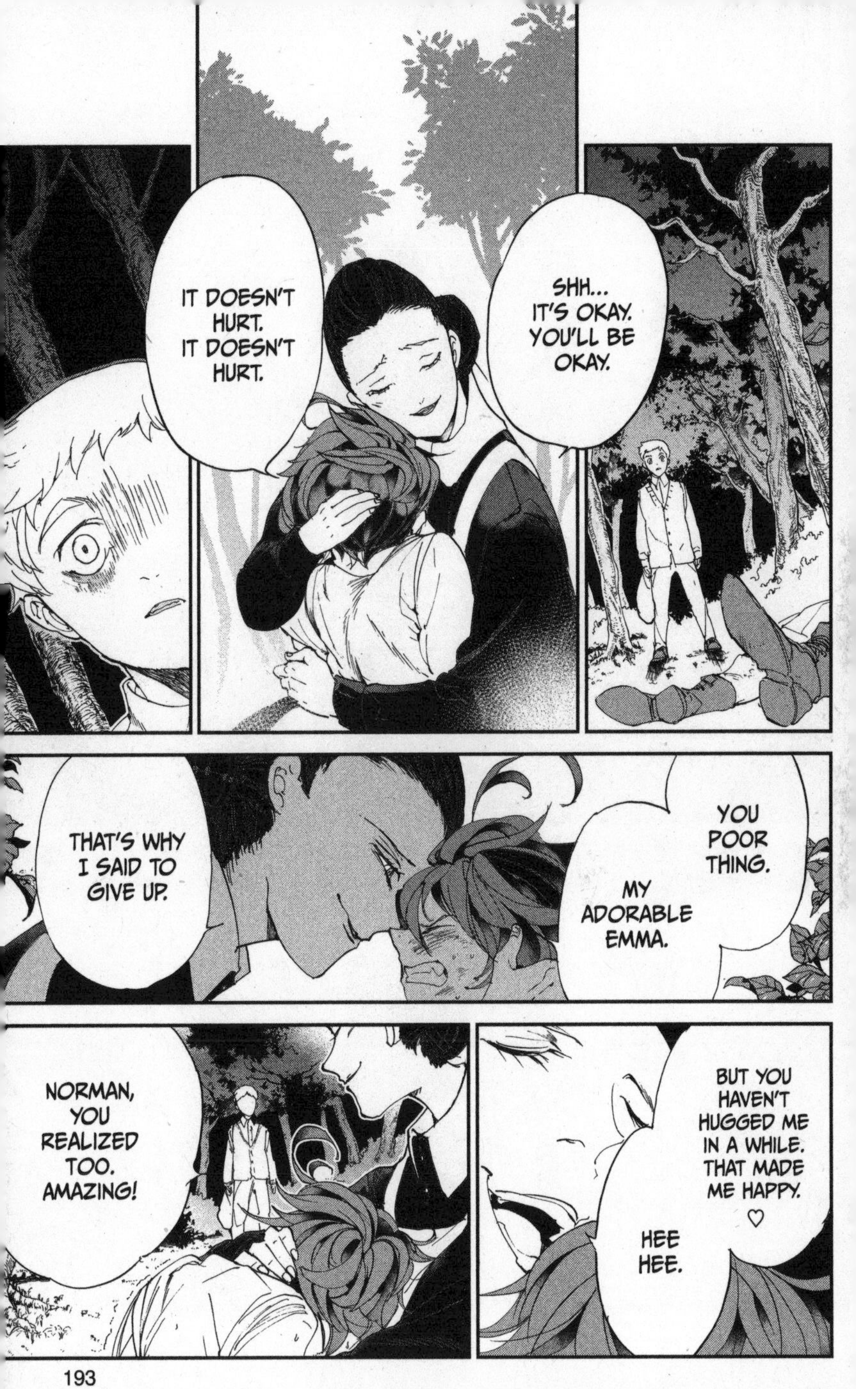
SHH... IT'S OKAY. YOU'LL BE OKAY.
IT DOESN'T HURT. IT DOESN'T HURT.
YOU POOR THING.
MY ADORABLE EMMA.
THAT'S WHY I SAID TO GIVE UP.
BUT YOU HAVEN'T HUGGED ME IN A WHILE. THAT MADE ME HAPPY. ♡
HEE HEE.
NORMAN, YOU REALIZED TOO. AMAZING!

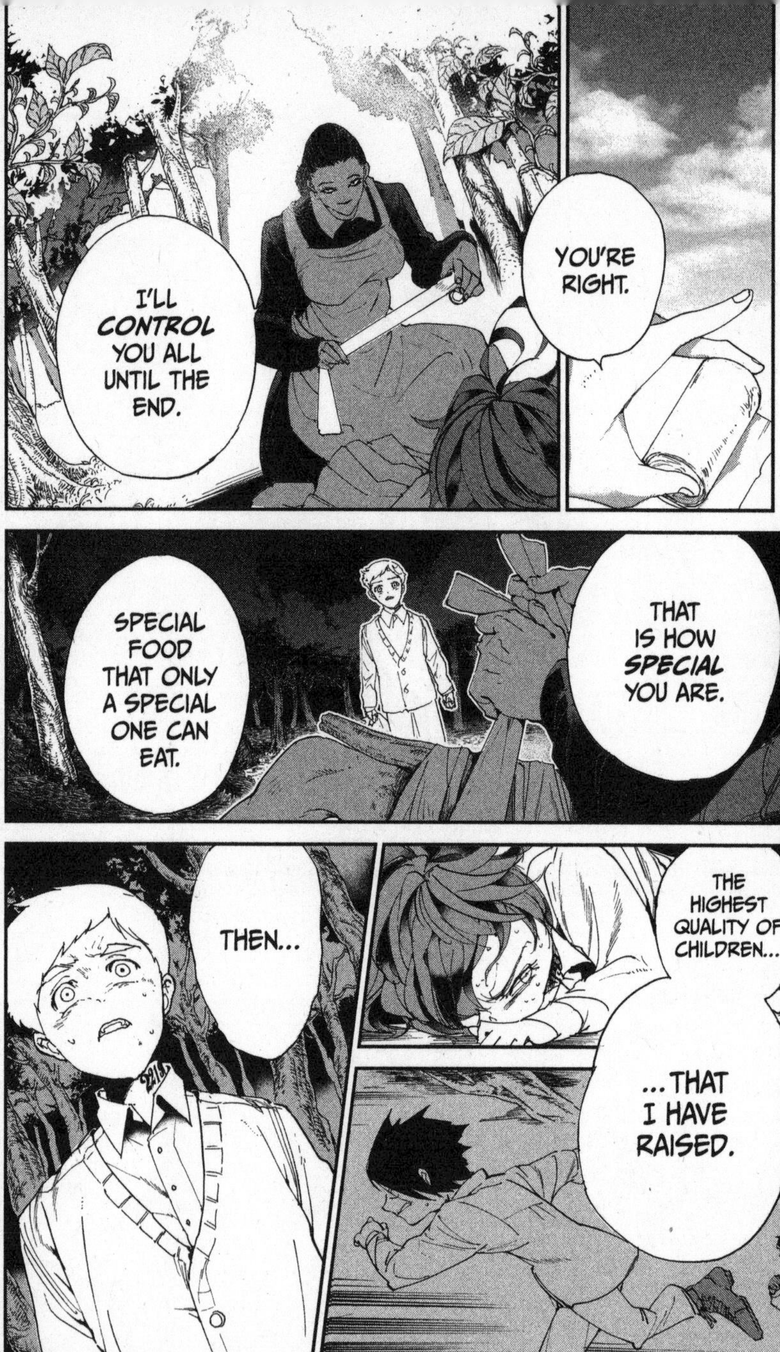
YOU'RE RIGHT.
I'LL CONTROL YOU ALL UNTIL THE END.
THAT IS HOW SPECIAL YOU ARE.
SPECIAL FOOD THAT ONLY A SPECIAL ONE CAN EAT.
THE HIGHEST QUALITY OF CHILDREN...
...THAT I HAVE RAISED.
THEN...

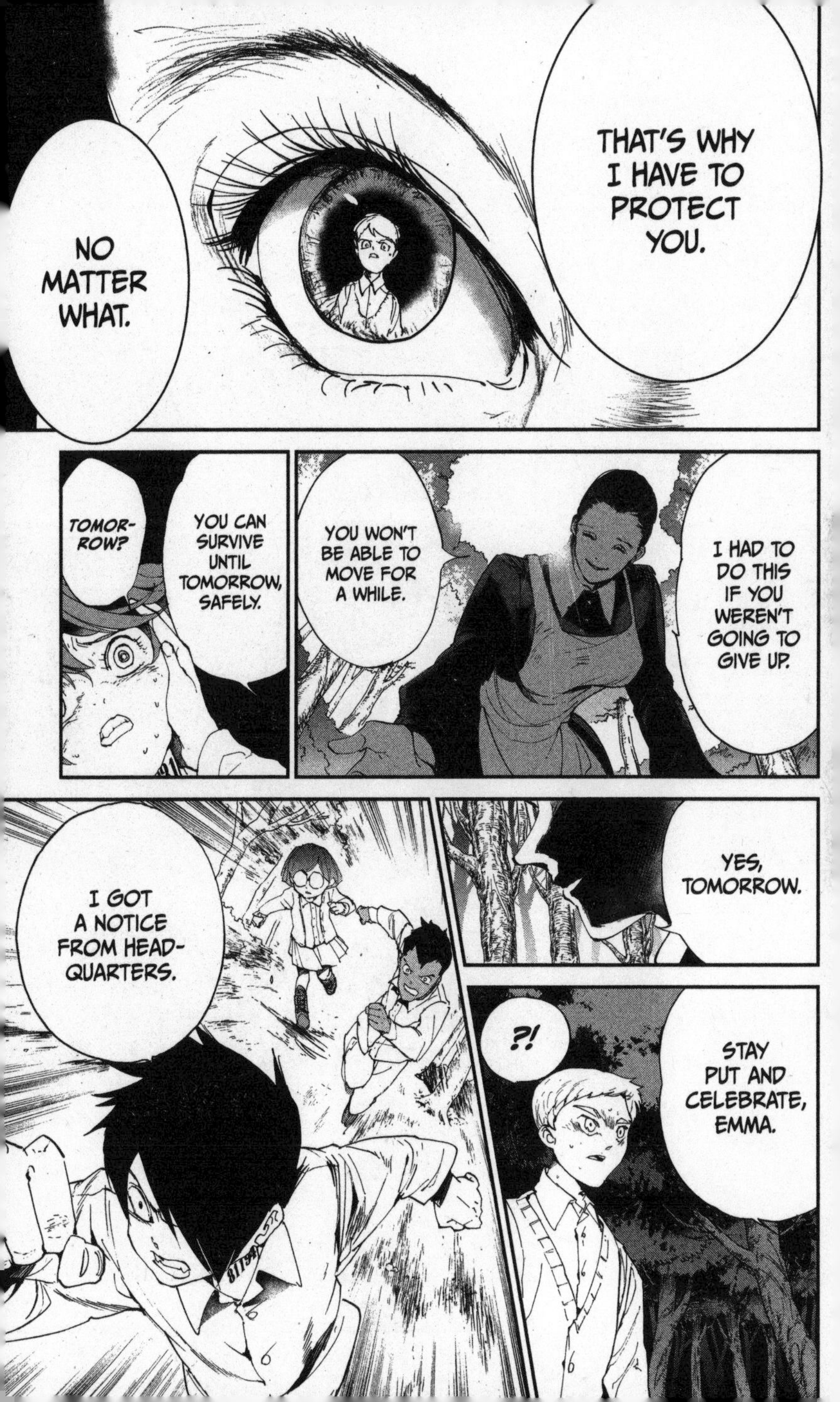
THAT'S WHY I HAVE TO PROTECT YOU.
NO MATTER WHAT.
I HAD TO DO THIS IF YOU WEREN'T GOING TO GIVE UP.
YOU WON'T BE ABLE TO MOVE FOR A WHILE.
YOU CAN SURVIVE UNTIL TOMORROW, SAFELY.
TOMORROW?
YES, TOMORROW.
STAY PUT AND CELEBRATE, EMMA.
?!
I GOT A NOTICE FROM HEAD-QUARTERS.

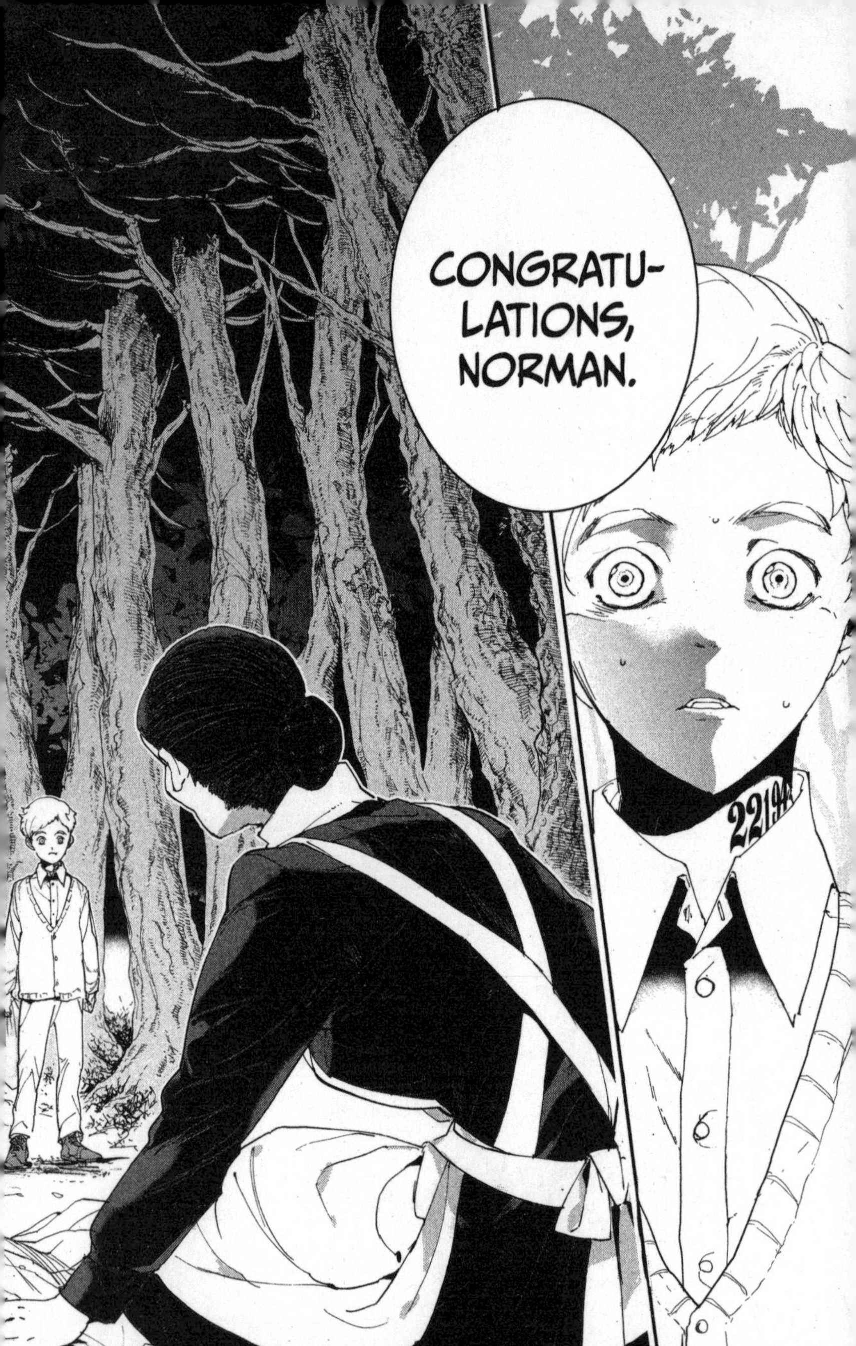
CONGRATU-
LATIONS,
NORMAN.
221194

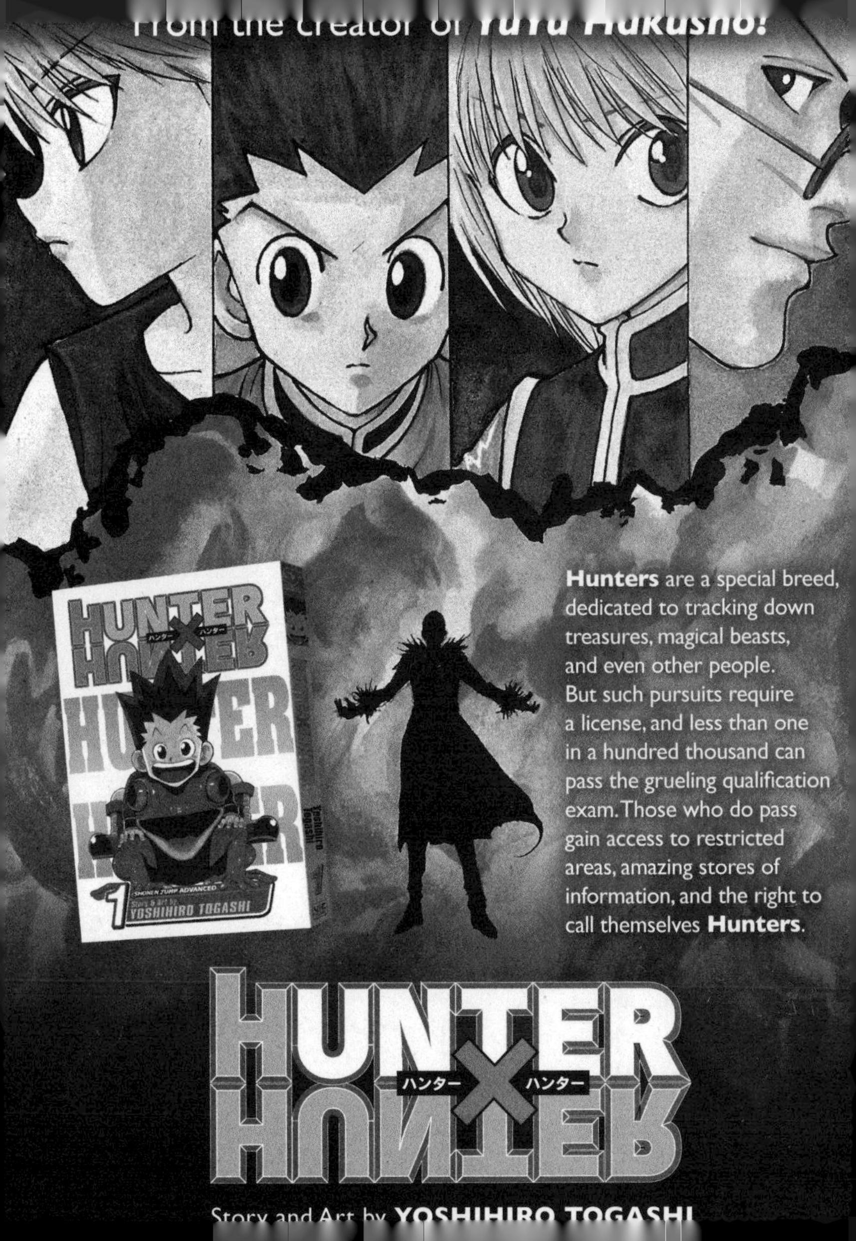
From the creator of YuYu Hakusho!
HUNTER × HUNTER
ハンター ハンター
SHONEN JUMP ADVANCED
Story & Art by YOSHIHIRO TOGASHI
Yoshihiro Togashi
1
Hunters are a special breed, dedicated to tracking down treasures, magical beasts, and even other people. But such pursuits require a license, and less than one in a hundred thousand can pass the grueling qualification exam. Those who do pass gain access to restricted areas, amazing stores of information, and the right to call themselves **Hunters**.
HUNTER × HUNTER
ハンター ハンター
Story and Art by YOSHIHIRO TOGASHI

YOU'RE READING THE **WRONG WAY!**

The Promised Neverland reads from right to left, starting in the upper-right corner. Japanese is read from right to left, meaning that action, sound effects and word-balloon order are completely reversed from English order.

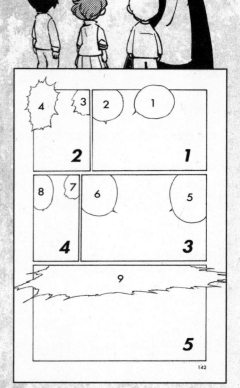